JOHN OF GAUNT
DUKE OF LANCASTER

John of Gaunt.
From a window in All Souls College, Oxford.

John of Gaunt

KING OF CASTILE AND LEON
DUKE OF AQUITAINE AND LANCASTER
EARL OF DERBY LINCOLN AND LEICESTER
SENESCHAL OF ENGLAND

BY

SYDNEY ARMITAGE-SMITH

*Late Scholar of New College, Oxford ; Fellow of
University College, London*

NEW YORK

BARNES & NOBLE, INC.

Publishers · Booksellers · Since 1873

V

Contents

vii

CONTENTS

CONTENTS

List of Illustrations

ILLUSTRATIONS

MAPS

NOTE.—The attempt to illustrate fourteenth century history from contemporary sources is almost hopeless. So far as illumination goes, the period was one of decadence, while portrait painting in England at least had not begun. Contemporary MSS. have scarcely anything worth reproduction. (*See* e.g. *Cotton Nero*, D. vi. and the engravings from it in Strutt's *Regal and Ecclesiastical Antiquities*.)

The face has perished from the drawing of John of Gaunt which formed part of the fresco in St. Stephen's Chapel, Westminster ; the sepulchral figure of the Duke and the Duchess Blanche in St. Paul's, which has often been engraved, has no authority, for it was not placed in the cathedral until the reign of Henry VII. It was destroyed in the great fire.

It is not impossible, however, that the window in All Souls' preserves some tradition, for the College was founded only a generation after the Duke's death, and the glass dates from the foundation.

The picture ascribed to Luca Cornelli is supposed to date from 1390. Internal evidence would place it between 1600 and 1650. Luca Cornelli is unknown to art, but if the picture is a Jacobean forgery it is interesting, for the face has character, and is of the true Plantagenet type.

The two MSS. from which most of the illustrations have been taken are Harl. 4379 and 4380, and 14 E. iv. Both are late fifteenth century. The first is French, and belonged to Philip de Commines ; the second is of Flemish workmanship, and was executed for Edward IV.

The blazons of the English, French and Gascon lordships of the Dukes of Lancaster are to be found brilliantly illuminated in the Great Cowcher of the Duchy (*Carte Regum*, Vol. ii.).

The Map of England attempts to provide a rough index to the political influence of the Duke of Lancaster, rather than a complete reconstruction of the Lancastrian estates.

xi

ILLUSTRATIONS

As no *Inquisition Post Mortem* appears to have been held on the death of John of Gaunt, the material has been compiled from the *Ministers' Accounts* (Duchy of Lancaster : Nos. 11, 986, 11,987, etc.) read in conjunction with the *Inquisition* held in A.D. 1361, and the evidence of the Register, the great Cowcher, Duchy of Lancaster deeds, leases, etc., and the Patent Rolls.

The shaded portions of the map represent the manors, etc., in the County of Lancaster and the four Yorkshire Honours, which are too numerous to be inserted in a map of this scale.

Sources and Authorities

CHRONICON HENRICI KNIGHTON, *Ed.* J. R. LUMBY (Vol. II
A.D. 1337–1395 ; A.D. 1367–1376 wanting). Rolls Series.
CHRONICON ANGLIÆ, AUCTORE MONACHO QUODAM SANCTI ALBANI,
Ed. E. M. THOMPSON (A.D. 1328–1388). Rolls Series.
THOMÆ WALSINGHAM HISTORIA ANGLICANA (A.D. 1272–1422).
YPODIGMA NEUSTRIÆ A THOMA WALSINGHAM, QUONDAM MONACHO
MONASTERII S. ALBANI, CONSCRIPTUM.
ANNALES RICARDI SECUNDI, A.D. 1392–1406 (with JOHANNIS DE
TROKELOWE ET HENRICI DE BLANEFORDE CHRONICA).
GESTA ABBATUM MONASTERII S. ALBANI, A THOMA WALSINGHAM,
COMPILATA (Vol. III, A.D. 1349–1411).
(*Chronica Monasterii S. Albani, Ed.* H. T. RILEY. Rolls Series)
EULOGIUM (HISTORIARIUM SIVE TEMPORIS) : Chronicon ab Orbe
condito usque ad Annum Domini 1366 ; a monacho quodam
Malmesbiriensi exaratum. Continuatio Eulogii AD. 1361–
1413 ; (Vol. III), *Ed.* F. S. HAYDON. Rolls Series.
POLYCHRONICON RANULPHI HIGDEN (Vols. VIII and IX), *Ed.*
J. LUMBY (Vol. IX JOHANNES MALVERNE, A.D. 1381–1394).
Rolls Series.
ADAMI MURIMATHENSIS CHRONICA (A.D. 1303–1346), CUM EORUN-
DEM CONTINUATIONE (A.D. 1346–1380), *Ed.* THOMAS HOG,
1846 (English Historical Society).
CHRONICON ADAE DE USK, A.D. (1377–1404). *Ed.* E. MAUNDE
THOMPSON. 1876.
HISTORIA VITAE ET REGNI RICARDI II, A MONACHO QUODAM
DE EVESHAM CONSIGNATA, *Ed.* T. HEARNE, Oxford, 1729.
THOMAS OTTERBOURNE, CHRONICA REGUM ANGLIAE, *Ed.* T.
HEARNE, Oxford, 1722.
FASCICULI ZIZANIORUM MAGISTRI JOHANNIS WYCLIF CUM TRI-
TICO, *Ed.* W. W. SHIRLEY. Rolls Series.
CHANDOS HERALD—LE PRINCE NOIR, *Ed.* FRANCISQUE-MICHEL,
London and Paris, 1883.
JOHANNIS CAPGRAVE LIBER DE ILLUSTRIBUS HENRICIS, *Ed.* F. C.
HINGESTON. Rolls Series.
THE CHRONICLE OF ENGLAND, by JOHN CAPGRAVE, *Ed.* F. C
HINGESTON. Rolls Series.
THE ORYGYNALE CRONYKIL OF SCOTLAND, by ANDREW OF
WYNTOUN, *Ed.* D. LAING, Edinburgh, 1872–9.
SCOTICHRONICON. FORDUN-BOWER, *Ed.* W. GOODALL, Edinburgh,
1759.

SOURCES AND AUTHORITIES

CRONICAS DE LOS REYES DE CASTILLA. PEDRO LOPEZ DE AYALA, *Ed.* EUGENIO DE LLAGUNO AMIROLA, Madrid, 1779–1780.

CHRONICA DE EL REI D. JOÃO I. FERNÃO LOPES (Bibliotheca de Classicos Portuguezes), Lisbon, 1897.

OEUVRES DE FROISSART, *Ed.* KERVYN DE LETTENHOVE, Brussels, 1868–77.

CHRONIQUES DE J. FROISSART. *Ed.* S. LUCE, Paris, 1876, etc. (Société de l'Histoire de France).

LES GRANDES CHRONIQUES DE FRANCE, *Ed.* P. PARIS, Paris, 1837–8.

CHRONIQUE DES QUATRE PREMIERS VALOIS (1327–1393), *Ed.* S. LUCE, Paris, 1862 (Société de l'Histoire de France).

CHRONIQUE DU BON DUC LOYS DE BOURBON PAR JEAN CABARET D'ORVILLE, *Ed.* A. M. CHAZAUD, Paris, 1876 (Société de l'Histoire de France).

CHRONIQUE NORMANDE DU XIVᵉ SIÈCLE, *Ed.* A. ET E. MOLINIER, Paris, 1882 (Société de l'Histoire de France).

CHRONOGRAPHIA REGUM FRANCORUM, *Ed.* H. MORANVILLE, Paris, 1891 (Société de l'Histoire de France).

CHRONIQUE DE RICHARD LE SCOT (continuation 1344–1364), *Ed.* J. LEMOINE, Paris, 1896 (Société de l'Histoire de France).

CHRONIQUE LATIN DE GUILLAUME DE NANGIS (continuation 1300–1368), *Ed.* H. GERAUD, Paris, 1843 (Société de l'Histoire de France).

CHRONIQUE DU RELIGIEUX DE SAINT DENYS (A.D. 1380–1422), *Ed.* L. BELLAGUET, Paris, 1840 (*Collection de documents inédits sur l'Histoire de France*).

CHRONIQUE DE BERTRAND DU GUESCLIN. CUVELIER: Le Libvre du bon Jehan Duc de Bretaigne. *Ed.* E. CHARRIÈRE, Paris, 1839. (*Collection de Documents inédits sur l'Histoire de France.*)

CHRONICQUE DE LA TRAÏSON ET MORT DE RICHART DEUX ROY D'ENGLETERRE, *Ed.* B. WILLIAMS, London, 1846 (English Historical Society).

LES DEMANDES FAITES PAR LE ROI CHARLES VI AVEC LES REPONSES DE PIERRE SALMON, *Ed.* M. CRAPELET, Paris, 1883.

PIERRE COCHON : CHRONIQUE NORMANDE, *Ed.* R. DE BEAUREPAIRE, Rouen, 1870 (Société de Histoire de Rouen).

PIERRE D'ORGEMONT (PARTIE INÉDITE DES CHRONIQUES DE SAINT DENYS), *Ed.* T. PICHON.

LIVRE DES FAITS DU MARÉCHAL BOUCICAUT, *Ed.* J. BUCHON, Paris, 1885 (Panthéon Littéraire).

ISTORE ET CHRONIQUES DE FLANDRES, *Ed.* KERVYN DE LETTENHOVE, Brussels, 1879.

RECUEIL DES CHRONIQUES, *Ed.* T. DE SMET (Collection de Chroniques Belges Inédites).

LE PETIT THALAMUS DE MONTPELLIER (Société Archéologique de Montpellier, 1840).

SOURCES AND AUTHORITIES

PETITE CHRONIQUE DE GUYENNE, *Ed.* LEFEVRE PONTALIS (Bibliothéque de l'École des Chartes, vol. XLVII).

ROTULI PARLIAMENTORUM. (Record Commission.)
SUMMONS OF THE NOBILITY TO THE GREAT COUNCILS AND PARLIAMENTS OF THE REALM. DUGDALE, London, 1785.
A RETURN OF EVERY MEMBER OF PARLIAMENT (*By Command*), 1878.
FOEDERA CONVENTIONES LITTERAE ETC, RYMER, London, 1704.
CALENDAR OF DIPLOMATIC DOCUMENTS : RECORD REPORT, XLV. Ap.
COLLECTION GÉNÉRALE DES DOCUMENTS FRANÇAIS QUI SE TROUVENT EN ANGLETERRE, *Ed.* J. DELPIT, Paris, 1847.
PROCEEDINGS AND ORDINANCES OF THE PRIVY COUNCIL OF ENGLAND, *Ed.* N. H. NICOLAS (Vol. I 10 Ric. II—11 Henry IV).
MUNIMENTA GILDHALLÆ LONDONIENSIS (Vol. II, Liber Custumarum), *Ed.* H. T. RILEY, 1859–1862.
MEMORIALS OF LONDON AND LONDON LIFE IN THE THIRTEENTH, FOURTEENTH AND FIFTEENTH CENTURIES, *Ed.* H. T. RILEY, London, 1868.
THE SCROPE AND GROSVENOR CONTROVERSY, *Ed.* N. H. NICOLAS, 1832.
ANTIENT KALENDARS AND INVENTORIES OF THE TREASURY OF HIS MAJESTY'S EXCHEQUER, *Ed.* F. PALGRAVE (1836).
LETTERS OF ROYAL LADIES, M. A. E. WOOD, London, 1846.
A COLLECTION OF ALL THE WILLS OF ROYAL PERSONAGES, ETC., J. NICHOLS, London, 1780.
THE EXCHEQUER ROLLS OF SCOTLAND (Vol. III, A.D. 1379–1406), *Ed.* GEORGE BURNETT, 1880.
CALENDAR OF DOCUMENTS RELATING TO SCOTLAND, preserved in the Public Record Office (Vol. IV, 1357–1509), *Ed.* J. BAIN (1888).
REGISTRUM MAGNI SIGILLI REG. SCOT (Vol. I, 1306–1424, *Ed.* T. THOMSON) (1814).
CHRONOLOGICAL LIST OF SCOTTISH DOCUMENTS : Record Report, XXXI, Ap. No. 6.
CALENDAR OF ENTRIES IN THE PAPAL REGISTERS, illustrating the History of Great Britain and Ireland, PAPAL LETTERS, Vol. III—1342–1362 ; Vol. IV—1362–1404 ; Vol. V—1396-1404. PETITIONS TO THE POPE, Vol. I—1342–1419, *Ed.* W. H. BLISS and C. JOHNSON, and J. A. TWEMLOW.

LOS ANALES DE LA CORONA DE ARAGON. GERONYMO ZURITA. ZARAGOZA. 1610.
COLLECÇÃO DOS DOCUMENTOS PARA AS MEMORIAS DEL REY. D. JOÃO I., *Ed.* SOARES DA SILVA, Lisbon, 1730-4.

xv

SOURCES AND AUTHORITIES

HISTORIA GENEALOGICA DA CASA REAL PORTUGUESA ; PROVAS. ANTONIO CAETANO DE SOUSA, Lisbon, 1735-49.

ARCHIVES MUNICIPALES DE BORDEAUX—
Vol. I, Livre des Bouillons.
Vols. III and IV, Registre de la Jurade, Bordeaux, 1861.

LES JURADES DE LA VILLE DE BERGERAC, Vol. I, A. CHARNIER, Bergerac, 1892.

PATENT ROLLS. Public Record Office Calendars—
EDWARD III : 1340-1345.
RICHARD II : 1377-1392.

CATALOGUE DES ROLLES GASCONS NORMANS ET FRANÇAIS, Ed. T. CARTE. London, 1743.

DESCRIPTIVE CATALOGUE OF ANCIENT DEEDS, preserved in the Public Record Office. 1890-1900.

ISSUE ROLL OF THOMAS DE BRANTINGHAM, 44 Edw. III, 1370. Ed. F. DEVON.

ISSUES OF THE EXCHEQUER, Henry III—Henry VI ; from the Pell Records. Ed. F. DEVON.

CALENDARIUM INQUISITIONUM POST MORTEM. (Record Commission.)

RECORDS OF THE BOROUGH OF LEICESTER. Ed. M. BATESON, Cambridge, 1901.

HISTORICAL MSS. COMMISSION REPORTS.

CHOIX DE PIÈCES INÉDITES RELATIVES AU RÈGNE DE CHARLES VI. Ed. L. DOUËT D'ARCQ. Paris, 1863-4. (Société de l'Histoire de France.)

LETTRES DE ROIS, A.D. 1301-1515, Ed. CHAMPOLLION-FIGEAC.

ITINÉRAIRES DE PHILIPPE LE HARDI, Ed. E. PETIT.

ACTES ET MANDEMENTS DIVERS DE CHARLES V.
(Collection de Documents inédits sur l'Histoire de France.)

COLLECTION DES PRINCIPAUX CARTULAIRES DU DIOCÈSE DE TROYES, Ed. C. LALORE. Paris and Troyes, 1875-90.

HISTOIRE DE BRETAGNE. LOBINEAU (Paris, 1707) and MORICE (Paris, 1750-56)—(Pièces Justicatives).

CALENDAR OF THE ROLLS OF THE CHANCERY OF THE COUNTY PALATINE OF LANCASTER. First to Twelfth Year of the Regality of Duke John (A.D. 1377-1389). Record Report XXXII, Ap. I (4).

CALENDAR OF PATENT ROLLS OF THE COUNTY PALATINE. From the Fifth to the Eleventh Year of the Regality of Duke John (A.D. 1381-1387). Record Report XL, Ap. No. 4.

CALENDAR OF PRIVY SEALS. Record Report XLIII, Ap. No. (3).

THE CHARTERS OF THE DUCHY OF LANCASTER. W. HARDY, London, 1845.

DUCHY OF LANCASTER. Calendar of Royal Charters. William II—Richard II. Record Report XXXI, Ap. No. 1.

SOURCES AND AUTHORITIES

DUCHY OF LANCASTER. Calendar of Ancient Charters or Grants.
Record Report XXXV, Ap. No. 1, and XXXVI, Ap.
No. 2.
DUCHY OF LANCASTER. List of MINISTERS' ACCOUNTS preserved
in the Public Record Office. 1894 and 1897.

RECORDS OF THE DUCHY AND COUNTY PALATINE OF
LANCASTER. (Public Record Office):—
REGISTER OF JOHN OF GAUNT.
Part I. Edward III.
Part II. Richard II.
DUCHY OF LANCASTER ACCOUNTS—
Receiver General Mich. 1376-Mich. 1377. (Bundle
III. No. I.).
Receiver General 2 Feb., 1392—2 Feb., 1393. (Bundle
III. No. 2).
Receiver General 2 Feb., 1394-2 Feb., 1395. (Bundle
XXXII. No. 21).
Receiver for Sussex (1393-1396). (Bundle XXXII.
No. 22).
ANCIENT CORRESPONDENCE. Nos. 29 and 30.
DEEDS, LEASES, CHANCERY WARRANTS, CHANCERY
FILES, ETC.
FOREIGN ACCOUNTS. Exchequer Accounts; Transcripts from
Foreign Archives, etc. (Public Record Office.)
PATENT ROLL, 22 Ric. II.
CHARTERS AND MSS. ETC. BRITISH MUSEUM. (References in
foot-notes).

THE COMPLETE WORKS OF GEOFFREY CHAUCER. Ed. W. SKEAT,
Oxford, 1894.
THE VISION OF WILLIAM CONCERNING PIERS THE PLOWMAN AND
RICHARD THE REDELESS. WILLIAM LANGLAND. Ed.
W. SKEAT, Oxford, 1886.
POLITICAL POEMS AND SONGS RELATING TO ENGLISH HISTORY,
FROM THE ACCESSION OF EDWARD III TO THAT OF RICHARD
III. Ed. T. WRIGHT. Rolls Series.

THE CONSTITUTIONAL HISTORY OF ENGLAND. W. STUBBS,
Oxford, 1897.
HISTORY OF ENGLISH LAW. F. POLLOCK AND F. W. MAITLAND.
Cambridge, 1898.
LA DÉSOLATION DES EGLISES EN FRANCE PENDANT LA GUERRE
DE CENT ANS. H. S. DENIFLE, Paris, 1897.
A HISTORY OF THE ART OF WAR.—THE MIDDLE AGES. C. OMAN,
1898.
HISTOIRE DE FRANCE. Ed. E. LAVISSE, Paris, 1902.

SOURCES AND AUTHORITIES

LES ANGLAIS EN GUYENNE. D. BRISSAUD, Paris, 1875.

HISTOIRE DU COMMERCE ET DE LA NAVIGATION À BORDEAUX. FRANCISQUE-MICHEL, Bordeaux, 1867.

RICHARD II. H. WALLON, Paris, 1864.

LES ANCIENS SEIGNEURS DE BEAUFORT. L. PIGEOTTE, Troyes, 1881.

HISTOIRE DE TROYES. T. BOUTIOT. Troyes, 1870–80.

BERGERAC SOUS LES ANGLAIS. E. LABROUE, 1893.

VARIÈTÉS BORDELOISES. L'ABBE BAUREIN. Ed. E. MERAN, Bordeaux, 1876.

MEMORIALS OF THE ORDER OF THE GARTER. F. BELTZ.

HISTORY OF THE HOUSE OF PERCY. G. BRENNAN, London, 1902.

ANNALS OF THE HOUSE OF PERCY. E. B. DE FONBLANQUE, London, 1887.

THE LIFE AND TIMES OF EDWARD III. W. LONGMAN, LONDON, 1869.

HISTOIRE DE FRANCE (MOYEN AGE). J. MICHELET.

HISTOIRE LITTÉRAIRE DU PEUPLE ANGLAIS. J. J. JUSSERAND, Paris, 1896.

HISTOIRE DE DON PÈDRE Ier ROI DE CASTILLE. P. MEMÉRIE, PARIS, 1865.

HISTORY OF THE DUCHY AND COUNTY PALATINE OF LANCASTER. E. BAINES, London, 1836.

ANNALS OF THE COINAGE OF GREAT BRITAIN. R. RUDING, London, 1817–9.

SUPPLEMENT TO THE ILLUSTRATIONS OF ANGLO-FRENCH COINAGE. G. R. AINSLIE, 1847.

ANGLO-GALLIC, NORMAN AND AQUITAINIAN COINS. H. C. DUCAREL, 1757.

DESCRIPCIÓN GENERAL DE LAS MONEDAS HISPANO-CRISTIANAS. A. HEISS, Madrid, 1865–9.

Preface

A N attempt has been made elsewhere to acknowledge
the debt which this book owes to published
authorities ; it is a pleasant duty to express also my
obligations to those who during the past three years
have given me help and advice.

All who venture into the field of military history, especially that of the Middle Ages, must be sensible of
the debt which they owe to Professor Oman's *History
of the Art of War*; my own debt is more considerable,
for I have also had the advantage of Professor Oman's
advice in dealing with the French and Spanish campaigns.

I have to thank Professor Arthur Platt for his kindness
in undertaking the laborious task of reading the proof-
sheets, and for much valuable criticism. To Mr. Hubert
Hall, of the Public Record Office, I am under no ordinary
obligations. Not only has Mr. Hall placed his knowledge
of mediaeval records and the mediaeval economy most
freely at my disposal, but he has contributed many valuable suggestions. It is impossible for me to express in detail
all my indebtedness to him, but in particular I must
thank him for a transcript of the Account of the Receiver-
General of the Duke of Lancaster, and for a collation of the
fragment of genealogical history printed in the Appendix.

My thanks are also due to Mr. Oswald Barron, who has
generously allowed me to avail myself of his genealogical
knowledge ; to Mr. Giuseppe, of the Public Record Office,
for guidance among the records of the Duchy of Lancaster,
and to Mr. Herbert, of the Department of Manuscripts
of the British Museum, for similar help in that department.

PREFACE

The Appendix on the Lancastrian coinage owes several suggestions to Mr. Grueber, Assistant-Keeper of Coins and Medals at the British Museum.

Finally, I have to thank the Duke of Beaufort for permission to reproduce the picture of John of Gaunt in his possession ; the Society of Antiquaries and their Assistant Secretary, Mr. St. John Hope, for lending me a cast of the Great Seal of Castile, and the Duke of Northumberland for his courtesy in placing at my disposal the manuscript in the Library of Alnwick Castle, an extract from which is printed in the Appendix.

I regret that it is impossible to print a very full itinerary which I have made out of the movements of John of Gaunt, a valuable corrective to the inaccuracies of the Chronicles, but this I hope to publish separately.

S. A.-S.

London, 1904.

Introduction

" OLD John Gaunt, time-honoured Lancaster."
What name on the roll of English princes is
more familiar ? What actor in the great drama of
English history has been watched with less attention ?

Two striking episodes in the Duke's history have
been related again and again, and from all points of view.
The defence of John Wycliffe and the attack on Sir Peter
de la Mare and William of Wykeham—these are the *loci
communes* of the history of the Church and of the Constitution. But for the rest, the Duke makes his exits and
his entrances, but it is upon the other players in the piece
that the audience fix their attention.

His strong and persistent craving for continental
royalty, the keynote to his character, has been strangely
neglected. The man has never yet lived and moved
among the historic figures of his age or nation. " Old
John of Gaunt, and gaunt in being old:" the words have
fixed in our minds the idea of a feudal magnate, the venerable uncle of a young and spendthrift king, but with
Richard II, who asks " Can sick men play so nicely with
their names ? " we do not listen, but go on our way and
leave him.

Yet, however inadequately conceived, the figure of John
of Gaunt, which filled so large a place in the story of his
times, has appealed to our imagination. Though the
man is almost a stranger to us, his name is a household

INTRODUCTION

word. Traces of his doings are met with on every side, for he seems to have been everywhere and to have attempted everything.

Long ago the last traces have disappeared of that magnificent building which once fronted the Thames between the Tower and the Palace of Westminster ; yet to whom does not the name of the Savoy recall John of Gaunt and the stately palace, where Jean le Bon spent his last days of exile, and where Geoffrey Chaucer listened to the " goodly softe speche " of Blanche the Duchess ?

Abroad, too, his name is not forgotten. In Ghent the Abbey of St. Bavon and the Château des Comtes still dispute the honour of ranking as his birthplace, and Gantois cicerones and English guide books keep up the quarrel.

In Bordeaux some old stone carving still displays the leopards of England quartering the lilies of France with the familiar label of three points ermine, and in the Abbey of Batalha the Duke's exploits are recorded on the tomb of his daughter, a Queen of Portugal.

Kenilworth, with its Lancaster tower, and the ruins of a score of castles proclaim the lavish hand of the builder and the power of the great feudatory. The Duchy of Lancaster is still a fact, and the Sovereign still bears the title of his far-off ancestor of the fourteenth century.

Yet the man whose territorial power stretched over a third of England, who in a sense may be said to have created the Duchy of Lancaster and founded the Portuguese Alliance, who was for fifteen years the titular King of Castile and Leon, and for a dozen years the uncrowned King of England, still moves through the realm of history in a region of half-lights and hazy outlines. For a moment, as he comes within their range, the military or constitutional historians turn their modern searchlight upon him. It is only for a moment ; again he is lost to sight. Now and then some enterprising essayist tries to penetrate the darkness, only to bring back anything but a reassuring report. We content ourselves with ill-defined notions both of grandeur and of wickedness. We acquiesce in unexplained contradictions, and are willing to accept the friend of Chaucer and the patron of letters as the enemy of the Church; the favourite son of Edward III and the favourite brother of the Black Prince, as the "wicked uncle" of Richard II. The "illustrious prince" of one writer is the "unscrupulous villain" of a second; historians of the Constitution, of the Church, of warfare, and of letters—each tell a different tale.

From this unmerited obscurity an attempt, however inadequate, has now been made to rescue him.

Of short notices in works of reference there is an abundance. Sir E. Maunde Thompson has a long article in the *Dictionary of National Biography*, and writers like Beltz (*Memorials of the Order of the Garter*) and Baines (*History of the Duchy and County Palatine of Lancaster*) review the more obvious and accessible facts of his life. The indefatigable Dugdale has compiled a list, incomplete it is true, of his estates; and of those who have transcribed from Dugdale the name is legion, but the Duke has never been accorded the distinction of a separate biography.

So far as the author is aware (and one cannot be wiser than the *Catalogue of the British Museum*), there is no extant biography of John of Gaunt in English, French, German, Spanish, or Portuguese.

In 1740 Arthur Collins appended an account of John of Gaunt to his *Life of the Black Prince*. It runs to some ninety pages of small octavo, the substance of which is for the most part an unacknowledged loan from Dugdale.

In 1803 William Godwin tacked on to his account of Chaucer's life and works " Memoirs of his near friend and kinsman, John of Gaunt Duke of Lancaster." The kinship to Chaucer is one of the least questionable of

INTRODUCTION

Godwin's facts, which by the way are based on the supposition that every writing of the poet must turn on some fact of his patron's life, the Chaucerian canon itself being enough to make a Chaucerian scholar shudder.

To Godwin John of Gaunt is everything that is good and great : the result is an uncritical eulogy, a lay figure of a fourteenth-century Maecenas.

From the first the Portuguese writers have shown a vivid interest in the exploits of the ally of Dom João of good memory, but to take a modern example, the Count of Villa Franca, in *João I, e a Allianç Inglese*, succeeds rather in evidencing than stimulating that interest, and the student is grateful to him chiefly for acting as a guide to the original sources.

The attempt, therefore, to present a connected account of the acts of a great historical figure, to analyze his admitted ambition and to gauge his character, is justified by the silence of others ; of the difficulties inherent in the task no one is more conscious than the author of these pages.

For better or for worse, Lancaster's name is connected with nearly every event and nearly every actor on one of the most interesting scenes of history. Within his lifetime (1340 to 1399) fall the first half of the Hundred Years War, the beginnings of the new economic system in England, the new literature, and the early Reformation. The Duke crosses swords with du Guesclin ; Sir John Chandos is his friend ; Sir Hugh Calverly fights under his banner, and Sir Robert Knolles is of his retinue. The unsuccessful general of the Hundred Years' War is the victim marked out for slaughter by the peasants in 1381 ; the friend of Chaucer is the patron of Wycliffe. The story of his life takes us from the Painted Chamber at Westminster to the Municipal Council hall of Bordeaux ; from the Savoy to Holyrood, to Malmaison, to the cathedrals of St. James of Compostella and of Burgos ; from the battlefields of France and Aquitaine to those of Castile ; from the struggle of Valois and Plantagenet to the death feud of the brothers Pedro the Cruel and Henry of Trastamare.

In all this the Duke, if a fascinating leader, is a dangerous guide. His biographer is led insensibly to precipice after precipice. He has to avoid the desperate suggestion of casting himself headlong into the abyss of the Hundred Years War, the early Reformation, the early Renaissance, or the County Palatine of Lancaster.

He must fix his eye upon one figure : the hero, or it may be, the villain of the piece. He must neglect all issues, however important, not his own. No underplot, however tempting, must disturb the unity of the story which tells of the ambitions of the protagonist and the events to which they led.

If the study of institutions is more important than the study of the lives of men and women, the large canvas a nobler work than the portrait or the cameo, the task of portraying personality has its own peculiar difficulties.

Foremost among these difficulties comes one peculiar to the period. For the riddle of personal character in the whole Middle Age is harder to guess than in any other. That age falls on the other side of the great dividing line drawn by that strange re-awakening, that re-discovery by man of himself and his place in the universe, which is summed up in the word Renaissance. After that epoch history has to deal with men and women ; before, with children, children who with little of the simplicity have much of the *naïveté* and incomprehensibility of childhood. The ages of faith and the ages of chivalry have passed away, and the seamless robe is rent. Between the modern and the Middle Age a great gulf is fixed. Therefore all estimates of character must be subject to doubt, and must be put forward with becoming diffidence. Dogmatism and easy assurance are less

INTRODUCTION

appropriate and less convincing than suggestion or at best a hesitating judgment. To these general considerations, true of the whole age, must be added one true of the particular period.

More perhaps than at any other time in English history our judgment of individuals must depend on the unravelling of a complex of intrigues, personal and political, which come down to us chronicled by men who united the passions of the partizan with the credulity of an age scorning evidence, greedy of the miraculous, ever ready to hear the devil speak with human voice, or to see blood flow at the tomb of a political martyr. Subject to these qualifications, the evidence both of the chronicles and of more formal documents is abundant and rich. There are those who record hearsay in the cloister, but there are also eye-witnesses and men of the world.

Froissart must have seen John of Gaunt and talked with him again and again. Ayala—courtier, soldier, statesman, and chronicler—met him in the field of battle and in the warfare of diplomacy; the Portuguese chroniclers, biassed doubtless in favour of the father of Queen Philippa and the father-in-law of the Master of Avis, the hero of national independence, have preserved in detail the record of his deeds in the great invasion, and, strangely enough, the only extant description of his appearance. After the men of affairs and men of letters come a mob of gentlemen who write with more or less of ease and more or less of prejudice : Henry Knighton and the nameless continuator of his chronicle, who, living in the shadow of the Lancastrian foundation at Leicester, testify to the Duke's piety ; the unknown monk of St. Albans, who testifies to his wickedness ; Adam of Usk, hard-headed lawyer and impartial critic, who sat in the reporters' gallery when the Duke as High Seneschal of England passed sentence on the conspirators of 1397 ; Chandos Herald, not altogether free from a herald's

INTRODUCTION

failings, who extols his prowess ; and a score of others, some with names, more without, a few interesting, the majority dull, but all having some fact to add to the story, some comment to show how the man appeared to those of his day.

Of formal evidence the amount is overwhelming. The Rolls of Parliament have of course long since been explored, though even here patient research can gather up crumbs that have fallen from the table.[1] For other sources similar in nature the student feels gratitude, tempered with despair. The records of the Duchy and County Palatine of Lancaster are almost inexhaustible, and suggest tempting lines of inquiry at every turn. Series like the *Collection de documents inédits sur l'histoire de France*, M. Delpit's *Collection des documents français qui se trouvent en Angleterre*, and the municipal records of Bordeaux—a monument of civic patriotism— are invaluable sources for the life of John of Gaunt. Often formal evidence succeeds where the professed chronicles are disappointingly inadequate. Froissart, with all his brilliance and charm, too often puts into the mouth of the Duke of Lancaster set speeches which would fit the Duke of Burgundy or the Count of Foix as well. Instead of the man, he gives us the type. Where Froissart fails, Walsingham is intolerable. Better the unmeasured abuse of the "scandalous chronicle" than Knighton's conventionality. It is from this curse of conventionality, as also from the barriers of prejudice, that formal evidence sets us free.

The Calendars of Papal Petitions and Papal Letters do far more than the *Fasciculi Zizaniorum* to explain the Duke's attitude to the early Reformation ; with the *Livre des Bouillons* in our hands we can watch the Duke fencing with the obstinate champions of municipal privilege and feudal independence ; the official records

[1] See Ch. xi. pp. 257–8.

xxvii

INTRODUCTION

of the township of Bergerac show us the mayor and échevins listening to news of their seigneur far away in Kenilworth or Pontefract ; the cartularies of Troyes conjure up the injured Abbot of " Chapelle aux Planches " fixing to the doors of his houses the arms of the Duke of Lancaster and Lord of Beaufort and Nogent ; the Register furnishes a picture of the daily life of the Duke and his stately household ; we watch his servants bearing gifts of firewood to the poor lazars of Leicester, or carrying gifts of wine to the prisoners of Newgate.

The type of the grand seigneur, the lay figure, warms into life and becomes the man of flesh and blood.

This man, who to the constitutional historian is only important as the persistent enemy of constitutional progress, and the author of the circumstances which produced a change of dynasty, has his faults—they are many and conspicuous—and also his virtues. We must not look for any one great and good. The age is not an heroic age ; it is one of *décadence*. The man is not a hero. But he is profoundly interesting. The great feudatory with princely wealth and an imposing retinue, appears now as the patron of letters, now as a knight errant in search of adventures, now as a general, usually unfortunate, now as the pretender aspiring to a throne. Military fame eludes him ; the laurels of victory wither at his touch. Royal dignity escapes him ; the crown and sceptre are beyond his reach. He stands by the steps of two thrones ; he cannot mount to either.

But judged by the standard of the time, the life is not altogether in vain. The roll of dignities and honours is long. Passion, whether of ambition or of love, claims its due. He enjoys great power, and he has enough of fighting and adventure to satisfy the cravings of one born in the age of chivalry.

Chapter I

BIRTH OF JOHN OF GAUNT

NEAR the Antwerp gate of Ghent, at the meeting place of the Lys and Scheldt, lie the ruins of the Abbey of St. Bavon.

Little but the cloisters and the baptistery now remains of the famous Abbey founded by Saint Amand, once one of the chief seats of Flemish learning, where Eginhardt had found a home, and the bones of the sainted Pharailde had been laid to rest.

For in 1540, to punish the rebellious city of his birth, Charles V ordered the destruction of certain ancient gates, towers and walls no longer needed, and those of the Abbey were among the number condemned. The canons removed their reliquaries to the Cathedral, henceforth to be known by the name of St. Bavon, and the walls of the Abbey were thrown down to build a castle which should overawe the turbulent subjects of the Emperor.[1]

But in the fourteenth century the Abbey was a rich foundation enclosing a large area within its precincts. At the beginning of 1340 there was unusual stir within its walls, for the ancient seat of Flemish learning was for the moment the scene of a Court, and the monks

[1] Kervyn de Volkaersbeke, *Les Eglises de Gand*. (Ghent, 1857-8.)

of St. Bavon were the hosts of Edward III of England and his Queen Philippa of Hainault.[1]

The Hundred Years War had begun, and King Edward, to quiet the conscience of his Flemish allies, had just assumed the royal style of France[2] and ridden into Ghent with the lilies of France quartered on his shield with the English leopards.[3] For in January a great Parliament was held in Ghent ; Holland, Brabant, and the three great cities of Flanders had been leagued together in alliance with England against Louis Count of Flanders, and his suzerain, Philip of Valois.[4]

The alliance was signed at St. Bavon, and the triumph of Artevelde's policy seemed complete, the commercial union of England and Flanders cemented by the strongest of political ties, when in the great piazza of the city, the Marché du Vendredi, the Flemings did homage to their new suzerain, and swore to obey Edward III as King of France. This was the prelude to the campaign which was to open in the spring, and Edward returned to England to prepare.

Leaving the Queen and her little son Lionel, born at Antwerp the year before, to the protection of St. Bavon and his new subjects, the King left Flanders on February 20.[5] In March his fourth son, John, was born.[6]

---

[1] Ende Edewaert, des seken sijt,
Sijn wijf ende sine kindere mede,
Bleuen te Ghend in de stede
Tsente Baefs int cloester geloïert.
—*Reimchronik von Flandern*, vol. i. 1, 8224–7.
(Ed. E. Kausler, Tübigen, 1840.)

[2] *Istore et Chroniques de Flandres*, I, 572.

[3] See *Edouard III, Roi d'Angleterre en Belgique*, translation of the rhymed chronicle of Jean de Klerk, by Octave Delepierre. (Ghent, 1841.)

[4] De Smet, *Collection de Chroniques Belges Inédites*, III. 151.

[5] See King Edward's Itinerary in M. Lemoine's Appendix to his edition of Richard Lescot.

[6] Mense Martii : Murimuth, 93 ; *Chr. Angl.* 11. Wals. I, 226.

BIRTH OF JOHN OF GAUNT

With a strange persistence, the name of his birthplace has clung to John Plantagenet from the first. Lionel " of Antwerp " is more familiar as Earl of Ulster, or as Duke of Clarence, but for his younger brother posterity has chosen to prefer, to an abundance of territorial titles, the name of the town known to English ears as " Gaunt," and John of Lancaster is John of Gaunt.

The little child born at St. Bavon in March was an early, if unconscious, witness of his father's democratic alliance inaugurated a few weeks earlier, for he was held at the font by James van Artevelde, nor did the burgesses of Ghent forget that their leader had been god-father to an English prince.[1]

The King remained in England until June. The day after he left, St. John the Baptist's Day, he won a battle memorable in the annals of the English navy, the crushing victory of Sluys, which destroyed the French maritime power, and gave England the command of the Channel for many years. Flushed with his triumph over the French and Genoese admirals, Edward rode to Ghent to greet the Queen and the son who had been born to him in his absence.

The Queen and her children remained at Ghent during the short campaign of the summer, which ended at the siege of Tournai, a campaign without a battle, for the French and English armies, after facing each other outside Tournai, made terms. King Robert of Naples had dreamed dreams and warned his cousin of France never

---

[1] [Regina] peperit filium, quem Jacobus de Artevella de sacro fonte levans, compater factus est regi Angliae. *Chr. Reg. Franc.* 93. Cf. *Istore et Chroniques de Flandres*, I, 574. Is this what Walsingham means when he says of Artevelde— Qui quondam consanguineus exstitit Anglorum Reginae Philippae ? (II, 61). Froissart says that John of Brabant was his godfather, and that the name John was given to him as a compliment to his sponsor. (*K. de L.* III, p. 207). Froissart also wrongly gives as his birthplace the Abbey of St. Peter at Ghent. *K. de L.* XVII, 78.

to engage an English army led by the King in person. Prophecy and policy for the moment agreed, and when Jeanne de Valois came from the cloister to make peace between her brother and her cousin, she succeeded. In September the truce of Esplechin postponed the struggle until June, 1341, and in November the King and Queen and the little Princes Lionel and John returned to England.

A courtly writer of the seventeenth century assures us that Queen Philippa's fourth child was "a lovely and lively boy." [1] Probably Philippa thought so, but it is safer to imitate the not unnatural silence of contemporary chroniclers, who had not yet learned to fix their attention on the King's fourth son. Isolda Newman, his nurse,[2] has left no reminiscences of the childhood of the great Duke of Lancaster, and curiosity must await his first appearance on the stage of public life. Impatience is soon set at rest, for it was not long before Edward III took the first step towards the family settlement completed twenty years later. In 1341 the King declared his intention of marrying Lionel, when of age, to Elizabeth de Burgh, daughter and heir of the Earl of Ulster.[3] Meanwhile, the English lands of John de Montfort, late Duke of Brittany and Earl of Richmond, were assigned for the maintenance of Lionel and John, and the King's daughters, Isabella and Joan, under the guardianship of the Queen.[4]

In 1342 John of Gaunt, only in his third year, was granted the Earldom of Richmond in tail, and was duly invested with the " girding of the sword." During his

[1] Barnes, *History of Edward III*, 158.

[2] Annuity of £10 to Isolda Newman, nurse of the King's son, John of Gaunt, February 22, 1346. Froissart, *K. de L.* XXII, 32, *note.*

[3] *Foed*, V. 247–8, dated May 5, 1341.

[4] *Foed*, V. 249, dated May 19, 1341 ; *Rot. Pat.*, May 25, 1341, and June 25 (15 Edward III, pp. 197 and 236, and 17 Edward III, p. 42).

minority the Queen was made his guardian.[1] Henceforth John of Gaunt bears the title Earl of Richmond until his alliance with the House of Lancaster brought him an ampler patrimony and a more famous name.

His youth falls in the first period, the heroic age of the Hundred Years War. A child of six when Prince Edward won his spurs at Crécy, his earliest memories must have been those of the great victories which filled men's minds. 1347 saw the defeat of the Scots at Nevil's Cross, King David a prisoner, the fall of Calais, and England holding " the keys of France." Then, after the victories which were quickening the people with a newly awakened sense of national life, came the Black Death. The age is one of sharply defined contrasts ; the brightest lights and the darkest shadows meet and touch on the canvas. Between Crécy and Poictiers the Great Plague swept over England, decimating the people.

Coming from the East—fruitful soil of disease and teeming populations—it had reached Italy in 1348, where Boccaccio raised to it a monument of graceful egoism and refined callousness in the *Decameron*. Traversing Germany and France, it provoked an outburst of gloomy mysticism, to which expression was given by the Flagellants.

If the faint recollections of childhood had any place in the thoughts of the grown man, these things formed their subject: wars and rumours of wars, plague, pestilence, and famine. But childhood did not last long. If life ended sooner in the fourteenth century than in later times, at least the business of life began earlier.

At eighteen Edward had avenged his father, overthrown the power of Mortimer and Isabella, and begun

---

[1] *Foed*, V. 348. The grant is dated November 20, 1342, and was confirmed March 6, 1351. The Earldom had been granted September 24, 1341, to John de Montfort as a reward for his attachment to the English cause (*Ibid.* V. 280 ; 299-300).

to rule. At fourteen his son had commanded at Crécy.
John of Gaunt saw his first battle at the age of ten. In
1350 an Invincible Armada of Castilian ships was lying
in the roads of Sluys. Nominally there was a truce between England and France and their allies, but a truce
made little difference at sea. Since the battle of Sluys
English sea-borne commerce had nothing to fear from
France, but the wine fleets coming from Bordeaux and the
wool fleets passing between England and Flanders had
suffered severely at the hands of the Castilians, who had
refused Edward's offer of a dynastic alliance, and disputed
his claim to the lordship of the seas — that " Dominium
Maris " which was recognized as the birthright of the
island kingdom.

To protect his commerce and complete the work done
at Sluys, the King got together a fleet and waited for the
enemy. Nearly all the principal feudatories were with
him, and it is with an evident relish that Froissart tells
over the names famous to chivalry : Derby, Hereford,
Arundel, a Holland, a Beauchamp, a Neville, and a Percy.
John, Earl of Richmond, now in his eleventh year, went
to sea with his peers, and was on board Prince Edward's
ship on the day of the battle.[1]

Among innumerable picturesque pages in the Chronicles,
perhaps one of the most striking is that in which Froissart tells how King Edward waited for the Spaniards
on that Sunday in August off the Sussex coast, between
Winchelsea and Rye. The King sits on the foredeck of

---

[1] For the battle of " L'Espagnols sur Mer " see *Chr. Angl.* 28.
Kn. II. 67, Cargrave, *Hist.* Chandos Herald, 499–501, forgets his
dates—

> Et là fut chivaler Johans
> Son frère, qui moult fut vaillantz
> Qui de Lancastre fut puis ducz ;
> Moult grantz parfurent ses vertuz.

Froissart is more convincing : " Mais cils estoit si jones que
point il ne s'armoit, mais l'avoit le princes avoecques lui en sa
nef pource que moult l'aimoit." E. de L. V. 258.

his flagship, the *Salle du Roi*, with his captains about him, while minstrels play an air brought back from Germany by the gallant Sir John Chandos. Suddenly music is interrupted by a shout from the look-out man : "A Sail!" The King, like Drake on the historic Devonshire green, will not be interrupted. He calls for wine, and pledges his knights. Soon the whole Spanish fleet, forty sail, with the afternoon sun striking on their canvas, bears down with a fresh north-easter towards the English ships.

With the wind in their favour and their greater tonnage and sail power, they might have swept down the Channel, but they chose to stay and fight. There was no manœuvring in naval warfare of the fourteenth century. Tactical instructions were comprised in three simple rules : grapple your enemy, board him, and fight it out.

From vespers to nightfall the battle was fought. At its close Edward had won another crushing victory; but it had been a hard fight, and there was scarcely a man in the English fleet who had not a wound to show.[1] One of the incidents of the battle was the danger of the Black Prince. He had grappled a Spaniard, and his own ship was sinking. For long his men could not board the enemy, and it seemed as though Prince Edward, and with him John of Gaunt and the whole crew, must be lost. With the cry of "Derby to the Rescue!" Henry of Lancaster laid his ship alongside and carried the enemy ; the Prince and his little brother were saved—not the last time that the fortunes of John of Gaunt were bound up with those of Henry Plantagenet.

When the battle was over, the King landed at Winchelsea to bring the news of the victory and the safety of her sons to Queen Philippa. *Si passèrent celle nuit les*

[1] Froissart, who got his facts from an eye-witness, put the Castilian loss at 14 ; Walsingham at 24 ; Capgrave at 30.

seigneurs et les dames en grand revel en parlant d'armes et d'amour.

This was the young Earl of Richmond's first taste of chivalry. Five years later the apprenticeship in arms was renewed. In the summer of 1355 John of Gaunt was attached to the expeditionary force placed under the command of the Duke of Lancaster with a view to co-operating against the French with Charles the Bad, King of Navarre — who, having quarrelled with his cousin, John, King of France, had concluded a secret treaty with Henry of Lancaster at Avignon the year before, agreeing to surrender his northern port of Cherbourg into English hands.[1]

The young Earl of Richmond doubtless wondered, with the rest of Duke Henry's captains, where the force would land, for the objective was kept as secret as the treaty which had brought this latest and least desirable ally into the circle of England's friends, and the Admiral lying with his fleet in the Thames had sealed orders.

In the end nothing was done, for when the fleet got under weigh at the beginning of July and reached the Channel Islands to wait for intelligence from the supposed ally which never came, Charles the Bad made peace with his adversary ; the fleet returned to pay off, nothing done, and the Treaty of Valognes saved Cherbourg for awhile from English occupation. France had parried the thrust, but Edward III returned to the charge, and at the beginning of November landed with an army at Calais to lead a raid through Picardy.[2] Again John of Gaunt took part in the expedition.[3] He was now more than fifteen years of age, old enough to begin fighting in earnest,[4] for this was the occasion on which

[1] Robert of Avesbury, p. 425-6 (Rolls Series).
[2] Wals, I, 280 ; Murimuth, p. 186.
[3] Robert of Avesbury, 427-9.
[4] Et se commençoient jà lì enfant à armer (Lionel and John). Froissart. K. de L. V. 321.

King Edward's sword laid knighthood on the shoulder of the young Earl of Richmond.[1] The Black Prince was younger when he won his name upon the field of Crécy; but no fame was to be won on this march, for the demonstration in Picardy failed to bring on an engagement, and accomplished nothing more than useless devastation. Further operations were effectually stopped by serious news from home.

On November 6 the Scots had surprised Berwick, the favourite pastime of the Border chiefs, and the King returned at once. After a hasty session of Parliament, Edward marched north, taking once more the Earl of Richmond with him. Christmas was kept at Newcastle-on-Tyne, the rendezvous of the army, and on New Year's Day the march began. There was little trouble in regaining the town, which was not garrisoned or victualled for a siege. On January 13 the keys were given up, and the King marched into Scotland to exact reprisals.[2]

At Roxburgh John of Gaunt witnessed the famous or infamous act of renunciation, whereby Edward Baliol sold his birthright for a mess of pottage, making over to the King of England his rights to the Scottish kingdom and the Baliol inheritance.[3] The first formal documents witnessed by the Earl of Richmond are the letters patent in which Baliol, pleading his age and failing strength, and disguising his hatred of David Bruce under the pretext of a statesmanlike desire of seeing the union of Englishmen and Scots under one ruler, transferred his rights to Edward III.

After Baliol's surrender the march continued without opposition, to Edinburgh, where the King took up his quarters in the house of that good burgess who, on the

[1] Kn. II, 80.
[2] Scotichronicon, IV, 104-5. Fordun's indignation runs away with him. Baliol addresses the King *tamquam leo rugiens*; Edward advances *velut ursa raptis foetibus in saltus sæviens*.
[3] Dated Bamburgh, January 20, and Roxburgh, January 20 and 25 (*Foed.* V. 832-43).

eve of the expedition ending at Nevil's Cross, besought David Bruce to make him Mayor of London.

There John of Gaunt must have seen the charming Countess of Douglas, whose prayers stayed the King's vengeance and saved Edinburgh from the flames, an act of clemency which thirty years later he himself repeated —saving, without the prayers of a Countess of Douglas, the city which Froissart calls the Paris of Scotland, " car c'est Paris en Ecosse comment que elle ne soit pas France."

After this lesson in warfare and chivalry for a time we lose sight of the Earl of Richmond. He was almost certainly in London when the Black Prince returned in the spring of 1357, and the city cheered the hero of Poictiers as he rode in triumph with his royal prisoner, John, King of France. In November of that year John of Gaunt probably shared in the conventional mourning for the Queen Mother Isabella, whose last years of disgrace since Mortimer's overthrow had been spent in a semi-captivity at Castle Rising, and who died when her grandson was in his nineteenth year.

But far more important than his early apprenticeship in the trade of war was Richmond's first meeting with one who was to be through life his friend and intimate, Geoffrey Chaucer. It was at Christmas, 1357, that John of Gaunt and Chaucer first came to know each other. Before this the poet may have come under his notice in the King's household, but at the Christmas feast of 1357 they met in a more intimate manner, for both were staying at Hatfield in Yorkshire with Lionel, now Earl of Ulster in the right of his wife, Elizabeth de Burgh.[1]

---

[1] Skeat, *Chaucer*, vol. I, xvii. (Introduction). Apparently the Earl of Richmond took his whole household with him. At least, the following entries occur in the account of the Earl of Ulster : Magistro Johanni Coq' comitis Richemundiæ pro consueto annono de consueto dono—13s. 4d. Johanni Lincoln clerico coquinæ dicti comitis pro consueto annono de consueto dono—13s. 4d. Brit. Mus. MS. Addit., 18,632.

FIRST MARRIAGE

Upon Chaucer's fortunes this meeting had a lasting effect, for the friendship of John of Gaunt secured to him the favour of the Court, so long as his patron lived, and after his death the protection of the new dynasty. But the advantage was not all on one side. It is scarcely fanciful to date from their meeting at Hatfield, and the friendship which then began, that interest in letters and men of letters which never forsook John of Gaunt among all the cares of military and political ambition. The soldier and politician is touched by the graces of "more humane" pursuits : it is this which differentiates him from the rough and uncultured type of men of the age, whose thin veneer of chivalry too often scarcely concealed a rough and brutal nature.

Hitherto the movements of King Edward's fourth son have been barely followed by a few scattered notices in the chronicles. After 1359 his position changes. All at once he becomes a public character, and for the next forty years he is never for long out of the public eye. The reason for this change lies in his marriage. In planning his children's marriages, Edward III kept two objects in view : that of strengthening his position abroad by political alliances, and of building up the royal power at home upon the solid basis of territorial power.

It was the first policy which led him to look to the Low Countries. Perhaps the husband of Philippa of Hainault had his prepossessions, but for his attitude to the princes of the Low Countries satisfactory reasons, military and political, could be adduced in support of the dictates of sentiment.[1] Flemish and English commerce were interdependent ; and since the short-lived imperial alliance had been discounted, it became all the more desirable to establish friendly relations with the powers lying near the French frontier. With these aims

[1] The Marquess of Juliers was created Earl of Cambridge May 12, 1340. *Foed,* V. 184–5.

in view, the King in 1340 had proposed to betroth his daughter Isabella to a son of the Count of Flanders,[1] and at the same time had asked the hand of the daughter of the Duke of Brabant for his eldest son, Edward.[2] Those negotiations came to nothing, but eleven years later the same policy was uppermost in the King's mind, when he despatched his cousin, Henry Duke of Lancaster, to the Count of Flanders, to arrange a marriage between the Count's daughter and John of Gaunt.[3]

Upon the success or failure of that mission depended the dynastic history of England for the next century. If John of Gaunt had married the Count's daughter and succeeded in time to the position of a continental potentate, the fortunes of England and of France must have been materially different. Perhaps Artevelde's dream of an Anglo-Flemish empire might have been realized. But at least one all-important factor would have been removed from the problem of English politics: the House of Lancaster might not have dethroned the Plantagenets; perhaps the Wars of the Roses would not have been necessary. But a speculative reconstruction of history, however tempting, is unprofitable. Duke Henry did not succeed in winning the daughter of the Count of Flanders for John of Gaunt. Eight years later he gave the hand of his own daughter instead. The first epoch in the public life of John of Gaunt had begun.

Some families owe both the beginning and the continuance of their power to fortunate marriages. That this is true of the Hapsburgs is a commonplace of history. It is equally true of the House of Lancaster, peculiarly so of John of Gaunt himself. His fate is

---

[1] Powers were given to the Earl of Salisbury Jan. 4, 1340. *Foed*, V. 155.

[2] May 3, 1340 (*Ibid.* 181); letter to the Pope dated Oct. 30, 1340, and Oct. 26, 1344. *Ibid.* 214–5; 432.

[3] Powers dated June 27, 1351. *Ibid.* 710.

moulded by marriage. The first made him a feudal magnate and shaped the next dozen years of his history. The second, equally momentous, converted the great feudatory into something more, making him the claimant to a continental throne and deciding the bent of his ambition for another dozen years. His public life begins and ends with marriage. To this are due his wealth, his power, and his prominence, and the multiplicity of those hereditary claims which make up so large a part of the interest of his life.

In this prominence of the dynastic element the story of John of Gaunt is typical of the age. For six years Parliament and the Privy Council are occupied with the dispute of two gentlemen about a certain coat-of-arms. For Sir Henry le Scrope and Robert Grosvenor substitute the Kings of England, France, and Castile; for the arms " *azure ov un bende d'or* "—the lilies, the castle triple towered, and the lion rampant; and the private quarrel becomes the international dispute. The nations had not yet learned to fight for religions or for markets: they fought for the hereditary rights of their sovereigns, Valois and Plantagenet fight for the crown of France. Burgundy and Trastamare for the crown of Castile, and minor potentates follow suit. For twenty years Brittany is torn by the dynastic quarrel of the houses of Blois and Montfort.

The dynastic importance of John's first marriage was the result of the extraordinary position won by the House of Lancaster. Henry Duke of Lancaster was the most prominent man in England. In the wars he had proved himself one of Edward's ablest generals. His vast wealth and power made him unquestionably the greatest feudatory of the Crown, but he had no male issue. Two daughters were co-heirs of his estates: the elder, Matilda or Maude, married to William Duke of Zealand; the younger, Blanche, whose hand he now gave to John of Gaunt.

The prospect of succeeding to a moiety of the Lancastrian inheritance would have been enough to make the match desirable. But the young Earl of Richmond, we are told, had other motives besides that of ambition.

If Chaucer's picture is true to the original, Blanche of Lancaster united unusual graces of disposition with a full measure of womanly beauty. The White Lady of the *Book of the Duchess* was the flower of English womanhood, a blonde with golden hair, tall, graceful, and with something of that ample richness of form so prized by the taste of the fourteenth century.

It is not unknown for Court poets to use both a poet's and a courtier's licence; and Chaucer doubtless wrote with the prepossessions of friendship, but he wrote for those who knew both John of Gaunt and Blanche of Lancaster. His attractive story of the courtship of the Earl therefore may perhaps be accepted : how he met with difficulties, and failed at first (for there is no royal road to love), but, haunted by the " goodly softe speche " and the eyes—

> Debonair goode glade and sadde,

which looked gentleness and forgiveness, persevered and at length succeeeded.

On Sunday, May 19, the marriage was solemnized at Reading[1] by papal dispensation, for John and Blanche

[1] Capgrave: *De Illustribus Henricis.* 164: Murimuth, 193. *Chr. Angl.* 39. Wals. I, 286.
To Thomas de Chynham, Clerk of the Chapel of Philippa, Queen of England, in money paid to him of the King's gift for his fee for the performance of three marriages in the same chapel, viz., Margaret, the King's daughter, the daughter of the Earl of Ulster and John Earl of Richmond—£10. Issue Roll. (Devon), July 15, 33 Ed. III, 1359, p. 170.
For jewels purchased for the marriage of the Earl of Richmond and the Lady Blanche : to wit, for one ring with a ruby, £20 ; and for a belt garnished with rubies, emeralds and pearls, £18 ; for a trypod with a cup of silver gilt, £20—£58. *Ibid.* July 6, 33 Ed. III, 1359, *Ibid.*
For divers jewels purchased for the marriage of the Earl of

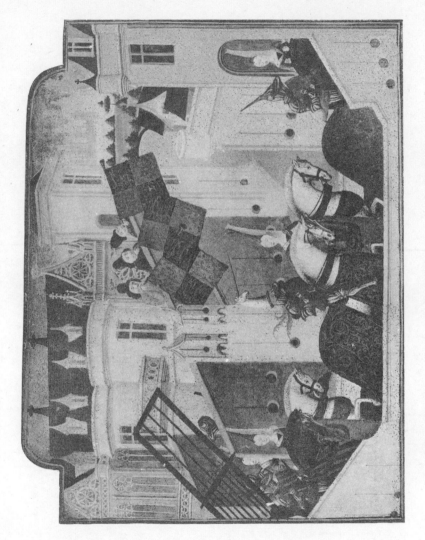

KNIGHTS AND LADIES RIDING TO A TOURNAMENT.

were related in the third and fourth degrees of consanguinity.[1] Taking place as it did at a time when
England was looking forward to a period of peace, the
marriage was eagerly welcomed as an excuse for national
rejoicing. Three days' jousting celebrated the event at
Reading, and for three days more rejoicings continued in
London. To mark its loyalty to the Sovereign and his
family, the City proclaimed a tournament. Mayor,
sheriffs, and aldermen undertook to hold the field for
three days against all comers. At the appointed time
twenty-four knights wearing the cognizance of the City
entered the lists. They made good their challenges, but
when the tournament was over a surprise was in store
for the people. To its astonishment and delight, London
found that, in place of the civic officers, the combatants
who had upheld the City's challenge were the King, his
four sons, Edward, Lionel, John, and Edmund, and
nineteen of the principal barons of England.[2]

Such at least is the tradition. If it is true, the situation
is one of the ironies of history ; before very long the
cheers of the London crowds were to turn to hisses, and
the citizens who in 1359 applauded John of Gaunt
as their champion soon came to look upon him as the
most determined enemy of their privileges and the foe
of all civic liberty.

Richmond and Blanche, daughter of the Duke of Lancaster,
£139 7s. 4d. Issue Roll, Oct. 26, 34 Ed. III, 1360, *Ibid.* p. 172.
For silver buckles given to the Countess of Richmond, £30.
Ibid. March 2, 1360, *Ibid.* p. 173.

[1] *Papal Petitions*, I, 337. Granted Avignon 8 Id. Jan. 7,
Innocent VI, 1359.

[2] Barnes, *History of Edward III*, quoting Holinshed from MS.
Vet. in Bibl. CCC, Cambridge, c. 230.

Chapter II

THE FIRST CAMPAIGN

AT daybreak on October 28, 1359, the flagship *Philip of Dartmouth* was hoisting her sails at Sandwich. Edward III was on board, bound for Calais : the last campaign of the first great epoch of the Hundred Years War was beginning.

Edward had determined to besiege Rheims. In the cathedral of the ancient city where, from time immemorial, the Kings of France had received unction and coronation, in the birthplace of the French monarchy, consecrated by tradition and surrounded by the halo of a peculiar sanctity, the King of England aspired to receive the crown of the " Fleurs de Lys."

The march from Calais to Rheims has little of military interest ; but the pomp and pageantry of the battle array still live in the pages of Froissart, who describes the English army marching out of Calais " so great multitude of people that all the country was covered therewith, so richly armed and beseen that it was great joy to behold the fresh shining armours, banners waving in the wind, their companies in good order, riding a soft pace." At this " soft pace " they advanced through Picardy, Artois, and Cambrésis to the ecclesiastical capital of France.

In the middle of the fourteenth century a walled city, strongly held and well garrisoned, was almost impregnable. Siege warfare reversed the judgment of the stricken field ; the advantage was on the side of the forces of defence. As Rheims was well garrisoned and well

16

provisioned, and the Archbishop made a stout resistance, Edward's seven weeks' siege proved fruitless. The camp was broken up, and the English army, turning to the south past Troyes, Tonnerre, and Noyers, marched to Guillon-sur-Serain, making a feint on Burgundy.

There, while the English captains amused themselves with hawking and hunting, and fished the streams and rivers for their lenten fare, Philip de Rouvre, Duke of Burgundy, made terms with the invader, and bought three years' immunity for his lands, which had not yet felt the scourge of the war, at the price of 200,000 francs— and his loyalty to France.

It was no part of the King's plan to invade Burgundy. He took the bribe and turned north-west to Paris. Challenge of battle was steadily refused. Taught by disaster, Charles, Regent of France, refused to risk battle, and was not to be tempted by a demonstration at his gates. From the walls of Paris, within which the populace of the suburbs St. Germain des Pres, Notre Dame des Champs, and St. Marcelle were gathered, his subjects watched the smoke rising from farm and homestead, and the whole country-side from Montlhéri to Chatillon in flames.[1] An attempt to besiege Paris was hopeless, and the army turned westward.

Meanwhile famine was wearing away the strength of the invaders. From the Seine to Etampes there was neither man nor food, and by the time that the English had reached Chartres their sufferings from privation and bad weather were intense. On Monday after Easter, one of the most mournful Eastertides that Paris has seen, a terrible storm overtook the army ; the English soldiers never forgot that " Black Monday," when fortune

[1] *Chr. Val.* 100–116 ; Richard Lescot, 142 *seq.* ; Continuator of Guillaume de Nangis (He was an eye-witness of the misery of Paris) ; II, 301 ; *Chr. Reg. Franc.* 289 *seq.* Froissart K. de L. VI. 203-294. Kn. II. 105–112.

seemed to have turned against them. The saints were surely punishing their impiety in violating the lands of Notre Dame de Chartres. The King allowed himself to be persuaded to listen to terms ; on May 8 the treaty concluded at Brétigni ended the first phase of the great war.

If the sufferings of the invading army had been great, those of the miserable crowds herded together within the walls of the capital had been greater.

On Sunday, May 10, the Regent took the oath to observe the treaty ; the act, humiliating as it was for France, was hailed " with a joy unspeakable " ; throughout Paris the church bells were set ringing, while in Notre Dame the " Te Deum " was chanted in thanksgiving for the deliverance.

The army returned to England. Apart from its political results, the campaign had done little to justify the judgment of the Valois Chronicler who calls Edward, " Le plus sage guerroier du monde et le plus soubtil." The political results, the terms of Brétigni, might with more justice be attributed to the campaign of 1356 than to that of 1360. It was really the captivity of his father which forced the Regent's hand. Judged from a strategic point of view, the campaign was a failure. The military education of John of Gaunt had opened with a most unfortunate example. Thirteen years later he was to put into practice the principles of his father, to be confronted with the same difficulties, and to suffer the same failure. But if there had been little generalship, there had been plenty of fighting, and in that the Earl of Richmond had played his part : he had taken his share in the skirmishes and raids on the march—at Rethel, where his friend Geoffrey Chaucer was captured, at the sack of Cernay-en-Dormois, and at the capture of Cormicy; and at Rheims he had commanded one of the three " battles " of the besieging army.[1]

[1] Kn. 107–8.

When in May he returned with the King to England, and the curtain fell on the first act of the Hundred Years War, his political life was just beginning. In 1360 he received his first summons to Parliament as Earl of Richmond.[1]

Within three years the king's fourth son was the greatest feudatory in England, and in power, wealth, and position there was no one to dispute his claim to rank as the first subject of the Crown.

John was ambitious ; but apart from ambition, he found " greatness thrust upon him." Forces beyond his control—partly fortune, partly policy—had shaped his destinies. The causes of this " greatness " were : first, the succession to the Lancastrian inheritance ; and second, the removal from England of his two elder brothers, Edward and Lionel.

War, plague, and famine succeed one to another in the Middle Ages with a fearful regularity. For a time war had ceased ; but in 1361 the Great Plague, which, since its first appearance in 1349, had never wholly passed away, broke out with more than usual malignancy. The death roll was long ; but among many notable victims the most illustrious was Henry the " Good " Duke of Lancaster,[2] and the Plague, which enriched William of Wykeham with a dozen prebends, brought to John of Gaunt the greatest inheritance in England.

Duke Henry left two daughters and co-heirs, the younger Blanche Countess of Richmond, the elder Matilda or Maude, who had been married first to Ralf, son of the Earl of Stafford, and afterwards to William of Bavaria, son of the Emperor Lewis, and Duke of Zealand.

The lands of Duke Henry were divided,[3] but not for

---

[1] By writ dated November 20, 34 Edward III. Dugdale, *Summons*, p. 262.

[2] Aeterna memoria dignus. Kn. II. 114. He died March 23, 1361 (Bateson, *Records of the Borough of Leicester*).

[3] Kn. II. 115, 116.

long. Matilda of Lancaster, coming to England to take possession of her patrimony, fell a victim, like her father, to the Plague, and died on April 10, 1362, and all Duke Henry's lands passed to his younger daughter, now sole heir, and in her right to her husband, John of Gaunt.

A few months later John of Gaunt, Earl of Richmond, in his own right and in the right of his wife Earl of Lancaster, Derby, Lincoln, and Leicester, and High Seneschal of England, was promoted to the dignity held by his father-in-law. In the Parliament of November, 1362, the King created him Duke of Lancaster, and formally invested him with the duchy, by " girding him with the sword and setting the cap upon his head." [1]

In the history of the House of Lancaster, with which John of Gaunt now became identified, it is possible to trace, with all due allowance for the difference of circumstance and divergence of personal temperament, a marked and permanent tradition. Towards the great problem of constitutional government which, since the end of the thirteenth century, the nation had set itself to solve, the Earls of Lancaster had contributed little or nothing. They had good service to record, but there was no constitutional fibre in the stock. All were men of great energy. They were pious, with the conventional piety of their age. They were men of strong purpose, and of great ambition. They were gallant soldiers, and perhaps the strongest passion of their race was the love of arms combined with thirst for adventure.

Edmund, the founder of his house, as a child had been trained to thoughts of continental sovereignty. By Papal grant the titular Kingship of Sicily and Apulia is

---

[1] *Rot. Parl.* II. 273. "Et puis nre dit Seign' le Roi ceinta son dity filz Johan d'un Espeie, et mist sur sa teste une cappe furre, et desus un cercle d'or et de peres, et lui noma et fist Duc de Lancastre ; et lui bailla un Chartre du dit Noun de Duc de Lancastre." The Charter is dated November 13, 1362, Hardy *Charters* VI.

I. THE HOUSE OF LANCASTER

Henry III. (1216–72)=Eleanor, daughter of Raymond VI, Count of Provence

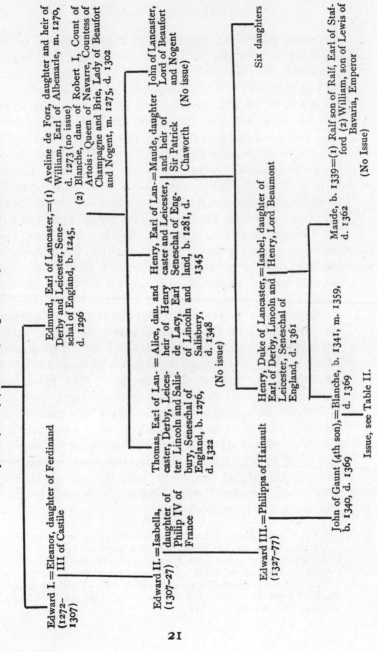

his until Henry III, repenting of a bad bargain, refuses to fight the battles of the Popes against the Hohen-stauffen. A grown man, he longs to exchange the ease of the Savoy for the hardships of the fields of Palestine ; he shares in the glorious illusions of the Crusades, draws his sword against the enemies of the Faith, and fights in the last great battle at Acre. His devotion is vouched for by many besides the Grey Friars of Preston, whose house he founded, or the Sisters of St. Clare at Aldgate. The second Earl, Thomas, shows less knight-errantry than any other of the house : with him home politics and the cares of a vast English domain thrust aside the calls of foreign ambition. For Earl Thomas, though no statesman, has a policy. He asserts the rights which his position, as the greatest feudatory of the Crown, seems to challenge. A council of magnates is to govern Eng-land and the King, and he is to exercise an irregular dictatorship in the Council. But the times are changing, and the ideals of Simon de Montfort no longer satisfy a people awakening to constitutional life. In one thing alone he has the sympathy of all parties—his bitter hatred of upstart royal favourites. He puts Piers Gaveston to death, and his own life pays the forfeit.

But the people do not forget. The hard man of few scruples and unmeasured ambition is transformed into a Saint. Blood still flows and miracles are wrought at the tomb of St. Thomas of Lancaster, and the Govern-ment of Edward II cannot prevent the worship of Piers Gaveston's murderer with Simon de Montfort among the martyrs of English liberty.[1]

---

[1] See the " Office of St. Thomas of Lancaster," beginning:
Gaude Thoma, ducum decus, lucerna Lancastriae.
Ad sepulchrum cujus fiunt frequenter miracula.
Caeci, claudi, surdi, muti, membra paralytica.
Prece sua consequentur optata praesidia. *Political Songs of England from the reign of John to that of Edward II.* Thomas Wright, Camden Society, 1839.

THE HOUSE OF LANCASTER

In the death of the favourite, Henry, third Earl, had no share. But the feud with royal favourites he makes his own. With his brother's arms he assumes his brother's quarrel. The Despencers and Mortimer share Gaveston's fate; Edward II falls, and Earl Thomas is avenged. Henry, too, has the piety of his father; the new hospital of St. Mary of Leicester is one of the many foundations which prove the devotion of the House of Lancaster to the Church.

His son Henry, the first Duke of Lancaster, was the best and greatest of his line. Known to his age as the " Good Duke," Henry was the very pattern of the " parfit gentil knight." Aspirants for chivalrous distinction came from all parts of Europe to perfect themselves in arms and knighthood in his household—the most magnificent in England, for even in peace Duke Henry retained two hundred knights and esquires in his service. He fought the enemies of England and of the Church. The heathen in Lithuania, and the Moors at Algeciras, Rhodes, Cyprus and the East knew his courage. The favourite of the nation and the hero of the French wars, he was the most notable of Edward's generals, until his fame began to pale before the rising brilliance of Prince Edward's star.

And in Duke Henry the adventurous daring of the Lancastrian blood was crowned with the ornament of personal saintliness and gentle piety. In a time of sickness he had written a book of devotion, " *Mercy, Grand, Mercy*," recalling the sins for which he prayed forgiveness, and the blessings for which he owed gratitude to Heaven. He built churches and endowed monasteries. The Church was enriched by his bounty and edified by his life, and the poor and oppressed found in him a protector and a friend.

Such were the traditions of the house with which John of Gaunt allied himself, and whose name he made peculiarly his own. The fifth Earl followed in the steps of his kinsmen, and with the heiress of their lands espoused their traditions.

With as little of real statesmanship as Earl Thomas, John of Gaunt stands the foremost of the great feudatories, his influence built on the solid basis of territorial power. In the stormy days of King Richard's rule he shows the same hatred of royal favourites. What Gaveston and the Despencers were to Earl Thomas and Henry, Robert de Vere is to him. He has the same conventional piety ; indeed, in foundations and endowments he surpasses all his predecessors. Above all, he has the Lancastrian love of arms and adventure. The days of the Crusades are over ; but as Edmund the Crusader had fought the infidel, John " Captain and Standard-bearer of the Church " fights the Antipope. Edmund, " King of Sicily and Apulia," reappears in John " King of Castile and Leon."

Was it policy or the mere caprice of fortune that thrust King Edward's third surviving son into the foremost rank ? Certainly it seems as though the King had from the first marked out for special favour the son who, with the Plantagenet build and features, inherited to the full the characteristics of his race. If this were so, fate conspired with the King's preference.

Lionel " of Antwerp " was two years older than John " of Gaunt." Betrothed in 1342 to the infant heiress of the Earls of Clare and Ulster, Lionel in 1363 went to Ireland as the King's Lieutenant. After three years' dreary exile he returned,[1] but not to play the part which might have fallen to him at the English Court. He went to Italy to seek a bride—and to find a grave. In April he married the daughter of Galeazzo, Lord of Milan. Six months later death cheated him of the Italian inherit-

---

[1] *Eulog.* 241.

ance. His end was mysterious ; there were dark hints of poison, and perhaps the Lord of Milan knew more than another of the mystery.

The Duke of Clarence scarcely finds a place in the annals of his time ; for history the only significance of his life lies in his first marriage. The heiress of Clare, before her death in 1363, had borne him a daughter, whose issue by the Earl of March came, on the failure of Prince Edward's line, to inherit the legitimate right to the English throne.

The Black Prince, who in 1361 had married his cousin Joan, the " Fair Maid of Kent," created Prince of Aquitaine, in 1362 left England to govern the Gascon dependency in the same year in which Clarence went to Ireland.

John of Gaunt was left at the King's right hand, with little rivalry to fear from Edmund of Langley, Earl of Cambridge, a colourless character with neither energy nor ambition, or from Thomas of Woodstock, fifteen years his junior. During the few years following his succession to the Lancastrian inheritance John of Gaunt remained in England, enjoying his new dignities and visiting with the Lady Blanche his new lands and lordships.[1]

Questions of the first importance were discussed in Parliament and in the Council ; as yet the Duke of Lancaster was content to listen. He was one of the " Triers of Petitions " in the Parliament of October, 1362, which recognized English as the language of the courts of law,[2] and again in October, 1363, when for the

[1] Tax of a custom given to the Lady of Leicester on her first coming. Tallage Roll quoted by Bateson, *Records of the Borough of Leicester* ii. 131.

[2] Parliament sat at Westminster from October 13 to November 17, 1362 (*Rot. Parl.* II. 268-274). John was summoned by writ dated August 14 as " Earl of Lancaster and Richmond." Dugdale, *Summons*, p. 266.

first time a Chancellor declared the causes of the summons of Parliament in the mother tongue.[1]

The most significant sign of the times was the growing hostility of England to the Papacy, now transplanted to Avignon, and acting in undisguised alliance with the Court of France. In January, 1365, Parliament forbade English subjects to obey citation to the Papal Court, and declared Papal " provision " to English benefices illegal,[2] and when Urban V made his ill-timed demand for the thirty-three years' arrears of tribute, the Parliament of May, 1366, repudiated once and for all the preposterous claim, which dated from the infamy of King John.[3]

At both these Parliaments Lancaster was present. He was the first on the roll of peers summoned to the Parliament which rejected the claim of Urban V to feudal suzerainty over England, the decision for which John Wycliffe, now a Royal chaplain, produced the official apologia. But the real significance of the changing relations between England and the Papacy he did not see; with the principle underlying " provisors " and " praemunire " he had little sympathy, and, as will be seen, in later years he regarded what was really the quarrel of the nation with Rome as the quarrel of the bishops, and his sympathy was more or less openly on the side of the Popes.

But this is a forecast. As yet far more engrossing than politics were the feasts and revels of King Edward's brilliant Court.

On St. George's Day, 1361, Lancaster for the first time

---

[1] This Parliament sat from October 6 to November 3, 1363. *Rot. Parl.* II. 275–282. John was summoned as " Duke of Lancaster." Dugdale, *Summons*, p. 268.

[2] Parliament sat from January 20, 1365, to February 25. *Rot. Parl.* II. 283–48. Lancaster was one of the Triers of Petitions in this and in all succeeding Parliaments which he attended.

[3] Parliament sat from May 4 to 12, 1366. *Rot. Parl.* II. 289–293.

filled a stall in the Chapel of the Knights of the Garter at Windsor, and took his place at the feast of the Order, clad in a " scarlet robe embroidered with garters of blue taffeta." [1] With his brothers Lionel and Edmund he was enrolled in the brotherhood of chivalry, which was to make Windsor another Camelot, to restore the faded glory of King Arthur's Court, and bind to one another and to the person of the English sovereign the first soldiers of the lands of chivalry.

England, now at the height of her military fame, was visited by knights from all the nations of Europe. After the Peace signed at Brétigni had been confirmed at Calais, the country was given up to rejoicing. At Smithfield and Windsor there were tournaments and jousts at which French and Bohemian, Spanish and Gascon knights vied with one another and with their English hosts. Hunting in the forests of Sherwood and Rockingham was as serious a part of the business of life as the meetings of Parliament.

In one year three kings met at King Edward's Court— Waldemar III of Denmark, David King of Scots, and Pierre de Lusignan, King of Cyprus. David had come to visit the shrine of Our Lady of Walsingham ; he was a suppliant for temporal fovours also, and was begging for a reduction of his ransom. Pierre de Lusignan, after visiting Avignon and Prague, Bruges and Paris, to preach his crusade against the infidel, was entreating King Edward to take the Cross.

---

[1] According to Beltz (*Memorials of the Order of the Garter*) John, Lionel, and Edmund succeeded to the stalls of Thomas Holland Earl of Kent, John Lord Beauchamp, and William Bohun Earl of Northampton, all of whom died at the close of 1360.

Thus Lancaster's stall would be the fourteenth, and he himself the thirty-seventh Knight of the Garter. Robes were first provided for him at the festival of 1361. *Ibid.*

There is no trace of his achievement in the Chapel, nor is it mentioned in any extant list.

JOHN OF GAUNT

At the Savoy, the "fairest palace in the realm," which Duke Henry had rebuilt from the spoils of Bergerac, and filled with all the precious things which fourteenth-century luxury could afford, the three kings and the French hostages were entertained by the Duke of Lancaster. There, doubtless, Chaucer met the Crusader who had won Attalia from the Paynim, and was soon to win Alexandria, and whose untimely end still points a moral in the "Monke's Tale." [1] There, too, the next year the King of France, returning to the land of his captivity, to take the place of the Duke of Anjou, who had broken his parole, lived for the few months that remained to him, and there on April 8, 1364, he died.

By that year the family settlement of Edward III was thought out and almost completed. One thing, however, remained to be done. Edmund of Langley, Earl of Cambridge, the King's fifth son, had no wife. The search for one brought to John of Gaunt his first experience of diplomacy.

In 1361 Philip "de Rouvres," Duke of Burgundy, died, and his line became extinct. Philip left a widow, Margaret, only daughter and heiress of Louis III, surnamed de Mâle, Count of Flanders, Artois, Nevers, and Rethel. On Philip's death his duchy of Burgundy reverted to the French crown, but the county of Burgundy, a fief of the Empire, was held by the Counts of Flanders, and was therefore part of Margaret's patrimony.

With the prospect of succeeding to this great inherit-

---

[1] O worthy Petro, King of Cypre, also
That Alisaundre wan by heigh maistrye
Ful many a hethen wroughtestow ful wo,
Of which thyn owene liges hadde envye,
And for no thing but for thy chivalrye
They in thy bedde han slayne thee by the morwe.
Thus can fortune his wheel governe and gye,
And out of Joye bringe men to sorwe.
Chaucer : *Monke's Tale*, 3581–9 (Skeat).

ance, comprising fiefs of France and of the Empire, the
wealth of Flanders, and lands stretching into the very
heart of France, Margaret was unquestionably the most
important heiress of the day.[1] Philip's death left her
hand to be the apple of discord at the feast of the Princes
of Europe—the prize of successful diplomacy.

Edward III took time by the forelock, and opened
negotiations as soon as decency allowed. The match
would provide for Edmund, and round off the family
settlement. It would strike a fatal blow at the Valois
dynasty, and do more for the English cause in the great
quarrel than ever Crécy or Poictiers had done.

Fortune seemed to be smiling on the King's efforts.
By 1364 he had arrived at an understanding with Count
Louis, and in the summer a special mission, consisting
of the Bishop of London, the Earl of Salisbury, and
Henry le Scrope, Warden of Calais, was appointed to go
to Flanders and conclude preliminary arrangements.[2]
On September 7 the Count met the English envoys at
Bruges and came to terms.[3] A fortnight later Lancaster
was on his way to Flanders, accredited as envoy extra-

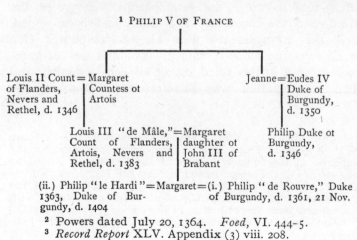

[1] PHILIP V OF FRANCE

Louis II Count = Margaret
of Flanders, | Countess ot
Nevers and | Artois
Rethel, d. 1346|

Jeanne = Eudes IV
       | Duke of
       | Burgundy,
       | d. 1350

Louis III " de Mâle," = Margaret
Count of Flanders, | daughter ot
Artois, Nevers and | John III of
Rethel, d. 1383 | Brabant

Philip Duke ot
Burgundy,
d. 1346

(ii.) Philip "le Hardi" = Margaret = (i.) Philip " de Rouvre," Duke
1363, Duke of Bur-   of Burgundy, d. 1361, 21 Nov.
gundy, d. 1404

[2] Powers dated July 20, 1364. *Foed*, VI. 444-5.
[3] *Record Report* XLV. Appendix (3) viii. 208.

ordinary. The Earl of Cambridge went with him to press the suit.[1]

Count Louis, who was by this time out of humour with his French suzerain, seemed eager for the English alliance. At Bruges and Ghent he entertained Lancaster and his would-be son-in-law. Then returning with them to Calais he crossed to Dover, and there, on October 19, formally ratified the marriage treaty.[2] It was agreed that Edmund should marry Margaret of Burgundy in the first week in February, 1365, and that the Earl should receive a suitable provision, consisting of Calais, Guines and Merk, and lands in England and lordships in Ponthieu.

Thus at the outset of his reign Charles V found himself face to face with a danger which threatened the very existence of his dynasty. The English scheme was far more than a revival of the policy put forward by Artevelde twenty years before. Political union between England and Flanders was only one of the consequences of an arrangement which would have placed some of the most important fiefs of the French crown in the hands of an English prince, and established the enemy on the frontiers of the kingdom. The treaty had been signed, and the arrangements were almost complete. One small formality alone remained. Edmund and Margaret were related in the third degree of consanguinity, and Papal dispensation was therefore required to legalize their union.

[1] *Chr. Angl.* 55 ; *Ypod. Neus.* 309 ; Wals. I, 300–1 ; Higd. VIII, App. 363 ; *Eulog.* 235. Lancaster received £400 for the expenses of the embassy (Issues of the Exchequer, November 22, 1365). Cf. " Foreign Accounts " 45 Ed. III, 5, m. " D "— the account of Robert Crulle, clerk of the King's ships for the expenses of the Duke's ships, *La Sainte Marie* and another, with 64 mariners from September 24 to November 3, 1364. [P.R.O.]

[2] Confirmed by the Black Prince as Prince of Aquitaine, February 20, 1365. *Feed*, VI. 461–2.

MARGARET OF BURGUNDY

But the Vicar of Christ, who held the power to bind and to loose, lived at Avignon, and Avignon obeyed the commands of Paris. Urban V listened to the representations of his ally, or his master, and refused dispensation.[1] It is true that a few months before he had granted it under exactly similar circumstances, but now it was found impossible to relax the strictness of canon law. The barrier of relationship could not be surmounted.

In vain the marriage was postponed from February to May, and again in May to a later date.[2] The Pope remained inexorable. Negotiations dragged on,[3] but to no purpose. Margaret remained a widow. Gradually the affections of Count Louis, never very stable, for the English alliance cooled, and the importunate demands of his mother, a bitter enemy of England, prevailed.[4]

Eight years later Margaret married Philip the Bold, to whom King John had granted the Duchy of Burgundy. French diplomacy had won the battle ; but it was a victory dearly purchased. In 1383 Louis de Mâle died, and the coveted inheritance was united with the Duchy of Burgundy, in the hands of the most ambitious of the Valois princes. Overgrown feudatories like the Dukes of Lancaster and the Dukes of Burgundy proved a thorn in the side of the French monarchy until the fatal success of Charles V was remedied by the policy

[1] Bull dated Avignon 15 Kal., January 3, Urban V. *Foed*, VI. 457.

[2] Powers to Sir Henry le Scrope, December 18, 1364, *Foed*, VI. 47–8. *Record Report* XLV. Appendix (3) viii. 205.

[3] October 24, 1365. *Foed*, VI. 479.

[4] In the *Chron. Reg. Franc.* II. 335-6, the negotiations of 1350 and 1364 are confused. The author thinks that the object of later negotiations was to marry Margaret of Burgundy to Lancaster " cuius uxor decesserat." But Blanche of Lancaster died September 12, 1369, and Philip the Bold married Margaret June 19 that year. The *Religieux de St. Denys* repeats the mistake, I. 159.

31

of Louis XI, and the ghost of the " Middle Kingdom," which had come back once more in the fourteenth century to haunt France, was laid once and for all.

To a man who had in him the makings of a statesman, insight into political conditions, and the power of measuring and using political forces, the embassy of 1364 would have been an invaluable experience. The wooing of Margaret of Burgundy brought to view a complex of political forces of the first importance. The relations, commercial and political, of England and Flanders ; the relations of the Count to his Flemish subjects on the one hand, and his French suzerain on the other ; the power and policy of the Papacy transplanted to Avignon and its value to the Kings of France—all these questions demanded thought of one who aspired to be a ruler in fourteenth-century Europe. That John of Gaunt had the capacity to become a statesman his history unfortunately disproves ; but one principle at least forced itself upon him during the mission of 1364.

Wycliffe would have seen, and seen with shame and anger, the incongruity between the theory and practice of the head of Catholic Christendom, now using and now withholding for political purposes a power claiming divine sanction. Lancaster felt no such incongruity, but he had learnt the value of an ally in the Papal Court. The Papacy had turned the scale against England and snatched the prize from her grasp. It was better to have the Pope for a friend than for a foe. This power he spared no effort to conciliate, and when the time came he was able to enlist the forces of the Papacy to serve his ambition and to use the spiritual weapons of the Church to fight in his cause.

Chapter III

THE INVASION OF CASTILE

AFTER the mission to Flanders in 1364 comes a period
of complete inactivity in the life of John of Gaunt.
The war was at a standstill, and attendance at two short
sessions of Parliament [1] exhausted the Duke's political
cares. Then in 1366 he abandoned this idleness,
forced upon him by circumstances, to play a part in one
of the great enterprises of the day.

> Or n'est pas raison que je faigne
> D'un noble voiage d'Espaigne ;
> Mais bien est raisons que hom l'emprise ;
> Car ce fut la plus noble emprise
> Que onques cristiens emprist—

So writes Chandos Herald [2] of the invasion of Castile
by the Black Prince, and though a less interested
spectator than the domestic herald of Sir John Chandos
may not hold, perhaps, that the undertaking rivalled
the Crusades, at least its political importance
cannot be exaggerated. The story takes us at once
from the Savoy and Kenilworth to Burgos and Valladolid ; and as its events left an indelible mark on the
character of John of Gaunt, and determined the trend

---

[1] The Duke was summoned to the Parliaments which sat at
Westminster from January 20 to February 24, 1365, and May 4
to May 12, 1366. *Rot. Parl.* II, 283–8 and 289–93 ; Dugdale,
Summons, 269 ; 272.

[2] Chandos Herald, 1638 42.

of his ambition, diverting it from its natural channels, it becomes necessary to plunge into the politics of the Spanish peninsula and to unravel the threads of the dynastic history of Castile and Leon which, a few years later, Lancaster himself helped to tangle.

In the fourteenth century the Iberian peninsula contained five independent kingdoms. Two centuries of uninterrupted conquest had driven the Moors, once masters of all but the impregnable highlands of the Asturias, southwards, and penned them within the narrow limits of Granada in the south-east, a refuge permitted to the waning fortunes of the Crescent, until a century later the united forces of the Christian kingdoms drove them out of Spain. In the east the three provinces of Aragon, Valencia and Catalonia made up the kingdom of Aragon : in the west, within the same frontiers as those of to-day, lay Portugal. The little kingdom of Navarre, leaning on the support of a foreign dynasty,[1] maintained its independence in the north, hemmed in on all sides by more powerful neighbours, from whom it was marked off by differences of race, language and tradition.

But Navarre, though inferior to the other kingdoms in material strength, was one of the most important factors in Peninsular politics, for the Lord of Pampeluna was also master of Roncevalles ; he held the keys of Spain in his hands, and could open or close the doors of the Pyrenees to the invader. The centre and south-west of Spain was subject to a ruler who styled himself " King of Castile, Leon, Toledo, Galicia, Seville, Cordova, Murcia, Jaen, Algarve and Algeçiras, Lord of Biscay and Molina," titles which, while indicating the steps by which his

---

[1] The House of Champagne, 1250–1283 ; the royal House of France, 1283–1328 ; then, owing to the absence of Salic Law, the House of Évreux, 1328–1425 ; the House of Aragon, 1425–1479 ; finally, the House of Foix and Albret, and dismemberment.

power had grown up, betray at the same time the looseness of its political organization.

When, in 1350, Alfonso XI, King of Castile and Leon, after winning Algeciras from the Moors and adding it to his dominions, died at the siege of Gibraltar, the great period of Castilian expansion ended. The kingdom now needed a period of quiet and orderly government, in which to consolidate its strength; at a time, however, when the firm hand of a strong ruler was required, the crown devolved upon a minor, and at sixteen years of age Alfonso's son, Pedro I, was called to the task of ruling the most ungovernable race in Europe. In Spain, where the soil had been won field by field, village by village, from the Moors, political organization inevitably took a military shape, and feudal government assumed a more extreme form than was to be found elsewhere in Europe. The mesne tenant owed obedience only to his immediate overlord : if a tenant in chief led his men against the Crown, what in him was treason was in them only loyal performance of feudal duty, while between vassal and vassal the right of private warfare had a legal sanction. When Pedro succeeded, the central authority of the Crown was a pretence and government might appear a visionary ideal. Yet, from the task of governing, a task far harder than that of his father Alfonso the Conqueror, or than that of Henry II and Edward I of England, who had the Church or the people to help them, Pedro did not shrink : he made a deliberate effort to crush disorder and its cause, the independence of the nobles, and for fifteen years struggled with the hydra of feudal anarchy. Unfortunately his most inveterate enemies were those of his own blood, for Alfonso had left to him the most fatal of royal inheritances—the legacy of a dynastic struggle. Alfonso, for political motives, had married his cousin Maria of Portugal, but his affections were bestowed elsewhere.

So soon as the Queen had borne an heir, Don Pedro, she was thrust aside to make place for the beautiful Leonor de Guzman, who became the mother of a line of royal bastards, nine sons and a daughter, the eldest of whom, Enrique, Count of Trastamare, inevitably became the rival of his legitimate half-brother. The position was invidious ; it was accentuated by the folly of Alfonso, who, leaving Queen Maria and Pedro the Infante in obscurity and neglect, allowed his mistress to keep open court as the uncrowned Queen of Castile, and trained his bastard sons to arms and a public career. Thus the earliest lessons taught to the Infante were those of a deep jealous hatred of the royal mistress and her sons, whose position was an insult to his mother and an injustice to himself. Yet Pedro began his reign with moderation and attempts to conciliate. It was only as his efforts were met with distrust and treachery that his temper hardened, and, wearied with sham reconciliations with Enrique, his brothers and their adherents, Pedro adopted harsher measures. Then the King's true character began to show itself ; ungovernable passion, whether of hate or love, swept away the last restraints imposed by conscience or policy ; meeting treachery on all sides, he answered it with cunning ; whoever thwarted his will was a traitor, and in the code of Pedro the Cruel there was only one penalty—death, without trial or sentence, without respite or delay.

One after another the noble families of Castile reckoned a kinsman struck down by the King's merciless hand on a charge of disaffection or rebellion ; blood-feuds multiplied, but anarchy continued. And, not content with declaring war on the nobles, the King alienated the second estate. The Church was the enemy of a ruler who cared nothing for ecclesiastical privilege, spared no one for the tonsure, and was reputed to be a scoffer at religion, while catholic sentiment and racial feeling alike were outraged by the conduct of a king who protected the Jews and chose his ministers from them, and who openly allied himself with the infidels of Granada. The Church and the nobles were against him ; the people alone recognised a method in his blood-madness, and applauded his severity to their oppressors, but in Castile the third estate was as useless in political life, as its levies were helpless on the field of battle. Pedro therefore stood alone, and, to complete his isolation, he had forfeited the support of foreign powers. He had consented to marry Blanche of Bourbon, but the day after the wedding he repudiated her to go back to his favourite Maria de Padilla, to whom he swore that he had been secretly married, and when Blanche died in captivity soon after, the guilt of blood was believed to rest upon the King. This France did not forget. Aragon, too, was a bitter enemy of the Castilian king, who had become involved in a long frontier struggle with his most powerful neighbour.

In 1365 Enrique of Trastamare, who had fled to France, found every circumstance favouring the attempt, which he had long been planning, to overthrow his brother and reign in his stead. When the Papal summons to Don Pedro to appear at Avignon and answer to the charges laid against him had been contemptuously disregarded, Urban V, declaring Pedro an enemy of the faith, "*bougre et incredule*," excommunicated him and gave his kingdom to his half-brother. The King of Aragon, smarting under the loss of his frontier provinces, offered sympathy, a passage through his dominions and financial support. But the determining cause of Enrique's success lay in the condition of France. From the time of the Peace dates the rise of the " free companies," who under their English, Gascon or Breton leaders were now overrunning France. In vain Urban V had backed the invitation of the King of Hungary, who wished to lead the companies against the Turk; at ease in "their chamber," as they called France, they preferred devastation of Christian provinces to the less profitable glories of a crusade. When, however, the prospect of enriching themselves in the yet un-plundered provinces south of the Pyrenees was offered, they accepted gladly.[1]

In December, 1365, Enrique found himself at the head of a formidable mercenary army, consisting of French men at arms, free companies and volunteers from Gascony, Brittany, and even from England, for Jean de Bourbon and the Marshal of France marched side by side with Sir Hugh Calverley, Eustace d'Aubrécicourt, and the Sieur d'Albret.[2] Urban V had bestowed his blessing and, less willingly, a contribution of two hundred thousand francs on the companies, whom a few months earlier he had cursed, and the army marched through Perpignan and the eastern gate of the Pyrenees to Barcelona, where on New Year's day, 1366, the King of Aragon fêted the leaders and paid a subsidy to the troops. Thence, with an insolent summons to Don Pedro to open the passes to the Pilgrims of God marching to avenge the faith and destroy the infidels of Granada, the invaders advanced to Saragossa, up the valley of the Ebro, which they crossed at Alfaro, to Calahorra, maintaining the name of Crusaders by plundering and murdering all the Jews whom they found. At Calahorra, on March 22, the bastard was proclaimed Enrique II; then, advancing unopposed to Navarette, he sacked Briviesca and continued his victorious march to Burgos

[1] Froissart, K. de L. vii. 80–95 ; Chandos Herald, 1668–1773 Ayala, i. 395–402.
[2] The loyalty of the English and Gascon contingent is not above suspicion. According to Ayala the Sieur d'Albret offered to detach the Gascons and join Don Pedro, but Pedro would not pay for his services : *non era usado de partir sus tesoros.* Ayala, i. 398, cf. i. 405.

itself. It was at Burgos that Pedro had been concentrating; but when the usurper was almost upon him, his nerve failed. The summons to arms had met with a poor response, and even among those who had come to protest their loyalty, Pedro knew that many were only waiting their time to desert.

On March 28, in spite of the entreaties of the city, Pedro abandoned Burgos and fled precipitately southwards to Seville.[1] In the hour of need the King bethought him of his cousin of Portugal, whose son had been betrothed to Beatrix, the eldest of Pedro's daughters, Infanta of Castile. But the King of Portugal declined to help him, and sent back the Infanta and her dowry, and the utmost that Pedro could obtain was a safe conduct through Portugal to the north. Taking his daughters with him, and as much treasure as he could collect, the King fled to Albuquerque, to find its gates shut in his face, and thence through Chaves and Lamego to Monterrey. There he stood at the parting of the ways, for in Galicia he was still king. Logroño, too, commanding the Ebro and the Burgos road, was still holding out for the legitimist cause. To march on this faithful city, and rally his forces for a campaign, was the advice of his trusted adviser, the governor of Galicia, Fernando de Castro, brother of the Inez de Castro famous in the annals of Portugal and the verse of Camoens. But Pedro despaired, and not without reason. For the Bastard's advance had been one of triumph : crowned at Las Huelgas on April 5, he had received the homage of nearly all the hidalgos of Castile at his court at Burgos, where he rewarded their support with a lavish generosity which won him the name Enrique "el Magnifico." Then, turning south, he had won Toledo, and as Pedro was flying north, had established himself in Cordova and

[1] Ayala, i. 402–406 ; Chandos Herald, 1774–1815 ; Froissart, K. de L. vii. 95–115.

Seville.[1] Pedro was convinced that resistance was hopeless. From Monterrey he had written the story of his misfortunes to Prince Edward; he now advanced to Coruña, and without awaiting the arrival of the envoys sent to meet him by the Prince, took ship, coasted to San Sebastian and landed at Bayonne, where he found Sir Thomas Felton, Seneschal of Aquitaine, waiting to receive him.[2]

Prince Edward himself rode out of Bordeaux to meet the royal exile, and by the cordiality of his welcome showed that he had already formed his decision on what was perhaps the most fateful issue ever presented to him—the decision to espouse the quarrel of the dethroned king.

The Prince's motives betray a mixture of policy and sentiment which is characteristic of the age. The Treaty of Calais, as every one knew, could not last for ever, and if, when war broke out again, France were to be supported by a friendly dynasty in Castile, and Aquitaine, fearing for her lines of communication by sea, were to be surrounded north, east and south by hostile powers, the Prince's position would be one of extreme danger. But apart from considerations of policy, two motives powerfully inclined the Black Prince to support Don Pedro—his feeling for royalty and his feeling for legitimate birth. To Spanish law and Spanish sentiment bastardy might be a matter of small moment, but in England and France this was not so. The Prince saw in Don Pedro the representative of legitimate royalty, and in the usurpation of Don Enrique an outrage upon the social order.

"*Ce n'est pas cose afférant deue ne raisonnable d'un bastart tenir royaulme et hiretage, et bouter hors de son*

---

[1] Ayala, i. 406–412 ; 421–430.
[2] *Ibid.* i. 430–33 ; Chandos Herald, 1816–1963 ; Froissart, K. de L. vii. 94–117.

*royaulme et hiretage un sien frère, roy et hoir de la terre
par loyal mariage ; et tout roy et enfant de roy ne le doient
nullement voloir ne consentir, car c'est uns grans préjudisces
contre l'estat royal."* [1]

So argued the Prince of Wales, who before all his
other titles styled himself " Eldest son of the King
of England."

The project of restoring a dethroned king was a matter
of policy and principle. It fell in too with the Black
Prince's humour of knight-errantry. Was there not a
prophecy, as old as Merlin's age, which foretold that
the Leopards of England, known to the fields of
Crécy and Maupertuis, should some day float over the
battlefields of Spain ? In vain the brave but cautious
Sir John Chandos, who had refused to take part in
the expedition of 1366, now gave his voice against a
policy which would divide the forces of England. Pedro's
appeal for help was accepted by a Parliament at Bordeaux
and referred to the home government. At the council
which listened to the Prince's proposal and the *apologia*
delivered by Don Pedro's envoys, the Duke of Lancaster
was present ; he gave his vote in favour of the project
to support the legitimate king and check the growing
influence of France in the Peninsula, and he accompanied
the envoys who returned to Aquitaine with the royal
assent. [2]

At Bayonne in September, 1366, a second Parliament
discussed the invasion of Castile. There were two routes
by which a mounted force could enter Spain : the eastern
door, by which Enrique had entered, and the western
door which alone was practicable from Aquitaine. Charles
the Bad, King of Navarre, therefore, was invited to the
meeting of the Gascon barons, and asked to name his

[1] Froissart, K. de L. vii. 107.
[2] Orders to arrest ships for Lancaster's passage, dated
September 16, 1366. *Rot. Gasc.* i. 154 (Carte).

price for opening the pass of Roncevalles.[1] The cession of a couple of provinces and half a dozen frontier towns on the part of Don Pedro bought Charles' adherence, and in consideration of two hundred thousand florins he agreed to open the passes and lead two thousand Navarrese troops in the invading army.

With the Gascon barons, as with the King of Navarre, the enterprise was purely a matter of business. They were perfectly willing to fight for Don Pedro, as many of their comrades had just fought against him, if he made it worth while, and when the exiled king talked freely of the hidden treasures of Castile, the Gascons needed no further argument to convince them of the divine right of kings. Pedro, however, was without resources for the time, and in a fatal moment Prince Edward undertook to advance not only Navarre's bribe, but the pay of the mercenary army.[2] This debt Pedro engaged himself to repay by the most solemn oaths, under pain of excommunication and interdict, and until the sum should be discharged he agreed to leave his daughters at Bordeaux, with the families of the Grand Master of Alcántara and the Chancellor of Castile by way of security, while, to mark his sense of obligation to his generous ally, he granted Prince Edward the province of Biscay and Castro-Urdiales in full sovereignty.[3] A

---

[1] L'an mccclxvi en hahost bengo lo rey Dempetro d'Espanha de Nabara e lo rey de Malhorguas e lo duc de Bretanha a parlamen a Bordeu. *Petite Chronique de Guyenne*, § 55.

[2] The articles of agreement between Prince Edward, Charles, King of Navarre, and Pedro, King of Castile, were confirmed at the Friars Minors, Libourne, September 23, 1366 (*Foed*, vi. 514–20). The Prince advanced 20,000 florins, the first instalment of Navarre's 200,000 for opening the passes, and 36,000 the first month's pay for Navarre's contingent (*ibid*. 512–4); the wages of the Prince's army, viz. 550,000 florins for six months' service, were to be repaid at Bordeaux by fixed instalments at specified periods within the next two years (*ibid*. 528–31).

[3] The donation, dated Libourne, September 23, was witnessed by Lancaster (*Foed*. vi. 521–3); on the same day letters com-

commercial concession and an honorary distinction completed the expression of Pedro's gratitude; he agreed that all English subjects should be quit of payment of taxes and customs (save ordinary *octroi* dues) throughout his dominions, and he granted to the King of England and his heirs in perpetuity the right of fighting in the vaward of Castilian armies, ordaining that in their absence the standard of England should be borne "*honorifice prout decet*" with the standard of Castile.[1]

The alliance was sealed and the die was cast. Prince Edward began to prepare without delay. Reminded by Chandos that taxation would be an unwise method of raising the supplies he needed, the Prince commanded his plate to be melted down, summoned back his Gascon and English subjects from Trastamare, and sent Chandos to negotiate with the leaders of the free companies, while John of Gaunt went back to England to raise a body of men for the compaign.[2] Lancaster spared no cost to appear worthily in his brother's army. To raise supplies he pledged his Honor of Richmond,[3] and at the beginning of November he left England in command of a compact force of four hundred men-at-arms and six hundred archers.[4] After crossing the

manding obedience were issued to the judges, alcaides and sheriffs of the ceded territories (*ibid*. 524–5), and powers were given to Sir John Chandos and Sir Thomas Felton to take possession (*ibid*. 525–7). All Pedro's obligations were again ratified at Bayonne, February 11, 1367 (*ibid*. 527–8; 528–31).

[1] Same date (*Ibid*. 531–3). Cf. *Brit. Mus. Cot.* Ch. v. 1, with a fine specimen of the leaden "bulla" of Castile.

[2] Chandos Herald, 1964–2013; Froissart, K. de L. vii. 115–117; 120–123.

[3] Delpit, *Collection*, ccii. Cf. Great Cowcher, ii. 413, dated Westminster, November 5, 1366.

[4] *Istore et Chroniques de Flandres*, ii. 102. Orders to seize ships for his passage, dated October 20. *Rot. Gasc.* 154 (12) (Carte).

Channel and landing in Brittany,[1] the Duke marched to Nantes, where the Duke and Duchess of Brittany gave him a send-off, crossed the Loire, advanced through Poitou and Saintonge, and crossing the Gironde at Blaye entered the capital of Aquitaine just a week after the birth of the Prince's second son, Richard of Bordeaux. On January 10 the Black Prince had left Bordeaux to take command of his army concentrated at Dax, and there three days later he welcomed John of Gaunt (who had stayed in Bordeaux only long enough to greet his sister-in-law), and the fine contingent marching under the Lancastrian banner, the only force in the army all ranks of which were English. On the eve of the march the Prince gave a banquet in honour of his brother's arrival, and there Lancaster for the first time met the Count of Foix. But in spite of festivities and the high hopes of the army, the moment was not without grave anxiety, for no one knew what game the King of Navarre was playing.[2]

At Bayonne, in September, 1366, he had sworn to open the passes to the Prince; at Santa Cruz de Campezo in January, 1367, for the same bribe he swore to close them. Committed so far as oaths could commit him, first to the Prince and then to Enrique, Charles the Bad was wondering which perjury would be more profitable and less dangerous.[3] But his dream of impartially malevolent neutrality suffered a rough awakening. Sir Hugh Calverly had been the last to leave the Bastard, in obedience to the Prince's summons, and on his homeward march through Navarre, knowing Charles' double-dealing, he sacked Miranda del Arga and Puente la

---

[1] Chandos Herald (2118) says he marched through the Cotentin; but according to Froissart's version (K. de L. vii. 149), the Duke landed at Saint Mahieu de Fine Poterne (i.e. Saint Mathieu Fin-de-Terre).

[2] Chandos Herald, 2014–2204.

[3] Ayala, i. 434–6.

Reina.[1] Navarre thus convinced as to the side on which his immediate interest lay, sent his right-hand man, Don Martin Henriquez de la Carra, to Dax with his excuses. With some difficulty a meeting was arranged between Navarre and Lancaster at St. Jean, when the Duke persuaded him to meet the allies, whom he had betrayed, at Peyrehorade, and in the end the old agreements were renewed, Navarre was held to his first promise, and nothing remained to hinder the advance.[2]

It was bleak winter weather when on Monday, February 15, 1367, the vaward of the Prince's army, some ten thousand strong, under the command of the Duke of Lancaster, began the ascent from St. Jean, and wind and hail beat upon horse and rider as the long line wound through the famous pass where more than five centuries before Roland the Paladin had fallen, and the Basques had cut up the rearward of Charlemagne's army. But the longest day's march comes to an end, and before nightfall the Duke had left Roncevalles behind him, and his force, descending the valley of the Arga, debouched upon the march of Pampeluna. The next day, when the Prince, with Don Pedro and the unwilling King of Navarre, led the centre column through the pass, was equally trying, but on Wednesday, 17th, the rearward, under the Gascon Albret and the dethroned King of Majorca, had better weather.[3] For the rest of the week the army remained round Pampeluna, enjoying an abundance of provisions, for which they were not too scrupulous in paying. Meanwhile Charles of Navarre was in an

---

[1] Chandos Herald, 2193–6. It is clear that this was done on his homeward march, for Calverly did not leave Enrique until after the meeting with Navarre at St. Cruz. (Ayala, i. 437.) Froissart's account is unintelligible, and leads one to suppose that Calverly rushed the pass of Roncevalles, which was of course, impossible (K. de L. vii. 150–3).

[2] Chandos Herald, 2205–2221.

[3] *Ibid.* 2221–2384.

uncomfortable position. In spite of his diplomatic efforts forty thousand men were in his kingdom, most without a keen sense of the rights of property, while he himself stood committed to a side, and he was by no means sure that it was the winning side. It was a case for finesse. From Pampeluna Tudela was not far distant, and a few leagues from Tudela lay Borja over the frontier, a castle given by the King of Aragon to Bertrand du Guesclin, and by him to his cousin Olivier de Mauni. Navarre arrived at an understanding with the lord of Borja, and, by accident, rode too near the frontier. Unfortunately he was captured, and therefore could take no farther part in the invasion; and while Martin de la Carra, a subordinate who could be disowned, took command of the Navarrese contingent, the Queen of Navarre went to the Prince with tears in her eyes to report the disaster and to beg for his rescue.[1]

While this comedy was being played in Navarre the Castilian scouts were not idle. Enrique on the first news of the Prince's movements had left Burgos and concentrated at Santo Domingo de la Calzada, on the Pampeluna-Logroño-Burgos road, where he found himself in command of some sixty thousand troops of all arms, heavy Castilian cavalry, light horse and infantry. His mainstay, however, was a picked body of French lances two thousand strong under the command of du Guesclin. The Bastard was confident of success, and wrote a spirited defiance to the English general.[2]

Henceforward the movements of three forces have to be followed : the usurper's army lying at San Domingo, the main body of Prince Edward's army lying at Pampeluna, and a flying column under Sir Thomas Felton sent to keep in touch with the enemy and report their

---

[1] Chandos Herald, 2476–99. Froissart, K. de L. vii. 163–4.
[2] Ayala, i. 438 ; Froissart, K. de L. vii. 159–61 ; Chandos Herald, 2385–447.

APRIL 5, 1966
ENRIQUE CROWNED

BAYOONNE
SEPT 1366
2ND PARLIAMENT TO DISCUSS
INVASION OF CASTILE

LIBOURNE SEPT 23
WITNESSED BY LANCASTER
EARLY NOV LANCASTER LEFT ENG
JAN 10 PRINCE LEFT BORDEAUX

FEB 11 BAYONNE
RATIFIED AGAIN

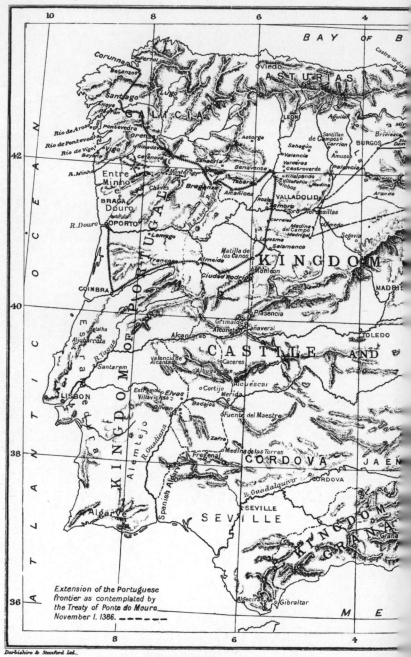

Extension of the Portuguese
frontier as contemplated by
the Treaty of Ponte do Mouro
November 1. 1386. – – – – – –

Darbishire & Stanford Ltd.,

English Miles

0   20   40   60   80   100

Scal

Invasion of Castile 1367,
March of Prince Edward ----------
March of Don Enrique ——————
Invasion of Castile 1387,
March of John of Gaunt ∿∿∿∿∿∿∿

The Oxford Geographical Institute.

Kilomètres
0 20 40 60 80 100

movements. This latter force struck south-west at once, and relying on the support of the legitimist stronghold of Logroño, crossed the Ebro there, and took up a position at Navarette.[1] Meanwhile the Prince, who had resolved to follow the Pampeluna-Vitória-Burgos road, was advancing through Guipuzcoa and Alava under the guidance of Martin de la Carra and his native guides. Traversing the pass of Arruiz, the army reached Salvatierra after a hard march, and after resting there six days continued unopposed to the outskirts of Vitória.[2] Don Enrique on his part, so soon as the line of the English advance became clear, broke up his camp at San Domingo, marched north to Bañares, crossed the Ebro, and took up a strong position at Añastro, near Treviño, thus throwing himself across the road from Vitória to Burgos, while Sir Thomas Felton, regaining the left bank of the Ebro, rode north to rejoin the army between Salvatierra and Vitória with the news of the enemy's movements.[3]

The two armies, though hidden from each other by the rising ground between them, were now within striking distance, and an action seemed imminent. Warned by his scouts of the enemy's arrival, the Prince marshalled his army for battle, and, in accordance with the usual custom, went through the ceremony of making new knights. With two hundred Englishmen and Gascons the King of Castile received knighthood at the

---

[1] Chandos Herald, 2448–75 ; Froissart, K. de L. vii. 161–3 ; Ayala, i. 438. I dissent from the conclusion of M. Luce (Froissart, vol. vii. Introduct. p. vii.), who thinks that the Navarette in question is a town of that name in Alava on the Salvatierra road. If the statement given above rested on the evidence of Froissart alone it might be rejected, but Chandos Herald is explicit, and cannot be set aside. Moreover, considering the position of the enemy, the other identification is impossible.

[2] Chandos Herald, 2500–21 ; Froissart, K. de L. vii. 164–6.

[3] Chandos Herald, 2523–78 ; Froissart, K. de L. vii. 166–9 ; Luce, vol. vii. Introd. ix.

hand of the Black Prince, while John of Gaunt also gave the accolade to a dozen captains of his division. It was an anxious moment, for the rearward of the Prince's army was some seven leagues away to the east, and had the enemy attacked they could never have come into action. But no attack was delivered, and after standing to arms until nightfall the troops were dismissed to their quarters.[1]

The next day an incident occurred which might have proved serious. Don Tello, the Rupert of the Castilian army, a dashing but untrustworthy leader of light horse, got together a body of some six thousand men, and left the Bastard's camp before dawn to reconnoitre the Prince's position, and to see what mischief could be done. Successfully evading the Prince's pickets, he fell upon an outpost of the first division, and then, after cutting up some of Calverly's men stationed there, advanced to the centre of the line. Soon, however, he had to beat a retreat, for at the first alarm Lancaster had come out of his tent fully armed, and displaying his standard had rallied his men. The attack, thanks to the readiness of John of Gaunt,[2] had failed, but Don Tello had not finished yet.

The chief disadvantage of the Prince's position was the difficulty of getting supplies, and it was the necessity of foraging far afield which led to the first and only reverse of the campaign. For while the army lay on the south-east side of Vitória facing Sant Roman, Sir Thomas Felton, with a couple of hundred men, had

---

[1] Chandos Herald, 2579–2641 ; Ayala, i. 447 ; Froissart, vii. 168–173.

[2] Là eust esté, si Dieux me garde
Forment supprise l'avant-garde,
Si n'eust esté li francs ducs
De Lancastre, plein de vertus. . . .

Chandos Herald, 2647–2720 ; Ayala, i. 445–6 ; Froissart, K. de L. vii. 173–7.

been sent westwards in search of provisions, and, as ill-luck would have it, at Ariñez he fell in with Don Tello's brigade fresh from their exploit in beating up Lancaster's camp. Felton was at once surrounded, but, in spite of fearful odds, fought the Spaniards with dogged determination from morning to nightfall. It was only after French men-at-arms had been brought up to reinforce Tello's genetours that the little band of English and Gascons was overpowered. Half of their number, including Felton's brother, had fallen; the rest were taken prisoners, after fighting all day with a heroic courage which has never been forgotten, for to this day the spot where they made their last stand retains the name of " Inglesmendi," or the " Grave of the English." [1]

These two successes, trivial as they were, buoyed the hopes of Enrique, who, hailing them as the prelude to a general defeat of the invading army, could not be brought to listen to the advice sent him by Charles V and urged upon him by his French officers—to avoid a pitched battle, and by closing the passes round Vitória to starve the English general into surrender. Only disaster had taught Charles V the lesson of inaction, and Enrique had yet to learn his lesson in the same school. It is true that, as often happens, the Castilian general was forced to qualify military conclusions by political considerations. The dynasty of Trastamare was only a year old ; it had yet to prove its title, and in view of the desertion [2] from the ranks which had taken place (and was to continue), it seemed imperative to strike a decisive blow. But the course actually adopted had all the faults of a compromise ; Enrique refused to block the passes and trust to inaction ; he refused also to sacrifice the advantage of a strong position and attack,

[1] Chandos Herald, 2642–6, 2721–2821 ; Froissart K. de L. vii. 177–84 ; Ayala, i. 446.
[2] Ayala, i. 439 and 454.

and he forgot that there was more than one road to Burgos.[1]

A cold, wet and stormy March had caused intense suffering in the Prince's camp, where every one was on short rations. The road *via* Miranda to Burgos was blocked, and every foraging party that left the lines was cut up. The enemy held a strong position, and showed no signs of intending to abandon it. So the Prince decided, after a week's delay before Vitória, to change his line of advance, and by manœuvre to regain the superiority of position. Suddenly breaking up his camp, he doubled back by a forced march to the south-east over the Sierra de Cantabria by the pass of La Guardia to Viana, and thence after breathing his army for a couple of days, marched into Logroño. The faithful city which commanded the passage of the Ebro deserved well of Don Pedro, for it was the loyalty of Logroño alone which enabled the Prince to undertake this brilliant flank march which had completely changed the position.[2]

The Bastard was compelled to abandon his position at Añastro, and crossing the Ebro at San Vicente to march to the south and throw himself once more across the line of the Prince's advance from Logroño to Burgos. The position which he chose was at Najera, where the river Najarilla, a tributary of the Ebro, protected his front.

Meanwhile the Prince advanced from Logroño to Navarette, and it was there that on April 1 he sent a letter[3] to the Bastard in answer to the challenge which had reached him at Pampeluna. The cause of legitimate royalty as much as Don Pedro's misfortunes and the traditional alliance of England and Castile had forced

[1] Chandos Herald, 2822–73 ; Ayala, i. 443–5.
[2] Chandos Herald, 2874–63 ; Ayala, i. 447–8 ; Froissart, K. de L. vii. 184–7.
[3] Chandos Herald, 2894–3140; Ayala, i. 448–50; Froissart, K. de L. vii. 187–91 ; *Foed*, vi. 554–5.

him to intervene in the struggle; Enrique was in arms
against the lawful sovereign to whom he had sworn
obedience, and unless he would consent to lay down
his arms and accept the Prince's mediation, the quarrel
must be referred to the arbitrament of the sword.

A dignified reply, dictated in the royal palace of Najera
on April 2, set forth the usurper's apology. Pedro's
misgovernment was notorious, and Enrique would not
abandon his self-chosen part of the deliverer of Castile.[1]

With this the Bastard crossed the Najarilla and took
up a position in the open plain between Najera and
Navarette, where he could have free play for his mounted
men, and prepared for battle, while the Prince on the
morning of Saturday, April 3, advanced to meet him.[2]

The Prince's army was marshalled in three divisions :
the vaward under the command of the Duke of Lancaster, with Sir John Chandos at his right hand ; the
centre under the Prince himself, with two wings commanded by the Captal de Buch and Sir Henry Percy
respectively ; the rearward under the King of Majorca
and the Gascon Armagnac, the three divisions and the
two wings being flanked on either side by a strong force
of archers, and the whole force, numbering some twenty
thousand men, half men-at-arms and half archers, all
dismounted. On the Spanish side only the vaward
was dismounted. This, consisting of about two thousand
men-at-arms, was composed of the French auxiliaries
and a picked body of Castilian men-at-arms, including
the Knights of the Scarf (the Castilian Garter), the
whole being under the command of Bertrand du Guesclin.

---

[1] Ayala, i. 450–53 ; Foed, vi. 556–7.
[2] See Professor Oman's exhaustive account in the *Art of
War (Middle Ages)*, pp. 637–48, and in addition to the authorities
quoted cf. *Chr. Reg. Franc.* ii. 324–30 ; Guillaume de Nangis
(Cont.), ii. 368 ; *Chr. Val.* 167 ; *Istore et Chroniques de Flandres*,
ii. 102 ; Petit Thalamus, 376 ; *Chr. Angl.* 57–60 ; Wals.
i. 302–6 ; Kn. 121–3 ; *Eulog.* 333–4.

JOHN OF GAUNT

Enrique commanded the centre in person; it consisted of about fifteen hundred mounted knights, and was supported by two wings, the left led by Don Tello, and the right by the Count of Denia and the Grand Master of Calatrava. In the rear was stationed a mob of Castilian infantry, who proved useless in the battle and an encumbrance in the flight.[1]

The battle array must have presented a fine picture. Chandos Herald had seen many a battle, but none like this, for in his own words—

> Unques tel mervaille ne fu,
> Ne tiel plenté dé poeple vu
> Come il ot à cele journée.
> Là ot mainte baniere ouvrée
> Qui fu de cendal et de soye [2]—

and Froissart, who, in spite of his eagerness to follow the army over the Pyrenees, had been sent back from Dax to Bordeaux when the march began, from the Abbey of St. Andrew conjures up the picture of the battlefield on that fateful day, when for the first time Castile was to feel the force of English archery, while even the dull prose of Ayala's narrative warms into life as he writes of the day when, bearing the banner of the Knights of the Scarf, he saw the red cross of St. George flutter over the crests of the English knights, and heard the battle-cries " Guyenne, St. George ! " and " Castile, Sant Iago ! " ring in his ears as the two hosts met in the shock of battle.

As the signal was given Lancaster pushed forward his archers, who poured a deadly fire into the ranks of the enemy, enfilading the Castilian vaward as it advanced. Yet in spite of this fusilade, for which the slingers and bowmen of the enemy were no match, Lancaster's division was borne back a spear's length

[1] " Pero aprovecharon muy poco en esta batalla, ca toda la pelea fué en los omes de armas." Ayala, i. 442.
Chandos Herald, 3075-9.

as du Guesclin's Frenchmen charged home, and for a moment the English van wavered. Soon, however, they held their own again, and the two lines remained locked together in a desperate struggle. It was the disgraceful conduct of the two wings which decided the battle. Appalled by the English archery, Don Tello never drove his charge home, and after the first onset galloped off the field. His loyalty to Don Enrique is not above suspicion, and it is more than probable that on the day of the battle he was thinking more of his own cherished ambition of maintaining an independent position in his northern lordship of Biscay than of the cause of Trastamare. However this may be, the right wing made no better show, the Count of Denia was wounded and captured, and the Prince, though he had made no attempt to outflank the enemy, was able by wheeling in his two wings to produce the same effect. When Percy and the Captal de Buch fell upon du Guesclin's right and left the issue was certain, and by the time the second lines got into action the battle was virtually decided. In vain Don Enrique with magnificent courage attempted to rally his men, three times leading a charge in person. The Spaniards were flying, and though du Guesclin's Frenchmen and the Knights of the Scarf stood their ground and fought until they were all killed or captured, the battle was lost, and the army was routed. It was in the pursuit, as usual, that the greatest carnage took place. The narrow bridge over the Najarilla was choked by the infantry, who had been the first to fly, and hundreds of the Bastard's cavalry were cut down as they fled or drowned as they attempted to cross the river, and eye-witnesses described how from Najera to the Ebro the stream was red with the blood of the slain.[1]

[1] Chandos Herald, 3141–3455 ; Ayala, i. 453 ; Froissart, K. de L. vii. 191–219.

JOHN OF GAUNT

So was won the last and greatest victory of the Black Prince, a victory which sent a thrill of admiration through Europe, compelling friend and foe to see in Edward Plantagenet what Froissart saw in him : " *la fleur de toute la chevalerie dou monde.*" Not only in England, where Najera was celebrated with a tumultuous extravagance of joy, but in Flanders and the Low Countries and in all the states of the Empire the prowess of the Black Prince was the subject of universal acclamation,[1] mingled in France alone with other feelings—regret for the hundreds of brave men who lay lifeless on the field of battle, dismay at the captivity of the heroic Bertrand du Guesclin. The victory which brought such fame to Prince Edward filled his ally with a savage exultation. One day had given him back his kingdom and placed in his hand the lives of those who had driven him from the throne to exile. So at least Pedro hoped, as, forgetting his oath that no Castilian should suffer death save for proved treason, he began to give way to the blood-thirst which possessed him. On the very day of the battle he had met one of the Bastard's most notable supporters, Iñigo Lopez de Orozco, who had surrendered to a Gascon knight, and in spite of the indignant protest of the captor, whose honour was pledged to protect the Castilian, the king had set upon him, and struck him dead with his own hand.[2] In vain the Prince complained of this violation of the compact, asking Don Pedro if such were the spirit in which he intended to fulfil his engagements, and warning him that he must learn gentler methods if he would keep his throne, for the next day the King put forward a transparent proposal to buy all Castilian prisoners from their captors, and when his offer was contemptuously rejected, passionately declared that the Prince was robbing him of

[1] Froissart, K. de L. vii. 227.
[2] Ayala, i. 458, 471.

the fruits of the victory. The restoration was only a day old, and already the allies were seriously estranged, for with Pedro gratitude was lost in the deeper feeling of disappointed revenge. In a few days this estrangement had ripened into a scarcely veiled hostility. On Monday, April 5, the king rode from the battlefield where the army had bivouacked in the enemy's deserted camp, straight to Burgos; the Prince halted for a couple of days in Briviesca, and did not reach Burgos until the 7th, when he was quartered in the Convent of Las Huelgas, where a year before the rebels had proclaimed Enrique II, while Lancaster was received in the Dominican Monastery of San Pablo.[1]

It was not long before further ill-feeling resulted from the false position of the allies.[2] Technically the Prince was merely a mercenary in the service of the Castilian King,[3] but he bore himself like a victorious general in a conquered country.[4] Nothing could have been more certain to arouse Perdo's jealous pride, while the Prince on his part did not scruple to show what he thought of the honour of his ally. It had been arranged that all the engagements entered into at Bayonne in September, 1366, and confirmed at Libourne and again at Bayonne just before the start, should be publicly ratified in Burgos, but before the Prince would consent to enter the capital of his ally he required that one of the city gates, with the wall flanking it, should be held by his own soldiers, and when the Prince and Lancaster entered Burgos for the ceremony of ratification they rode at the head of five

---

[1] Ayala, i. 461 ; Froissart, K. de L. vii. 222–3 ; Chandos Herald, 3583–88, 3621–722.

[2] Ayala, i. 471–83, 493–8.

[3] *Ibid.* i. 458–61.

[4] Avoecq tout chou li prinches de Galles tint son jugement et son gage de bataille devant Burghes siques on puet bien dire tout notoirement que toutte Espaigne par concquès fu à lui et à son commandement. Froissart, K. de L. vii. 223.

hundred trusty men-at-arms. However, the promises, for what they were worth, were repeated, and on Sunday, May 2, in the Church of St. Mary the Greater the several instruments were read alone, and Pedro standing before the high altar, with his hand upon the gospels, solemnly swore to fulfil his engagements.[1] Half of his debt to the Prince Pedro was to discharge at the end of a period of four months, during which the army was to remain in the province of Valladolid, while the other half was to be paid at Bayonne in a year's time. After this compromise Pedro set out for the south, ostensibly to raise supplies to pay the army. Unquestionably the feat of raising the money forthwith would have tasked the powers of a conscientious monarch, but Pedro chose to intensify the difficulty and to disregard the obligation. His progress southwards to Seville was traced in blood; everywhere those who were barely suspected of sympathy with the usurper were cut down without mercy; even kinship with a rebel was a death warrant, while the cities which were compelled to deliver up hostages to their rightful king were not induced by open suspicion to loose their purse-strings. But financial embarrassment alone cannot excuse Pedro's delay, and only the grossest disloyalty can explain his conduct. If the whole sum required could not be raised at once, Pedro might have advanced a portion; but, in fact, he had no intention of keeping his word. He began by haggling over the value of the treasure, consisting chiefly of jewels and precious stones, which he had carried with him in his flight to Bayonne and had surrendered before the army started. These valuables had been realized at once at enormous loss by the Prince's captains, but the King insisted on reckoning their value at a full, if not fancy price. After long parleyings between the King's treasurers and the Prince's agents over this piece of

[1] *Foed,* vi. 559–60; *Record Report,* xl. App. (3), ix. 252.

sharp practice, there came an impudent attempt to evade indisputable obligations. The grant to the Prince of the province of Biscay and Castro-Urdiales was nominally made good when Pedro issued letters commanding his officers to deliver possession, but these letters were accompanied by others less official and more sincere, and when Lord Poynings went to take over the lands in the Prince's name he was met by a determined resistance, which was admitted to be countenanced by royal authority. Even more shameless and undisguised was the fraud practised upon Sir John Chandos, who had been named Count of Soria. The grant was admitted, but before issuing the necessary letters patent Pedro's chancellor demanded a chancery fee of ten thousand marcs.

Meanwhile the army remained in the neighbourhood of Burgos, finding provisions daily more difficult to obtain. At first, with a rare and laudable restraint, the Prince had forbidden plunder, refusing, as he said, to make the poor folk pay for the debts of their ruler. But gradually, as Pedro's ill-faith became more certain, the Prince's temper hardened, until, faced with the alternative of starvation or plunder, he gave a loose rein to his mercenary forces. The maxim of necessity needs no justification, and, as Chandos Herald tersely puts it—

> Un proverbe aï oÿ noncier,
> Que hom doit pur sa femme tencier
> Et pur sa viande combatre.

When Burgos was exhausted the army marched on and occupied Amusco, which found supplies for another month, thence moving on to Valladolid, Medina del Campo and Madrigal, levying blackmail on the towns, and plundering the villages far and wide. Meanwhile the privations suffered on the march through Guipuzcoa and Alava, combined with the effects of climate and excess, produced the inevitable outbreak of dysentery. Hundreds of men-at-arms and archers perished, while in the Prince himself symptoms appeared of the lingering illness which nine years later was to prove fatal. Clearly the position could not last. The latest representations to Don Pedro brought back nothing but the request that the Prince would lead his mercenaries, "*ces maledites gens de compagnes*," out of Castile, as no subsidy could be raised while they were living on the country, while to the Prince's demand for a score of strongholds by way of security the King returned a curt refusal.[1]

This reply put an end once and for all to relations between the "allies," and the Prince, mobilizing his army which was lying round Madrigal, marched eastwards to Soria, near the Aragon frontier.[2] There were indeed imperative reasons for beginning the return march, for disquieting news came from Aquitaine.

For weeks after the battle no one, but a few faithful adherents, knew what had become of Don Enrique.[3] In point of fact he had ridden for his life across the mountains to Soria, narrowly escaping capture, and thence by the Calatayud road to Saragossa.[4] Trastamare had no stauncher friend than the House of Luna, and among the members of that House no partizan more devoted than Pedro de Luna (afterwards Pope by the name of Benedict XIII), who guided the fugitive north through Jaca. Once safe across the Pyrenees, Enrique breathed more freely, and looked for a resting-place at Orthez with the Count of Foix. But Foix, while welcoming the foe of Don Pedro, was embarrassed by the enemy of the Black Prince,[5] and hastened to speed the parting

[1] Froissart, K. de L. vii. 224–6, 236–9.
[2] Chandos Herald, 3723–44.
[3] On April 15 Pedro writes: "E el traydor non sabemos si es preso ó muerto." Ayala, i. 461.
[4] *Ibid.* i. 461–3 ; Froissart, K. de L. vii. 227–31.
[5] "Ca veia que el principe era estonce uno de los mayores omes del mundo entre los Christianos." Ayala, i. 462.

guest with money and horses to Toulouse. Something
in the chivalrous daring of the fallen king struck the
imagination of his contemporaries, who soon weaved
round his figure the web of a cycle of romance, telling
how in the guise of a pilgrim he wandered from the hills
of Lerida to the Biscay shore and to the Mediterranean,
how he paid a secret visit to the King of Aragon at Perpignan, and spoke with the great Bertrand in his captivity at Bordeaux.[1] But the legends of the trouvère are
indeed less interesting than the facts of history, for
Enrique, indomitable where another would have despaired, was no sooner overthrown than he began again
to plan, to intrigue and work for his restoration. So
great was the terror of the Prince's name that none of
the friendly powers dared openly to receive him ; his
interview with Urban V at Villeneuve, near Avignon,
was secret,[2] and official correctness constrained Charles V,
who gave convincing if furtive encouragement to the
usurper, to place the Count of Auxerre under arrest for
excess of zeal in his cause. But the strongest support
came from Louis, Duke of Anjou and Lieutenant of
Languedoc. Between Anjou and Trastamare a secret
treaty was concluded, directed not only against Prince
Edward, but also his brothers, and Lancaster in particular ; nor was it long before the alliance began to show
practical results. Financed by Anjou, Enrique gathered
a few hundred lances about him, and began forthwith
to harry Aquitaine from the side of Bigorre.

The manœuvre succeeded. Anxious messages from
the Princess Joan recalled the Prince to the protection
of his own lands ; but to return direct by the route of
the invasion would be both to lose all hold on Don Pedro
and to invite the usurper to return by the eastern gate
and to repeat his victorious march of 1366.

[1] See Cuvelier 444–55 and Froissart, K. de L. vii. 515–7, *note.*
[2] Ayala, i. 503–5.

JOHN OF GAUNT

Hence the Prince's move to the confines of Aragon and the beginning of a new chapter in the history of English relations with the Peninsular powers.[1] So far as foreign affairs are concerned there were two phases of political opinion in Aragon. One party, led by the Infante Don Pedro, the Archbishop of Saragossa and the powerful House of Luna, was devoted to the interests of Trastamare; it was this faction which had obtained a refuge for Juana, Enrique's Queen, and her children, the eldest of whom, Don Juan, was betrothed to Doña Leonor, daughter of the King of Aragon.[2] "Pedro, the Ceremonious" himself, however, was not inclined to sacrifice his kingdom to a losing, if not a lost cause, and when Sir John Chandos and Sir Hugh Calverly arrived on a mission from the Black Prince, they found it no hard task to expel the *émigré* family of the usurper of Castile. For a time the House of Luna felt their influence paralyzed : Juana finding Saragossa uncomfortable, went north to join her husband on a more friendly soil.[3] But much more than a strict neutrality in the quarrel of Trastamare and Burgundy was required of Aragon by the English envoys, for the Prince, infuriated by Pedro's treachery, was contemplating something like a partition of his dominions. Chandos found Aragon in a state of panic ; his master's name was one to conjure with throughout the peninsula. So soon as Najera was won and Enrique overthrown, Aragon had feared the worst. *Proximus ardet Ucalegon.* The rumour of invasion had grown precise enough to fore-

---

[1] Ayala, i. 465–6. Chandos Herald knows, as he admits, nothing of the negotiations but the fact of their existence. The gap is filled by Zurita (*Anales de la Corona de Aragón*, ii. 348–50). Zurita was not contemporary ; he lived A.D. 1512–80. But he worked from originals, and though dull, is accurate and not lacking in the critical sense.

[2] Ayala, i. 463 ; Chandos Herald, 3589–622.

[3] Ayala, i. 562.

cast the exact intentions of the Black Prince : while he himself looked to the eastern frontier, John of Gaunt, supported by the King of Majorca, so it was believed, would attack Aragon via Tarrazona, and attempt a systematic conquest of the kingdom. These fears and the sense of relief consequent upon the revelations of Prince Edward's true intentions, made the task of nego- tiation easy. The King of Aragon welcomed the Prince's proffered alliance, at once disowned Don Enrique and annulled the betrothal of his daughter to Enrique's son, agreed to oppose Enrique's restoration if necessary by force, and seriously discussed the proposal that, if Don Pedro did not make good his promises of repay- ment and the cession of Biscay and Castro-Urdiales,[1] and did not also pay an indemnity for the losses suffered by Aragon in the former war, he should unite his forces with those of the Prince in a confederation into which Navarre and Portugal were to be called, should attack Pedro, and partition his dominions. The Infanta Leonor, divorced from the usurper's son, was by this arrange- ment to be married to Edward Plantagenet, elder son of the Black Prince, and an Anglo-Aragonese dynasty was to be set up in the central kingdom, or what was left of it after partition between the allies.

Thus in August, 1367, England appeared to be on the brink of a new and revolutionary Peninsular policy. That these proposals were never carried further was due to the condition of the Prince's health and the danger of Aquitaine. But at least for the moment the Prince's object was served ; he had shut the doors of Aragon on Trastamare, as it seemed, and he had prepared the way for punishing the perjured Castilian King. He was free therefore to return to Aquitaine. No difficulty hampered the retreat. Navarre was unable to offer

[1] The Prince never obtained possession, but continued to style himself Lord of Biscay and of Castro-Urdiales.

D

resistance, and Charles the Bad, having now emerged from his sham captivity at Borja (and, by the way, having cheated Olivier de Mauni of the reward promised for his complaisance), hastened to place himself at the disposal of the successful general, and to atone by obsequiousness for treachery. Conducting Prince Edward from the southern to the northern limit of his dominions,[1] he bowed the English army out of Navarre at Roncevalles, and the Prince and Lancaster returned through Bayonne to Bordeaux.

So ended the great Castilian expedition of 1367, an episode which marking as it does an epoch in the history of the Hundred Years War, marks also a crisis in the lives of Prince Edward and the Duke of Lancaster. Of its disastrous effects upon the Prince and through him upon the fortunes of English Aquitaine, more will have to be said hereafter. In the life of John of Gaunt also its importance is scarcely less. He had gained a new and invaluable experience of men and affairs. He had borne himself bravely in battle, so that the Herald of the gallant Chandos could say of him—

> Et d'autre part li noble ducz
> De Lancastre, plein de vertuz
> Si noblement se combatoit
> Que chescun s'en emerveilloit
> En regardant sa grant prouesse
> Coment par sa noble hautesse
> Mettoit son corps en aventure :
> Car jeo croy que nunques creature
> Poevre ne riches, ne se mist
> Cel jour si avant come il fist.

Well served, as he had been, by the ablest of English leaders, the Duke had won some credit as a divisional commander : in a critical moment he had shown courage and presence of mind. But the experience of 1367 was not confined to the art of war ; it furnished also a lesson

---

[1] Froissart, K. de L. vii. 240-243 ; Chandos Herald, 3745-814.

in statecraft. The Black Prince had overwhelmed all material opposition to his will ; he had shown himself arbiter of the destinies of kings. Lancaster who, while lacking the force and strength of purpose which alone secure permanence to the work of the statesman, had yet in imagination and in reserve two qualities essential to the diplomatist, burned to imitate the example of one who at a touch had made the whole fabric of the new dynasty collapse, who made and unmade alliances at his will, and by his mere fiat rearranged the relations of the powers. That example was not forgotten, and it worked in the mind of the ambitious Duke, as in October he returned to England and dismissed his men-at-arms and archers to fight all their battles o'er again and to tell the story of Najera to their comrades in the chaces of Derbyshire and the Lancashire forests.

It seemed then an easy thing to set up and dethrone kings, but, in truth, the brilliance of the Prince's achievement was illusory and its results ephemeral. No sooner had the Prince crossed the Pyrenees than the reaction began. Enrique soon found himself in command of a second army ; in spite of the protests, sincere but inoperative, of the King of Aragon, the usurper a second time crossed the frontier and invaded Castile. A short campaign recovered Leon ; Oviedo and the Asturias accepted the counter-revolution, and though Logroño again held out for the legitimist cause and Galicia made only a nominal surrender, there was nothing to check Enrique's advance or to hinder his progress to the south. At Toledo du Guesclin, now at liberty, again joined his standard with a body of fine French troops, and the army advanced to the south.

On March 13, 1369, the issue was decided. Instead of the invincible army led by Prince Edward two years before, Pedro had to rely on a heterogeneous mass of untrustworthy Castilian levies, Moorish cavalry, and armed Jews. When the two armies got into touch the legitimist superiority of numbers was useless, for Pedro's forces were taken by surprise and defeated in detail. Du Guesclin's Frenchmen easily accounted for the Castilian division ; the Jews fled at the first onset, and the splendid courage of the Moors of Granada, who only came into action when the battle was already decided, only availed to swell the numbers of the slain. Pedro's own ferocious bravery was useless ; his last army was routed, and there was no alternative to flight. With a few faithful followers he reached the Castle of Montiel, but his movements were known and the place was surrounded. The hope of getting past the enemy's pickets on a dark midnight after the battle proved forlorn. As a last expedient the King sent an emissary to du Guesclin's camp with the offer of an immense bribe if he were allowed to escape. The great Breton soldier despised the treachery, but used it. He enticed the King to his tent, and there, with the aid of Olivier de Mauni, du Guesclin's cousin, Enrique of Trastamare stabbed his brother, the last monarch of the House of Burgundy.

In later days, when the memory of Pedro's disloyalty to the Black Prince was less present to men's minds than the motives, both personal and political, which made England the enemy of the usurping dynasty, Geoffrey Chaucer, learning it doubtless from the lips of Constance of Castile, told the story of Pedro's death—

> O noble, O worthy Petro, glorie of Spayne,
> Whom fortune heeld so hy in magestee,
> Wel oughten men thy pitous deeth complayne !
> Out of thy lond thy brother made thee flee ;
> And after, at a sege, by subtiltee,
> Thou were bitrayed, and lad un-to his tente,
> Wher-as he with his owene hond slow thee,
> Succeding in thy regne and in thy rente.

THE INVASION OF CASTILE

The feeld of snow, with thegle blak ther-inne,
Caught with the lymrod, coloured as the glede,
He brew this cursednes and at this sinne.
The " wikked nest " was werker of this nede ;
Noght Charles Oliver, that ay took hede
Of trouthe and honour, but of Armorike
Genilon Oliver, corrupt for mede,
Broghte his worthy king in swich a brike.[1] //

Like those of old upon whom the curse of blood-guiltiness had fallen, Pedro the Cruel had been driven from crime to crime, never suffered to rest, involving others in his own fall, driven by the results of his deeds to expiate the curse with his own life. Yet in spite of his savagery there is something of real tragedy in his life and death. He stood for a true principle, and he failed, not only because his own character was wanting, but because anything save failure was impossible.

History in Spain was written not by monks, but by gentlemen, and therefore in the verdict of history for Pedro, the enemy of the nobles, there are no extenuating circumstances. But to the people, who remembered his stern justice and forgot the cruelty only shown to their oppressors, Pedro the Cruel was Pedro the Justiciar.

Thus in two years the work of Najera was undone at Montiel ; but the dynastic struggle continued, and the blood feud of Burgundy and Trastamare remained, to be renewed a generation later by the son of Enrique the Magnificent and the daughter of Pedro the Cruel, when English soldiers were to fight once more in Spain under the standard of John of Gaunt, and as the old prophecy foretold, the English Leopards were again to be seen on the field of Castile.

[1] Chaucer, " The Monke's Tale," 384–400. The " feeld of snow," etc., describes du Guesclin's arms ; the " wikked nest " is Sir Oliver de Mauni " Mau " " ni." See Skeat, Chaucer, vol. v. Notes to the Monke's Tale, p. 238–40. Ayala (i. 551–557) is, as usual, more trustworthy than Froissart.

Chapter IV

THE OUTBREAK OF WAR

IN the *Livre des faits et bons moeurs du sage Roy Charles V*, Christine de Pisan, the first of literary ladies, has an excellent story which illustrates the character both of the King who, she persuades herself, is the pattern of knightly accomplishments, and of the Duke of Lancaster.

Once the court of Edward III was discussing the merits of his " adversary of France," and Lancaster remarked— " Notre adversaire n'est pas un sage prince : ce n'est qu'un avocat." The *mot* coming to the ears of Charles V provoked the retort : " Si nous sommes avocats, nous leur batirons tel plaid que la sentence les ennuiera." The royal " attorney " made good his threat : he lived to see England weary of the struggle. But if history has justified the King's retort, the events of 1369 testified to the Duke's judgment. The phrase touched a weak spot in the King's armour. It was a hit—a very palpable hit. King John had fought his enemies in the field. He had failed, and failed disastrously, it is true, but England and France, foe and friend, respected " Jean le Bon " even in failure. When a prince of the " Fleurs de Lys " had broken parole, King John, it was remembered, had returned of his free will to captivity, to redeem the forfeited honour of France. He was a man of action and a man of his word.

John, if a poor king, was a good knight ; Charles was a " politique," and policy rather than chivalry was

66

needed to deliver France out of the hand of her enemies. But the contrast between father and son was striking, and seemed to many besides the Duke of Lancaster far from favourable to Charles V.

From the point of view of chivalry, and to men imbued with the prejudices and prepossessions natural to a military society, in all of which the Duke shared, Charles V was a craven. Weighed in the balance of feudal thought, he was found wanting. It required a standpoint more detached, an insight into policy more clear and penetrating, to appreciate the kingliness of the man who now sat on the throne of the Valois, the friend of scholars and priests, the lover of books, of fasts and masses, the king who never bore arms in battle or tourney, who rarely travelled more than fifty miles from Paris, and who won his victories from the council chamber.

Devout and orderly in his life, monastic in the regularity if not in the simplicity of his habits—for he loved a measure of kingly magnificence and did not spare France the burden of a costly household—Charles had taken for his model his ancestor Louis IX. But he inherited neither the real grace and goodness of Louis the Saint nor the frank manliness of John the Good. If his subjects could interpret caution as timidity, his enemies may be excused for finding in his subtlety something underhand.

The attorney's nature had shown itself in manipulating the Treaty of Calais. The engagements entered into at Brétigni in May, 1360, and confirmed by the treaty at Calais in October, had never been fulfilled. The really vital issue was mutual renunciation on the part of the King of France of his claim to the suzerainty of Aquitaine ; on the part of the King of England of his claim to the throne of France. There were doubtless faults on both sides, but it may be accepted as a fact that the then Regent of France had no intention of handing over territories as great as his own kingdom to the enemy. In spite of formal orders, he had made no effort to restore Limousin, Périgord, Querci and Rouergue to effective English rule. A new pretext was ever at hand for delaying the performance of treaty obligations, until the time-limit fixed by treaty was passed. The "attorney" had won his legal point. He could wait.

For nine years he had been content to wait, while the peace was observed with doubtful faith and on both sides with mutual distrust. With malevolent neutrality he had watched the Black Prince cross the Pyrenees and oust Don Enrique. The Marshal of France and a French army had fought for Don Enrique, himself a pensioner of the French court, but between France and England there had been no overt hostilities. The peace was shaken, not broken.

Then came the day of reckoning. Don Pedro's promises proved worthless. How was Prince Edward to pay the army which had followed him on the strength of under-takings for which he had made himself responsible ?

It was with the free assent of the Estates that the Black Prince had espoused Don Pedro's quarrel ; the promised gain had proved a loss, and those who had coveted the spoils were not willing to share the cost.

The Estates which met at St. Émilion in October, 1367, and at Angoulême in January, 1368, granted a *fouage*, a tax of ten sous on each hearth, to run for five years, but they were not speaking with the voice of Aqui-taine. Owing to the unsettled state of the country, for one reason and another many deputies of the towns had been prevented from coming to the Parliament ; others deliberately stayed away. Armagnac and his nephew Albret, the most powerful of the Gascon barons, refused to come, and swore that the *fouage* should never run in their lands.

The Prince insisted. It was in vain that Sir John Chandos protested, pointing out that he was taking the surest means to shake his subjects' wavering loyalty and to throw the malcontents into the arms of France.

Was it that Prince Edward's illness had clouded his view of a plain political issue ? Or did he despise the meanness of those who repudiated what was virtually their own action, and refused the tax which was to pay a debt in which the honour of their suzerain was at stake ?

The Prince would not give way, and Chandos, the best and greatest of King Edward's captains, withdrew to St. Sauveur, his lordship in the north, only to leave it two years later to draw sword and die in the quarrel he had striven to avert. The fatal step was taken. In April, 1368, Armagnac and the disloyal party appealed from the Black Prince to the King of France as overlord of Aquitaine. The spring of that year saw a throng of *emigré* Gascon barons at the French Court, fêted and caressed by the King, who had fair words, promises, and gifts for each. Some received money bribes ; others rich fiefs. To Albret himself the King gave the hand of his sister-in-law, Isabella of Bourbon. Charles had accepted the appeal, but while treating the Gascon barons as subjects, he still hesitated to take the last step.

At length he was persuaded by the counsels of his advisers, backed by the devastations of the free companies who, unemployed since their return from Spain, and now dismissed frrm Aquitaine, were living at ease in their " chamber " of France.

Charles would have all the law gave him. The " attorney " looked into his bond. The bond said that the King of England was still his vassal for Aquitaine. He cited Prince Edward to Paris to answer to the complaints of his Gascon subjects. The summons, given publicly in the Abbey of St. Andrew at Bordeaux, stung the Prince to fury.

His answer is one of the many boasts which history has

preserved only to belie. He would come to Paris, but with helmet on head and sixty thousand men behind him.

Then at length Charles defied the King of England, and Edward reassumed, with the sanction of Parliament, the style and title of King of France. The most timid of the Valois had " cried havoc and let slip the dogs of war."

The nine long years of waiting since Brétigni had not been wasted, and Charles, with a true instinct for the needs of France, had given proof of the wisdom which Christine claims for him.

When the struggle opened again in 1369, he had a policy, an ally, and the sinews of war—a fleet and army ready to use. His policy—inaction—was his own. His ally was given to him by the Black Prince. In more ways than one the policy of the Black Prince in supporting Don Pedro was fraught with fatal results. The ruin of his own health, the loss of Aquitaine, and the downfall of English naval supremacy were all, wholly or in part, the consequences of the momentous decision of 1366. In 1340 and 1350 Edward III had cleared the Channel of enemies, and had done something to win the proud title—" Lord of the Seas." The Spanish policy of his son threw Castile into the arms of France, and made the alliance of the Houses of Trastamare and Valois a political necessity. Henceforth the naval force of Castile and Leon is added to that of France ; the existing balance of naval power is overthrown. In the second epoch of the Hundred Years War the fleets of Charles V and Don Enrique make common cause. England has lost the mastery of the seas : she cannot even hold the Channel.

Meanwhile, in France itself, all through these years of peace, preparations had been made for war. Charles had worked hard to supplement the feudal levies which had failed so signally at Crécy and Poictiers by the creation of a royal army, and taking a leaf from his rival's book, he had begun to take the people into partnership, and to place burgess and citizen in the field beside knight and man-at-arms. Co-ordinate in the King's policy with the creation of a royal army was the attempt to create a royal navy. Side by side with du Guesclin stands Jean de Vienne, soon to be Admiral of France, and worthy to be ranked with the great Breton soldier among the heroes of French emancipation.

At Clos des Galées, the royal arsenal and dockyard on the left bank of the Seine, there were busy preparations in the autumn of 1369. The King himself was at Rouen, superintending, with Philippe le Hardi, Duke of Burgundy, the preparations for the struggle. Vexin and Beauvais swarmed with soldiers. From Harfleur to Rouen the river was crowded with ships and vessels, large and small, for Charles meant to make a great demonstration in the Channel, his plan being to ravage the south coast of England, and to keep Edward engaged in protecting his home ports, while, communications being thus severed between England and Bordeaux, the Dukes of Berri and Anjou pushed back the English frontiers in the south and drove Prince Edward out of Aquitaine.

To this England replied by despatching the Earls of Cambridge and Pembroke south with reinforcements, while Lancaster was sent to Calais, to engage Burgundy's attention and to make a diversion in Picardy.[1]

[1] Lancaster's powers as Lieutenant of the King in the North and Captain of Calais, Guines and Merk, with the duty of supervising fortresses, etc., are dated 12 June, 1369. *Rot. Franc.* ii. 100, m. 11. Cf. orders to Adam de Hoghton and four of the commissioners of array to enrol 400 archers in Lancashire. *Rot. Vasc.* 43 Edw. III, m. 5.

For the raids in Picardy in August and September, 1369, I have followed Froissart K. de L. vii. 420–443; xvii. 480–3, and the French chroniclers *Chron. Bourb.*, 72–43; *Chron. Norm.* 190–1; *Grandes Chroniques*, vi. 318–320. Cf. *Istore et Chroniques de Flandres*, II. 106. *Chr. Reg. Franc.* ii. 341. *Chr. Val.* 205. *Chron. Angl.* 63. *Eulog.* 336.

Walsingham's i. 307–8 account seems intended as a eulogy of the Earl of Warwick, and does not square with the known facts.

JOHN OF GAUNT

In July John of Gaunt landed at Calais with some six hundred men-at-arms and fifteen hundred archers—his first independent command. The army was too small to do much ; it was just strong enough for a " reconnaissance in force," capable of the usual devastations, and large enough to postpone for a time Buigundy's projects of invasion.

It numbered some soldiers of note—Sir Walter Manny and the Earls of Salisbury and Warwick; and the duke's friend, Sir Henry Percy, a splendid fighting man, was among the number. Some notables of the Low Countries, the Marquess of Juliers, the Duke of Gueldres and Robert of Namur, who had done as much as most men to start the Hundred Years War, joined the duke's standard at Calais.

Lancaster soon made his presence felt.[1] The week in which Burgundy should have mobilized his fleet in the Seine, the whole country side from Calais to Boulogne and Licques was reported in flames, and the Count of St. Pol was shut up in Thérouanne and dare not move.

Burgundy, recalled from his preparations to check English depredations in the north, marched from Rouen through Abbeville and Hesdin to Tournehem.[2] This was the news for which Lancaster was waiting. The Duke had returned to Calais after a couple of raids, but hearing of Burgundy's advance, he at once marched south to Tournehem and took up a strong position opposite the enemy.

The French outnumbered the Duke's army by at least seven to one, and no one doubted that they would attack.

---

[1] Cf. *Mandements et actes divers*, No. 566. On 16 Aug., 1369, Charles had already heard that Lancaster " had landed at Calais with a great force of men-at-arms and archers, and had raided Picardy."
[2] See Itineraires de Philippe le hardi, 58.

But no attack came. From August 25 to September 12, 1369, the two armies faced each other, the English in daily and hourly expectation of the assault which was never delivered. Burgundy's movements were controlled from headquarters ; the new policy of inaction had begun. In spite of their vast superiority of numbers, the French did nothing. The sum total of military operations amounted to a few irregular encounters between individual knights, desirous of " advancing themselves," and one half-hearted surprise attack on the English camp, which was easily beaten off. At length, after a fortnight's inaction, Philip " the bold " obtained permission to end a situation little to his taste. One night—September 12— covering his movements by a long line of fires, Burgundy broke up his camp and marched away to Paris. Lancaster's camp was roused by the glare of French fires. At length the expected attack was coming ! After standing to arms for half the night the Duke's force became convinced of the truth. Lancaster had refused to believe that Burgundy would withdraw without battle, but his spies confirmed what his council had told him. The enemy had retreated.

The next day he bivouacked in the French camp, and after a halt carried out his original plan. His objective was the Seine : he intended to see what damage could be done to the French shipping.

The line of march lay past St. Omer, Thérouanne, Pernes and St. Pol, and the country was swept clear as the army advanced.[1] Without stopping to besiege strong places, Lancaster, on reaching Lucheux, turned westwards to St. Riquier and crossed the Somme near Abbeville at the historic ford of Blanchetaque. Meeting no opposition,

---

[1] For the march through Picardy *Pierre Cochon* (p. 123) is worth reading. He wrote a generation later than the events, but he was a native of Caux, and preserved the tradition of things which happened there with the greatest interest.

he struck due west to the sea coast,[1] looting as he went and embarking his spoils on board the ships which followed his march, guided by the smoke and flame of burning farm and village. This went on till the army reached St. Adresse, the most important port on the Seine before the existence of Le Havre de Grace. Montivilliers was assaulted, but Harfleur itself was too strong to be attacked. Had the Duke been in greater force it would have been tempting to assault Rouen and try to cross the Seine and burn " Clos des Galées." But happily for the French the Duke had only a handful of men and no siege engines, and the arsenals, being on the south side of the river, were safe. After a few days before Harfleur the army returned through Estouteville, Gomerville, Étienville, Bolbec, Oisemont, Rue and Montreuil to Calais.[2]

Outside Abbeville the Duke had captured Hugh de Châtillon, captain of Abbeville and Master of the French crossbowmen, the man who nine years earlier had been in command of the French fleet which burned Winchelsea. This was the one success scored on the homeward march, for, as in most of the operations of the second part of the great war, there was little military result to show. The enemy's attack had been postponed but not prevented, for the next month a French fleet ravaged the south coast and burnt Portsmouth. After providing for the proper custody of Calais and the neighbouring fortresses, Lancaster returned to England in November.[3]

Bitter tidings awaited him on his return. During his short absence in Picardy two events had taken place

[1] The Duke appears to have struck the coast near Dieppe. See *Mandements* de Charles V, No. 657, a letter addressed to the royal "grenetier" at Dieppe reciting that the salt-pan industry at Boutcilles had been stopped owing to the ravages of the English army.
[2] Froissart Luce, VII, lxxxiii–lxxxv.
[3] *Foed*, VII, 640–1, and *Calendars of the Exchequer, I*. 223.

in England, both significant in their results upon his fortunes and the fortunes of England—the death of his mother and the death of his wife.

On August 15 Queen Philippa died, and within a month, on the very day on which Burgundy's camp fires at Tournehem had given the alarm to the English army, England was mourning for the Duchess of Lancaster.

The year 1369 had seen another outbreak of the great plague, severe enough to be remembered as " the third pestilence," and Blanche of Lancaster had fallen a victim to the disease which had already proved fatal to her father and her sister. The two noblest women of the English court had passed away, and it was fitting that Froissart should place together in his lament the names of Philippa of Hainault and Blanche of Lancaster—

> La bonne, qui pourist en terre,
> Qui fu roïne d'Engleterre ;
> *   *   *
> Aussi sa fille de Lancastre—
> Haro ! Mettés moi une emplastre
> Sus le coer, car, quant m'en souvient,
> Certes souspirer me couvient,
> Tant sui plains de melancolie.—
> Elle morut jone et jolie,
> Environ de vingt et deux ans ;
> Gaie, lie, friche, esbatans,
> Douce, simple, d'umble samblance ;
> La bonne dame ot à nom Blanche.[1]

Of the gentle consort of Edward III, whose last thoughts were for those of her household, whose last prayer that the King, when his hour came, would be buried at her side, history has nothing but good to relate. To many beside Froissart Philippa " of good memory " was " la plus gentil roine, plus large et plus courtoise que oncques regna en son temps." Her death marked a climax in the reign of Edward III. Of Philippa it might truly have been said that she was " felix oppor-

[1] Le Joli Buisson de Jonece (*Poésies*, vol. ii, p. 8).

tunitate mortis." She lived to see her husband and her sons attain the pinnacle of military fame ; she had welcomed her husband back from the victories of Sluys and L'Espagnols-sur-mer and Crécy, and her son from Poictiers. She died before the great failures of the war : before the Good Parliament and the Peasants' rising, and she left a place that no one could fill. The most brilliant court of Europe became the most corrupt. After the reign of Philippa comes the reign of Alice Perrers.

To John of Gaunt the death of Blanche of Lancaster was a momentous loss. In his life also the death of his consort draws the dividing line. Before it all had gone well. Of the dangers which were soon to beset the Duke's path she could foresee nothing. Those belong to a later epoch.

Of the sincerity of the Duke's grief there need be no question, though there is no evidence and little probability that we have his own words in the lament of Chaucer's Man in Black, the " wonder wel-faringe knight," who sits refusing to be comforted, and mourning her whom he had lost—

> I have of sorwe so gret woon,
> That Joye gete I never noon,
>   Now that I see my lady bright,
>   Which I have loved with al my might,
> Is fro me deed, and is a-goon.
>
> Alas, o deeth ! what ayleth thee,
> That thou noldest have taken me,
>   Whan that thou toke my lady swete ?
> That was so fayr, so fresh, so free,
> So good, that men may wel ysee
>   Of al goodnesse she had no mete ! [1]

The *Book of the Duchess* is a tribute alike to the chivalrous love of John of Gaunt for Blanche and to the affection of the poet for his earliest patroness. Who

[1] Chaucer, *The Book of the Duchess*, 475–486.

so fit to offer consolation to one who had loved and lost
as he who himself knew, if dark hints are rightly interpreted, the sorrows of unrequited affection? But
Chaucer does not attempt to console. The poet's
tact saves him from offering " vacant chaff well meant
for grain." Master of a subtle sympathy, he knows
that the only true consolation is to dwell on and recall
the image of the departed. Therefore Chaucer speaks
of the graces of person and of character, of the simplicity,
gentleness and beauty of the " Whyte " lady—Blanche
the Duchess. It was only ten years since their marriage.
Well could Lancaster cry with the widowed queen of
Chaucer's story : " To litel whyl our blisse lasteth."
Blanche had borne her husband five children : two died
in infancy ; of the three who survived two were to play
a leading part in the story of these times, for Henry
was destined for the throne of England, and Philippa
for that of Portugal.

Blanche was buried in the " Cathedral Church of St.
Paul at London." There, near the high altar, the Duke
raised over her body a costly tomb of alabaster.
That men might not forget the form and features
of the dead Duchess, a painted effigy of marble was placed
there, a monument, as time has proved, less durable
than Chaucer's elegy, and all the year round two priests
chanted masses for her soul at an altar built beside
her tomb, and furnished with rich missal and chalice.
Once a year, on September 12, the anniversary of
her death, a solemn celebration was held in St. Paul's.
The Duke and his household attended, or if the Duke
were out of England his high officers took his place.
Gratitude to the memory of his first wife never failed :
so long as he lived the rites due to religion and affection
were observed, and in his will[1] the Duke's first injunction
is that he shall be laid by her side. " My body to be

---

[1] See *Appendix* I. p. 420.

buried in the Cathedral Church of St. Paul of London, near the principal altar, beside my most dear late wife Blanche, who is there interred." [1]

But for the time there was little leisure for mourning. The war had begun in grim earnest, and there was work to be done. Charles V had planned a two-fold invasion of Aquitaine. The Duke of Anjou, concentrating at Toulouse, was to advance by the line of La Réole and Bergerac. The Duke of Berri was to invade Limousin, and the two columns converging at Angoulême, were to besiege the Prince of Wales there. The English King, on the other hand, resolved to harry the enemy in the north, and to send Lancaster to the south to reinforce his brother. The northern command was given to Sir Robert Knolles, and soon Champagne and Brie were again in flames and the pennon of St. George was waving under the walls of Paris.

In the south the outlook for English arms was gloomy. The plan of campaign of the French had been skilfully conceived; it only failed because at the last moment their nerve failed, and no one dared to come within striking distance of the Black Prince.

England sadly lacked the generalship which could alone save a losing cause and counteract the errors of a fatal policy. Prince Edward himself, wasted by disease, and broken in all but spirit, was quite unfit to control the operations of a campaign. Chandos, the best general on the English side, had fallen mortally wounded on January 1, 1370, in a skirmish at the bridge of Lussac, in his last hour saving his prisoners from the vengeance of his men, with his last breath commending to God the King,

---

[1] Warrants to pay for the annual celebration and for the services of the chantry priests extend over the whole period covered by the Register (1372–1382), and similar notices are found in the Receiver-General's Accounts for 1391–2. *Duchy of Lancs. Accts.* iii. 2. They are too numerous to quote, but they show the Duke's solicitude for the memory of his first wife.

and Prince, and the lady he loved. England had lost the one man whose advice could have saved Aquitaine and whose skill might even then have retrieved her losses.

But while the English forces had no man of genius left to lead them, France had recalled du Guesclin from Castile, where, in his new lordship of Molina, he was detained, so rumour said, not by loyalty to his new master alone, but by the yet more potent spell of Castilian beauty, a triumph not foreseen by the prophetic vision of his Breton wife.

At the end of June John of Gaunt was at Plymouth in command of a force of 300 men-at-arms and 500 archers ready to sail for the south. [1]   But the government did not rely on force alone.   The time had come, so it appeared, to try the effect of persuasion on Gascon discontent.   In the vain hope that the removal of the fiscal grievance would at the same time remove its results, the King revoked the objectionable *fouage*. Further, he empowered Lancaster, with the concurrence of the Prince, to pardon and reinstate all rebels who would return to their allegiance. [2]   In England it was recognized

---

[1] Froissart, K. de L. vii, 480-2, viii, 13-15.   Orders for men-at-arms and archers to be ready at Southampton and Plymouth by the Sunday next before the Feast of Pentecost. *Rot. Franc.* 44 Edw. III, m. 25.

Payment to sergeants-at-arms, etc., sent from the Thames to Lyme, Hull, Newcastle, Bristol and the Severn, Weymouth and the coasts of Cornwall and Wales, to arrest ships. *Issue Roll*, May 15, 44 Edw. III.

The Duke received over £9,000 for the expenses of his army, and something over £2,000 for freight (*Issue Roll*, May 9 and 22, June 15 and 20, 44 Edw. III.), but he had to borrow heavily as well. (Reg.).

The payments to the Duke and his retinue were :—The Duke, 26s. 8d. a day ; three bannerets, 8s. ; eighty knights, 4s. ; 216 men-at-arms, 2s., and 500 archers, 12d. a day. (*Issue Roll*, 44 Edw. III. May 9).   Sir Hugh Calverly was among the bannerets.

[2] For the Duke's powers, dated July 1, 1370, see *Rot. Vasc.*

that the Black Prince had become unfitted by his illness for public business. Hence the large discretionary powers granted to John of Gaunt by the King. As yet events had not made the Duke of Lancaster the unpopular figure which he appears a few years later, but subsequently his enemies were quick to seize upon this point and to attempt to twist it into evidence of unscrupulous ambition. The grant of these legal powers, however, remained a matter of purely academic interest. The *fouage* had done its work ; revocation had no effect upon the political situation.

Step by step, castle by castle, and town by town the French were gaining ground and pushing back the frontiers of English Aquitaine. In the autumn the Duke of Berri scored a great success. He had been in communication with Jean de Cros, Bishop of Limoges, and on August 24 the Bishop surrendered the town to the enemy and received a French garrison. Apart from the military importance of the gain, English prestige had suffered a severe blow. The example of Limoges was sure to have weight wherever loyalty to the English crown was wavering, and it seemed as though with the defection of the capital the whole of Limousin would be lost. The loss of Limoges roused the Prince to one last burst of passionate energy. Suffering in body and in mind, embittered by the loss of his physical strength and the humiliating sense of failure, and infuriated by the treachery of Jean de Cros (for the Bishop had been his friend and councillor, and had held his first-born son at the font), the Black Prince made a vow of vengeance, and unhappily for himself and for others, made it good. He swore " by his father's soul, by the which he was never forsworn," that he would have Limoges and with it the lives of every one who dwelt in that city of traitors.

I, 158. 12. They are printed in *Lettres de Rois*, p. 176, No. xcviii. Cf. *Record Report*, xxxi. App. I. p. 36.

THE SIEGE OF LIMOGES

Lancaster landed at Bordeaux in the late summer of 1370. For once du Guesclin's generalship failed him. By the middle of July he had reached Toulouse. The obvious duty of the French general was to prevent the junction of Lancaster's comparatively small force with the main body of the Prince's army, some five thousand of all ranks, lying at Cognac, but he let the golden opportunity pass. The Duke joined his brother at Cognac, and their united forces marched on the doomed city.[1] At the news of the English advance Limoges began, too late, to repent its choice. Berri had taken possession of the city on August 24. The next day he left it to its fate, and no entreaties induced him to attempt to raise the siege. But he had left a stout garrison under Jean de Villemur, and the besieged fought with the courage of despair. From the day the English Army left Cognac to the end of the siege the command was virtually entrusted to Lancaster, for the Prince was too ill even to ride : he was carried in a litter, and was forced to leave the conduct of siege operations to his brother.

Limoges was well victualled and provided with artillery. The besiegers also had artillery with them, but they relied chiefly on mining operations to carry the city, and there Lancaster directed in person. One of the French chronicles has a strange story of how once miners and counterminers met beneath the ground when the Duke was present. Lancaster and Jean de Villemur for a long time fought hand to hand. Then the Duke

---

[1] For the siege of Limoges see *Chr. Val.* 209. *Chr. Norm.* 195 ; Froissart, K. de L. viii. 29–43, 54 ; xvii. 502. Cf. Delpit, *Collection*, ccxviii., ccxxi., and ccxxxi. *Petite Chronique de Guyenne*, § 62, L'an MCCCLXX en jun fo destruita la siutat de Lemodoges per monsehnor lo prince de Anglaterra. The *Chronique Romane* of Petit Thalamus is the only authority for the date : Item, aquel au meteyss a xix jorns del mes de setembre, fou preza e destrucha la ciutat de Lymotoges per lo princep de Galas lo qual y avia tengut ceti per alcun temps petit p. (385). Cf. *Livre des Coutumes*, p. 688.

says : " Qui es tu qui si fort te combas à moi ? Es tu comte ou tu es baron ? Nennin, dist Vinemeur, mais je suis ung povre chevalier. Adonc dit le Duc de Lancastre : Je te prie que tu me diez ton nom, puis que tu es chevalier, car tel porras estre que j'auray honneur de m'estre essayé à toy, ou tel que non." Donc dit Vinemeur : " Saches Angloiz que oncquez en armes ne regniez mon nom. J'ay nom Jehan de Vinemeur." A donc dit le Duc de Lancaster : " Monseigneur Jehan de Vinemeur, j'ay bien grant joye que je me suy esprouvé contre si bon chevalier comme vous estes. Si sachiez que je suys le Duc de Lancastre." The story may be only a confused version of a better-attested duel fought above ground, but the account is singularly circumstantial and minute, describing how the Duke was wounded by a prop which gave way in the mine. However this may be, it was Lancaster's mine which brought about the fall of Limoges, one of the few instances in the history of the Hundred Years War of a successful attack on a walled city.

After a month's work everything was reported ready. The word was given and the mine fired. A hundred feet of rampart and wall crashed to the ground, and over the ruins the invaders rushed to the assault. The first attack was beaten off ; with the second Limoges was carried. The Prince's vengeance had begun. He had issued his orders in person. They were ruthless, and they were obeyed. Neither age nor sex, neither man, woman nor child was to be spared. Limoges was a city of rebels and traitors, and the Prince had hardened his heart : the whole population was given up to the vengeance of the besieging army. For once the Black Prince, the pattern of chivalry, stained his name and his knightly honour. For once even Froissart's *insouciance* forsakes him. Usually so indifferent to the miseries of the " povre gens," Froissart melts at the picture of weak women and children crying out for mercy and crying in vain. " La eut grant pité ; car hommes, femmes et enfans se jetoient en genouls devant le prince et crioient : ' Merci, gentils sires, merci ! ' Mais il estoit si enflammés d'aïr que point n'i entendoit. . . . Il n'est si durs cœrs, se il fust adont à Limoges et il li souvenist de Dieu, qui ne plorast tenrement dou grant meschief qui y estoit, car plus de trois mille personnes, hommes, femmes et enfans, y furent dévyet et décolet celle journée. Diex en ait les ames, car il furent bien martir."

The carnage was greatest near the Cathedral of St. Étienne. There, in later days, men raised a statue to Notre Dame de Bonne Délivrance, the Madonna holding the Child in her arms, and with one hand covering His face to shut out the sight of the slaughter. History would willingly follow the example and draw the veil over the darkest day in the life of the Black Prince.

At length the massacre was stopped, and that in a way characteristic of the hardening caste feeling of the fourteenth century. What had been refused to the poor and helpless citizens of Limoges was granted to the courage of a few knights and gentlemen of the garrison. Some eighty of these, with Jean de Villemur the captain, withdrew to one place, put their backs to the wall, and resolved to sell their lives dearly.

Lancaster fought the captain of the garrison hand to hand, while his brother Cambridge and the Earl of Pembroke each singled out his man. It happened that in the thick of the fight Prince Edward was carried past in his litter. Touched by the gallantry of the French garrison, who knew that they were doomed and were fighting heavy odds, the Prince spared their lives and ordered the slaughter to cease.

So soon as the town was carried the first care of the besiegers was to find the arch-traitor who had brewed the mischief. Jean de Cros was caught in his palace, and taken chained and bareheaded before the Prince, who swore by God and St. George that he would have his life. It was a great thing to hang a bishop, even if that bishop were the traitor who had surrendered the key of a whole province to the enemy. But in the heat of Prince Edward's fury it is doubtful if his tonsure could have saved Jean de Cros, and Froissart evidently thinks that his life lay in the balance. It was Lancaster who saved him. The Duke, who had not yet learnt to hate political bishops, begged that the traitor might be given to him to deal with at his pleasure, and when the first burst of the Prince's resentment had passed, and he was left to look on the ruin he had wrought, Lancaster was allowed to send the Bishop a prisoner to the Papal court.

The Prince's vengeance was achieved. He had fulfilled his vow; the English army marched back to Cognac, leaving Limoges a desert and a ruin.

The feverish burst of energy which had carried the Black Prince to Limoges was succeeded by the usual reaction. The strain had been more than his health could bear. His vengeance was satisfied; he had saved his word; he could not save Aquitaine.

On reaching Cognac at the beginning of October, the Prince made a grant in tail to his brother of the castles and towns of Bergerac and of Roche-sur-Yon.[1] It was his last act of sovereignty. Three days later he abandoned the government of the Principality, formally appointing Lancaster his Lieutenant and surrendering Aquitaine into his hands.[2] Both the Prince and his brother must have been aware that to hold what remained

---

[1] Dated Cognac, 8 Oct. 1370. Delpit *Collection*, ccxviii. and ccxix.

[2] Dated Cognac, Oct. 11, 1370. Delpit *Collection*, ccxx. Froissart, K. de L. viii. 60–64; xvii. 505.

was a difficult task, to recover what was already lost well-nigh impossible.   The treasury was empty.   Those of the Gascon barons who had accepted French suzerainty were committed hopelessly and beyond recall, and the struggle between the English Gascons and the French Gascons was fought out with all the bitterness of a civil war.[1]

A stroke of the pen could not undo the past, nor stop the slow but sure advance of the enemy east and north and south.

By the terms of the indenture of agreement drawn·up between the Prince and his Lieutenant it is expressly stipulated that under no circumstances is Lancaster bound to continue in office after June 24, 1371.   Then, failing the appearance of a new lieutenant, the Constable and Steward of Aquitaine are to assume charge of the Principality.   At the root of the political situation lay the financial embarrassment of the country.[2]   Men-at-arms, as Froissart reminds us, cannot be expected to fight without their wages.   If the Duke's forces find their

---

[1] Chandos-Herald regards the war as a civil war—

> La véissez guerre mortele
> Et en plusours lieux moult cruele
> Le frere fut contre le frere
> Et le fitz fut contre le piere
> Chescun de eux sa part tenoit
> A quel part que meulx li plesoit
>   (3926–3931).

There was no principle at issue : a good instance is to be found in the Pope's own family.   One kinsman, Jean de Cros, had betrayed Limoges to the French ; another, William Viscount of Turenne, he protests, had always been faithful to the English cause. (See letter to Lancaster dated Villeneuve, Non. Aug. 1371, *Papal Letters*, iv. 96).

[2] The wine duties levied in the Isle of Oleron produced a small revenue for the war chest. Cf. Warrant dated 3 May, 1371, to Sir Thomas Percy, Steward of Poitou and Governor of Oleron to pay 600 franks from this source to the Marshal of Aquitaine (Delpit *Collection*, ccxxviii.).

pay in arrears for more than a month he is to be at once free from all responsibility.

So with feelings of disappointment at the past and misgivings for the future, Prince Edward laid down his burden. No other course was possible. His doctors were despairing of his life, and ordering his immediate return to England. At Bordeaux the Duke of Lancaster was presented to a Parliament of the loyal barons, and received from them the oath of fealty ; the Prince was free to go back to the lingering death which awaited him in England. Yet the cup of bitterness was not even now filled to the brim ; one more sorrow was in store for him. To the bitterness of failure and the loss of health and strength was added the death of his elder son, Prince Edward, a child of six, who died on the eve of the departure for England. Prince Richard alone survived to continue the eldest line of succession.

Lancaster was left at Bordeaux to bury his nephew, for the Prince was too ill to stay for his funeral,[1] and then to take up the task of holding Aquitaine.

The work began without delay. No sooner had his brother hoisted sail, than news came to Bordeaux that the Breton garrison of Périgueux had made a sally and captured Montpont-sur-l'Isle.[2] Lancaster began his task with energy. He marched out to Montpont,[3] invested

---

[1] Kervyn de Lettenhove. Froissart. Note, vol. viii., 432. The body was brought to England later by the command of Richard II.

[2] *Chr. Val.* p. 208, *Chr. Norm.* p. 200. The town in question is Montpont-sur-l'Isle (Dordogne arr. de Riberac), not Montpont in Rouergne, with which it has often been confused. It was taken by a column from Périgueux, which helps to fix the situation ; *Chr. Norm.* is explicit as to the site—" bien avant vers Bordeaux." Gregory XI, in his anxiety for peace writes to Charles V asking him to forbid the Duke of Anjou to attempt the relief of Montpont, *at least in his own person* (*Datum sub signeto nostro secreto*, 14 Kal. Feb. Avignon 1371 (*Papal Letters*, iv. 92).

[3] Froissart K. de L. viii, 64–76 ; xvii. 506–7, Cf. Petit Thala-

the town closely, and after a vigorous siege lasting some weeks, won it back from the French. Montpont was only a pawn in the great game of the French conquest of Aquitaine, but in one respect its capture was a triumph for the new Lieutenant. For the second time he had scored a success over the great Breton general. Du Guesclin had marched to raise the siege, but he came too late—only in time to find the English flag floating from its walls.

For six months after the capture of Montpont Lancaster fought on the ever-shifting frontier of Aquitaine with varying fortune. Montpont fell in February; he is back at Bordeaux in March ; in April he is at Niort in the north ; in May at Saintes and Pons, and he is back again at Bordeaux in the summer. Here and there a Gascon baron turned French and carried over his lands and castles to the enemy ; here and there the English won back some stronghold from the French. The campaign, if it deserves the name, was one of sieges and desultory fighting. There were no pitched battles ; there was nothing like a sustained plan of operations. But the general result is clear enough. Little by little the French were gaining ground, and pushing back the frontiers of the Principality.

Time passed, and with it the term of Lancaster's lieutenancy. The terms of the engagement had been more than fulfilled on the Duke's part, for since February his men had not had a day's pay from the exchequer of Aquitaine. The Duke had been fighting his brother's battles at his own cost, and the financial burden could be borne no longer. In July he summoned a meeting of the barons and explained his position. On June

mus (385): Item aquel an meteyss, en lo mes de febrier, fou pres e destrug lo castel de Montpaon en Peiragorc per lo duc de Lencastre e mossen Aymo frayre del dich princep los quals y avian teugut ceti per alcun temps ; and *Livre des Coutumes*, 688, and *Petite Chronique de Guyenne*, § 63.

24 his legal responsibilities had ceased. Although for the last six months his men-at-arms and archers had not been paid, and he would therefore have been justified in laying down the command, he had consented to remain at the head of affairs. Hitherto, out of consideration for the exhaustion of the country, he had levied no aid or tax. If he stayed on he would be compelled to " live on the country " with his army, a course which did not tend to the honour of the King his father, or the Prince, and which was not for the interest of the Principality. So long as he remained in Aquitaine he was ready to defend its territories against enemies without or rebels within, but he wished to be relieved of formal responsibility.[1] On July 21 the Duke resigned his powers, and the control of affairs was taken over by two of the most trusted officers of the Black Prince, Jean de Graily Captal de Buch and Sir Thomas Felton, Constable and Seneschal of Aquitaine.

This surrender of the Lieutenancy of Aquitaine is bound up with one of the events which had the most profound influence upon the Duke's life—his second marriage. Ambition has been admitted on all sides to have been the dominant note in the character of John of Gaunt, but satisfied with this general impression, none too explicit, history has not always consented to dwell for a moment on her judgment and analyse the motives at the root of this ambition. It is easy to take a statical view of a man's character, to hit upon some striking moment, some notorious and clearly understood phase, and by a hasty but unsafe generalisation to read all events previous and subsequent in the light of this alone. In 1371 it was John's ambition to play a great part among the Princes of Europe. He had not yet attempted to dominate the domestic politics of England, and some years were to elapse before the illness which

[1] Delpit *Collection*, ccxxx

effaced the Black Prince, and the dishonoured dotage of the King, forced Edward's favourite son to act as the representative of the Crown.

In 1371 the Duke had set his heart on Continental sovereignty, and to realize the dreams of foreign ambition natural to the son of Edward III, he endeavoured first to exploit to the full the dynastic claims of his inheritance, and then when this failed to create new claims by foreign alliance.

On the shadowy borderland of the great Lancastrian patrimony there were several claims which a man ambitious of power and dignity might wish to assert. One of these was the right to the Earldom of Moray, which David II had granted to Henry Duke of Lancaster, with remainder to his co-heirs for their lives, and which therefore should have descended with the other Lancastrian titles to Blanche and John of Gaunt.[1] The grant is indisputable. It passed under the great seal of Scotland and was witnessed by the leading magnates of the kingdom, but not even John of Gaunt dreamt of asserting his right to the Scottish earldom.

With another claim even more remote and more difficult to make good, it was otherwise. The Duke claimed the County of Provence. To revive a long-dormant and half-forgotten right like this is characteristic both of the Duke's temper and of his age—an age in which dynastic considerations determine foreign policy, and kings and princes haggle like lawyers over every clause in the family title deeds.

Such as it was, the claim arose in this way. Raymond VI of Provence had four daughters. All were beautiful, and all were wooed by royal suitors. Margaret, the eldest, married Saint Louis ; the second daughter, Eleanor, married Henry III of England ; while Sanchia,

---

[1] Dated Dundee, April 5, 30 David II. (*Record Report*, xxxv. App. (1) No. 119).

89

the third, married his brother, Richard Earl of Cornwall. The County of Provence passed with the hand of the youngest, Beatrice, to Charles of Anjou, brother of Saint Louis. Charles, thus Count of Provence in the right of his wife, became in 1268 King of Naples and Sicily. The Angevin inheritance, robbed of one kingdom by the Sicilian Vespers in 1282, passed through the descendants of Charles to Joanna Queen of Naples and Countess of Provence, who held it when John of Gaunt put forward his claim.

Though the youngest of Raymond's daughters had been allowed to carry the County to her husband and her children, her elder sister Eleanor, Queen of Henry III, retained or claimed to retain certain rights in Provence. These she made over to her grandsons Thomas and Henry, Earls of Lancaster, and their issue, and from Henry they passed with the rest of the patrimony to Blanche of Lancaster and her husband. Queen Eleanor's grant had been confirmed by Edward I and Edward II.[1] It remained a dead letter, but it was not forgotten, nor was John of Gaunt a man to lose sight of any claim which inheritance might bring him. When he came back to England from the council at Bayonne, at which Don Pedro had poured out his sorrows and his promises to the Gascon barons, he procured a renewal of the time-honoured grant of his ancestress.[2] The moment chosen to revive this visionary right is suggestive. At the council of Bayonne there was another royal suitor besides Don Pedro entreating Prince Edward's help, Dom Jayme, the *de jure* King of Majorca, and husband of the same Joanna who now called herself Queen of Naples and Countess of Provence. Was some concession as to the Lancastrian claim to be part of the

---

[1] Dated York, June 5, 1313 (Delpit *Collection*, xcix.).
[2] *Inspeximus* of the letters patent of Edward II, dated Westminster, 30 October, 1366 (Delpit *ibid*. cci. p. 124.)

price to be paid by Dom Jayme for his restoration to his Balearic kingdom ? The conjecture is tempting, but if there is anything in it, it is more than probable that Dom Jayme was reckoning without his consort, for Joanna of Naples had no intention of being dispossessed of the County of Provence. The disastrous ending to the campaign of 1367 put an end once and for all to the knight-errantry of the Black Prince. With Aquitaine in arms he had enough to do in setting his own house in order, and was compelled to abandon the succour of distressed monarchs, Dom Jayme among the number. Had it been otherwise, the Prince might perhaps have been engaged by his brother in an attempt to make good this far-fetched claim.

What is certain is that Lancaster's ambitions became known, and that Queen Joanna took alarm. For the Kingdom of Sicily she owned the suzerainty of the Apostolic See, and the Pope took up the cause of his vassal. The next year Urban sent a legate to the English court with a Bull of remonstrance.[1] The Duke's rights were denied in round terms, and the King was entreated not to allow his ambitious son to take up arms in an unjust quarrel and so to disturb the peace of princes. Negotiations dragged on for several years, of course to no purpose. As late as 1371 Gregory XI issued a mandate to the Bishops of London and Worcester to inform themselves as to the Duke's rights and to report to the Curia,[2] but needless to say no English army invaded Provence, and the Duke never took any practical steps to become Count of Provence.

[1] Dated Viterbo, vii. Kal. August, 5 Urban V. 1367 (*Foed* VI. 569). Baines confuses the claim to the County of Provence with an impossible claim to the Kingdom of Sicily (*History of the Duchy of Lancaster*, 351).

[2] Dated Avignon, 2 Kal. April, 1371. *Papal Letters*, iv, 169 ; 99. Cf. Warrant to Ralf de Erghum his Chancellor to pay 40*d*. to a messenger who brought the Pope's Bull touching his right to the County of Provence, dated The Savoy, April 17, 46 Edw. III) (1372) Reg. I. f. 146.

Nevertheless, the foreign ambitions remained. John of Gaunt had not given up the game. The luck was against him ; he doubled the stakes. There were bigger prizes than Provence to be won ; one of these was the throne of Don Pedro, the crown of Castile and Leon.

In the flight from Castile in 1366 Don Pedro had brought with him to Bordeaux his three daughters, Beatrice, Constance, and Isabel. The eldest took the veil and died soon after. The second remained the heiress of Castile, and with her sister Isabel the sole survivor of the House of Burgundy.

An *émigrée* Princess, living on the charity of a foreign court, without dynastic alliances, and having for friends only the few courtiers who still clung to the fortunes of the fallen House, Constance must have found her position at Bordeaux doubtful and difficult. She must have seen about her the evidence of her father's ill faith in the ruin of the Black Prince and the rebellion of Aquitaine.

But if she inherited nothing else, the heiress of Don Pedro had something of that fierce tenacity of purpose which had sustained her father single-handed in his life-long struggle with the feudal anarchy, and she had in no small measure the pride of race and instinct of royalty, and all the exile's bitter love for her native land.

Lancaster's ambition, or as Froissart puts it, his council, suggested a match. To the Duke, Constance of Castile stood for boundless possibilities of adventurous ambition. To Constance, the alliance presented a ready means of escape from the difficulties of her position, and perhaps the only possibility of making the dream of her youth a reality—the overthrow of the usurper, the traitor who had stabbed her father after the fatal day of Montiel, and the restoration of the legitimate line.

Though the succour of distressed princesses might fall in perhaps with the Duke's humour—for motives are often mixed and even politicians are men—there was no pretence on either side of any motive but convenience. Chaucer has no delicate idyll of a romantic courtship, no meed of a melodious tear when thirteen years later the " Queen of Castile " followed Blanche the Duchess to the grave.

" For better or for worse " the die was cast. In September, 1371, at Roquefort,[1] the Duke married his second wife. Constance of Castile became Duchess of Lancaster and, with a less certain title, John of Gaunt became " King of Castile and Leon." When soon afterwards Edmund Earl of Cambridge married her younger sister Isabella the sole survivors of the House of Burgundy had carried their rights of royalty to King Edward's sons.

In November Lancaster landed at Plymouth with his bride. As the cortege passed through Exeter, Winchester and Guildford to London, curious eyes might have noted new faces in the retinue of " Monseigneur d'Espaigne," Spanish knights wearing the Lancastrian livery, and a train of Spanish ladies-in-waiting of the " Queen of Castile."

---

[1] Froissart, K. de L. viii. 104-7 ; but according to xvii. 514, the marriage took place at St. Andrew.

E

II. THE FIRST AND SECOND MARRIAGES OF JOHN OF GAUNT

(1) Blanche of Lancaster, = John of Gaunt = (2) Constance, daughter of Pedro I of Castile,
b. 1341, m. 1359, d. 1369   b. 1354, m. 1371, d. 1394

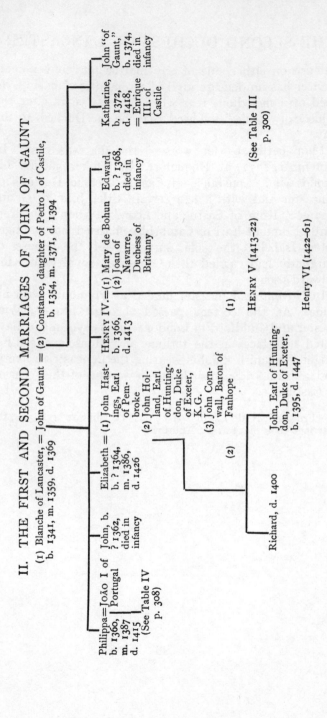

Chapter V

THE NAVAL QUESTION

THAT Lancaster's second marriage had any immediate result upon the relations of France and Castile is extremely doubtful.

It has been argued that Lancaster's claim threw Don Enrique into the arms of France and engaged England in a struggle with two enemies instead of one ; but this argument overlooks the fact that in 1372 the offensive and defensive alliance of the Kings of France and Castile was three years old.[1] Najera was a defeat for the French : Montiel was a victory for the French. Don Enrique held his throne by the grace and favour of the French King, and to him at least the alliance with the ultramontane neighbour was from the first a cardinal point of policy, and indeed a political necessity. To the action of the Black Prince in 1366 and 1367, not to that of Lancaster in 1371, is it due that England began the second period of the Hundred Years War against a combination of enemies.

At the root of the Franco-Castilian alliance lay the burning question of naval supremacy. Once only in the wars did a Castilian army march across the Pyrenees to reinforce the French ; there were negotiations for such assistance in 1374, it is true, but they came to nothing. On the other hand, never in the dynastic struggles which

---

[1] Dated Toledo, Nov. 20, 1368, *Foed*, VI. 598, 602. Cf. 602–3.

convulsed Castile was an important battle fought without the aid of French troops. It must not be supposed that the alliance was a one-sided bargain, or that Charles V was guilty of political philanthropy. He got as good as he gave, and he got what he needed—Castilian ships to make common cause against the enemy, who in 1340 and 1350 had defeated France and Castile in detail. Since 1350, however, the naval situation had changed, for, with a want of forethought which in the greatest military power of the day is little short of extraordinary, England had neglected her navy and let the power won at Sluys and Winchelsea slip from her grasp.

In the fourteenth century there was, for England at least, no " Mediterranean question." Only once, and then by accident, did an English battle fleet pass through the Straits of Gibraltar ; only once—in 1355—did an English army march to the shores of the Mediterranean. It was left to Genoese and Venetian, Catalan and Portuguese to dispute among themselves, with occasional protests from the corsairs of the African coast, for the mastery of the seas in which Great Britain now maintains her most powerful battle fleet. But then, as now, England had maritime interests at stake second in importance to those of no other European State. Naval force exists for one purpose, and one purpose only—to maintain lines of communication ; to destroy any hostile force which can menace them. In the period in question those lines lay between Bayonne and Bordeaux and the home ports ; along the Channel, and between Dover, Sandwich and Yarmouth and the mouths of the Scheldt and Rhine. Here, therefore, on the routes followed by the great sea-borne commerce, the naval battles of the period are fought—at Sluys in 1340, off Winchelsea in 1350, off Rochelle in 1372.

Although Edward III knew that commerce furnishes the sinews of war, he did little or nothing to create a royal navy, or to maintain in numbers and efficiency the ships of the English mercantile marine. In spite of protests on the part of Parliament, the oppressive system of seizing merchant ships for transport purposes went on as before—an abuse which did as much as the depredations of enemies to discourage maritime enterprise. England had no naval policy as such, for there was no fleet capable of being mobilized without delay and of keeping the sea for a continuous period.

Faced, therefore, with the united naval force of France and Castile, England was found wanting. In this naval combination, which marks the second period of the war, lies the true significance of the alliance of Valois and Trastamare. It was this condition of affairs which a dozen years later enabled John of Gaunt to make out a case for the invasion of Castile, and to plead with some show of plausibility that he was doing for England what Charles V had done for France. English archers fight the battles of Portuguese independence, and help to set up the House of Avis, as French men-at-arms had set up the House of Trastamare. Portuguese galleys come across the bay to reinforce English fleets. In the eighties John of Gaunt can persuade Parliament that the answer to the coalition of Valois and Trastamare is the alliance of Portugal and Lancaster.

But this is an anticipation. In 1372 England fought single-handed, and with disastrous results. On his return Prince Edward had surrendered the Principality of Aquitaine to the King, and in June, 1372, the Earl of Pembroke was sent south as the King's Lieutenant.

Off La Rochelle Pembroke's ships fell in with the Castilian Admirals, Boccanegra and Cabeza de Vaca, in command of a powerful fleet. A two days' action, stubbornly fought against heavy odds, decided Pembroke's fate. His ships were sunk or captured. His treasure, the war chest which was to pay for the coming campaign in Gascony, fell into the hands of the enemy, and the Earl himself was carried away into captivity.

Meanwhile du Guesclin, now Constable of France, with energy almost amounting to genius, was pressing on with the reduction of Aquitaine. Town after town, castle after castle, surrendered to the Constable and his Lieutenants, Clisson, Kerlouët, Mauni and Beaumanoir—the Breton heroes who inspired Cuvelier's interminable epic. Chizé, Niort, Lusignan, Cognac and Lancaster's town Roche-sur-Yon had fallen already. Poitou and Saintonge were as good as lost. Chauvigni, Lussac, Moncontour, Sainte Sévère fell in August. Thouars, hard pressed by the besiegers, had agreed to surrender if no help came by September 30.

The King resolved to save Thouars, and avenge Pembroke. Every ship that could be pressed from the mouth of the Thames to Newcastle and to the ports of Lancashire was swept into the harbours of Portsmouth and Sandwich.[1] Every tenant in chief was summoned to join the king's flag. Lancaster brought his whole retinue.[2] Even the Prince of Wales was carried from his sick bed at Berkhamstead on board the *Grace de Dieu,* the King's flagship. On the last day of August, when there was just a month to save Thouars, the fleet weighed anchor : but a month was not enough. The Channel in September is not a good sea for little vessels dependent solely on sail

---

[1] Orders to collect ships February 6 and 7, 1372 (*Foed,* VI. 708-9; 715-6); hastened, April 4 (ibid.). The date fixed for departure was originally May 1, but it was the end of August before the ships were ready.

[2] The Duke orders ships to be collected Feb. 10, 1372 ; levies an aid Feb. 7 ; contracts for provisions March 3. Reg. I. f. 19-51. He receives 6,000 marcs for the expenses of the expedition (Register, Aug. 10). The King orders the guardian of the privy wardrobe in the Tower to give him " de nostre artillerie quatre mill quarelx " (*Lettres des Rois,* p. 181, No. ci. Dated Westminster, August 26, 1372). Cf. Froissart, K. de L. viii. 205-7 ; xvii. 529.

power, and before Edward's ships were out of sight of the Hampshire coast they met the full strength of the equinoctial gales. For a month or more the ships were storm-tossed on the Norman and Breton coasts, trying to beat up against contrary winds. They could never make Cape Ushant. The costly expedition proved futile: Thouars was perforce abandoned to its fate, and the fleet returned to pay off, nothing done.

At the close of 1372 the military position was deplorable. Before the end of the year Angoulême had fallen; La Rochelle had received a French garrison, and Thouars was in the hands of the enemy. Aquitaine was as good as lost. Only in the North the English cause seemed less desperate, where the Earl of Salisbury was gallantly holding out against the Constable for Edward's ally, the Duke of Brittany. In the spring of 1373 Montfort came to England in person to concert a plan of action.[1] It was arranged that in the summer a strong army should be despatched to invade France; the restoration of the Earldom of Richmond rewarded Montfort's promise to lead his Breton levies in the English army, which was to be placed under the command of John of Gaunt.

The summer of 1373 marks the zenith of Lancaster's ambition. Of late years English arms had suffered reverse after reverse; there had been no victory since Najera, and at Najera the Duke, though acquitting himself well, had held a subordinate command. The short campaign in Picardy in 1369 had been controlled by him, it is true, but the army only amounted to a handful of men. In 1370 and 1371 again he had fought for a losing, if not a lost, cause with few men and no money.

Now he found himself Commander-in-Chief of as fine an army as ever left English shores during the Hundred

---

[1] Froissart, K. de L. viii. 249–50; 266–8.

Years War, with the sole and independent command of the flower of English soldiery. What wonder that the son of Edward III and brother of the Black Prince dreamt of victories and burned to win a place beside his father, his brother, and Good Duke Henry among the nation's heroes ?

But this is not all. Strong as the desire for military fame was with the ambitious Duke of Lancaster, there was one desire even stronger, that craving for Continental sovereignty, which Edward III had transmitted to his son and encouraged by his own example.

Fascinated in 1367 by the spectacle of Castilian royalty, though in ruins, as in 1396 Richard II became fascinated by the spectacle of French royalty, Lancaster from the first had formed the resolve of winning back Pedro's heritage, enforcing the just claims of his consort, and building up again the fallen fabric of the House of Burgundy.

Thus the invasion of France in 1373 was, in the Duke's mind, but the prelude to the piece ; the drama which was to begin on the fields of Picardy was to have its closing scene upon the battlefields of Castile.[1]

Because the event belied his hopes and frustrated his intention, the intention itself has escaped notice. That interference in home politics, which in conjunction with military disaster produced his extraordinary unpopularity, has usually been placed half a dozen years too soon, while the foreign ambitions which give the keynote to his character and policy have been placed at least ten years too late. From the day when in the village near Bordeaux Constance of Castile united her fortunes to his, to the day when sixteen years later his army of invasion left Plymouth bound for Coruña, the single aim

---

[1] The great invasion was to have taken place in the previous year, but was postponed on account of the Thouars expedition. Froissart, K. de L. viii. 91-3 ; 118-207.

JOHN OF GAUNT.

(From a Picture Ascribed to Luca Cornelli.)

of the Duke of Lancaster was to win the throne of Castile.

The first and most obvious ally for a would-be invader of Castile is the sovereign who holds Oporto and Lisbon and commands access to the long and exposed Castilian frontier. Lancaster recognized the fact, and shaped his policy accordingly.

So soon as the marriage was solemnized the work began. From 1371 to 1386 envoys are passing to and fro between the court of "Monseigneur d'Espaigne" in England or Aquitaine and the court of the King of Portugal.

By 1372 a treaty of alliance had been concluded between John and Constance, King and Queen of Castile and Leon, on the one part, and Fernando and Leonor, King and Queen of Portugal, on the other,[1] by which the allies bound themselves to attack the House of Trastamare.

From the ratification of that treaty onwards the Duke has a stream of emissaries constantly flowing to the Portuguese court bound on diplomatic missions.[2]

Just before the unlucky attempt to relieve Thouars offensive action against Castile was expressly contemplated, for the Duke's indenture of service mentions a possible invasion, and goes so far as to fix the numbers of his retinue to meet that event.[3] Further, on the eve of his departure for France in July the Duke empowers his consort to pardon rebels in his kingdom of Castile, an attempt to profit by the chronic

[1] Duchy of Lancaster, Ancient Correspondence, No. 29. Dated Nov. 27, 1410 (i.e. A.D. 1372). Cf. also No. 30, dated July 10, 1372, and *Foed*, VII. 15–22 and 263.

[2] Warrant to his Receiver-General to pay Mons. Lambard de Weston £20 and to John Mere 10 marcs for their expenses on their voyage to Portugal, dated Hertford, Jan. 10, 1373, Reg. I. f. 169; do. to pay the Dean of Segovia 100s. which he had given him for his expenses, dated The Savoy, April 3, 1373. Reg. I. f. 177.

[3] Reg. I. f. 12.

discontent among the semi-independent feudal nobles and to detach waverers from the usurper's cause, and on the same day he empowers his Chamberlain, Sir Robert Swylyngton, and his Steward, Sir William Croyser, with Sir Godfrey Foliambe, a trusted retainer, and that faithful adherent, Juan Guttierez, Dean of Segovia and afterwards Bishop of Dax, to negotiate as plenipotentiaries and make alliances in Castile.[1]

The Duke's intentions, therefore, are beyond the range of doubt. They comprised far more than an invasion of France. Lancaster's midsummer madness—for such the sequel proves it—was the dream of following up the conquest of France by the conquest of Castile, of winning some great victory which should make him the popular hero of the hour, and then with the acclamations of the nation of leading his victorious army from Bordeaux across the Pyrenees, to cast the usurper from his throne, and to be proclaimed in the Cortes by that title to which he clings—John, King of Castile and Leon.

With such high stakes it is not surprising that the Duke watched the game with feverish interest. Froissart does not exaggerate when he says : "Li dus de Lancastre et li consauls dou roy d'Engleterre avoient entendu à appareillier les pourvéances si grandes et si belles, que merveilles seroit à penser." [2]

The details of preparation fill the Duke's mind ; they are arranged months beforehand with elaborate forethought. He is careful to give orders that his archers shall be picked men ; they are to have their wages paid in advance ; there is to be no pretext for failure to appear at the rendezvous on the appointed day.[3]

Early in the year the Duke is pledging his credit with

---

[1] Register I. f. 61. Dated Norbourne, July 14, 1373.
[2] Froissart, K. de L. viii. 268.
[3] Warrants dated Hertford, April 17, 1373. Reg. I. f. 179.

friends lay and clerical to raise money for the war ;[1] in the Eastern counties, in the Midlands and the North, the Duke's receivers have urgent orders to send all the money in their hands to the Savoy. In March his avener is buying horses ;[2] his stewards are contracting for supplies and his commissioners of array are recruiting men-at-arms, and his foresters are choosing archers wherever men are to be found who can shoot true.[3]

The first rendezvous was Plymouth, the date May 10.[4] The choice of the Western port shows that the Duke's original idea was to land somewhere on the Breton or west Norman coast, effect a junction with Montfort and his men, and after relieving the beleagured garrisons of Brest, Becherel, St. Sauveur and Derval, to advance between the Loire and the Seine, perhaps on Paris, but at any rate to deliver an attack from the west.

This plan was abandoned. In the first place, England had lost command of the sea ; from Cherbourg to Plymouth and from Plymouth to Brest the Channel was swept by Amaury de Narbonne, Admiral of France, and his lieutenant, Jean de Vienne.[5] Then there was the usual delay in getting the transport ships together ;[6] unhappily for the Duke and his army, it was near the end of July

[1] Warrant to the Receiver in Yorkshire to borrow £200 of the Bishop of Durham and 200 marcs of the dowager Lady Neville until March next, dated The Savoy, March 23, 1373, Reg. I. f. 175. The Earl of Arundel lent him 2,000 marcs, and he received from the Treasury £3,977 5s. 6d. and 2,000 marcs on account of the late campaign in Aquitaine. (Reg. I. f. 171 and 178).

[2] Reg. I. f. 176-7.

[3] Warrants to the Receivers in Stafford, Lincoln, Yorkshire, Norfolk, and Suffolk, and to the Forester of the Frith of Leicester, dated Hertford, April 19, 1373. Reg. I. f. 159. See Note of the delivery of munitions of war to the Duke, dated July 28, 1373. *Lettres des Rois*, p. 193.

[4] Reg. I. f. 179.

[5] See *Jean de Vienne*, by Terrier de Loray, p. 61.

[6] Orders dated April 28, 1373. *Foed*, VII. 7-8.

instead of the beginning of May before the freight fleet was mobilized—a delay which had the most disastrous effect on the fate of the expedition.

Instead of Plymouth, Dover and Sandwich were chosen as the ports of embarkation,[1] and the line of advance was changed accordingly.

By the end of July everything was ready. The Duke had appointed new constables for all his castles, for most of his officers were going with him to the wars ; he had prepared Tutbury Castle for his children and the " Queen of Castile " ;[2] he had named his attorneys and chosen his executors—among them, be it noted, William of Wykeham, Bishop of Winchester.[3]

The army had mustered—something like fifteen thousand men, including 6,000 archers, all ranks being mounted.[4] There was a good transport service and a useful body of sappers and miners. Nothing had been forgotten.

With full powers as Commander-in-Chief of the King's forces, as Lieutenant in the realm of France and in Aquitaine,[5] with the prayers of the Church[6] and the hopes of the nation, the Duke set sail from Calais at the end of July, bound on the adventure so bright in its inception, so gloomy in its sequel.

At Calais Montfort's men, and soldiers of fortune from Hainault, Brabant, and Germany added a few hundreds to the Duke's forces, and his popularity across the Border

---

[1] For the rendezvous at Dover and Sandwich see orders dated May 20, 1373. Reg. I. f. 59.

[2] Order to prepare Tutbury Castle, dated Norbourne, July 6, 1373 (Reg. I. f. 181).

[3] Appointed May 11, 1373. *Foed,* VII. 7–8.

[4] The numbers given by *Chr. Bourb.* are 16,000.

[5] The Duke's Commission is dated June 12, 1373. *Foed,* VII. 13–15.

[6] For "Prayers for King John in his Expedition of Arms " see letters dated June 16, 1373. *Foed,* VII. 15.

brought a contingent of some three hundred Scottish lances to forget the national quarrel and fight under his banner.[1]

On August 4 the great march began. With banners and pennons flying, to the blare of trumpets and the beating of drums, the Duke's army marched out of Calais and debouched on the plains round Guines and Ardres in three divisions or " battles." With the first were the Marshals, the Earls of Warwick and Suffolk. The Duke of Brittany was with Lancaster in the second ; so was Sir Hugh Calverly, the veteran campaigner, who now acted as " chief of the staff " to the Duke, as Sir John Chandos had done six years before. Then came the transport and baggage train. The Constable, Lord Despencer, brought up the rear.

Straggling and irregular fighting were strictly forbidden—a soldierlike precaution which, though difficult to enforce in an army of the fourteenth century, saved the Duke from considerable loss. For the first third of the march, from Calais to Troyes, the line of advance was roughly that followed by Edward III in the campaign of 1360, viz. through Picardy, Artois, Vermandois, Laonnois and Champagne.[2] After leaving the marches of Calais the division into three " battles " was changed for a formation more convenient to an invading army on the march, viz. that of two columns. The western column, under the Duke of Brittany, followed a fairly straight line to the south-east.[3] Lancaster, who led the

---

[1] Froissart, K. de L. viii. 450.

[2] For Lancaster's March see *Grandes Chroniques de France*, vi. 339–341 ; *Chr. Val.* 245–48 ; *Chr. Reg. Franc.*, 346–7 ; *Istore et Chroniques de Flandres*, ii. 136–9 ; Froissart, K. de L. viii. 280–296 ; xvii. 542–5 ; Luce viii. (1) lxxxiii.–ciii. ; and *Chronicon Briocense*, quoted by Morice, *Histoire de Bretagne* (*Preuves* i. pp. 47–8).

[3] The itinerary given by the *Grandes Chroniques de France* (vi. 339), is evidently that of the western column:—Calais, La

eastern column, advanced in a direction forming a very irregular parallel to Montfort's line, keeping his men as long as possible in the fertile river basins, the valleys of the Authie, the Somme and the Oise. The two columns converged near Vailly-sur-Aisne, but Lancaster's right wing and Montfort's left wing were never far out of touch with each other. The area enclosed between the two lines represents roughly the sphere of devastation.

The western column marched past Licques, Thérouanne, Hesdin, crossed the Authie at Doullens, which beat off an attack, and the Somme at Corbie. Meanwhile, Lancaster at a leisurely pace had marched past Ardres, St. Omer and Aire, ravaged the lands of the Count of St. Pol, and after calling a halt for a couple of days near Arras, where he stayed in the Abbey of Mont-St.-Eloi, had turned due south, getting into close touch with his ally at Bray-sur-Somme.

It was here that the greatest havoc was wrought. Santerre, Noyon, all that " fair and rich land of Vermandois," as Froissart calls it, were swept by the invading army. Roye, Essigni, Vendeuil and Rémigny were burnt to the ground. So thorough was the work of destruction that long after the invasion was over the French King's exchequer had to abandon all hope of a revenue from these towns, and the Receiver of Noyon was ordered to remit their taxes.[1]

From the ruins of Roye Montfort wrote a defiance to his French suzerain ; there could be no longer any doubt as to the side which the Duke of Brittany chose. Throughout Noyon, Soissons and Champagne there was a reign of terror. It was now the time of harvest and

Marche, Hesdin, Doullens, Beauquesne, Corbie, Roye, Vailly-sur-Aisne, Oulchie; then of the two columns combined, Gyé, Marcingny-les-Nonnains, etc. Cf. *Chronicon Briocense.*
[1] *Mandements de Charles V*, dated Paris, Jan. 4, 1374. (No. 1091.)

English Miles

Scale

0 20 40 60 80 100

Darbishire & Stanford Ltd.,

Lancaster's march on Harfleur, (1369) - - - - - - - - thus ....
The March on Limoges, (1370)   - - - - - - - ,, + + + + +
Lancaster's march from Calais to Bordeaux,(1373) ,, ▬▬▬▬
Burgundy's pursuit   - - - - - - - ,, — — —

The Oxford Geographical Institute.

0,000   Kilometres
        0 20 40 60 80 100

vintage, but the year's labour and hopes went for nothing. To add to the misery of the crowds herded from all the country side into the strong places (the weak had been abandoned), they could mark the progress of the work of devastation by the flame and smoke of their burning farms and houses.

From Nesle-notre-Dame to Rheims and from Rheims to Châlons and from Châlons to Troyes sentinels watched night and day from the walls of the defensible positions for the signs of the English advance.

On August 20 the Duke's army was signalled at Bray and Cappy; in hot haste the Captain of Nesle sent a courier to the Governor and Échevins of Rheims. Rheims passed on the word to Troyes. Just as the Governor was sealing his letter the news came in of the occupation of Roye, while from the east Châlons on August 25 reported another body of the invaders across the Oise then camping between Pont l'Evêque and Vailly.[1]

From Calais to Vailly the Duke had only met with one sign of activity on the part of the enemy. The captain of Ribemont had led a sortie and by a successful ambush cut up the retinue of Sir Hugh Calverly, to whom, however, no blame attached, for he was with the Duke and the main body of the army at the time.

But the French had not been idle. Charles V had a policy, thoughtfully conceived and persistently enforced. It was not heroic, but events proved its wisdom. The " attorney " was " pleading his cause," and he pleaded long enough to weary the English general. Charles chose persistent inaction; he had made up his mind to bow before the storm, until it should have spent its fury

[1] The letters are printed in M. Arbois de Jubainville's *Voyage Paléographique dans le département de l'Aube,* pp. 148–150. (Troyes, 1885.)

and worn itself out. " Laissez-les-aller "—Froissart is
speaking for the King's Council—" Par fumières ne
peuvent-ils venir a votre héritage ; il leur ennuira,
et iront tous à neant. Quoi que un orage et une tem-
pête se appert à la fois en un pays, si se depart depuis et
degâte de soi-même, ainsi adviendra-t-il de ces gens
Anglois."

At all costs the hazard of battle was to be avoided.
To hang upon the rear and flank of the invading army,
to cut off stragglers and foraging parties, and in some
measure to " contain " the movements of the enemy
was all that Charles was prepared to attempt.

This policy did not pass without comment. There
were hot-headed critics who construed inaction as
cowardice, and forgetting Poictiers, longed for the days
of " Jean le Bon." To those without the King's fore-
sight, to all who had failed to learn the lessons of the war,
Charles was the dastard son of a brave if unfortunate
father. But at least the Council was unanimous. Thanks
to the Black Prince and English archery, the belief of
the invaders in their own invincibility was a creed un-
questioned by the invaded. Not a voice was given for
accepting Lancaster's challenge of battle.

To carry out the King's policy, Philip Duke of Burgundy had been sent to Amiens as soon as the rumour of
the coming invasion reached France. He was supported
by Jean de Vienne, a brave and dashing captain both
ashore and afloat, whose merit was soon to be rewarded
by the office of Admiral of France.

Philip the Bold, in spite of his name, was statesman
first and soldier second. Perhaps, like Lancaster, he
lacked the real essence of statesmanship. The Duke
was playing his own game. His predecessor in
1360 had bribed Edward III not to ravage Burgundy,
and had left the Regent and the rest of France to
their fate. With equal preoccupation for the safety

of his own lands the Duke showed now plainly enough his anxiety to get to the south. He left Amiens on August 17 ; the English did not reach Bray till the 20th. When the Duke of Brittany was burning Roye, Burgundy had reached Soissons. It is true that he cut up an English outpost at Oulchy-le-Château, but that was by the way. The Duke could not rest until, throwing himself into Troyes a few days ahead of the enemy, he was within easy distance of his own dominions.[1]

Thus the Duke, who for the time represented the defensive force of France, had marched in line roughly parallel to but shorter and more direct than that followed by Lancaster, in advance of the invaders, and only three times coming into contact with them—at Ribemont and Oulchy, mere matters of outposts, and at Plancy, where there was a trifling encounter at the *Barrières Amoureuses*.

Meanwhile, the Court of Avignon, always anxious for the peace of Christendom, doubly so when the French King was in difficulties, had been roused to one more effort to stop hostilities.[2]

Two Cardinals, the Archbishop of Ravenna, and the Bishop of Carpentras with this object in view had been sent from Avignon to Paris, where their efforts were welcomed, if they had not been invited. The peacemakers followed Burgundy to Troyes, charged with the duty of mediation, and parleying began so soon as Lancaster came within sight of Troyes. But there was no real basis for negotiations. The Duke listened but paid no attention, and the cardinals returned with their rebuff.

Lancaster now stood at the parting of the ways :

---

[1] From this point onwards see *Chron. Bourb.* 50–51, which says the English lost 120 killed, 180 captured, in the fight round suburbs of Troyes.

[2] *Papal Letters*, IV. 125.

the advance from Calais to Troyes had produced no engagements and no military result. He could go back, which would be inglorious, or he could go on, which would be useless. So much was clear, for the tactics of the enemy had paralyzed the English attack. But the general failed utterly to realize the altered conditions under which he had now to conduct the campaign.

He had avoided one possible but disastrous mistake— to fritter his strength away on isolated sieges. His fault was of omission, not of commission. The Duke, remembering Rheims, refused sieges. The French, remembering Poictiers, refused battle. John of Gaunt, a respectable tactician, as he had shown at Najera, was as incompetent a strategist as his father, and had learned little from the generalship of the Black Prince.

Only accident and circumstances for which he was not responsible saved King Edward's campaign in 1360 from ending in disaster. Then the captivity of King John and the exhaustion of France forced the hands of the Regent, and Brétigni saved the credit of the English King. Now fortune, which had smiled on the father, frowned on the son. A repetition of the treaty of Brétigni with its wildly favourable terms was impossible in 1373. The Duke could not have peace with honour. He chose honour with disaster, and went on.

If he was not prepared to besiege Troyes (and sieges were difficult and rarely successful), he might have threatened Paris and tried to compel Charles V, that carpet knight, to don his armour for once and do battle for his throne. The Black Prince would have manœuvred until he had the advantage of the enemy. Then he would have attacked and driven the charge home. There was something to be said for going back : there was still more to be said for forcing the enemy's hand and compelling him to fight. For the course which the Duke chose, there was little or nothing to be said. It meant the ruin of the army.

So the advance continued, but under very different conditions. About six hundred horse had followed the Duke as far as the line of the Seine. Now Anjou Clisson and the famous Constable of France, recalled from the siege of the Breton towns (so much the Duke's invasion had done) to reinforce Burgundy, with their combined forces, were free to harry the Duke's flanks and rearguard and to cut up stragglers and foraging parties.[1]

It was the time of vintage and harvest when the English had advanced through Picardy, Artois, Vermandois Laonnois and Champagne ; when they left Troyes, September was nearly over ; the land of corn and wine was behind them ; in front of them lay two-thirds of the journey ; the barren mountains of Auvergne, the Loire, Authie, Dordogne, Lot, and Garonne, all swollen by the rainfall of an unusually wet season.

Leaving Troyes behind him, Lancaster marched up the valley of the Seine as far as Gyé, where he crossed, while Brittany with a detached force crossed the river just below Troyes itself and marched on Sens only to fall into a cleverly laid ambush of Clisson and to suffer accordingly.[2] The first week of October found the two columns combined again, and preparing to waste the *entourage* of Avallon.

On October 1 the Bailiff of Auxerre, writing to the Duchess of Burgundy, reported that the invaders had just occupied Pothières, Pontaubert and le Vault de Lugny, and were destroying everything that they could find.[3] There was little enough left for them, for the same

---

[1] Froissart, K. de L. viii 307–21 ; xvii 546–50.
[2] *Chr. Bourb.*, p. 54.   Et fut la plus grosse destrousse que les Anglois eussent en cellui voyage.
[3] See M.E. Petit *Avallon et l'Avallonnais*, vol. ii p. 246 (Aux-

district had been ravaged only the year before by Breton free companies, and the Burgundians had learnt the lesson. More fortunate, too, than the men of Vermandois and the northern provinces, they had been given time to get their harvest in, and the corn, with every sort of movable property—" jusqu'aux fers des moulins "—which could tempt destruction or plunder, had been carried off and stored in strong places.

After leaving Avallon the real nature of the great march appeared in its true light : that of a disastrous military promenade. The fighting, such as it was, was over. The captain of Marigny-le-Châtel, it is true, plucked up courage to lead a sortie, but failed to do much damage.[1] True to the King's policy, the " containing force " kept in touch with every movement of the invaders but steadily refused to come to close quarters. Leaving Troyes on September 26, the Duke of Burgundy had marched through Joigny, Auxerre, Varzy, Premery and Decize in a line parallel to Lancaster's route. From Decize Burgundy made a spurt, and getting ahead of the English, crossed the Loire at Roanne, a point a good deal south of the crossing place chosen by Lancaster, with the idea of heading off the English army to the west. But Lancaster, instead of striking westwards from Marcigny-les-Nonnains, as might have been expected, turned sharp to the south, and in spite of the time of the year (it was the beginning of November) faced the fearful prospect of leading an army to Bordeaux through Auvergne in the winter.

At Clermont Philip the Bold gave up the pursuit. His lands had no more to fear from the invasion, and

erre 1867); quoting *Comptes de l'Auxois*, and M. A. Chérest *Étude Historique sur Vézelay*, vol. ii p. 245-6 (Auxerre 1863); quoting *Archives de la Côte-d'or*.

[1] Boutiot. *Histoire de Troyes* ii. 234-5, quoting *Arch. Dep. de St. Pierre.*

knowing that the enemy were doomed, he was content to leave them to their fate. Cold and privation would henceforth deal with the invaders.

The miseries of this last stage of the march can well be imagined. It is no longer possible to trace Lancaster's movements by the records of the villages which he burnt, the despairing petitions of ruined communes praying for remission of taxes. In that rugged volcanic region of the Puy de Dôme, the barren hills and scarcely less barren plateaux of lower Auvergne, there was little damage to be done. But the hardships of the march were intensified tenfold. The crossing of the Loire and Allier had accounted for the baggage train and transport ; now the horses began to get knocked up, and many of all ranks, high and low, had to march on foot, while provisions became daily more hard to find.

Just at the time when at Westminster Sir John Knyvett, the Chancellor, was assuring Parliament that Lancaster's forces had " stayed the malice of the King's adversaries and by their good and noble governance and deeds of arms had wrought great damage and destruction to the enemy in France,"[1] hunger and cold were thinning the ranks of the army ; horse and man were dropping out to perish of cold, disease, and starvation in the defiles and passes of Auvergne.

With stubborn endurance and indomitable courage, which even their enemies extolled, the army, or what was left of it, struggled on. By December 14 Mur-de-Barrez and Montsalvy were reached ;[2] a few days later

---

[1] " Et ore tard' l'an passe manda celes parties son filz le Roi de Castil et de Leon et duc de Lancastre, ove plusours grantz et autres en sa campagnie a grant nombre a aresteer la malice de ses dits adversoirs : queux parmi lour bon et noble governement et fait d'armes ont fait grantz damages et destruction as enemys par dela . . . *Rot. Parl.* ii. 316a.

[2] See *Le Rouergue sous les Anglais,* p. 271 (L'Abbé Rouquette Millau, 1887).

and Lancaster was at Tulle and Brive-la-Gaillarde and on friendly soil, for Brive had not lost the old Gascon sentiment, and its inhabitants were " traitors to the King of France." Here, if the *Bourbon Chronicle* can be trusted, Lancaster called a muster of his forces. Of the 15,000 men who had marched out of Calais with such high hopes, only 8,000 were left, and of these only half were still mounted.

The rest had perished, few by the hand of the enemy, almost all of the hardships suffered in that last fearful stage of the journey, from Clermont to Mur-de-Barrez. It was a pitiable condition to which one of the best-equipped of English armies had been reduced. " Il y avoit plus de trois cens chevaliers à pié, qui avoient laissiées leur armeures, les uns jetées en rivière, les autres les avoient despéciéés pour ce que ils ne les povoient porter, et afin que les François ne s'en peussent aidéer." [1]

As though to mock the intentions of the invaders, a few insignificant successes were now achieved. Martel, Belloc and Demanac reverted to the English cause, the first result of the invasion since at the outset it had indirectly relieved the Breton towns besieged by Clisson and du Guesclin. Even this success, trivial as it was, was only momentary, for within a few months all Limousin and Rouergue were lost for good.

From Brive Lancaster advanced to Sarlat, crossed the Vezère, occupied Limeuil [2] by agreement , and captured Lalinde by force, and thence marched through his own town of Bergerac to Bordeaux. [3]

---

[1] *Grandes Chroniques de France*, vi. 339.

[2] The Pope's brother Nicholas de Beaufort was Lord of Limeuil. See *Papal Letters*, iv. 128.

[3] For the last stage of the march see *Chronicon Briocense* and *Le Libvre du bon Jehan Duc de Bretaigne* (with Cuvelier) ii. 489. I have assumed that for the last stage of the march Lancaster's itinerary was the same as that of Brittany. According to Guillaume de St. André (*loc. cit.*) the two leaders quarrelled about the

THE GREAT MARCH

" Ensi fu traitté ceste grant chevaucie à chief."

To contemporary judgment the great march of '73 was the most pretentious effort of the war. " Il avoit fait," says the *Chronicler of the Valois Kings* of Lancaster, "la greignour reze et le greignour hostoiement qui fust fait en France puis le commencement des guerres dessus dictes." The author of the *Grandes Chroniques de France* agrees: " Et jà soit que la dite chevaucheé leur feust moult honorable, elle leur fut moult domageuse."

There was something in the feat which struck the imagination, especially of the French—something which appealed to the love of daring and adventure which marks the age.

From Calais to Bordeaux through the heart of France the Duke had led his army, wasting cornland and vineyard, burning and putting to ransom château, manor and village. For five months he had offered the enemy whose lands he insulted constant challenge of battle, and that challenge had been constantly refused. From start to finish no opposition worth the name had been offered, no army had dared to meet him in the field.

This seeming triumph obscured, in the minds of the invaded, at any rate, if not also of the invaders, the utter futility of the whole proceeding. No military result had been achieved. An incalculable amount of misery, it is true, had been inflicted on the French peasantry, but Edward III had been brought no nearer to the throne of the Valois by his son's efforts. And this campaign without battles, upon which so much had been built, this great military promenade, so far from achieving any positive result, in truth amounted to a disaster to English arms. The Duke's point-to-point race across France had cost an English army.

payment of their troops (more probably about Brittany's pretensions in Limousin), but this seems to have been exaggerated. See Delpit *Collection*, cclvii.

How severe the hardships of the campaign had been may be judged from the result.

On reaching Bordeaux the men began to desert in scores ; the King was compelled to issue a writ to the Mayor and Sheriffs of London ordering the arrest of all who returned without the Duke's licence.[1]

With what remained of his army Lancaster, after spending Christmas at Bordeaux, prepared to take the field again in the spring against the Duke of Anjou, who had been sent to the south in command of a considerable force. In spite of his losses, Lancaster managed to secure a few gains in the debatable land of the Gascon frontier. Though without any permanent influence on the fate of English Aquitaine, they were considerable enough to alarm Anjou, who entered into communication with his ally south of the Pyrenees. Don Enrique had promised to lead 30,000 men to his assistance, and a day had been fixed for a pitched battle near Moissac in the spring, when further hostilities were postponed by a truce. Once more the Pope had attempted the thankless task of peace-making.[2] Threats of excommunication, coupled with the fact that plague and famine[3] were ravaging the south of France and that both sides were weary of the struggle, produced the desired result.

At Périgord the French and English generals patched

---

[1] Dated Jan. 8, 1374. After Lancaster reached the Duchy : " Nous est dit que pour tant ascuns de gentz du dit hoste se sont tretz et pensent de soi trer deins brief d'illoeques en tapizon et autrement de nostre dit fitz, sannz son congie, en nostre roialme d'Angleterre, en deshonour et contempt de nous et de mesme nostre fitz et arrierissement qe Dieu defende de notre dite guere, au damage de nostre roialme avant dit (Delpit *Collection*, ccl. p. 190).

[2] Mandate to the Patriarch of Jerusalem and the Archbishop of Bordeaux, dated Avignon, March 6, 1374 *Papal Letters*, iv. 108 and 135.

[3] L'an MCCCLXXIIII fo grant carestra de blat en Guasquonha que bale lo bochet deu fromen x. (*Petite Chronique de Guyenne*, § 65.)

up a truce, and Lancaster prepared to abandon the command of Aquitaine to Sir Thomas Felton.[1]

The invasion of France had failed; the invasion of Castile was out of the question. England was disappointed ; the Duke's hopes were dashed to the ground.

Crippled in resources (for he had to borrow heavily before leaving Aquitaine),[2] and with the disappointment of the great failure, Lancaster returned to England in April, 1374.[3]

According to Christine de Pisan, who, however, had no love for the Duke, and may be romancing, the King openly reprimanded him for his mismanagement of the campaign.[4] At any rate, for nearly a year he took no part in affairs. There was no Parliament between November, 1373, and April, 1376, and the half-hearted attempt to continue the war in Brittany was entrusted to others.

The Duke's ten months' retirement from public affairs, which he spent chiefly at Hertford and in his northern estates,[5] gave him leisure to think about the political situation and his own position. What his thoughts were may be judged from the result, for when he emerged from

[1] Lancaster agrees to pay John Cresswell and Geoffrey St. Quintin 6,000 florins for keeping the Castle of Lusignan (indenture dated Bordeaux, April 4, 1374), Delpit *Collection*, p. 191, No. cclii. *Calendars of the Exchequer*, i. 243.

[2] Lancaster had borrowed 500 francs (gold) from the Chapter of St. Andrew at Bordeaux (Warrant for repayment dated The Savoy, June 13, 1374, Delpit *Collection*, p. 192, No. cliv.) ; £20 from Nicholas Duchayn, Aquitaine King at Arms (Warrant dated Jan. 17, 1375, ibid. No. cclviii.) ; 200 marcs from Benet Bodsawe (ibid. ccliii. Warrant dated June 11, 1374), etc.

[3] Warrant dated June 11, 1374, to pay John Snelle, Master of the *Grace de Dieu*, £140 for freight on account (Delpit *Collection*, p. 192, No. ccliii.), also £180 to Marcellini Albertson for freight from Bordeaux to Dartmouth. Reg. I. f. 205.

[4] " Si fu moult blasmé de son pere et a petite feste receu pour ce que si mal ot exploictié." Christine de Pisan quoted by Kervyn de Lettenhove. Froissart viii. 460 (note).

[5] Register *passim*.

retirement to exchange the rôle of Commander-in-Chief for that of Ambassador, he appeared as the exponent of a new policy.

The conclusion had forced itself upon him that the struggle with France was hopeless. His readiness to abandon the first dynastic struggle is the measure of his determination to continue the second. The dream of winning the crown of Castile has not left him. He has not yet learnt its unreality.

As the forces of England cannot be divided, the enemies must be divided, or if this is not possible, one must be neutralised. " *Qui trop embrasse mal etreint.*" Hostilities with France must cease. That is the keynote to the Duke's foreign policy for the next dozen years.

The financial exhaustion of England gave him his chance. In spite of repeated rebuffs, the Papacy had never ceased trying to bring about peace ; in the spring of 1375 England listened to the proposals, and a meeting between envoys from both countries was arranged to take place on neutral ground.

The Dukes of Anjou and Berri represented France ;[1] Lancaster met them at Bruges as the King's Lieutenant.

---

[1] The Duke's first absence was from about March 10 to July 10, 1375. His powers are dated February 20 and 21, and June 8, and letters of attorney March 1, 1375. *Foed*, VII. 58–60, 61, 66-7.

His second absence was from the end of October, 1375, to the end of March, 1376. His powers are dated September 20 and 23, and Oct. 10, 1375. The commission of the Dukes of Anjou and Brittany is dated Feb. 18, 1376.

The first Truce concluded at Bruges June 27, 1375, lasted until June 31, 1376, Foed, VII. 68–9, 80, 82–3 ; the second concluded on March 12, also at Bruges, prolonged the first until April 1, 1377.

King Edward confirmed the first Truce Aug. 24, 1375 ; the second, April 1, 1376. *Foed*, VII. 88–91, 99, 100–102 ; *Record Report*, xlv. App. (*Diplomatic Documents*), x. 279.

Froissart, K. de L. viii. 327, 338–9, 343, 349–51, 335 ; xvii. 559.

THE NEW FOREIGN POLICY

Insuperable difficulties lay in the way of a definite peace. The Duke stood on his royal dignity as King of Castile. Don Enrique was the ally of Charles V, and Charles' representatives refused of course to acknowledge the Duke's pretensions, and in the official documents that passed, denied him his royal title. Again, the Duke of Brittany was in arms against his suzerain and in open alliance with England. As yet there was no solution possible to the difficulties created by the position of Castile and Brittany. But there was no real hindrance to a truce. England was anxious for it, while France acted on the principle " reculer pour mieux sauter."

After three months' parleying, the envoys concluded a truce at Bruges on June 27, 1375, to last for a year.

In July Lancaster returned to procure the ratification of his terms ; in November he was back again at Bruges, working hard by personal efforts to bring about a better understanding.

The routine of diplomatic negotiations was relieved by feasts and banquets, which gave to Louis, Duke of Anjou, the opportunity for the lavish display in which he delighted, and which provoke the horror of the French chroniclers, who complain that there is little to choose between peace and war, the money saved in soldiers' wages being poured out by the wanton extravagance of the King's envoys.[1]

On this occasion the Duchess of Lancaster accompanied her husband, and it was at Ghent, his own birthplace, that the Duke's son John, also called " John of

---

[1] *Chron. Reg. Franc.*, 361. The English chronicles echo the complaints. Lancaster stayed at Bruges " in gravibus expensis regni " . . . Nullas gratias reportavit. *Cont: Eulog.* 336.

The Duke received 500 marks for his expenses on the first mission. Receipt dated Bruges, June 28, 1375 (Reg. I. f. 36).

Cf. Warrant to the Clerk of his Great Wardrobe to send him at once by a safe messenger his collar and circle of gold and £100 in gold. Dated Oct. 22, 1375 (ibid.).

F

Gaunt," was born, on the return of the Duchess from a pilgrimage to Saint Adrien de Grammont.[1]

On March 12 the truce was prolonged until April 1, 1377, and the Duke returned to England after nearly six months' absence.

Kervyn de Lettenhove: Froissart, viii. 466-7 (note).

Chapter VI

THE " GOOD " PARLIAMENT

THE Duke of Lancaster was never peculiarly sensitive to public opinion. Secure in the consciousness of his own power, he was usually contemptuously indifferent to the feelings with which the people regarded him, neither courting their favour nor fearing their hostility. Yet, as he rode from Windsor after the feast of the Garter on St. George's Day, to Westminster, where Parliament was to meet on April 28, his *insouciance* must have been to some extent affected by the prevailing sense of uneasiness.

It was possible, indeed, without the gift of prophecy, to foretell an uncomfortable session, for various causes had contributed to produce a large measure of discontent in the country. There had been no Parliament since that of 1373, when, almost at the close of the Duke's disastrous campaign, every one had been deluded by the Chancellor's assurance that all was going well at the front. In view of the strong feeling in favour of annual Parliaments, a feeling by no means confined to constitutional purists, this three years' interregnum was sufficient to cause alarm.

Further, the country, which had again and again given expression to the feelings of hostility with which it regarded Papal exactions, and the relations subsisting between the courts of Avignon and Paris, received with surprise and disappointment the results of the negotiations which had been carried on in Flanders by the Bishop of Bangor and his colleagues, concurrently with Lancaster's negotiations with France, and the anti-papal or national party contended with some show of reason that the effect of the concordat of Bruges was merely to stereotype some of the worst ecclesiastical abuses which it had been intended to remove.

More general, however, and more serious than either of these sources of discontent was the disappointment caused by the military failures of the last half dozen years. A series of brilliant victories, Sluys, Crécy, Winchelsea, Poictiers and Najera, had reconciled England to the heavy burden of taxation involved in Edward's military ambitions, but, so soon as failure took the place of the success which had come to be regarded almost as the right of English arms, discontent at once appeared, and people demanded an explanation for this succession of misfortunes—the rebellion of Aquitaine, the costly fiasco of 1372, and the great failure of the following year.

Nor was the administration of home affairs less unpopular. The King had of late years abandoned himself to pleasure and the control of affairs to ministers who failed to command the confidence of any one but an indulgent or indifferent master. The country suspected them of abusing their trust, and did not hesitate to express the opinion that the shortcomings of the administration were due quite as much to corruption as to incompetence.

All this discontent found expression in the national assembly held in April 1376, which, on account of its well-meaning (though inoperative) efforts at administrative reform, has achieved, somewhat cheaply perhaps, the title of the " Good " Parliament. As the episode which has now to be related marks a crisis in the history of John of Gaunt, and as his acts in this Parliament are responsible for the usually accepted tradition of his character, it may be well to define his position at the time when the eventful session began.

THE "GOOD" PARLIAMENT

In the first place it is clear that the attack delivered on the administration was not aimed at Lancaster in person, and that at the outset there was no quarrel between the Parliament and the Duke. John of Gaunt had not chosen his father's ministers, and there was no obligation upon him to accept responsibility for their doings. It is important to remember the directions in which the Duke had exercised his influence. Hitherto he had used the position which his territorial power as much as his birth gave him, to secure the command of armies and the control of foreign relations. Indeed, up to the year 1376 there had been little opportunity for that supposed interference in home politics which is usually included in the vague phrase " Lancastrian influence," for during the last six years John of Gaunt had never spent twelve consecutive months in England. From July to November, 1369, he was fighting in Picardy ; then, after staying in England just long enough to get another army together, he left for the south, where the campaign and lieutenancy of Aquitaine kept him fully occupied for the eighteen months between June, 1370, and December, 1371. The year 1372, a year without a Parliament, the Duke spent in England, save for his two months' absence with the fleet in the autumn, but in July, 1373, he left England once more, not to return until the end of April, 1374, while from that date to the opening of the " Good " Parliament two diplomatic missions to Flanders account for nearly a year's absence.

If the country held the Duke responsible for the conduct of military operations and negotiations with foreign powers he could not complain, for that was the sphere of action which he had jealously marked out for himself. Even here, however, one reservation has to be made. In the Church question the Duke's sympathies were certainly on the side of the Papacy as opposed to the national party, as his later action shows, but as yet he

123

had not betrayed this inclination or formulated an ecclesiastical policy, and he was therefore free as yet from the unpopularity which such sympathy would entail with a large section of the nation.

In April, 1376, therefore, the Duke's unpopularity, such as it was (and it was in no way comparable to the feeling with which he was regarded three months later), arose from one main and principal cause. He stood before the country as the unsuccessful general, the leader whose promises had proved delusive and whose policy had failed, the commander who had poured out blood and treasure lavishly in the war without achieving any result, who had impoverished the country and led an English army to ruin, where others had brought back king's ransoms and won victories which stirred the reluctant admiration of Europe. To this must be added the dislike of his countrymen for the Castilian marriage and their fear of the international difficulties which it appeared to involve, and the natural suspicion which they felt for one who, not content with his extraordinary position as the wealthiest subject of the English crown, surrounded himself with royal state and claimed also the respect due to the King of Castile and Leon.

Such was the position of John of Gaunt when the session of Parliament began : he came to Westminster with the consciousness of failure ; his pride as a soldier touched, his ambition cruelly disappointed—a disappointment the bitterness of which can only be measured when it is remembered that for five years he had given his whole strength to the Castilian scheme, and that before another opportunity occurred of attempting to carry it out, he had to work and wait for thirteen years.

On Monday, April 28, the " Good " Parliament[1]

---

[1] For the "Good" Parliament see *Rot. Parl.* ii. 321–60 ; *Chr. Angl.* 68–108 ; lxvii.–lxviii. ; lxx.–lxxii. ; 391–4. Wals. i. 320–321. Murimuth, *Contin.* 218–20.

opened in the Painted Chamber at Westminster, but, as the zeal for reform which animated its members failed to bring them to Westminster punctually, the usual adjournment was necessary in order to allow late-comers to take their places. The next day their duties were explained to them by the Chancellor, Sir John Knyvett : to provide for the good government of the realm, the safety of the King's dominions and the prosecution of the war—a sufficiently comprehensive programme. On all grounds a liberal subsidy was necessary, and the Commons were invited to sanction it without delay. The Commons, however, had no intention of doing any such thing, and preferred to assert the sound constitutional principle that redress of grievances should precede supply. Before the King could have his votes there were scores to settle with his ministers, and, as a prelude to the attack which they intended to deliver, following the precedent set in 1373, they invited a committee of Peers to join their deliberations. Among those on whom their choice fell, the Bishops of London, Norwich, Carlisle, and St. David's, the Earls of March, Stafford, Warwick and Suffolk, and Lords Henry Percy, Guy Bryan, Henry le Scrope and Richard Stafford, John of Gaunt had two supporters at least, for Adam Houghton, Bishop of St. David's, was an adherent, and Henry Percy, though not yet a declared partisan, must from the first have been drawn to the side of the Duke by kinship, common service in the wars, and class feeling.

Having thus stiffened their ranks with these twelve lords spiritual and temporal, the Commons next selected a "Speaker." Their mouthpiece was Sir Peter de la Mare, one of the knights of the shire for the county of Hereford, and steward to the Earl of March, a man whose courageous bearing justified their confidence, and whose sacrifices in the cause were to win him a place among the martyrs of Parliamentary freedom.

JOHN OF GAUNT

It was no easy task which their choice laid upon him, for, true to the maxim that " the King can do no wrong," the Speaker, in attacking the royal ministers, had to avoid the semblance of attacking their master, and while denouncing the administration to show due respect to the sovereign himself. Sir Peter discharged his duty without hesitation, and without mincing words.

The Commons had been asked to vote supplies : every one must be aware how heavy was the burden of taxation hitherto borne by the country. Yet that burden, heavy as it was, would have been borne cheerfully, had the country derived from it any proportionate advantage. The conduct of military operations had not been successful. (Here the Duke of Lancaster must have turned colour.) But the nation would have acquiesced even in failure, had the moneys voted been spent upon the war. That the reverse was the case was notorious. The King was poor because his Ministers were greedy and corrupt ; the constant need for taxation was the result of ministerial dishonesty. It was imperative that a close scrutiny should be held of public accounts.

Sir Peter sat down. The boldness of his attack had made a great impression. The manifesto was a sufficient achievement for one day's session, and the House adjourned. So far nothing had been said which could be construed as an attack on the Duke of Lancaster. The single casual reference to military failure was the only point at which Parliamentary criticism had touched him, and at the end of the first day's session John of Gaunt stood absolutely free to choose his course. He might have stood aloof and watched the efforts of the Commons to assert some sort of control over the executive ; on the other hand, he might have thrown his influence into the scale of reform, and given his sympathy to the popular party, as the Prince of Wales was understood to have done. Unhappily for himself and for the peace of political life, the Duke chose neither the liberal side, nor the cautious and safe alternative of neutrality. With any theory of popular control of the administration he had no vestige of sympathy, and, over-rating his own strength and under-estimating that of the opposition, he was not inclined to stand aside in the quarrel.

The Ministers who had been, as yet covertly, attacked, were his father's servants. Criticism of the administration was, in the Duke's eyes, criticism of the Crown, and the King's son was the representative of the Crown and the natural champion of the court party.

Yet, when the session was resumed on the following day, the Duke's demeanour was remarkably gracious. It is quite clear that by the exercise of his personal influence he still hoped to avert anything like a definite conflict between the popular party and the court, and as yet not fully conscious of the extreme bitterness of feeling which animated the opposition, or of the strength of their cause, he relied on compromise.

Acknowledging the sacrifices which had been made by the country, the Duke, in a sympathetic address, invited the Commons to declare their grievances, and promised to use all his influence to secure redress.

But the Commons were in no mood for conciliation or half-measures : they took the Duke's invitation literally, and through the mouth of Sir Peter de la Mare proceeded to make a sweeping condemnation of the administration. The first victims to be impeached were William Lord Latimer, Chamberlain to the King and a member of the Privy Council, and Richard Lyons, a wealthy London merchant.

Latimer was charged with oppression and extortion in Brittany, and with wholesale embezzlement of public money. In particular he was said to have sold the castle of Saint Sauveur to the enemy, to have prevented the relief of Becherel, and to have appropriated eight thousand marcs out of a fine of ten thousand marcs inflicted on Sir Robert Knolles, which had passed through his hands, and to have perpetrated a similar fraud in connexion with a fine levied on the city of Bristol.

Conjointly with Latimer, Richard Lyons was charged with similar misappropriation of public funds ; they had lent to the King, it was said, twenty thousand marcs, at a time when no loan was needed, and had repaid themselves twenty thousand pounds, the whole transaction being cloaked under fictitious names, and they had made a " corner " in imported goods, raising the price for their own profit to such an exorbitant scale that the poor had been starved in consequence.

Even now, when the Commons had declared war, the Duke hesitated to join in the struggle : he attempted to gain time, and after these sweeping charges had been heard, postponed judgment to a further sitting. In the meantime the Commons, for the first time, fell foul of one of the Duke's personal friends. Lord Latimer was of course well known to Lancaster, who had occasionally employed him in positions of trust, but he was not one of the Lancastrian party. Terrorized by the indictment of the Speaker, he had attempted to enlist the sympathy of one who was united to the Duke by the strongest ties, John Lord Neville of Raby, a constant companion of the Duke, who had enrolled him in his retinue. When, however, Neville hinted to the Speaker that the violence of his attack on one of the officers of the royal household might expose him to unpleasant consequences, he was met with the open threat that his own case would shortly be dealt with, a threat which the Commons made good by petitioning for the removal of Lord Neville from the position of Steward of the King's household.

It is impossible to say, on the evidence which has survived, how far Latimer and Lyons were guilty of the charges brought against them ; what is certain is that the Commons believed them guilty, and the Duke was compelled to allow them to be punished. Latimer was deprived of the office of Chamberlain and placed under arrest, a number of peers going surety for him. Lyons was to be condemned to forfeiture and imprisonment.

When the Commons proceeded to attack Alice Perrers, they were adopting a course which, bold as it was, probably commanded the sympathy of all sections of the House. The royal mistress had completely dominated the court, and abused the influence which she exercised over the King in the most shameful manner, interfering with the course of justice, and enriching herself at the expense of others, after the manner of her kind. One of the victims of her oppression was the Abbey of St. Albans, a fact which is not without its influence upon the history of the proceedings. The prosecution of the royal favourite came nearer to a direct attack upon the King than any other act of the session ; it also placed Lancaster in a position of the utmost difficulty. The influence of the mistress was the only serious rival to his own power with the King, who was completely infatuated with the woman, and could not bear to be parted from her. Personally the Duke had nothing to gain from her presence at the court, and everything to lose, for her connexion with the King discredited the court party, and, as will be seen, stood in the way of the Duke's own projects. Probably, therefore, he was not sorry when, upon the unanimous petition of the opposition, Alice Perrers was condemned to banishment from the court and to confiscation of property.[1]

In the middle of this conflict between parties, on Trinity Sunday, June 8, died Edward Prince of Wales,

[1] On January 19, 1378, John of Gaunt obtained a grant (afterwards surrendered) of the forfeited property of Alice Perrers in London. *Rot. Pat.*

and England was thrown into mourning for one whose career is among the most brilliant and the most sad of whom her annals tell. If, as has been conjectured, the Black Prince had been the strength of the opposition in the battle with his father's Ministers, his death would assuredly have dealt the party a blow from which it could scarcely have recovered. Since 1370, however, the Prince had been unable to take any part in affairs, and apart from the tradition that he openly sympathized with some effort at reform, there is no sufficient evidence for the view which represents him as a violent partisan of those who were attacking the court, or for drawing an imaginary line of cleavage between the Prince of Wales on the one hand and the King and the Duke of Lancaster on the other. The immediate political result of the Prince's death was not to discourage the popular party, which, on the contrary, redoubled its efforts, but to bring Prince Richard one step nearer to the throne and to intensify the suspicions of the Duke's enemies on the delicate question of the succession. On this subject all kinds of rumours were rife, one of the most improbable being to the effect that John of Gaunt chose this critical moment for a proposal to set aside the right of succession through females, in order to remove from the direct line the heirs of Lionel of Clarence, Philippa and her husband the Earl of March. No position more invidious than that of John of Gaunt at this time could well be imagined. He stood before England as Viceroy of a dying king whose heir apparent was a helpless minor. It was inevitable that to the least ambitious of men, situated as he was, designs on the throne would be imputed. The Black Prince at least harboured no such thoughts with regard to the loyalty of the brother who had been his constant companion and comrade-in-arms from boyhood onwards, for on the day before he died the Prince named first among his executors his " very dear and well-beloved

brother of Spain," [1] and the best friend whom the Duke
had to rely on in the troubled days after his nephew came
of age was the Princess Joan. But the suspicion which
the Prince repudiated the Commons chose to publish and
emphasize. The last act of the " Good " Parliament was
to request that Prince Richard should be introduced to
Parliament forthwith, while to neutralize the Duke's power
it was proposed that a permanent body of ten or twelve
peers should be added to the council, some of whom were
always to be attached to the King's person. In com-
plying with the former request and causing the lands
and titles of the Prince of Wales to be at once bestowed
on the infant Prince, John of Gaunt never forgave the
thoughts which had prompted it ; the slur on his
honour roused him to fury.

A man of stronger purpose and weaker principle might
have been tempted to some such treason as the Commons
suspected, but Lancaster was true to the ethical code of
his age and his class. John of Gaunt was of a different
mettle from Henry of Bolingbroke, nor was England in
1376 prepared for that change of dynasty which twenty
years of ill government made welcome in 1399.

A false imputation of disloyalty is the greatest wrong
that a man can suffer, and Lancaster's thirst for revenge
hurried him into a course of action which violated law and
justice alike. No sooner had the members dispersed than
the Duke, assuming an authority which no King of England had dared to exercise, and for which no precedent
could be found since the first beginnings of constitutional
government, declared the " Good " Parliament to be no
Parliament at all, and condemned its acts as null and void.
He dismissed the council which the Commons had tried
to place about the King, restored those who had been
impeached, and allowed the King's mistress to return to
the court.

[1] *Royal Wills*, p. 75.

JOHN OF GAUNT

Not content with undoing the work of one of the longest and busiest sessions in the history of Parliament, he determined to punish the leaders in such a way as should serve as a warning to others for all time.

Two men in particular were singled out to bear the brunt of his wrath. It was by the mouth of the intrepid Speaker of the Commons that the defiance had been uttered; among all the denunciations of Sir Peter de la Mare that of Alice Perrers had been the most vehement. For once the royal mistress and the only rival of her influence with the King found themselves agreed: Sir Peter was sent to imprisonment in Nottingham Castle.

The second victim was more illustrious and more difficult to reach. Among those who had prompted the impeachment of Lord Latimer, William of Wykeham had shown the greatest bitterness, even proposing, it is said, to refuse the prisoner time and counsel for his defence.

But apart from his prominence in the attack upon the court, there were reasons which had suddenly changed the feelings of John of Gaunt towards the man who had hitherto in a special degree shared his confidence.[1]

William of Wykeham had risen from obscurity to such a position of influence at the court, that Froissart records with astonishment that without the advice of this single priest nothing of importance was done in England.[2] Such preferment the Bishop owed to his own administrative capacity and to royal favour. That the power of the great feudatories should be equalled by that of an official hierarchy was bad enough : that this power, created by

---

[1] The name of the Bishop of Winchester appears with those of five others who were all friends and household officers of the Duke, as sureties on the pledging of the Honor of Richmond in 1366. (Delpit *Collection*, p. 124. ccii.) William of Wykeham also appears as Attorney for the Duke in 1375. *Foed.*, vii. 61. The only notices of Lancaster in the Bishop's Register are purely formal, viz. mandates to the clergy of his diocese to pray for the success of the Duke's military expeditions.

[2] Froissart *K. de L.*, vii. 232.

royal favour, should be used to oppose the King's government and criticise the King's ministers was intolerable.
So argued the Duke of Lancaster, regarding the Bishop's
part in the opposition as a double treason, to his sovereign
and to his benefactor. So must be explained, but not
excused, the treatment accorded by the Duke to the great
minister, whose services to his sovereign, however considerable, were surpassed by those services to the cause
of learning to which his two noble foundations have
erected an imperishable monument.

The Duke's vengeance was thorough. He chose two
weapons to attack his enemy. The first was a charge of
malversation, difficult to prove, impossible to disprove,
and certain to carry conviction with those who were
anxious to be convinced. It is needless to examine the
charges in detail.[1] Probably Lord Latimer was innocent
of several of the counts of the indictment upon which
he was condemned ; certainly the accusations launched
against William of Wykeham were merely the expression
of political hatred.

The Bishop was condemned to lose his temporalities,
which were granted to Prince Richard, and he himself
was forbidden to come within twenty miles of the court.[2]

The second mode of attack was more subtle in conception, more far-reaching in effect. William of Wykeham
did not stand alone. He was one of the class of political
bishops with whom on more occasions than one the court
had come into conflict in the past, and with whom there
were to be bitter feuds in the near future.

John of Gaunt, who had a habit of discovering interesting people, had met at Bruges a year before a certain
priest John Wycliffe, who had formed decided views

[1] One may deserve notice in this connexion. Among those
whom the Bishop was charged with oppressing were Sir Thomas
Fogg and Sir John Seyntlowe, both retainers of the Duke. *Foed,*
VII. 164–70.
[2] *Foed,* VII. 142. Cf. 132.

about priests who neglected the cure of souls for the care of castles, devoting to the secular service of the state lives consecrated to the service of religion.

John Wycliffe, born near Richmond in Yorkshire (until 1372 a Lancastrian Honor), and connected with a family one member of which at least was known to the Duke,[1] had made an impression on the man who had discernment enough to see much merit in Geoffrey Chaucer and none in Walter of Peterborough. There were other views besides those in question, which Wycliffe held and published, but in order to secure co-operation on the lines of a particular policy it is not necessary to sympathize with a man's whole scheme of thought.

Two months after the close of the " Good " Parliament a courier was riding from Westminster to Oxford, with a summons to Wycliffe to appear in London before the King's council,[2] and for the next six months, by the mandate and under the protection of the Duke of Lancaster, the reformer was busied in exposing, with the all power of his moral earnestness and unrivalled dialectic, the abuses and evils of a corrupt church. Such was the answer of the Duke of Lancaster to clerical zealots for administrative reform, and so ended one of the most deeply interesting episodes in the political history of England.

It is unfortunate that by far the most graphic account of the events of these three months comes from a source which is rendered wholly untrustworthy by the violence of its bias. The story of the Monk of St. Albans, however dramatic and full in detail, forms a most unsubstantial basis for sober history.

The tone of his writing may be gauged from its introduction. Nothing short of a miracle would be a fitting consecration of the efforts of the reforming party. There-

[1] Warrant to the Chief Forester of Knaresborough to deliver one buck to Sir Robert de Wycliffe, Reg. I. f. 197.
[2] *Issue Roll*, p. 200.

fore a miracle is forthcoming. One of the knights of the shire, our author's informant, on the eve of the impeachment, goes to bed, his thoughts full of the evils of the times. Naturally he dreams. With his fellow members he is sitting in the Chapter House at Westminster (though by a slip of the pen the Monk of St. Albans says St. Paul's). He sees on the floor seven golden coins, picks them up, and being an honest man, goes about trying to find the owner. Strangely enough, no one claims the money, and when the finder, in his quest, reaches the Choir, he discovers a number of monks conspicuous by their black robes (worn also by our Benedictine author) and their pious and godly bearing. To his question if any one of them has lost the coins their leader replies : " My son, those seven coins have not been lost ; they are the seven gifts of the Holy Spirit, bestowed upon you and the other faithful Commons who are to reform the abuses of Government." Such is the proem : the rest is in keeping.

The *Chronicon Angliae* for this period indeed reads like the " Annals " on the reign of Nero. Like Tacitus, the Monk loves bright lights and dark shadows, and abhors semitones. The reformers are men of saintly life and inspired wisdom ; the court party are villains, traitors, adulterers and murderers. With an eye for contrast and a love of antithesis, the author cannot refrain from seeing some occult meaning even in the names of the hero and the villain of the piece. Peter, the name of the Speaker of the Commons, suggestive of apostolic boldness and eloquence, is worthily borne by one whose cause is built upon a rock of popular good will ! But as for John Plantagenet, *Quantum mutatus ab illo !* His words and deeds belie the name borne by the evangelist. Is he not altogether devoid of grace human or divine ?

When, however, the Monk of St. Albans comes to describe Lord Latimer, his own words fail him. Conjuring up the picture of another patrician equally abandoned, equally pernicious to his country, the monk borrows the language of Sallust and dresses up Latimer in the rags of Catiline.[1]

Unfortunately no Lancastrian account of the year 1376 has survived. Knighton's history breaks off abruptly ten years before, and there is no chronicle, however fragmentary, to balance the prejudice of St. Albans with the bias of the Savoy. Walsingham's narrative, toned down to respectability when the son of John of Gaunt had become King of England, surprises the reader not so much by its omissions and alterations as by the large amount of abuse which has been suffered to stand, and it is not unnecessary to place upon record a protest against the too literal interpretation of a chronicle inspired by the double acrimony of the churchman and the political partisan.[2] Though the staunch courage of Sir Peter de la Mare and the calm dignity of William of Wykeham must win the admiration and claim the sympathy of all impartial minds, it must also be admitted that the popular party adopted an extreme and somewhat vindictive attitude, and that it was their suspicion which drove John of Gaunt from unwise obstruction to violent and unjustifiable revenge.

There can be little doubt that to him the boldness of the attack was a surprise, an unwelcome revelation of a power the extent of which he had never realized, and the destiny of which he never even dimly discerned.

The Duke's conception of political life was old-fashioned, not to say obsolete. The prerogative of the Crown and the predominance of the *noblesse*, especially of the royal *noblesse*, were among the presuppositions of his political creed, while, in his view, the sphere of the faithful Commons was merely to register the decisions of the Crown and to vote supplies for the King's necessities.

---

[1] Sallust, *Bellum Catilinae*, Ch. 5, *Ed.* Eussner. *Chr. Angl.* 84.
[2] See Sir E. Maunde Thompson's valuable introduction to the *Chronicon Angliae*, pp. lxii. lxiii.

LANCASTER AND THE HOUSE OF COMMONS

Hitherto he had taken little interest in the proceedings of Parliament, but taught by Sir Peter de la Mare, he begins to give his attention to questions of Parliamentary representation. If public opinion could not be ignored, at least its expressions could to some extent be controlled in the Commons, nor was the task one of extreme difficulty. Henceforth a Lancastrian party is a permanent factor in the composition of the " Lower House," as well as in that of the Lords or the King's council ; for year after year the counties where the Duke's interests predominate,[1] send his friends, retainers or administrative officers, to Parliament as knights of the shire. A year later John of Gaunt will be found receiving legal powers to nominate the members for the County of Lancaster, but the power which in that county possessed a legal sanction was exercised *de facto* in a score of other constituencies. The representation of Yorkshire was a matter of the Duke's discretion as entirely as that of the County of Lancaster. In successive Parliaments the electors for the county of Derby chose Sir Avery Sulny, one of the Duke's master foresters, Sir Esmon Appleby, Sir Thomas Marchington, Sir Philip Okonore, Sir Thomas Wennesley, Oliver de Barton, or John de la Pole, all knights or esquires of his retinue, while Lincoln in like manner sent now a retainer of the Duke, now his feoder for the county, and now his chief steward.

Time after time Sussex returned Sir John Sentcler and Sir Edward Dalynrigg, one a retainer, the other a friend of the Duke, while in Kent Sir Thomas Fogg found as safe a seat as John Mautravers in Dorset, or Sir Thomas Fychet and Sir Thomas Hungerford in Wiltshire and Gloucester. These are certain and obvious instances of an influence which must have been exercised also in many directions

[1] See map illustrating the territorial interest of the Duke of Lancaster.

137

less easy to follow, and it is not surprising that the Duke
was able to command the support of a respectable minority
at least in the Commons, whenever he might desire to
issue some manifesto or urge a cherished scheme upon
the country.[1]

Not the least difficult of the tasks devolving upon this
Lancastrian party was to defend the honour and good
name of their leader among their colleagues. For his
high-handed treatment of the popular leaders, coupled
with existing causes of unpopularity and reinforced by
the hostility of the Church which had already been
challenged, created for a time a fever of hatred for the
Duke, for which it would be difficult to find a parallel in
English history. Henceforth every word and act of John
of Gaunt becomes the object of rooted suspicion on the
part of enemies constantly on the alert to catch some
rumour likely to damage his name, or to discover some
fact capable of being twisted into evidence of criminal
ambition, and where the slight foundation of fact which
gives stability to calumny is wanting, imagination
sharpened by " odium theologicum " or political passion readily supplies the deficiency.

Dark stories of treason and crime crowd the pages of
the " Scandalous Chronicle " ; John of Gaunt is branded
as an abandoned libertine, an unscrupulous intriguer, a
traitor false to his country and to those of his own house,
a murderer whose hands are red with innocent blood.

The Duke's personal morality, if no better, was certainly
no worse than that of the court ; the standard of English

---

[1] These are the most obvious instances which strike one on
comparing the " Return of every Member of Parliament " with the
Register.

It is impossible to say exactly where the Duke's political influence ended, and I recognize a number of names in the lists of
Sheriffs (P. R. O. Lists and Indexes, No. IX.) which are familiar
as those of members of the Lancastrian Household and Civil
Service.

society in the fourteenth century was not exacting in such matters, and putting it at the worst, the Duke conformed to the standard. One *amour* in early youth, and in later life a *liaison* which lasted nearly thirty years, and was eventually covered by an honourable marriage, do not constitute a very heavy indictment against a man whose position exposed him to the temptations of one of the most luxurious courts of Europe. But the Monk of St. Albans launches reckless charges of gross licentiousness, pretending that John of Gaunt insulted the memory of the Duchess Blanche and outraged the feelings of the Duchess Constance in the most callous and shameful manner,[1] while, in the pages of his inveterate enemy, the Duke, who though a hardened is an inconsistent villain, sins and weeps, errs and repents with a tiresome and suspicious regularity.[2]

Again, the proudest of Plantagenet princes, a "vial full of Edward's sacred blood," trained to arms by the Black Prince and Sir John Chandos, inured to hardship and danger from tender years, the man whose livery some of the bravest soldiers of the day were not ashamed to wear, and whose knighthood was more to him than his royal blood—this man placed by Froissart among the "preux" with Duke Henry, the Black Prince and Edward III, is, according to the "Scandalous Chronicle," a coward. It is his habit to say "Go!" not "Follow!" and to hang back out of the reach of danger while his men rush to the assault.[3]

This is merely the venom of the cloister, and could mislead no one, but charges of political crime are more insidious.

---

[1] *Chr. Angl.* 75.

[2] E.g. *Chr. Angl.* 328 ; Wals. ii. 43, 194, etc.

[3] *Chr. Angl.* 205, describing the siege of St. Malo, 1378. The parallel passage in Walsingham (i. 374) is softened down to innuendo.

JOHN OF GAUNT

To the author of the *Chronicon Angliae* it was axiomatic that directly or indirectly the Duke of Lancaster was at the root of any base intrigue that came to light. For instance: in 1370 a Gloucestershire knight, Sir John Minsterworth, after betraying a position of trust in the army of Sir Robert Knolles, turned traitor and sold himself to the French. Seven years later, while engaged in a plot of that irreconcilable Celt, Owen of Wales, he was captured in Navarre red-handed, carrying despatches from France to Spain relative to the invasion of England. When brought home he was very properly hanged, drawn and quartered, but before his execution he was allowed to write a letter to the King. This letter, which probably contained an appeal for mercy and the usual kind of promise of information, was opened by Henry Percy as Earl Marshal, and no more was heard of it. But the Monk of St. Albans must of course drag the Duke in, and leave it on record that the dying appeal of Sir John Minsterworth was suppressed by Lancaster and Percy because it betrayed the secret of some infamy with which both were stained.[1]

Once more : in 1380 a charge of treasonable correspondence with the enemy was brought against Sir Ralf Ferrers, a man who had for many years served the country in responsible positions. The supposed treason rested on the evidence of letters purporting to be under his seal, containing state secrets and addressed to Bureau de la Rivière, Chamberlain of the King of France, Clisson, and Bertrand du Guesclin. These letters were sent by John Philipot to the Duke, then on the Scotch border, and the Duke caused Ferrers to be arrested and sent for

---

[1] *Chr. Angl.* 65–6 ; 135–6 ; 399.   Wals. i. 310–1 ; 326.   Froissart, *K. de L.* vii. 481 ; viii. 16, 50–51, 90, 430 ; ix. 508.   Minsterworth held lands of Lancaster on the Welsh border, and the Register contains a warrant to the feoder to seize them on the ground of the tenant's treason.   *Reg.* i. f. 91 and ii. f. 15.

trial to the Parliament then sitting at Northampton. The Monk of St. Albans is quite satisfied of Ferrers' guilt, and relates how Lancaster himself, implicated as principal in the conspiracy, was secretly encouraging his agent ; but in point of fact the incriminating letters, when examined by a judicial committee in Parliament, were proved to be forgeries, and Sir Ralf Ferrers was acquitted, the Earls of Warwick, Stafford, Salisbury, and Northumberland, Lord Grey de Ruthyn, and the Prior of St. John going surety for him.[1]

This running comment of malice is kept up for the next dozen years, but it is in relation to the critical years 1376-7 that the charges are most definite and most malevolent.

It was at this time that the famous changeling story came into vogue, according to which John of Gaunt was no true son of Edward III, but really the child of some Flemish woman, juggled into the place of the infant whom Queen Philippa had born and overlain at birth. To shelter herself from the King's anger " good " Queen Philippa had practised this fraud, only confiding the shameful secret, under seal of the confessional, to the Bishop of Winchester, and enjoining him to reveal it if ever the changeling should come near to the royal succession.[2]

It is not likely that John of Gaunt cared to challenge any views which might be held as to his personal morality, his courage, or his legitimate birth, but on one score he showed himself keenly sensitive, and there was one charge which he took the pains to rebut. It took various forms, from the crude version of St. Albans that Lancaster was

---

[1] *Chr. Angl.* 210, 278-9, 281 ; Wals. i. 447-8 ; *Rot. Parl.* iii. 90-93. Froissart, *K. de L.* xii. 378.

[2] For the changeling story see *Chr. Angl.* 107, 398. The Baron Kervyn de Lettenhove, accepts it ! After all, *N'était il pas un étranger dans la maison royale ?* Froissart, xxii. 34 (note).

plotting to murder his nephew,[1] to the more elaborate fiction of a deep-laid international conspiracy. An examination of the version current abroad may give some idea of the difficulties in which Lancaster found himself in the unhappy days following the " Good " Parliament.

The great march of 1373 had proved a signal failure. What more obvious than to ascribe failure to corruption ? Between 1372 and 1376 envoys were passing between the Count of Flanders and the King of Navarre, an indefatigable intriguer, whose latest scheme was to organize a confederacy of Flanders, Foix and Brittany under his own leadership, and of course for his own ends, against Charles V. From the Navarrese court the Count's envoys brought back to Flanders a truly sensational rumour. There was a secret treaty, they had heard, between Charles V on the one part and the Duke of Lancaster on the other. Edward III was dying : Prince Edward's days were numbered. The early matrimonial adventures of Princess Joan offered scope not only for scandal, but for legal difficulties. A bull from Avignon would declare Prince Richard illegitimate. (In point of fact the Pope had threatened to issue such a bull when the life of Jean de Cros was in danger after his capture at Limoges, but Lancaster's intervention had prevented things reaching extremities.) John of Gaunt, with the support of Charles V, would then supplant his nephew, and, assured of the throne of England, would proceed to seize the throne of Spain, while, as the price of abandoning the French war, he was assured of the benevolent neutrality of Charles V.[2]

If sensational reports such as this found a place in the

---

[1] Consideravit enim senectutem regis cujus mors erat in januis, et juventutem principis, quem, *ut dicebatur*, impotionare cogitabat, si aliter ad regnum pervenire non posset. *Chr. Angl.* 92.

[2] *Archives of Lille*, quoted by Kervyn de Lettenhove. Froissart, viii. 460 (note).

diplomatic despatches of a foreign court,[1] it is not surprising that the rumours which have been noticed were current in England, and we read without extravagant surprise that in 1362 the Duke poisoned Maude of Lancaster, his sister-in-law, to re-unite the inheritance of Duke Henry, and that in 1376 he was plotting to poison Richard his nephew to secure the succession to the throne of Edward III ! [2]

It would perhaps be scarcely worth while to repeat and examine the unsupported charges launched by the " Scandalous Chronicle," but that at the time they had a real political significance in increasing tenfold the difficulties of Lancaster's position, and that since they have tended to give a real if unconscious bias to history. Severally unconvincing, they have had a cumulative effect upon the judgment afforded by posterity to the man who was their victim, for, though first cast out at random with the saving clause " ut dicitur," " ut fertur," " ut quidam asserunt," they have been repeated not as rumours but as facts, and at first holding by a most precarious tenure, they have in course of time and by dint of repetition acquired prescriptive rights, and have become history by courtesy.

If John of Gaunt, by setting himself for a while above the law, helped to create this prejudice and played into the hands of the prosecution, it is only fair that his words and acts should be taken also as evidence for the defence.

On Christmas Day, 1376, six months after the death of the Black Prince, six months before the death of Edward III, there was a great gathering at Westminster Palace. There the King, or rather John of Gaunt acting in his name, had summoned the great feudatories and all the men of note at the court, and there he pre-

---

[1] For other echoes of these suspicions in foreign chronicles see *Chr. Val.* 257–8 ; *Istore et Chroniques de Flandres*, ii. 144.
[2] Kn. 116.

sented to them Richard of Bordeaux as the heir to the throne and kingdom, while the Duke of Lancaster, first of all as the greatest of the Lords Temporal, knelt down before the throne where his brother's child sat at the King's side, and swore to accept him as sovereign.[1]

How John of Gaunt kept his oath and how he replied to those who held him guilty of intended treason, he was soon to show.

[1] Froissart, *K. de L.* viii. 384–5.

Chapter VII

THE LAST PARLIAMENT OF EDWARD III—TRIAL OF WYCLIFFE—QUARREL WITH THE CITY

THE last Parliament of Edward III met at Westminster on January 27, 1377.[1] Rank and file had been carefully recruited, and the whole army was officered by the Duke's partisans. Just before the session began he had given the great seal to Adam Houghton, Bishop of St. David's, an old friend in whose foundations both he himself and the Duchess Blanche had shared. The Speaker of the Commons was Sir Thomas Hungerford, a man who owed his knighthood and his whole fortunes to the Duke, and who was entirely devoted to his master's interests.[2] The acts of a carefully packed Parliament, with Chancellor and Speaker in the Lancastrian interest, may fairly be regarded as the acts of the Duke, and a scrutiny of what was said and done in it will reveal the Duke's thoughts and intentions. The result is clear. On the one hand, Lancaster meant to answer the challenge

[1] Parliament was summoned by writ dated Dec. 1. 50 Edward III for the quinzaine of St. Hilary following, and sat from Jan. 27 to March 2. Dugdale *Summons to Parl.* 291 ; *Rot. Parl.* ii. 361–75 ; *Chr. Angl.* 108–9 ; 395 111–4. Higd. viii. 387 ; Murimuth 221. Wals. i. 323-4.

[2] Sir Thomas Hungerford was not the Duke's Steward, as is usually stated. He was successively Chief Steward North and South of Trent, an administrative office in the Lancastrian service.

The Stewardship of Lancaster's household, an honorary position of some dignity, was at this time held by Sir William Croyser.

of the "Good" Parliament in the most unmistakable manner ; on the other, he intended, while his father yet lived, to give the lie once and for all to the calumnies which had been circulated about his designs on the succession. The acts and words of the Parliament form a manifesto of loyalty to the court and loyalty to the legitimate heir.

In the first place, the Duke had insisted on the young Prince Richard being introduced into Parliament as the King's Lieutenant, and made a point of treating the child with pronounced deference.[1] In the second, he had carefully coached his friend the Bishop of St. David's, and addressed Parliament through his mouth.

The Chancellor opened proceedings in the Painted Chamber at Westminster with a speech, or a sermon, in which the words of the spiritual father and the courtier are somewhat grotesquely blended, beginning with an affectation of humility which is more conventional than convincing, seeing that he had the whole homily entered on the Rolls of Parliament.

Compared with the wisdom of Lords and Commons, his own words can be but foolishness. Yet he knows they will willingly hear him—" Libenter suffertis insipientes cum sitis ipsi sapientes "—the more so as he has good news to tell. The King has been afflicted with a grievous sickness ; that is not surprising, for whom God loveth He chasteneth. But now happily he is on his way to recovery.

This was scarcely the fact, but it served to introduce the real subject of the Bishop's discourse. For the mention of the King's name is the signal for a eulogy not only of Edward himself, but of the whole royal family. The onslaught of 1376 had been an attack on the King and the court. This is Lancaster's reply. " Consider, my lords,"

---

[1] *Chr. Angl.* iii.

says the Bishop, speaking for John of Gaunt, " if any Christian King or any other Prince in the world had ever so noble and gracious a lady to wife, or such sons as our Lord the King." The reference to Queen Philippa was singularly ill-judged when the *affaire* Perrers was fresh in every one's memory ; and it was going a little far in view of 1373 to say, as the Bishop proceeded to do, that the King's sons had not only made the name of England dreaded abroad, but had enriched the country and realm. But the Bishop knew his points ; he was working up to the climax. The country should be grateful for King Edward and for the Duke of Lancaster. But not only was the King blessed in seeing his sons about him, but in his son's son. Turning to the royal throne where the child Richard sat, the Chancellor pronounced a eulogy upon the heir who was to succeed to the throne of the glorious Edward. Then for the practical application of the text. Just as the wise men from the East had brought gifts of gold and frankincense and myrrh to the Child at Bethlehem, so the faithful subjects of the King should bring their gifts to the cherished heir of England, in liberal subsidies for the defence of the realm and in their true service and obedience.

The political object served, the manifesto of the Duke's loyalty published, the Chancellor concluded in a brief sentence with the causes of the summons of Parliament —provision for the exigencies of national defence. Under colour of the truce the French had been preparing for war, and when war broke out again the enemy would not be single-handed. The Scots would be with them ; and finally (the reference is significant), Spain—that is, Castile under the usurping dynasty— would help to fight their battles.

The Chancellor sat down, and Sir Robert Aston, the King's Chamberlain, rose to define in a few words the policy of the Government to the Papal See—to find a compromise between Papal claims and the King's regality.

As the business of Parliament began, everything seemed to be working well. The obedient Commons voted a poll-tax of fourpence, and refused to listen to the protests of the small minority who, in spite of Lancastrian electioneering, had retained their seats from the last Parliament, and were demanding a fair trial for Sir Peter de la Mare.

On the committee of peers chosen (it is not clear by whom) to deliberate with the Commons the Duke's interests were sufficiently safeguarded. Arundel and Warwick, if not partizans, were at least friendly at this time ; Lords Percy and Fitzwalter were firm adherents, and Lord Roos was among the Duke's retainers.

But the opposition smothered in Parliament found a voice outside : the Bishops gallantly continued the quarrel.[1] When Convocation met (February 2) William of Wykeham was not in his place. Obedient to the sentence of exile from the court, he had ignored the mandate to attend, issued by Courtenay as Dean of the Province. Lancaster had several firm friends on the episcopal bench, but whether it was from professional feeling or from want of nerve they did not disturb the unanimity with which the clergy declared their intention of refusing to proceed to business until their brother of Winchester was present.

Yielding to pressure, the Primate appealed to the King, and William of Wykeham appeared and took his place.

Courtenay had scored his first successes. He was not content. If the great Duke of Lancaster was for the time beyond the reach of spiritual or temporal weapons, if he could not be attacked in person, he could be attacked in the person of his friends. Having championed the Duke's victim, the Bishop of London undertook to make

---

[1] *Chr. Angl.* 114.

a victim of the Duke's champion : he would bring John Wycliffe to book.

Wycliffe was cited [1] to appear before the Bishops at St. Paul's on February 19, Parliament yet sitting.

For six months the London pulpits had been ringing with denunciations of clerical wealth, luxury and worldliness, which were none the less galling because they were well deserved, and with anathemas of episcopal shortcomings, the application of which was obvious. For these crimes, the attack on the wealth and worldly ambitions of the prelacy, and for these alone, Wycliffe was arraigned.

The step was a bold one. It would never have been taken on the initiative of the Primate, for Sudbury, a man of peace and far from unfriendly to Lancaster, was not unenlightened, and for some of the abuses denounced by Wycliffe had scant sympathy. But Courtenay was a man of different metal. In his eyes the Primate was a weakling who was self-deceived. He was one of those crying peace where there was no peace : and there could be no peace while Wycliffe was allowed to preach with impunity doctrines subversive of the whole ecclesiastical and social order. But the dangerous fanatic did not stand alone. In the Court he had the most powerful support. As well as Lancaster, the Princess Joan was an adherent ; and more than half London openly sympathized. Therefore when Courtenay resolved on the prosecution he was playing a dangerous game. He was pushing the quarrel with the Court party to extremes, and running the risk of alienating the sympathy of his own diocese. But the game was worth playing, for Wycliffe was not only an enemy of the Church, but a friend of the Duke of Lancaster.

John of Gaunt took up the challenge. His first step

---

[1] For Wycliffe's trial, see *Chr. Angl.* 115–21 ; 397. Murimuth, 223–4. Wals. i. 325–6. Higd. viii. 389–90.

was to retain four friars, one from each of the great mendicant orders, to defend the prisoner.[1] Because, later, Wycliffe and the friars were bitter enemies, this has been questioned. But there can be little doubt of it. In the first place it rests on the strongest possible evidence, that of the Monk of St. Albans,[2] who hated Lancaster and Wycliffe about equally. In the second place, there is nothing antecedently improbable in the friars defending Wycliffe in 1377. The friars loved Lancaster and hated the Bishops. Wycliffe was attacking political bishops and the principle against which, in theory at least, the whole mendicant organization protested—clerical wealth. Here then was a chance of gratifying their patron and their animosities—and a fine chance for ecclesiastical polemics !

The trial was to take place on the afternoon of Thursday, February 19. Long before it began St. Paul's was crowded to overflowing ; all who could had found places, but there was a mob of expectant sightseers outside, for half London was burning with excitement about the trial, the greatest *cause célèbre* of the day. At length the cortege arrived : Courtenay and his brother bishops, and the prisoner, supported by Lancaster, Percy, and other notables, and followed by the four mendicants who held briefs for the defence.

The first difficulty was to get Wycliffe through the crowd into the Lady Chapel, and Percy, Earl Marshal, cleared the way with perhaps unnecessary violence. This was the beginning of a scene. Percy's rough methods and indeed the use of the Marshal's authority at all within the precincts of St. Paul's roused the Bishop of London, who ordered him to stop, and told him that had this been foreseen he would never have allowed him to enter the Cathedral. Lancaster joined in the quarrel, and told the

---

[1] *Chr. Angl.* 118.

[2] [Wycliffe] ordinibus adhaesit Mendicantium eorum pauper tatem approbans, perfectionem extollens. *Chr. Angl.* 116.

Bishop that Percy would continue to act as Marshal whether the Bishop liked it or not !

By the time the Lady Chapel was reached every one was fairly heated. But the trial was even yet not begun. The prisoner had taken his place ; his friends were encouraging him. The scene was memorable ; one which has most strangely repeated itself in the drama of history. A century and a half later, in the ancient hall of audience at Worms, Martin Luther stands at the bar before a Diet of the Empire ; as the Landgrave of Hesse and George of Frondsberg encourage the monk who single-handed has defied the thunders of the Church, so now Lancaster and Percy support the secular priest who has dared to expose the sins of the clergy.

At Worms George of Frondsberg said to Luther : " Little monk, thou hast a fight before thee which we, whose trade is war, never faced the like of." [1]

So now : hard soldiers like Lancaster and Percy must have admired the courage of the poor scholar who had dared to defy the whole official hierarchy of the Church.

Whatever their own views might be, Lancaster and Percy were going to see fair play.

Percy began the next episode by ordering Wycliffe to be seated. The indictment was long, and the prisoner would need rest. The Bishop of London refused to allow it ; Wycliffe as an accused priest in the presence of his ordinary must stand.

As Percy and the Bishop raged at each other the crowd in St. Paul's grew more and more excited. There was a curious mixture of parties in London, for while the citizens were loyal to their Bishop, Percy was as yet a popular hero, and Wycliffe had half of London for him. The mob in St. Paul's began to take sides and make an uproar. When Lancaster joined in the quarrel it was worse. The

---

[1] Froude. *The Council of Trent,* p. 53.

G

Duke abused the Bishop, and the Bishop replied in kind ; as his admirers claim the victory for him, it may perhaps be conceded that the episcopal language was on the whole more powerful.[1] The Duke's temper was up ; he swore that he would humble the pride of the Bishop of London and all the bishops in England. "You trust in your family," said Lancaster (the Bishop was a son of the Earl of Devon), "but they shall not help you ; they will have enough to do to look to themselves," to which Courtenay replied with unction that he trusted in God.

When a muttered threat of the Duke to drag the Bishop by the hair from St. Paul's was overheard, the uproar in the Cathedral became a riot. Sympathy for Wycliffe might divide the mob, but in a quarrel between the Bishop and the Duke they were united. It had long been clear that there would be no trial. The meeting now broke up in confusion ; for the time Wycliffe was free. The devil had known how to save his own ![2]

For a moment Wycliffe was forgotten. The insult to the Bishop of London excited the citizens to fury. It was taken as an insult to the city itself, and, as it happened, it confirmed their worst fears. The Duke was plotting against civic liberty and privilege. The "trial" took place in the afternoon. That very morning, so the citizens heard, a petition had been presented in Parliament by Thomas of Woodstock and Henry Percy to replace the Mayor by a captain, of course a royal officer, and to extend the Marshal's jurisdiction to the city.

The next day (February 20) the citizens held a meeting : [3] their privileges were at stake ; their corporate existence was threatened. In the middle of the debate, enter Lords Fitzwalter and Guy Bryan. Fitz-

---

[1] Erubuit Dux quod non potuit praevalere litigio. *Chr. Angl.* 120.

[2] *Chr. Angl.* 119.

[3] *Chr. Angl.* 121–129; 397–398.

walter was himself a civic officer : he was a Standard-bearer to the City ; both had property in the city, and were entitled by citizenship to be present. But they came at the risk of their lives, for anti-feudal feeling ran high. Fitzwalter had news to tell : he came to add fuel to the flames. In violation of civic liberty the Marshal was detaining a prisoner in his house. A fatal precedent. Let the City beware ! It is not clear what game Fitzwalter and Brian were playing, for both were supposed to be friends of the Duke. Perhaps they wanted to see what was going on, and it is just possible that Fitzwalter had some old score to wipe out with Percy. The history of the period is a perfect tangle of personal quarrels, and such an explanation is always antecedently probable. Whatever his motive, his story had a magical effect. The meeting broke up in a moment : the citizens flew to arms and made a rush for the Marshalsea. Percy's doors were beaten in ; the prisoner was found in the stocks and rescued, and his stocks were burnt in the street. The mob searched the house from cellar to attic; pikes were thrust through every curtain, and every cupboard was examined. Happily for himself the Marshal could not be found. As it happened, that day Lancaster and Percy were dining in London with Sir John d'Ypres, a rich London merchant, who had risen to knighthood and to so high a position of trust in the royal household that King Edward made him one of his executors. The mob did not know their movements, and failing to find Percy at the Marshalsea, made for the Savoy. It was this false scent which saved the life of the Duke and the Marshal, for while the mob was howling outside the gates of the Savoy a knight of Lancaster's retinue rode to Ypres Inn to give the alarm. Breathless with haste the knight told his news : the Marshalsea was gutted, the Savoy besieged, London in arms and at the heels of the Duke. Dinner had only just begun ; in fact, according

to the Monk of St. Albans, who has a most graphic
and detailed account of the whole episode duly embel-
lished with ornaments of his own setting, the *hors
d'œuvres* had just been served. But there was not a
moment to be lost. Lancaster and Percy rose and
made for the river. The Duke took his barge up the
river as fast as oars could carry it, and did not stop
till he reached Kennington, where Princess Joan and
the little Prince Richard were staying.

They were well out of danger, for the blood of the
Londoners was up. Stray retainers of the Duke found
it prudent to hide their badges; one, braver or less prudent
than the rest, who refused to hide the proud emblem of
the Lancastrian retinue, Sir John Swynton, a Scottish
knight, was badly mauled by the mob, who dragged him
from his horse and tore the badge of Lancaster from
his neck. A priest who asked what the riot was
about, being told that London was going to make the
Duke release Sir Peter de la Mare, in a rash moment
said that Sir Peter was a traitor, who ought to have
been hanged long ago. The mob beat him to death.
At length the Bishop of London, roused by the riot, came
out to quiet his disorderly diocese. It was February 20,
the middle of Lent, and the Bishop entreated the citizens
not to disturb the sanctity of the lenten season. The
promise of satisfaction succeeded in restoring some
degree of calm—a result which speaks well for his influence, and the rioters promised to return to their homes.
One more picturesque episode before the day closed.
Outside a shop in Cheapside there was hung up an escut-
cheon bearing the Duke's arms—the familiar blazon
Castile and Leon quartering England and France. Here
was a chance of insulting Monseigneur d'Espaigne.
The mob hung the shield up reversed, as was done with
the arms of a traitor!

It was no easy task which the flight of Lancaster and

Percy to Kennington had laid upon the Princess Joan, but the widow of the Black Prince and the mother of Prince Richard was popular in the city, and she used her influence to the full to make peace.

Three of her knights, Sir Aubrey de Vere, Sir Simon Burley and Sir Lewis Clifford were despatched to the city. Vere belonged to the family that gave to Richard when King his greatest favourite : Burley was to lose his life through his devotion to his young master, and Clifford was notorious for his Lollard opinions. The choice of emissaries was politic ; but they found the task of conciliation difficult. The citizens returned an answer at once respectful and firm. " The Bishop of Winchester and Sir Peter de la Mare must have a fair trial " : and they would "have the traitor wherever he were found " : a rather obscure threat, to which Lancaster found a ready explanation.[1]

A deputation followed to explain and excuse the riot. For a long time they were denied the King's presence, but at length the Duke consented to receive them, adding that the King was too ill to be disturbed. But John Philipot, spokesman for the city, stuck to his point. His message was for the King alone, and he was not empowered to convey it through an intermediary. Brought before King Edward, Philipot declared the grievance of the City :—the rumour that the Mayor was to be replaced by a captain, and the threats levelled at the city privileges. As for the riot of the previous day, and the insults heaped on the Duke, that was the work of a few disorderly persons for whom the city was in no way responsible, people who had nothing to lose and were bent on making mischief. He protested, however, that neither the Duke nor his men had suffered any material

---

[1] Here the Monk of St. Albans is sarcastic : "Hoc" ait [Dux] "de me dicunt" : *tamen non est credibile eos de eo hoc dixisse* (*Chr. Angl.* 127).

damage. Perhaps Sir John Swynton would have taken a different view! With that gracious demeanour which always won the confidence of his subjects, King Edward dismissed the deputation with the assurance that he had never intended to cancel the liberties of the city, but on the contrary, was prepared to extend them.

As the emissaries left the presence they met the Duke, and promised him that those guilty of the insults to his name should be punished when found. Of course no one was found. So far from any discouragement to such insults being given, matters went from bad to worse. Lampoons, composed in terms calculated to rouse popular passion, were posted about in the principal streets, and the Duke, still more infuriated, demanded that their authors should be excommunicated.

By this time the civic dignitaries had become genuinely alarmed ; thinking things had gone far enough, and intent on showing their innocence, they stood by while the Bishop of Bangor formally excommunicated those who had defamed the Duke's good name.

Wycliffe's trial and the next day's riot had effectually stopped the business of Parliament. When peace and order were sufficiently restored, the session was continued, but the Duke and the Marshal took the precaution of riding to Westminster with a strong armed retinue, and gave the city a wide berth.[1]

The opposition of the clergy had only served to exasperate the Duke. Inside Parliament he could at least do what he would ; the majority he commanded would secure that. He used it to undo the last remaining acts of the previous parliament. Among the victims of the reforming party some were illustrious and others were obscure. The Duke insisted on restoring one and all to their former estate. The restoration of petty

[1] *Chr. Angl.* 130.

offenders could certainly not benefit him; on the contrary, it could only damage his reputation. Only one of the impeached, as has been seen, was a friend of the Duke. But in spite of this, Lancaster insisted on a complete reversal of the acts of 1376; nothing less would satisfy his vengeance, and without this the challenge to the opposition would be incomplete.

The answer to the city was equally decisive. Sir Peter de la Mare remained in prison. On February 23 a selected body of lords and commons went to Sheen to hear the answers given by the King to the petitions which had been presented, and to listen to the general pardon which the King had granted to mark the jubilee of his reign. The interest of the charter of pardon lay in the last paragraph, in which " Sir William of Wykeham " was excepted by name.

The exchequer provided with funds and the work of " restoration " completed, Parliament dissolved. Lancaster had achieved his objects, but at a great cost. He was involved in a bitter quarrel with the City and the Church.

Since the riot the citizens had lived in a state of painful expectancy. It must have been something of a relief when a royal mandate arrived, summoning the Mayor, Sheriffs and Aldermen to the King's presence at Sheen.[1] At least they would soon know the worst. King Edward had only a few weeks to live, and when they arrived they found him propped up in his chair, and scarcely able to speak. In his name Sir Robert Aston, the royal chamberlain, addressed them.

They must know the cause of their summons. Insults had been heaped upon the Duke of Lancaster. The Duke was the King's son; more, he was the King's representative. Therefore an insult to the Duke was an insult

---

[1] *Chr. Angl.* 131-4.

to the King himself. The citizens would be well advised to submit themselves without more ado to the Duke's grace.

This proposal did not commend itself to the officials of the city. In reply they could only protest their entire innocence of the events of the 20th ; for the disorders, which they lamented, they were in no way responsible. On the contrary, they were ready to do anything in their power to compel restitution.

No one, of course, supposed that the Mayor had thrown stones at the Savoy, or that the Sheriffs had with their own hands posted up lampoons about the streets of the city. The fact remained that these disorders had been committed within their jurisdiction, and that they had done nothing to stop them, and to protest inability to maintain order was unfortunate at the very moment when the continuance of civic jurisdiction was one of the points about which they had shown such concern.

To prove their sincerity, however, the citizens determined to make some demonstration ; though the form which this took was peculiarly ill-advised. If, as is stated, the suggestion came from the King's advisers, it seems almost as though some mischief-maker had deliberately chosen a measure calculated to embitter the quarrel.

A candle was procured, bearing Lancaster's arms, and the city magnates forming themselves into procession, which the common people, in spite of the crier's proclamation, refused to follow, solemnly bore their peace-offering to St. Paul's, where they deposited it before the altar of the Virgin.

A ceremony performed in memory of the dead inevitably suggested the wish that the Duke might shortly be in a position to require that honour, and to subtle minds conveyed a hint of his political annihilation !

The City was disappointed. The procession had proved a failure, and the penance was performed by the civic dignitaries alone. The Duke was not conciliated ; he chose to regard the whole effort as a deliberate insult. No one had been brought to book for the disorders of the riot ; there was no intention of so doing. The parties to the quarrel remained exasperated.

Nothing would satisfy the Duke, said the citizens, short of making him King !

All this is petty enough, but the quarrel with the Church leads us to larger issues.

In the fight with the Bishops Lancaster and Wycliffe had stood side by side. What was the true relation between them, and what was the Duke's real attitude to the Church ?

Chapter VIII

LANCASTER AND THE CHURCH

IN the latter half of the fourteenth century the condition of the Church was such as to inspire thoughtful men with feelings almost amounting to despair. From head to foot the body of the Church seemed smitten with disease, and there were no signs of a healthy and vigorous life in any member. Papacy, secular clergy, and "religious"—all were alike discredited.

When in 1305 the head of Catholic Christendom removed his court from Rome to Avignon, deserting the Eternal City for a town on the borders of France, that "sinful city of Avignon," as the English Commons called it, something more than mere dignity was lost, something more than the prestige of immemorial tradition. Innocent III had aspired to universal dictatorship, to the arbitrament of the affairs of Christian Europe; with Urban V and Gregory XI the interests of the Papacy during the war are no longer Catholic; they are parochial. The universal arbiter has become the political partisan. In 1377 the Papacy was already standing on the verge of the abyss, for no sooner is the "Babylonish captivity" over than the Great Schism begins. To the political quarrels of Europe, which they are powerless to prevent or to compose, the Popes add an ecclesiastical quarrel. The seamless robe is rent, and Christian Europe is divided into two hostile camps. The infidel is pressing on their frontiers, but Christian princes waste their strength on internecine

160

struggles; while French and English, Castilian and Portuguese struggle one with the other, and Urbanist and Clementist spill Christian blood, the Crescent triumphs over the Cross, and Bajazet crushes a crusading army under the walls of Nicopolis.

But while the Papacy abated nothing of its pretensions, in the unhealthy moral atmosphere of the day it had caught the infection of that "covetise" which, as Chaucer in a serious moment tells us, was the predominant vice of the age; [1] the spirit of Lady Meed of the Vision of Piers Ploughman corrupting all classes of society. This indeed was nothing new. Had not Dante [2] at the beginning of the century written of the Popes—

> . . . La vostra avarizia il mondo attrista,
> Calcando i buoni e sollevando i pravi.
> Di voi pastor s' accorse il Vangelista,
> Quando colei, che siede sopra l'acque,
> Puttaneggiar coi regi a lui fu vista.
>
> . . . .
>
> Fatto v'avete Dio d' oro e d' argento:
> E che altro è da voi all' idolatre,
> Se non ch' egli uno, e voi n' orate cento?
> Ahi, Constantin, di quanto mal fu matre,
> Non la tua conversion, ma quella dote
> Che da te prese il primo ricco patre!

Fifty years later Boccaccio, in the frivolous setting of the Decameron, [3] has the story, profoundly significant in spite of its cynicism, of Abraham the Jew, who, pressed by a proselytising Christian friend, goes to Rome, sees the spectacle of the Papal Court, and in spite of this revelation, demands baptism, convinced that a Church

---

[1] Allas, allas! now may men wepe and crye!
For in our dayes nis but covetyse
And doublenesse, and tresoun and envye,
Poysoun, manslauhtre, and mordre in sondry wyse.
(Chaucer, *The Former Age*, 61-4).
[2] *Inferno*, xix. 104-119.
[3] *Decameron*, Giornata Prima; Novella II.

which could survive in spite of such depravity must be built upon the rock, and can indeed claim a divine sanction.

The facts of the chronicler are stranger than the fictions of the novelist. Adam of Usk, a prosaic lawyer, who had no love for Lollards or doctrinal reform, echoes the same cry : " Romae omnia venalia."

Adam, who, like Abraham the Jew, himself went to Rome, says : " There everything was bought and sold, so that benefices were given not for desert, but to the highest bidder. Whence, every man who had wealth and was greedy for empty glory, kept his money in the merchants' bank to further his advancement. And therefore, as, when under the old testament the priesthood were corrupted with venality, the three miracles ceased, namely the unquenchable fire of the priesthood, sweet smell of sacrifice which offendeth not, and the smoke which ever riseth up, so I fear will it come to pass under the new testament. And methinks the danger standeth daily knocking at the very doors of the Church "[1]—words which most strangely anticipate the warning of the later reformation—

> That two-handed engine at the door
> Stands ready to smite once, and smite no more.

If things were bad at the metropolis of Christendom, they were little better in the outlying provinces of the Church.

In England two abuses in particular called aloud for remedy—plurality and non-residence. William of Wykeham, who in 1362, even before he was ordained priest, held a deanery of St. Paul's and of Hereford as well as twelve other prebends, was only an example, if an extreme example, of the prevailing system which Wycliffe denounced. He was only one offender out of many, and

---

[1] *Adam of Usk*, p. 201.

his practice was the rule not the exception. To the prejudice alike of principle, of ecclesiastical discipline, and of learning, the Church was invaded by an army of men, who, so far from devoting their lives to their profession—it would be absurd to say their "calling"— had no intention of giving any portion of their time to the duties of the priesthood. Orders formed the necessary preliminary to a civil career ; the reward of clerical labour, whether in departments of government, the household of the King, or that of some great feudatory, was, according to the dignity of the service, a bishopric, prebend, canonry, or living—more often a number of benefices held concurrently. The result was inevitable : on the one hand, a body of ecclesiastics, differing in rank but agreeing in their interests, those of a secular ambition, from the Bishop who presided over the Chancery or Treasury, down to the absentee clerk who held a single benefice ; on the other hand, a laity alienated from the secular clergy, consisting of the rich who looked to others—the monk or the mendicant—to satisfy their spiritual needs, and of the poor whose spiritual condition was too often one of entire neglect. The duties of the parish priest were left to a substitute : a "curate," ignorant, poor, often the father of a family which canon law refused to recognize, struggling for existence in competition with the friar, who deprived him of the profits of the confessional, and the chantry priest, if possible more ignorant than himself, who absorbed the offerings wrung from the rich by family sentiment and superstition.[1]

Such is the picture of the secular clergy of England, painted by contemporary hands. If some portions of the canvas are overcoloured, there can be little doubt that the general impression is faithful to fact.

Against the regular clergy, the "religious," the charges

[1] See the valuable introduction to vol. ii. of the *Monumenta Franciscana* (Rolls Series).

are different. The chief sins of the monks are those of omission. Such services as the monastic system had been able to render to the cause of learning and civilization belong to the dark ages of ignorance and insecurity long since past. In this age the monks stood condemned because, in spite of their enormous wealth and ample opportunity, they were doing little or nothing for Society. Doubtless in some places the standard of conduct was not what might have been expected of monastic profession, but on the whole the complaints made against the monks by the men of their day are not so much those of ill-living as of idleness and luxury. With their wealth and power their pretensions had grown and their sense of responsibility had diminished. The wealthiest class of the community was aiming at exemption from the burdens of national life ; privilege had taken the place of duty.

Side by side with the secular clergy and the monks, stands the third great division of the forces of the Church militant, the mendicant orders, organized in four great battalions—Franciscans, Dominicans, Augustinians, and Carmelites.

It was a true instinct which caused Innocent III to hesitate before sanctioning the scheme laid before him by the saintly enthusiasm of Francis of Assisi ; for the religion of St. Francis was in its essence spiritual, and therefore, had it been able to preserve the purity of its founder, destined to prove a solvent of the papal system ; and, on the other hand, the mendicant organization was incompatible with the existing machinery of the Church. But the doubts of the thirteenth century had been long since laid to rest ; first one then another mendicant order had come into existence, to become a devoted militia of the Pope, to challenge the spiritual monopoly of seculars and monks and to earn the hatred of both. In England for more than a century the friars had secured an established position ; they had won their battle against episcopal control, and were emancipated from the diocesan system. They had their own independent organization, a hierarchy consisting of wardens or superiors, and Provincial, the Provincial responsible to the Minister General at the Papal Court, the Minister General responsible directly to the Pope.

Like the monks, the friars had forgotten the early strictness of their rule ; a legal fiction which vested their property in the Pope evaded the literal interpretation of the vow of poverty, and the principle of "accommodation" disposed of the duty of manual labour. But in spite of shortcomings which poet and satirist are never tired of denouncing, the friars prospered. It was in vain that FitzRalf, Archbishop of Armagh, had fought his campaign against mendicancy and had been himself to Avignon to denounce the corruption of the orders. The friars, who had once seemed superfluous, were now indispensable. The Pope could not spare them. The laity were in their power, for they had wrested from seculars and monks the weapon of the confessional. Two-thirds of the laity of England confessed to them and received absolution at their hands.[1]

The vices of all orders of ecclesiastical society did not pass without criticism.

Chaucer, the genial man of the world, laughs at them ; Langland, the brooding mystic of the Malvern hills, weeps over them ; Gower, the sententious moralist, lashes them—and every one else who comes within reach of his arm. The age condemned them ; the age found a voice in one man—John Wycliffe. This

[1] "Tertio quoque nobis imponunt quod major pars dominorum et populi, sicut nobis praecipue confitentur, ita et nostro, ut fingunt consilio in agendis potissime regulantur." Letter of the four claustral orders to John, Duke of Lancaster. *Fasc. Ziz.* p. 294.

is not the place to tell the story of Wycliffe's life, or to trace the development of his thought, the growth of his system. It is necessary only to indicate the point at which the lines followed by the great reformer and his patron intersect, to show how sharply they diverge and to what different poles of thought they point. Suffice it to say that Wycliffe, like Luther, offended by practical abuses, was led by intense moral conviction and by the positive and rationalistic bent of his mind first to challenge the existing administrative organization of the Church, and finally to question its fundamental doctrines ; first to assail the outworks of the ecclesiastical camp, and finally to lay siege to the very citadel of the Catholic faith. Wycliffe condemned the Papal system, with its exactions and " provisions," its weapons of excommunication and interdict ; he condemned the monastic system and the mendicant system, and contrasted the wealth and luxury, the secular ambition and temporal power of the clergy with the apostolic purity of the early Church. But while his doctrinal doubts and beliefs belong to the history of thought and the history of the Church, there is one belief that now claims examination, the belief that in John Plantagenet he had found the chosen minister to reform the abuses of the age, and to set right a time out of joint.

How little justification there was for such a belief, how far John of Gaunt was from the position of an ecclesiastical reformer, how scant his sympathy with the ideals and theories of Wycliffe, will appear from a brief review of the circumstances which throw a light on his dealings with the Church and the ecclesiastical problems of his day.

What was the Duke's attitude to the regular clergy, the monks and the friars ? To judge by the rumours afloat in 1378, or from the impression created by the sensational author of the *Chronicon Angliae*, it might be thought that the monks regarded John of Gaunt as their peculiar enemy, the sworn foe of the monastic system and of ecclesiastical property. The credulous reader of the Monk of St. Albans will conjure up the vision of some Abbot or Prior, meeting the cavalcade of the Duke of Lancaster on the King's highways, crossing himself with horror at the sight of the Church's arch-enemy, and, with a muttered prayer to his patron saint, turning his bridle for the nearest way of escape. Such is the fiction ; the fact is otherwise. The Abbot, let us suppose, was a mitred abbot among the number of those who sat in Parliament and knew the Duke at Westminster. If so, he would know him as a man always ready to use his influence with the King or the Pope on behalf of a monastic foundation. It is more than likely that he would also know him as a host, for abbot and bishop jostled knight and baron in the castle halls of Leicester and Kenilworth whenever the Duke had a party to hunt in the Lancastrian forests. So far from appearing as an enemy of the regular clergy, or a " suspect " person in their eyes, the Duke is on the best of terms with them. He is an indulgent landlord ; he visits their houses constantly in his endless journeyings to and fro in England,[1] and the visit is usually remembered by the monks with satisfaction, for by Papal indulgence religious persons may eat meat in his presence,[2] and he leaves behind him some mark of favour, a remission of rent or grant of lands or privilege.[3] Licences for alienation in mortmain the Duke, like other lay tenants, scatters

---

[1] John of Gaunt certainly availed himself of the "indult to enter any monasteries of religious men and women once a year with thirty persons of good repute " (a wise qualification). *Papal Letters*, iv. 167.

[2] John, Duke of Lancaster, and Blanche, his wife : That religious persons may eat meat in their house or presence. *Petitions to the Pope*, i. 422.

[3] E.g. The Abbey of Cristall, i.e. Kirkstall, *Hist. MSS.* 8th Report App. p. 413, and Register *passim*.

with a lavish hand;[1] he is constantly backing the petition of Abbots and Convents to the Papal court.[2]

The man whom Wycliffe in 1376 thought to be sincerely opposed to the undue wealth of the religious orders, whom the country in 1378 believed to be plotting a wholesale expropriation of Church property, is the patron of more than a score of abbeys. He is constantly giving gifts, not only the small marks of favour like timber and venison from his forests, but gifts of land, solid endowments, manors, and the advowsons of churches and chapels. He protects the clergy from the rapacity of the King's officers and from oppression by his own purveyors.[3] He acts as their champion in difficulties and as arbiter in their disputes.[4]

Something of course must be allowed for the Lancastrian tradition. The heir of Duke Henry could scarcely abandon foundations like Leicester, and the great monasteries of Furness and Whalley looked to the Duke of Lancaster as their natural protector. But the Duke showed no inclination to break with the Lancastrian tradition, and Duke John in continuing the Hospital and Collegiate Church at Leicester [5] continued Duke Henry's policy, and besides those anciently associated

---

[1] Register I. f. 31–6, etc.

[2] E.g. The Duke supports the petition of the Benedictine Priory of St. Faiths, Norfolk, cell to the Abbey of Conches to be considered an English and not an alien Priory (*Rot. Pat.* 17 Dec., 1390); he is the patron of the Austin Priory of St. Mary's Norton and of the Cistercian Abbey of St. Mary's, Kirkstall, and supports their petition to the Pope (*Papal Letters*, iv. 405; and v. 16); he is the present founder of Biddlesdon Abbey (Brit. Mus. *Harl. Ch.* 84. c. 17.) and supports their petition and that of the Benedictine Abbey of St. Peter's, Gloucester (*Papal Letters*, v. 598, cf. 157).

[3] Reg. II. f. 137.

[4] E.g. St. Frideswyde's, Oxford. *Rot. Pat.* July 22, 1377.

[5] Lancaster gave the Dean and Chapter of the New Church at Leicester 100 marcs a year. For marks of his favour to Leicester see Register *passim*.

with the Lancastrian name, a score of foundations, Cistercian and Benedictine alike, scattered over all England enrolled Duke John among their patrons.

As the birthplace of the *Scandalous Chronicle*, St. Albans has a peculiar interest for the history of John of Gaunt. His relations to this great Abbey may be taken as a typical example of his real attitude to the monks.

Thomas de la Mare, perhaps a kinsman of the hero of the "Good" Parliament, thirtieth Abbot, reigned there from 1349 to his death in 1396—a reign of terror to erring brethren, for the Abbot, equally renowned for his flagellations, his bad handwriting, and his hatred of sport, was as merciless to his flock as to himself. Next after hunting, the Abbot, who had supported FitzRalf in the anti-mendicant crusade, hated Lollard and friar with an equally unmeasured hatred. The Duke loved sport, protected Wycliffe, and was the firm friend of the friars. But this difference of taste did not prevent friendly relations. An early case of disputed jurisdiction, in which the Duke had shown a very conciliatory attitude, was terminated in favour of the Abbey,[1] and in more than one legal difficulty the Abbey chose John of Gaunt as arbitrator.[2]

When the Abbot petitioned the Pope for remission of the yearly payment and dispensation from the duty of personal attendance at the Curia, Lancaster used his influence in favour of the request, and gave testimony to the sanctity of the brotherhood.[3]

[1] The dispute turned on the question whether the Abbot, in virtue of his tenure of the Manor of Norton near Boroughbridge, owed suit to the Duke's Court of Frendles Wapentake.

The Duke's officers, for the Honor of Richmond, had amerced and distrained on the Abbot for refusal, but an Inquisition held with the Duke's assent found in favour of the Abbot (42 Edw. III) *Gesta Abbatum Sancti Albani*, iii. 97.

[2] Ibid. iii. 241–6.

[3] The Duke writes: "Ego qui honorem et bonum statum dictorum monasterii Abbatis et conventus . . . ob dicti Sancti

JOHN OF GAUNT

One of the burning questions of monastic politics, one on which the Abbot Thomas held strong views, was the relation between the Abbey of Saint Albans and the Priory of Christ Church, Canterbury. The Prior claimed exemption from the duty of sending proctors to the Chapter of the Benedictine Order, on the ground of Papal indulgence. St. Albans had never admitted this claim, or succeeded in enforcing its own. The Abbot Thomas, being a man of energy and nothing if not a disciplinarian, insisted. In 1376 a formal summons to the Capitular meeting reached Canterbury. The Prior showed his independence by beating the Abbot's envoys and then locking them up. As it happened, the Black Prince was in Canterbury at the time, and heard of the indignity. The result was a reprimand to the Prior for this open affront to the head of the order. The Prior, finding court influence against him, hastened to agree with his adversary by the way, and sent his proctor to the Chapter, but as the Abbot was not likely to forgive or forget, he went further, and tried to enlist sympathy at Court also. He appealed to John of Gaunt, who went to St. Albans, interceded for the offending Prior, made peace between these angry sons of the Church, won the gratitude of the Prior and the friendship of the Abbot, and was received into the brotherhood of the Benedictine Order.[1]

Four years later we find the Duke backing a petition from the Abbey to the King for commutation of the fine levied on " vacation " for a yearly payment,[2] and eleven years later still it is the Duke who, acting out of " love and charity to the Abbey," satisfies the King in his

reverentiam et honorem et elegentiam meritorum et vitae monachorum inibi degentium non inmerito desidero augeri . . ." *Gesta Abbatum Sc. Albani.*
[1] " *Cum summa devotione.*" Ibid. ii. 403.
[2] Ibid. iii. 135–137).

extortionate demands for a forced loan from St. Albans.[1]

Friendly relations were not broken by the hostile attitude of the Abbot to the Duke's crusade in 1386 ; the Abbot, forcibly as usual, expressed his opinion of the sale of papal chaplaincies, but the Abbey still regarded John of Gaunt as a friend and patron. In the official list of benefactors the Duke's picture is still to be found. In the margin above a miniature of the Duchess Constance is a miniature of the Duke ; in the text a grateful acknowledgment of his gifts to the foundation—in particular a gift of one hundred pounds towards the restoration of the gate at Tynemouth Priory—and this sentence : " This prince had an extreme love and affection for our monastery and Abbot ; many a time he gave us gifts of wine ; he promoted our interests and greatly enriched the Church with his magnificent and oft-repeated oblations." [2]

The Abbot Thomas died in September, 1396, and Lancaster was among those who came to visit him in his sickness and to ask for his blessing and his prayers.[3]

So much for Lancaster's hostility to the monks and the monastic system. But it was upon the other great body of the regular clergy that the Duke bestowed his favour preeminently. To the friars he entrusts his soul while he lives and his body when he dies. Friars Preachers, Friars Minors, Austins, and Carmelites—to all his patronage extends, but it is the Carmelites which he singles out for especial favour.[4] One after another his confessors

---

[1] Wals. ii. 403. Cf. *Gest. Abb. Sc. Alb*. iii. 363. *Rot. Pat.* 23 Feb. 1390.

[2] Liber de Benefactoribus Monasterii Sancti Albani. *Ann. Ric. II*. p. 434-5, and British Museum MS. Cotton Nero. D. vii. Wals. ii. 403.

[3] *Gesta Abbatum Sc. Albani*, iii. 412.

[4] Among the Friars mentioned in the Register as recipients of presents, etc., are the Carmelites of Nottingham, of Sandwich, of Doncaster, and of London ; the Minors of Richmond and of

are chosen from that order, William de Reynham, John Badby, Walter Dysse, and John Cuningham. The last was a man of some importance, for he was twenty-first Provincial of the English Carmelites. But long before Cuningham had become the Duke's confessor, and had repented of that uncourtly reference to the House of Herod [1]—made in the days when he did not, and Wycliffe did, enjoy the Duke's favour—Lancaster had a powerful body of supporters in the order. The results of a lavish generosity and unmistakable preference of the Carmelite order [2] had been to place at the Duke's

York, the Preachers of Pontefract and of Derby, the proctors of the Hospital of "Our Lady of Runcyvale," etc. See also Appendix I. p. 424-5, and Appendix IV. p. 449.

William de Reynham, Carmelite and Master in Theology, was his confessor in 1366 (Lancaster petitions for plenary absolution for him and for three of his relations. *Petitions to the Pope*, i. 528-9).

John Badby, another confessor, received an annuity of £10 in 1372 (Register I. f. 73 ; 169).

Walter Dysse, Carmelite and Doctor in Theology, of Cambridge, was his confessor from 1375 to 1386 (Reg. II. 116, annuity of £10 ; present of 100s., etc.). *Fasc. Ziz.* p. 508 and 286.

John Cuningham succeeded Walter Dysse. He was confessor at the time of the Council of Stamford, 1392. *Fasc. Ziz.* p. 3.

[1] Nec Herodis domus dux mihi est (*Fasc. Ziz.* p. 14).

[2] Johan, etc., A touz, etc., Saluz. Come par le chapitre provinciale del ordre des frers caresmes d'Engleterre pleinement celebrez a Cauntebrugg le jour de l'assumpcion notre Dame darrein passe nous fumes devoutement et humblement suppliez par lettres des ditz provinciale et chapitre d'estre foundour del meson et covent des ffrers caresmes de Doncastre et de accepter en noz mains la fundacion del dite meson de Doncastre en eide et socour del dite meson et covent en temps avenir a cause depuis que leurs especiales foundres del dite meson ove successours liniales sont a dieux comandez. Sachez nous al honure de Dieu et notre Dame et de Seinte Religion et mesment pour la grande especiale affection quele nous portons au dit ordre et ensement al humble et devout request et supplicacion del dite chapitre provinciale avoir ottroiez notre plein assent et bone volentée d'estre foundour de meisme la meson et accepter en noz mains et les mains de noz heirs successours de la duchee de Lancastre la fundacion del dite meson de Doncastre

command the services of a powerful and highly disciplined army, invaluable for its effects on public opinion, unswerving in its devotion to its greatest lay patron. It was the Carmelites who preached the Duke's crusade against Spain in 1386. When in 1384, for reasons which will appear later, a Carmelite Friar brought charges of treason against the Duke, he was at once disowned by the brotherhood, and those who would have made political capital out of the man's arrest and death were promptly suppressed by orders from headquarters.

The friars had no illusions about the Duke's heterodoxy and revolutionary ideas. They were willing at first to defend his agent in an attack on ecclesiastical wealth theoretically condemned by their own rules, and later, when the reformer of administration became the heretic, while attacking Wycliffe to defend his patron. The Duke shared both their friendships and their hatreds. He was inclined to regard the Pope as an ally; the friars were the Pope's devoted servants. He hated political bishops; the friars were the enemies of the whole secular clergy. Unlike the temporary alliance with Wycliffe, the Duke's connexion with the friars lasted to the end of his life; it was founded on similarity of interests, and had all the elements of permanence.

Had the Duke any sympathy with Wycliffe's ideas of administrative reform? There should be little doubt on this point, for the man who possessed the largest ecclesiastical patronage in England had ample opportunities of doing something to remedy the evils of plurality and

en maniere come appient a ffondour de tiele meson de reson et par ycestes nous voulons et acceptons en noz mains et en les mains de noz heires et successours de la duchee de Lancastre la fundacion de la dite meson et d'estre leur foundour en tout temps avenir en eide et sustenance et promossion del dite meson ove l'eide de notre Seigneur le toutpuissant Dieu.

En tesmoignance, etc. Donne, etc., a Everwyk le xiii jour de Septembre, l'an . . . etc., sisme. Register II. f. 143, in tergo.

non-residence. What, however, is the fact ? The Duke
in these matters, as in all others, conformed to the practice of his day ; the Lancastrian household, like the
King's government, is supported by the very abuses
which Wycliffe denounced. The diocese of Salisbury
shifted for itself while its Bishop, Ralf Erghum, presided
over the Ducal Chancery, and if William de Sutton, who
was the Chancellor in 1363, did not hold a canonry and
prebend of Salisbury concurrently with the Church of
Trimingham in Norfolk by the Duke's presentation that
was not the fault of his patron.[1] In 1359 the Duke's
treasurer, Walter de Campeden, rector of Somercotes,
gets a Canonry of York, with expectation of a prebend ;[2]
in 1363 the Duke does his best to get for another
treasurer, John de Lincoln[3] (who, by the way, had been
ordained by Lancastrian influence in spite of the canonical
ban of illegitimacy), a canonry of York, with expectation
of a prebend, concurrently with the free chapel of Wykes.
The Duke petitions that William de Horneby[4] his Receiver
for Lancashire, may hold a Canonry of Lincoln, with
expectation of a prebend notwithstanding that he has
the church of Ribchester. While John de Yerdburgh[5] is

[1] *Petitions to the Pope*, i. 423.

[2] Ibid. 337.

[3] Petition of John, Duke of Lancaster, etc. : on behalf of John
de Lincoln, the son of a priest, for dispensation to be ordained
and hold a benefice or dignity and exchange or resign the same and
accept another, do, on behalf of the same, who has been ordained
priest and has obtained the Chapel of Wykes, which belongs to
the presentation of the said Duke, to retain the Chapel and
hold canonry or prebend. Ibid. 480 and 496.

[4] Ibid. 423.

[5] Presentation of John de Yerdeburgh to the Church of Ribchester in the archdeaconry of Richmond and of John de Lincoln to the Church of Leadenham in the diocese of Lincoln by
exchange, 18 Dec. 1374 ; ditto of John de Yerdeburgh to the
Church of Stoke in the diocese of Lichfield and Coventry, 21 Jan.
1375. Reg. I. f. 47.

Similarly Robert de Whitby, Receiver General, is parson

cumbered about the furs and jewels and cloth of gold and all the precious things of the great wardrobe of the Savoy, the churches of Ribchester and Stoke, which he held by the Duke's gift, were left to the care (or otherwise) of some poor curate; so also is the case with the Church of Bradford, held by the Duke's gift by William de Burghbrigg,[1] Receiver General, who lived in London, and spent his time in struggling with the perplexities of mediaeval arithmetic, while the duke's auditors who checked Burghbrigg's figures and those of all the local receivers are, like him, absentee holders of one or more benefices. For this use of ecclesiastical patronage (the instances are only a few out of many, taken at random for an example), the Duke seeks Papal sanction, and a benefice rewards the envoy[2] who brings back the " bulls of grace " from Avignon, and a benefice pays the labour of the Duke's secretary who wrote the petitions.

William of Wykeham himself, the arch-pluralist, was an intimate of the Duke right up to the time of the " Good " Parliament, and whatever cause may be assigned for their quarrel, it was certainly no question of principle. All these facts were notorious; they were in no way exceptional. Did Wycliffe know the use which Lancaster made of ecclesiastical patronage? And if so, could he distinguish between the case of the man who rose to high ecclesiastical position by keeping the Duke's furs and jewels, and the man who rose to the Episcopate by keeping the King's hounds and overseeing his castles?

The contrast between the principles of the reformer and the practice of the patron is glaring: not that the

---

of Bassingbourn in the diocese of Ely. Confirmation May 3, 1391. *Rot. Pat.*

[1] Presentation of William de Burghbrigg to the Church of Bradford in the diocese of York, 30 Sept. 1375. Reg. I. 47. Cf. *Petitions to the Pope,* iv. 544; and *Papal Letters,* iv. 502.

[2] *Petitions to the Pope,* i. 337.

Duke was in any way below the standard of his age. That is not so. He did the same as other lay patrons, only being more important than the rest, the result is more conspicuous.

Nor had Lancaster any quarrel with the bishop or parish priest as such, but, in common with the men of his time, he preferred to subsidize the non-effective forces of the Church—hence his expenditure on chantry priests, and his solicitude for the comfort of hermit and recluse. To the parish priest he gives gifts of brushwood for fuel from his woods, conies from his warrens, and now and then a fat buck from his parks. He rebuilds his parsonage, and now and then, when some sacrilegious thief has broken into a church and stolen the altar furniture, he makes good the loss. He is particularly careful of the fabric of his churches and parsonages, and visits his wrath on the incumbents who let them decay. For the humbler ranks at least of the secular clergy he has much sympathy ; but he is devoid of any sense of the abuses which are making their position intolerable, any appreciation of the evils of accepted practice, which would assuredly have been found in one who understood Wycliffe's aims.

Evidently, then, the point of agreement between Wycliffe and Lancaster is not to be found in the desire for administrative reform.

Can it be found in doctrinal opinion, in religious thought or practice ? Wycliffe thought that for a penitent of " a broken and a contrite heart " the external act of confession was superfluous and useless.[1] Not so the Duke of Lancaster. To him the act of confession was one of the first of religious duties. His confessors are among the most important officers of the household. From two successive popes he obtains permission to choose

---

[1] Kn. ii. 158. Haeresis, 5.

them at his pleasure; Urban V grants him licence to change them at will. That there may be no interregnum in the reign of the spiritual father who grants absolution to the Duke for his sins, he importunes the Pope to grant licence that his chaplain, too, may listen to his confessions and those of his household, and minister to them the sacraments, and both for himself and for his intimates he craves plenary remission at the hour of death.[1]

Wycliffe denied the divine sanction for the institution of the mass.[2] When foreign envoys or the King's ministers had occasion to visit John of Gaunt, they could testify that the celebration of mass was the invariable prelude to public business in the Lancastrian household. That household breathes an atmosphere of conventional piety. When the Duke leaves the Savoy for Hertford, Leicester, or Pontefract, a body of chaplains, the Dean, and the clerks of his chapel go with him. His religious officers have a definite and permanent place in the household : their number is considerable ; among them are foreigners as well as Englishmen, seculars as well as friars, and one at least, in spite of canon law and propriety, is openly and unblushingly married![3]

Again, when the Duke goes to the wars, his chaplains go with him. There is no break in their ministrations, and everywhere they find prepared for them in England, or take with them abroad, the rich and comely furniture of the chapel, vestments and altar trappings, missal and chalice. So far as the outward observances of religious life go, the Lancastrian household is a model. Blanche the Duchess had perhaps the real piety of her

---

[1] *Petitions to the Pope*, i. 337 ; 528–30 ; 422. Cf. 401.
[2] Kn. ii. 158. Haeresis 6.
[3] Reg. II. f. 40, 42, 53, 56, 58, 63, 72, etc. John Crowe, Clerk of the Chapel, and his wife Alexandra are both in receipt of pensions. Reg. II. f. 29. Cf. Wycliffe's fourth heresy. Kn. ii. 158.

father; it is piety which marks the contrast between the Duchess Constance and the Duchess of York. Katharine of Lancaster, the Duke's daughter, astonishes the Castilians by the tenacity of her ecclesiastical principle; Philippa of Lancaster, her half-sister, is an ensample of godly living, and the Portuguese chroniclers remark her assiduous attention to the duties of religion, her daily care to recite the offices after the custom of Sarum.

Wycliffe had denied the special efficacy of "particular prayers" recited for the benefit of one person singled out of the whole congregation of the Church.

From the date of the death of the Duchess Blanche, throughout the Duke's life he pays two chaplains to sing daily for her soul by the altar and tomb in St. Paul's; and his last wishes are that obits shall be celebrated each year for his own soul and for the souls of Blanche and Constance on the anniversaries of the day of their death.[1] Not only for himself but for others he builds chapels and founds chantries;[2] he pays for masses to be sung for the souls of his brother Knights of the Garter at their decease.[3] To Wycliffe it seemed that he who offered money for participation in the benefits of the prayers of convent or priory was guilty of the sin of Simon Magus, holding such an act to be more truly simoniacal than even the purchase of benefices. But Lancaster, in accordance with the conscience of his time, felt no scruple in carrying

[1] Appendix I: pp. 423, 429, 435.
[2] *Record Report*, xxxv. App. 353, etc.
[3] E.g. Warrant to the Receiver General to pay to Brother Walter Dysse, his confessor, £4 3s. 4d. for 1,000 masses sung for the souls of Sir Guichard Dangle and Sir Thomas Banastre, Knights of the Garter (dated Kenilworth, April 15, 3 Rich. II); do. to his auditors to allow in the R.G.'s account £4 3s. 4d. for 1,000 masses sung for the souls of Ralf, Earl of Stafford, and Humphrey, Earl of Hereford, K.G. (dated Savoy, April 24, 1373); do. to pay to Brother Walter Dysse 2,500 pence for so many masses to be sung for the souls of five of the companions of the Garter lately deceased, Register, I. f. 227 and II. f. 30.

the contractual spirit of feudalism into the things of religion. There were a score of heads of religious houses who, like " John, Abbot of Barlings Abbey, with the convent at that place," entered into a formal bond [1] " for the performance of divine service by five canons of the house at the feast of Pentecost yearly, for the good estate of John, King of Castile and Leon, and Duke of Lancaster, their great benefactor, during his life, and for the performance of divine service by four canons of the house for the benefit of his soul on the anniversary of his decease."

To Wycliffe, penetrating to the spiritual reality of things which lay beneath and were often concealed by the external form and ceremony, excommunication meant the veritable severance of the sinner from the body of the Church, a cutting off of the diseased branch from the stem of the True Vine in which alone Christian men could have true life. Hence his condemnation of the use and abuse for personal or political ends of the sentence of excommunication.

Lancaster saw nothing incongruous in the use of the power for mundane purposes. It was a political fact of the first importance ; sometimes convenient, sometimes the reverse. In 1377 he had used it against the turbulent citizens of London; in 1386 he used it against the usurper of his kingdom of Castile. In other words, excommunication was a weapon to be wielded by a complaisant prelacy at the request of the temporal power for personal or dynastic purposes. It was part of the political as well as of the ecclesiastical system ; a man of the world would accept the fact, and a statesman would not desire to have it otherwise.

Lastly, we come to the crowning act of revolt, the fundamental heresy—the denial of transubstantiation. Lancaster, though far from uncultured, was no scholar,

[1] Dated April 1, 1386. Hist. MSS. Com. Ninth Report, App. 54b.

and the metaphysical argument of the impossibility of the existence of substance without accidents, upon which Wycliffe based his denial of the accepted Eucharistic doctrine, must have sounded in his ears like the raving of a madman. Any paltering with so sacred a truth was impossible ; when the enormity of this latest conclusion was put before him, he bade Wycliffe be silent.

To sum up : John of Gaunt in no point differed from the average of religious thought and practice of his day. From the days of Archbishop Stratford onwards there had always been a party jealous of the influence of an episcopal ministerial class. In 1376 events forced on Lancaster the leadership of that party. He had no quarrel with the secular clergy as such, apart from their share in political opposition. The parish priest found him an indulgent landlord ; the monastic orders a munificent patron ; to the friars he was something more, for their leaders looked to him for support, and their armies fought his battles. From them he chose friends and councillors, and to every rank and division of the mendicant army he showed unstinted favour.

He was free on the one hand from any touch of the rationalism which questioned accepted doctrine ; on the other, from cynical indifference to religious duties and observances. Conventional in all things, in none was he more conventional than in religious practice ; though his piety, like that of others then and since, was not inconsistent with a certain laxity of moral practice.

The great issues raised by Wycliffe he did not understand ; could he have done so, he would have viewed the whole scheme of Wycliffe's thought with horror. The early reformation was still-born ; an angel had troubled the waters, but they were not waters of healing. Wycliffe came not to bring peace but a sword. His doctrine, ecclesiastical and civil, was a wild flight of idealism. Lancaster was no enthusiast, but a practical man of the world. With Lollard doctrine he had no sympathy, and it does not mark an inconsistency in the Lancastrian tradition that Henry IV should place upon the statute book the Act "De heretico comburendo," or that Cardinal Beaufort should help at the Council of Constance to burn John Huss.

Whether Wycliffe, led away by enthusiasm for reform, misunderstood Lancaster as Lancaster misunderstood him, and mistook the conventional and conservative politician for an apostle of reform, or whether, keenly observant of the Duke's mode of life as well as of the signs of the times, he was astute enough to use Lancastrian support against a worldly prelacy, and, making friends, like Wykeham, with the mammon of unrighteousness, consented to use for a moment a power which he knew could not be his for long—this depends upon an estimate of the reformer's character which would be out of place here.

On the other hand, the issue which concerns us at present is plain.

The connexion of Lancaster and Wycliffe was a political mistake ; it alienated more support than it gained. It did not divide the Londoners, who continued to hate Lancaster more than any man in England. It infuriated the episcopal party. It was unnatural and perplexing.

Lollardry was from the first a cross current in politics. Corresponding to no existing division of political thought, it only made the confusion of parties worse confounded. The short-lived " unholy alliance " proved to be not only an encumbrance to the Duke himself, but an embarassment to his friends. Knighton, sharing the prejudices of the *religiosi possessionati* and the benefits of Lancastrian bounty, must not allow himself to forget that while Wycliffe is the heresiarch, his supporter is the " pious Duke." Brother Stephen Patrington, who, if he did not write, at least had a hand in much of the

JOHN OF GAUNT

Fasciculi Zizaniorum, while regarding the reformer as
the forerunner of anti-Christ, has no scruple in declaring
that "illustrious prince, gallant soldier and wise councillor, John, Duke of Lancaster," to be a faithful son of the
Church,[1] a judgment which may conceivably be affected
by the fact that Brother Stephen was in receipt of a pension from Wycliffe's patron.[2] Brother Walter Dysse, the
Duke's confessor, and the Bishop of Salisbury, the Duke's
Chancellor, sign the condemnation of Wycliffe's heresies ;
so does John Cuningham, who succeeded Walter Dysse,
and was one of the first "harvesters" who took sickle in
hand to mow down Wycliffe's tares.[3] The Friars, at first
the reformer's friends and afterwards his most inveterate
enemies, turn for support to the supporter of Wycliffe,
and regard the Duke as peculiarly their champion.[4] The
alliance has all the marks of a temporary and make-shift
expedient, adopted in haste, repented of at leisure.

At first a puzzle to friend and enemy, it became understood later, and then those of the Duke's admirers who
wrote a record of the events were bound to use measured
language and choose their words with care. Hence the
caution of the Canon of Leicester and the apparent contradictions of the *Fasciculi.*

In this explanation there is nothing antecedently
improbable. Indeed, it is what might have been expected from the character of the man. The Duke was a
man of expedients, not of principles. In politics as in
warfare he was a good tactician, a bad general. He
could strike hard ; he could not plan ; he won battles,
and lost campaigns. The advocacy of Wycliffe won a
momentary success at immense cost. *Inter alia* it has

---

[1] *Fasc. Ziz.* p. 114.
[2] Confirmation of a grant of an annuity to Brother Stephen
Patryngton. *Patent Roll,* 22 Rich. II, Part 2, Membrane 3.
[3] *Fasc. Ziz.* pp. 286 and 357.
[4] Letter of the four claustral orders (*per Patryngton*) to the
Duke, *Fasc. Ziz.* p. 292.

helped to secure for John of Gaunt five centuries of persistent obloquy.

On the other hand, the story illustrates one quality of the Duke's nature. After 1382, at any rate, Wycliffe's position was clear. Even to the least careful observer the reformer was now a dangerous heretic whose mouth must be closed. But John of Gaunt would not abandon the man who had been led to look to him for protection. The Church was balked of its prey. It touched the Duke's honour to protect John Wycliffe as he would have protected the humblest of those two hundred knights and esquires who had sworn to serve him in peace and war.

Wycliffe was suffered to die in peace.

H

Chapter IX

DEATH OF EDWARD III

IN spite of optimistic assurances in Parliament it
must have been clear that at the end of 1376 Edward
III had not long to live. For a few months after
October 7, when he made his will, naming John of
Gaunt his chief executor,[1] the King lingered on. While
he lived there was one influence and one alone
stronger than that of the Duke. The King's son had one
rival, the King's mistress, for to the end Alice Perrers
preserved her power over her dying lover. The fact was
recognized by all, including William of Wykeham. The
Bishop was a practical man. It was for the interest
of the Church as well as for himself that he should recover
the temporalities of the see. The Bishop went to the
all-powerful favourite and bought her favour.[2] In spite
of Lancaster's protest the confiscated temporalities were
restored. That the Bishop should thus stoop to make
friends with the mammon of unrighteousness has shocked
many good people and all good Wykehamists. The fact
is scarcely open to doubt, but the judgment need not
be too severe. The Bishop was the representative of
a cause, and in a good cause one must make sacrifices.
William of Wykeham sacrificed his pride. Moreover
there was precedent for the course. Should a Bishop be

---

[1] Dated Havering-atte-Bower, 7 Oct. 1376. *Royal Wills*,
59–64.
[2] *Chr. Angl.* 136–7. Itaque *invito duce* redonari sibi tempo-
ralia sua jussit. The evidence of the Monk of St. Albans is here,
I think, conclusive. He would never slander one of his own
party, an enemy of Lancaster.

more punctilious than the Pope himself ?   Who would
dare to cast the first stone, when the head of Christendom
had besought the King's mistress to use her influence in a
personal quarrel ? [1]

This restoration of his persecuted servant was the
last political act of Edward III.   In spite of his feebleness
he was able to hold one last feast of the Garter at Windsor,
and there he made his grandson and heir knight.[2]

After that his strength gradually sank.   The end
came at Sheen on Sunday, June 21, 1377, the jubilee
of his reign.   In spite of the misfortunes of his last years
and one discreditable *liaison* which cast a shadow over his
good fame at the end, Edward never lost the affections
of his people.   Even the chroniclers who lament his
fatal infatuation save their censures for its unworthy
object, and pour out the vials of righteous wrath upon
the heartless and greedy favourite who deserted the King
in his last moments and, if rumour speaks truth, robbed
him of the very rings on his fingers.[3]   As for Edward
himself his faults and shortcomings are forgotten.   The
callous and selfish ambition which embarked England
upon the Hundred Years War did not appear in its true
light to his subjects.   They were dazzled by his victories.
They loved him for his past glories, for his courage and
clemency, his affability and generous, openhanded
character.   His end was edifying, for at the last, the monks
are careful to record, a sincere repentance smoothed the
way to that bourne from which no traveller returns.

---

[1] Jean de Graily had got Roger Beaufort, brother of
Gregory XI, in his possession ; Roger had been his prisoner ever
since the Pope's election.   The Pope writes on his behalf to the
Black Prince, John of Gaunt, Aubrey de Vere, the Prince's
secretary, William of Wykeham, Richard, Earl of Arundel, *and
Alice Perrers.   Papal Letters*, vol. iv. p. 96.

[2] Wals. i. 326.

[3] For the death-bed scene see *Chr. Angl.* p. 142-6, Wals.
i. 326 ; for Edward's character, Murimuth, 225-7.

The King had many qualities which endeared him to his subjects, who soon learned to point the contrast between his martial spirit and the effeminate weakness of his successor.

The glories of the great war were remembered, its failures and miseries forgotten ; its fatal consequences could not be foreseen. Therefore history, which like fortune deals out good and evil things in unequal measure, has consented to deal tenderly with the memory of the third Edward, and Froissart is only expressing the thoughts of his subjects when he says of Edward III : " He had been a good King to them : never had they the like since the time of King Arthur who was aforetime King of England," [1]

Le Roi est mort ; Vive le Roi ! The city of London at least was not slow in declaring its loyalty to the young King. When the news of Edward's condition was known, even before the end came, the city sent a deputation to Prince Richard, who with his mother was staying at Kingston. John Philipot, as spokesman for the citizens, was charged to protest their unwavering loyalty to the person of the heir,[2] to recommend the city to his favour, to entreat him to come to London, and finally to compose the quarrel between the city and the Duke.

The next day a gracious reply was returned, and Lord Latimer, Sir Nicholas Bonde, Sir Simon Burley, and Sir Richard Aderby were sent to London with a formal announcement of Edward's death and the greetings of the new King.

In compliance with the citizens' request the King would shortly come to London. Meanwhile he had already tried to compose the quarrel, and the Duke had submitted

[1] Froissart, K. de L. viii. 389.
[2] *Chr. Angl.* 146-7, Wals. i. 329-30. The words " Qui in proximo eritis noster rex, quem solum regem recognoscimus," etc., are significant.

without reserve to his will. The citizens were invited to do the same.

A storm of opposition greeted this suggestion. The citizens were on their guard; they suspected a trap. Only after six hours' argument, and upon the King's envoys swearing on their honour that submission should not prejudice life, limb or privileges, did the citizens consent.

At length they screwed their courage to the sticking point and went to the young King at Sheen, where Richard received them in the presence of his mother and his uncles and the whole royal family. Lancaster did everything in his power to disarm suspicion. Falling upon his knees before the young King, he entreated him to take the quarrel into his own hands. He even asked pardon for those who were awaiting punishment on account of the late disorders. Then rising, the Duke swore to forget the quarrel, and gave the kiss of peace to each of the city magnates in turn. Such an edifying spectacle moves the contemporary chroniclers to pious thanksgiving. Once more the Monk of Saint Albans [1] loses control of his feelings, and cries out—" Haec est mutatio dextrae Excelsi ! "

On Friday following the Duke met his late enemies at Westminster, and a herald publicly proclaimed the welcome news of the pacification.[2]

Policy required one more reconciliation, and justice cried aloud for one act of restitution.

Richard made peace between his uncle and the Bishop of Winchester, and released Sir Peter de la Mare from prison. The Duke had no choice but to be reconciled.

---

[1] The point of his story, however, is rather spoilt by the fact that it was *not* St. Albans Day, and therefore the Saint's mediation need not be invoked to supplement political causes. *Chr. Angl.* 147-9.
[2] *Chr. Angl.* 150.

To smooth the way for his nephew's accession was the only practical way of rebutting the charges of disloyalty. But he must have been galled at the reception given to the persecuted Speaker of the Commons.

From his prison at Nottingham to London, Sir Peter's journey was a triumphal progress, for persecution, as usual, had made a martyr, and Lancaster had gained nothing by a flagrant act of injustice to a bold political opponent.

For the moment, however, old quarrels were buried, and all parties combined to welcome the new King.

The Duke of Lancaster was not a man to forego any dignity to which his territorial position gave him a claim. There were reasons of policy, however, as well as of etiquette, which induced him to play a prominent part in the coronation. The Council had admitted his legal right as Earl of Leicester to act as High Seneschal of England, as Duke of Lancaster to bear the Curtana on the day of the coronation, and as Earl of Lincoln to carve before the King at table.

All these duties he undertook in person or by deputy. The coronation was the outward and visible expression of the beginning of the new reign. As the Duke had smoothed the way for the accession, he was determined to play his proper part in the ceremonial also.

As High Seneschal his first duty was to hear and decide claims to perform the traditional coronation services. Under the Duke's presidency the Court of Claims began to sit in the White Hall of the Palace at Westminster, near the King's Chapel, on July 9th. As the ceremony itself had been arranged for the 16th this left only a week for the work, and it is not surprising that the Seneschal found himself hard pressed. Out of nineteen claims preferred fourteen were clear, and were granted forthwith. One was ruled out of court, but the remaining four, claims which raised complicated issues of hereditary right, had to be settled "without prejudice" by a provisional ruling.[1]

After the Seneschal himself the most important officers were Thomas of Woodstock, Constable in the right of his wife, a daughter and co-heir of Humphrey de Bohun, the last Earl of Hereford of his name, and Henry Percy, Marshal, an office which in spite of the right of Margaret, Countess of Norfolk, the Crown claimed to dispose of at will. Robert de Vere, Earl of Oxford, although a minor, was allowed to act as the King's Chamberlain—a mark of that friendship which, dating from childhood, was to be the curse of Richard's later years. Among the coronation services one innovation marks the peculiar condition of politics at the time : by Richard's special desire the Mayor was allowed to serve the king with a golden cup and the citizens to serve in the butlery. Even in the ceremonial the spirit of compromise showed itself, for the Mayor served beside his foe Lord Latimer the Almoner. The lion and the lamb lay down together and a little child led them.

The claimants satisfied, or the reverse, London got ready for the ceremony of the 16th.[2]

On the day before the coronation the Peers, with their retinues, and the Mayor and Sheriffs assembled at the gates of the Tower, and amid the blare of trumpets conducted the King down Cheapside and Fleet Street, where fountains were running with wine, and the houses were hung with cloth of gold and silver or hangings of gay colours, to Westminster Palace, while the fickle London crowd, delighted with the gracious bearing of the Seneschal and Marshal, forgot their grudge and for one day cheered Lancaster and Percy as they headed the cortege.

[1] *Munimenta Gildhallae Londoniensis* (Liber Custumarum), p. 456.
[2] *Chr. Angl.* 152–163 ; Wals. i. 331–9 ; Murimuth, 228 ; *Mon. Eve.* i. Froissart. K. de L. viii. 392.

JOHN OF GAUNT

That night the King slept at Westminster Palace. The next morning after hearing mass the procession passed over scarlet cloth, laid down by the King's Almoner, from the great Hall of the Palace to the Abbey.

Even in his tender youth the King seems to have possessed the strange beauty of the Plantagenets, and eye-witnesses described the child dressed in white robes symbolical of his innocence, as "fair among men as another Absalom." [1] Before him were Lancaster with the Curtana, the Earls of March and Warwick with the second sword and the gilt spurs, the Earl of Cambridge and Thomas of Woodstock, each bearing a sceptre surmounted with a dove. The Bishops of St. David's and Worcester, Chancellor and Treasurer respectively, walked before the King, bearing a rich chalice, and the Primate with the Bishops of London and Winchester followed.

Then came the elaborate ceremonial consecrated by tradition for the coronation of an English King. The King takes the oath to keep faith, to preserve and maintain the laws of the realm, in particular those of St. Edward, to do justice and show mercy. He is accepted by acclamation. Solemnly the Primate gives him his blessing. He receives the holy rite of unction. He is invested with the tunic of St. Edward, the sword and bracelet, the robe and the spurs. Finally the crown is placed upon his head and the ring upon his finger. The sceptre is handed to him, and again invoking divine blessings the Primate leads him to the throne. After the enthronement mass is sung; the King makes his offering, receives the Eucharist, confesses, and is absolved.

Among many impressive coronation scenes that of July 16, 1377, is peculiarly moving. The helplessness, the youth and innocence of the child upon whom King Edward's crown had devolved, had done what the will of a grown man could scarcely have effected. For a moment

[1] *Adam of Usk*, 1.

all parties had laid aside their quarrels. The Bishop of Rochester, in his sermon addressed to the city the next day, could hold up before the people the ensample of a life as yet unspotted by the world. But time failed to keep its promises. The King, whose advent was hailed with loyal enthusiasm on every side, could not win and keep his subjects' affection. Generous instincts and childless innocence disappeared in a premature manhood, giving place to callousness, levity and vice. The oath to do justice between man and man and show mercy, to observe the laws and live according to right, was soon to be broken; the reign begun with such bright promise was to end in disaster.

But the future moulded by Richard's yet unformed character could not be foreseen. For the moment London and the Court was given up to rejoicing.

A state banquet closed the coronation day; and before feasting began the King made four grants of peerage. His youngest uncle, Thomas of Woodstock, was made Earl of Buckingham; Guiscard d'Angoulême, Earl of Huntingdon; Thomas Mowbray, Earl of Nottingham, and the Marshal Henry Percy, Earl of Northumberland. Thomas of Woodstock, though a son of Edward III, was far behind his brothers in territorial dignities; he had seen a nephew, Lancaster's son, Henry, Earl of Derby, admitted to the Order of the Garter before him: the Earldom of Buckingham was a tardy recognition of the claims of the blood royal. The other creations show Lancaster's influence and the young King's own preferences. The new Earl of Huntingdon had been his tutor; Mowbray, like Vere, was of his own years and had been brought up with him, while Henry Percy was as yet a firm partisan of the Duke.[1]

[1] At the end of the detailed account of the Coronation in the Liber Custumarum :—Memorandum quod praedictus Rex Castellae et Legionis Dux Lancastriae et Seneschallus Angliae istum processum per manus suas proprias in Cancellarium Domini

JOHN OF GAUNT

Three days later the King, or rather his advisers, named the Council.[1] All interests were represented ; no single party predominated. The royal family was represented by the Earl of Cambridge, a man entirely under his brother's power, but too feeble to have any influence. William Courtenay, Bishop of London, was balanced by Ralf Erghum, Bishop of Salisbury, the Duke's Chancellor ; the rest were the Earls of Arundel and March, Lords Latimer, Cobham, Roger Beauchamp, and Richard Stafford, Sir John Knyvet, Sir Ralph Ferrers, Sir John Devereux and Sir Hugh Segrave. Lancaster himself was too wise to claim a place.

This spirit of compromise which had marked the accession inspired the acts of the young king's first Parliament, which met at Westminster on October 13th.[2] It was undoubtedly an anti-Lancastrian Parliament. A large proportion of the Knights of the Shire who had sat in the " Good " Parliament and had lost their seats in January, were returned again,[3] and Sir Peter de la Mare was again chosen Speaker.

This being so, the Commons showed an altogether extraordinary friendliness to the Duke. Perhaps the correctness of his attitude at the accession had told in his favour ; probably the rumours of disloyalty had not been believed by those who for political purposes had consented to give them currency. At any rate the first act of the Commons was to conciliate their former enemy. Following the precedents set in the last two Parliaments,they prayed that certain peers would form an advisory committee.

Regis liberavit, ibidem in rotulis ejusdem Cancellarii irrotulandum.

[1] *Foed* VII. 161, dated July 20, 1377.

[2] Parliament was summoned by writ dated 4 August, 1 Richard II, for the quinzaine of St. Michael (Dugdale, *Summons*, 29A). *Rot. Parl.* iii. 3–31.

[3] A return of every member of Parliament. *Chr. Angl.* 171 ; Wals. i. 343.

LANCASTER'S MANIFESTO

The name of the "King of Castile and Leon and Duke of Lancaster" headed the list. This gave the Duke his chance. No sooner was the Commons' bill read than Lancaster rose in his place and walked up to the throne. There was a flutter in the House. All parties were anxious for peace, and nervous members wondered what was in store. Falling upon his knees before the boy King, the Duke prayed humbly that he would listen for a while to words which concerned his own person as well as his sovereign.

The Commons had chosen him to be one of their advisors. By the King's favour he would not act as their advisor until he had cleared himself of charges current among the people, charges which touched his honour. Unworthy as he was, he was a son of Edward III, and after the King one of the greatest peers of the realm. The malicious rumours spread by his enemies would, if true (which God forbid) amount to open treason. Until the truth were known he could do nothing. None of his ancestors had ever been traitor ; they had all been true and loyal subjects of the crown. He himself had more to lose by treachery than any other man in England ; apart from this, it would be a strange and marvellous thing if he should so far depart from the traditions of his blood. If any man, whatever his degree, dared to charge him with treason, disloyalty or any act prejudicial to the realm, he was prepared to defend himself with his body as readily as the poorest gentleman in England.[1]

The Duke ended. It was a striking scene—the greatest feudatory of the realm kneeling before the child-king, protesting his innocence, defying his unknown slanderers, and offering to defend his loyalty by wager of battle.

It was a repetition in a hostile parliament of the manifesto, which in the Lancastrian Parliament of

[1] *Rot. Parl.* iii. 5.

January he had issued in the Chancellor's opening speech, and it produced a marked effect. Lords spiritual and temporal crowded round the Duke before the throne and entreated him to be appeased. They were sure that no one would dare to pronounce the charges which he denied. The Commons joined the entreaties of the peers. Could any one doubt that they held the Duke innocent ? Had they not selected him to be their " principal aid, comforter and councillor ? "

With a protest against the nameless authors of these calumnies, the real traitors who were endeavouring to wreck the peace of England, Lancaster allowed himself to be pacified. For himself he was willing to forgive the guilty. He did not ask that any man should be punished for the past. But he urged Parliament to prevent the recurrence of conduct which might imperil the peace and quiet of the realm.

Following up this moderate conduct Lancaster acquiesced in the wishes of the Commons. They petitioned that Acts of Parliament should not be repealed by irregular influence out of Parliament ; that eight members should be added to the Council, that Lord Latimer should be removed and that William Walworth and John Philipot, merchants of London, should be appointed treasurers to receive the monies voted for the war. When the Commons insisted on bringing Alice Perrers to trial, the Duke, so far from interfering, gave evidence against her.[1]

These petitions were granted, and after a liberal vote, two tenths and two fifteenths, Parliament dissolved. Lancaster had offered no opposition. He had put forward no claim to the regency or to a preponderant influence on the council. Leaving the affairs of state to others Lancaster retired for a while from public life.

To avoid responsibility was to avoid suspicion. The

[1] *Rot. Parl.* iii. 13a.

LANCASTER'S RETIREMENT

Duke had other interests in life besides the control of the King's council, the Chancery and the Treasury. What these interests were will appear from a short survey of the Lancastrian estates.

Chapter X

THE LANCASTRIAN ESTATES

" JOHN, by the grace of God, King of Castile and Leon, Duke of Lancaster, Earl of Derby, Lincoln and Leicester, Lord of Beaufort and Nogent, of Bergerac and Roche-sur-Yon, Seneschal of England and Constable of Chester "—such was the style in which Lancaster Herald could proclaim John of Gaunt.

The titular sovereignty of Castile forms one of the most interesting portions of Lancastrian story, and of this we shall speak at length later; the lands in France and Aquitaine deserve at least a passing notice.

On the fringe of the great Lancastrian inheritance lay two seigniories in France, Beaufort and Nogent; and these, with two others, Bergerac and Roche-sur-Yon, which came not by inheritance from Duke Henry, but by grant from Prince Edward, make up the sum of Duke John's territorial interest in France and Aquitaine.[1] Beaufort and its connexion with John of Gaunt have for generations proved a stumbling block and rock of offence to the genealogist. Unfortunately, there is a Beaufort in Anjou, in Artois, in Picardy, in Champagne, in Dauphiné and in Savoy. With this " embarras de choix " compilers of Peerages and others[2] have usually fixed upon Beaufort in Anjou, which has never had the remotest connexion with John of Gaunt.

[1] He had also certain tenements in Calais (Delpit *Collection*, pp. 83, 189, ccxlix; 200, cclxxviii; 202, cclxxx; 208-9, cccvi). In 1489, the Lancastrian tenements in Calais were worth 40*l*. 4*s*. Flemish.

[2] e.g. Collins' *Peerage*, etc., and *Dict. Nat. Biog.* Art. Henry Beaufort. Kervyn de Lettenhove. Froissart, xx. 282, etc..

THE LANCASTRIAN ESTATES

It is perhaps worth while to rescue the name of Beaufort[1] from the limbo of romance.

At the present time in the Canton of Chavanges (Aube), between Châlons and Troyes, there is a village called Montmorency. Before the family of Montmorency held it and gave it their name the village was called Beaufort. In 1270 Blanche of Artois, niece of Saint Louis and wife of Henry III, Count of Champagne and King of Navarre, bought the lordship of Beaufort and of Nogent.[2] Blanche married *en secondes noces* Edmund, Earl of Lancaster, and on Edmund's death Blanche's lands were divided between her second and third sons, Henry, third Earl, and John " of Lancaster." When John died in 1336 without issue, Beaufort and Nogent became the sole property of Henry, third Earl of Lancaster, and passed from him through Duke Henry to Blanche of Lancaster and John of Gaunt.

[1] BEAUFORT AND THE LANCASTRIAN INHERITANCE

Henry III. Count of = Blanche of Artois = Edmund, Earl of Lancaster,
Champagne; King   bought the lord-   Count Palatine of Cham-
of Navarre, m. 1269,   ship of Beaufort   pagne and Brie, m. January,
d. 22 July, 1274   1270 (June)   1276

Thomas, Earl   Henry, Earl   John "of Lancaster," = Aalis de
of Lancaster   of Lancaster, Lord Lord of Beaufort,   Joinville
                     of Beaufort,   d. 1336   (no issue)
                     1336–45

Henry, Duke of Lancaster,
Lord of Beaufort

Blanche = John of Gaunt,
Lord of Beaufort

[2] Lancaster's lease quoted below (L. 962) describes the town as Nogent-sur-Marne. There are two towns of this name on the Marne, 'Nogent-sur-Marne' *arr.* Sceaux. *cant.* Charenton, and 'Nogent-l'Artaud,' on the left bank of the Marne *arr.* Château Thierry *cant.* Charly. It was the second which belonged to the Count of Champagne. See Pigeotte, *Seigneurs de Beaufort*, 16, 17.

It is clear that John of Gaunt could not in the nature of things exercise much influence in an outlying part of the Lancastrian inheritance situated in the heart of what was for the greater part of his life an enemy's country.

His lordship perhaps saved the lands from devastation when Champagne was raided time after time by English armies marching from Calais to the South, but there is no evidence that he ever set foot in either of the towns which called him lord,[1] or ever spent a day in the castle where romance tells us that his children were born. A charter still exists, however, by which the Duke takes under his protection the Abbot and Convent of Chapelle aux Planches, who, in 1364, were being persecuted in a local feud, and grants the Abbot licence to affix the arms of Lancaster to the houses of the Convent, in token of his favour.[2]

Beaufort only once draws upon itself the attention of history during the Hundred Years War. That is upon the outbreak of the hostilities in 1369.

The duke was unfortunate in his choice of a tenant, for John Wyn, to whom in 1365 he had leased the castles and lordships of Beaufort and Nogent for ten years, at a yearly rental of £100 sterling,[3] turned French and sold his trust.[4] Wyn was a friend of Owen of Wales, Froissart tells us ; that he had a reputation for gallantry we may perhaps infer from his nickname " Poursuivant d'amour," but little else is known of the last tenant who held Beaufort and Nogent of a Lancastrian overlord except the treason with which Beaufort and Nogent pass into the

[1] He passed near his lands in 1373.
[2] Dated the Savoy, October 28, 1364, Lalore *Cartulaires de Troyes*, iv. 85–6. The mandate is addressed " Aux premiers sergens de nos terres de Beaufort *et autres en France*."
[3] Indenture dated Leicester, June 6, 39 Ed. III. 1365. [P.R.O Series L (Duchy of Lancaster Royal Charters and ancient deeds) 962].
[4] Froissart, K. de L. viii. 324–5, 539. Boutiot, *Histoire de Troyes*.

hands of the Kings of France, become part of the royal domain, and disappear from Lancastrian story. If it had not been gravely stated that the " Beauforts " must have been born before 1369, when the castle was lost, it would scarcely be necessary to add that no argument as to the date of the *liaison* with Katherine Swynford can be based on the Duke's tenure. Katherine never saw Beaufort, and her children were certainly not born there. The explanation of the choice of this name for the Duke's illegitimate family must be found in the fact that among the many territorial titles which came by descent to John of Gaunt it was found convenient to choose one which would not prejudice the rights of his legitimate heir. The names of the English Honors being impossible, it was found convenient to assume for them the name of a French seigniory long since lost, and after the legitimation to retain a name long familiar to England, and not unknown to the chivalry of Europe.

Bergerac and Roche-sur-Yon were both granted to John of Gaunt by the Black Prince on the same day, October 8, 1370, just after the destruction of Limoges.[1] Both were granted to the Duke and his heirs male in tail, with reversion to Prince Edward as overlord. The French soon got possession of Roche, but while the Duke held it, the town was worth 500 marcs a year to his exchequer.[2]

Bergerac, as well as being a source of revenue, was a place of considerable strategical importance, for it commanded the Dordogne, and the lines of communication between Bordeaux and central and southern France.

Captured in 1345 by Henry Duke of Lancaster,

---

[1] Delpit *Collection*, ccxviii. and ccxix.

[2] Indenture dated La Rochelle, September 25, 1371, leasing the lordship to Sir Thomas Percy and Sir John Harpeden, Seneschals of Poitou and Saintonge and to Sir Regnault Vivonne. Delpit *Collection*, ccxxxi.

Bergerac had been granted in tail to him and his heirs male by Edward III two years later.[1]

Having reverted to the Crown on Duke Henry's death, Bergerac, being parcel of the Duchy of Aquitaine, came into the hand of Prince Edward, and by the grant of 1370 John of Gaunt held it with the same powers and privileges as his father-in-law had held it from Edward III. When the Black Prince renounced the Principality Edward III renewed the grant,[2] and one of the first acts of Richard's minority was to confirm it.[3]

But it was one thing to hold the town by charter and another to hold it by the sword, and the importance of Bergerac as a strategical position exposed it to the brunt of all the fighting in the South. Anjou and du Guesclin took the town after a great siege in September, 1377,[4] and after that date it was taken and retaken a dozen times by French and English forces, until in the end it shared the fortunes of the whole Gascon dependency of the English Crown. In 1381 the Duke makes a charge upon its revenues, to reward one of his feudatories who had suffered in the wars, but the town was then in the hands of the French, and the grant is conditional on its recovery.[5] At different times three members of the family of Buade were charged with its custody. A certain Heliot Buade was appointed Governor in 1371,[6] and ten years later Pierre Buade and

[1] June 1, 1347. Cf. Delpit *Collection*, clii.
[2] November 8, 1376. Delpit *Collection*, cclxvii:
[3] September 15, 1377. Delpit *Collection*, cclxviii.
[4] L'an m.ccc.lxxvii a iii de Setembre lo duc d'Ango e mossenhor Bertran de Claquin Conestable de Fransa prengoren Bragueyrac Sancta Fe e Castelhon de Peyregorc e aprop anet a Basax. *Petite Chronique de Guyenne* § 73. The siege began August 22.
[5] Warrant to the Governor, Receiver and other officers of the town of Bergerac in favour of Mondon Ebrad, Esquire, dated Hertford, May 6, 1381. Register II. f. 97.
[6] Warrant dated Montpont, January 15, 1371. Delpit *Collection* ccxxv. Gift to Heliot Buade, Captain of Bergerac, April 28, 51

Miot Buade appear as Governor and Châtelain respectively. Their loyalty is not above suspicion. The Duke thought they had an understanding with the enemy, and commanded them at their peril to restore their trust, appointing Bertongat de la Bret to supersede them.[1] Whether Bertongat recovered the stronghold is doubtful, but as late as 1395 the Duke appears to have been in possession, for it was at Bergerac that he received the French envoys in that year.

The history of the town with its vigorous civic life and its military importance is rich in interest; and John of Gaunt knew its value, and he speaks of the town " come de ville et chastel que nous aviens bien pres au cuer." In the great Cowcher book of the Duchy of Lancaster, among a series of richly illuminated blazons of his lordship, the arms of Bergerac mays till be seen : " Deux pattes de griffon de sable sur un champ d'or."

Leaving these outposts, let us advance to the citadel itself, and examine the foundation of the Duke's greatness, the broad and solid basis of territorial power upon which was built his preeminence in English politics. The bulk of his lands, as has been seen, came to him by inheritance ; they were the fiefs of Edmund Crouchback, the broad acres of Ferrers Montfort, Lacy, and Chaworthe—the accumulated result of lavish royal grants and a succession of politic marriages.

But though the Lancastrian patrimony formed the bulk, it was not the whole of the Duke's possessions.

In 1360, after the death of Queen Dowager Isabella, Edward III granted to his son the castle, town and Honor of Hertford, and the towns of Beyford, Essendon, and

Edw. III ; payment to Arnald Buade, Captain of the Castle and Townof Bergerac (Duchy of Lancs.). Accounts Various, Bundle III. No. I,) Confirmation of indenture of service with Arnald Buade, *Rot. Pat.* 22 Ric. II.

[1] Commission and warrants dated Hertford, May 6, 1381. Delpit *Collection*, cclxxxii. and cclxxxiii. and cclxxxiv:

Hertingfordbury, "with all their members and appurtenances, and the endowments and issues thereunto belonging." [1]

The object of the grant was to provide the Earl of Richmond, as he then was, with a residence until he should inherit some other dwelling befitting his station. But when the Earl of Richmond had become Duke of Lancaster and the master of the Savoy, he still retained his Honor of Hertford, and Hertford Castle was to the last one of his favourite residences.

This addition is inconsiderable in relation to the total of the Duke's estates ; not so the next.

The Honor of Richmond had been the first appanage granted to John of Gaunt. The Earldom and Honor since the Conquest had belonged to the family of Montfort, which, besides claiming the Dukedom of Brittany in France, had also taken a place in the ranks of the English baronage. In 1372, to attach John de Montfort, who was wavering between England and France, definitely to the English cause, it was resolved to restore the Earldom and Honor to the original holders. It was found to be " for the advantage of the King and the quiet and honour of the whole realm " of England that the Earldom and Honor of Richmond should be restored, and John, " like a grateful son, preferring his father's pleasure and the honour and convenience of the kingdom to his own private advantage," surrendered lands and title. Such sacrifice did not go unrewarded. He received in exchange the castle of Pevensey, the castle, Honor, and manor of Tickhill, and of Knaresborough. and the castle and manor of the High Peak, together

---

[1] *Record Report*, xxxi. App. p. 32. The charter is dated May 20, 1360. It was renewed October 8, 1376 (ibid. p. 37). Great Cowcher, 228 (1, 2 and 4). The manors of Beyford and Essendon more than once had been granted in the twelfth and thirteenth centuries to the Lord Treasurer of England.

with manors, franchises, and advowsons in half a dozen counties, Nottingham, Huntingdon, Cambridge, Norfolk, Suffolk and Sussex.[1]

These two additions, the Honor of Hertford, and the Honors of Tickhill, Knaresborough and the High Peak and the rest form the greater part of the second Duke's additions to the Lancastrian patrimony, but throughout the reign of his father and that of his nephew, the Duke's possessions were in one way or another swelled from time to time by royal bounty.

The mere extent of lands, however, extraordinary as it was, would never have given to the Lancastrian inheritance its peculiar distinctiveness. The Duke is differentiated from his compeers as much in the nature as in the extent of his power.

In 1377 he was Duke and Count Palatine of Lancaster. As for the title of Duke it meant nothing more than a certain primacy of dignity among the lords temporal. When Edward III made his eldest son Duke of Cornwall in 1333, the title was new to England. The creation of Duke Henry in 1351 was the second precedent, and the creation of John of Gaunt in 1362 is the third. A few years later the title used so sparingly by Edward III was scattered broadcast by the prodigal hand of his grandson, and Richard II's *Dukètti* or "Dukelings" made this cheapened dignity ridiculous in the eyes of all good conservatives. The title as such was "vox et praeterea nihil." A breath could make it and unmake it. At the most, before the lavish creations of

---

[1] Hardy, *Charters*, viii. dated June 25, 1372. Cf. *Parl. Petit* 4678. *Foed*, VI. 728–737 ; Gt. Cowcher, 222 (1) ; the Earldom was given to Montfort on July 20. *Foed*. Warrant to the Receiver of Richmond to bring all the accounts to London, May 13, 1372.

Some of the rolls appear to have gone astray. Warrant to pay to men to go and search for them, Aug. 30, 1372.

The search appears to have been successful. Warrant to deliver muniments, standards and measures to the Duke of Brittany, February 18, 1373. Register, I. f. 151, 174.

Richard II, it could call attention to an existing pre-eminence. It did not create that preeminence.

The title of Duke then is comparatively unimportant. As for the Duchy of Lancaster, it did not exist. It may seem at first sight a paradox, but it is none the less true that in the modern sense the Duchy of Lancaster did not and could not exist in the lifetime of John of Gaunt. When the Duke in letters and warrants speaks of his "Duchy of Lancaster," he always means not the sum total of his vast possessions but merely one portion of them—the County of Lancaster ; before 1377, the county pure and simple, and after 1377, the County Palatine. One and the same officer is referred to now as the Receiver " in Lancashire," now as the Receiver " of the County of Lancaster," now as the Receiver of " the Duchy of Lancaster."

It was only after the Dukes of Lancaster became Kings of England that the Duchy, as distinct from the County Palatine, came to exist. Then Henry IV, desiring to mark off the princely inheritance which came to him by hereditary right, from the royal estate, which he had acquired by usurpation, conquest or election, or by all together (he was careful not to distinguish), gave a unity to his father's lands which did not exist in his father's lifetime : lands in Sussex or Yorkshire which would now be spoken of as " parcel of the Duchy of Lancaster," would in the life of John of Gaunt have been referred to as " parcel of the Honor of Eagle," or " parcel of the Honor of Tickhill, or of Knaresborough," held by the Duke of Lancaster in chief.

Remembering then that the " Duke " of Lancaster is only the more dignified style of the Earl of Lancaster, and that for present purposes the Duchy of Lancaster means, in 1377, no more than the County of Lancaster, which county was also a County Palatine, we must examine the nature of the first great source of the Duke's power and wealth—the Palatinate.

In earlier days, when England was threatened by invasion from over sea, and was hard pressed by enemies on her own borders, it had been found highly convenient to allow the feudatories, whose territorial power lay in the districts most exposed to attack, certain powers and privileges of royalty. Hence the erection of the Counties Palatine.

But even in those days of insecurity the creation of a Palatinate had been recognized as a dangerous remedy, and measures had been taken to limit the risk. The Palatinate of Chester, for instance, soon became a royal appanage, never going further out of the King's hand than to the hand of the heir-apparent.

In 1351 Edward III recognised the debt which he and England owed to his cousin, Henry of Lancaster, by erecting the county of Lancaster into a Palatinate. The grant was for life only, and therefore became legally extinct in 1361.

The position of Duke Henry did not differ greatly from that of his son-in-law, and John of Gaunt was determined to regain all that his predecessor had held. Ever since his succession he had exercised one act of regality : he had nominated the Sheriffs of the County of Lancaster.[1] In 1377 he recovered the whole of the *jura regalia* conceded to his predecessor, and after an abeyance of sixteen years the Palatinate was again called into existence, and again the grant was for the Duke's life.

John of Gaunt, possibly, had his own reasons for seeking this aggrandizement : if ever there were to be a repetition of the " Good " Parliament it might be convenient to have a quasi-royal jurisdiction in the North, where he might entrench himself against his enemies.

[1] Reg. I. 48, 65, etc.

JOHN OF GAUNT

What had been granted to Duke Henry as the reward of state service was obtained by Duke John to satisfy his ambition and to guard against contingencies. But the concession made in 1351, equally with that made in 1377, was politically indefensible. For the Palatinate of Lancaster no necessity could be adduced, military or political. It was and always has been an anachronism. It never had a *raison d'être*, and has never served a useful purpose; it was a glaring example of Edward III's indifference to constitutional considerations, if not of his incapacity in statesmanship, for the step was a departure from the sound policy of Henry II and Edward I— the statesmanlike effort to build up a central system of royal justice and administration.

If the old idea of a Palatinate had still had any significance, a case might perhaps have been made out for erecting on the southern borders of Wales, in Hereford, Monmouth, Glamorgan, and Carmarthen, where Lancaster held a group of fortresses of the first rank, a palatinate jurisdiction, to join through the lands of the Earls of March with the Northern Palatinate of Chester. A still more plausible case might have been made out by the Percies for a Palatinate in Northumberland. At least the lords of Alnwick could plead a real danger on the Scottish border. But the Scots never got so far as the Duke's lands ; if they crossed the border at the northern end of the Cheviots they ravaged Northumberland ; if they marched across the southern border they overran Cumberland, and Westmorland. Berwick, Carlisle, and Penrith were attacked : but the Duke's castles of Lancaster and Hornby never stood a siege, still less Clitheroe and Liverpool.

Politically, therefore, the Palatinate of Lancaster was useless, and could only be harmful. The charter of 1377 was an act of retrogression. To measure the extent of that retrogression the question must be asked :

THE LANCASTRIAN ESTATES

What were the rights and privileges appertaining to a Count Palatine ?

Let the royal charter of donation speak for itself.[1]

It opens with the usual preamble, a mere matter of form, reciting the conspicuous merits of the grantee, his strenuous goodness, excellent wisdom and readiness to serve the King with labour and charges, and his intrepid exposure to the dangers of war—merits for which the benefit and honour now bestowed are some, howbeit an inadequate, reward.

Then we come to business. " Of certain knowledge and with cheerful heart, with the assent of the prelates and nobles in Parliament assembled," the King grants for himself and his heirs, " that for the whole of his life John Duke of Lancaster may have within the county of Lancaster his chancery and his writs to be sealed under his seal to be deputed for the office of chancery ; his justices to hold as well the pleas of the Crown, as all other pleas whatsoever touching the common law and the cognizance thereof, and all manner of execution to be made by his writs and his ministers there, and all other liberties and *jura regalia* pertaining to a Count Palatine, as freely and entirely as the Earl of Chester is well known to obtain within the County of Chester."

Certain *regalia*, however, are reserved by the Crown. The Count Palatine shall not have the tenths and fifteenths granted by Parliament and Convocation ; his jurisdiction shall not preclude the King from pardoning those condemned to lose life or limb ; it shall not derogate from the " superiority and power of correcting those things which shall have been erroneously done in the Courts of the Count Palatine." In other words, the King reserves for himself Parliamentary subsidies, the royal prerogative of pardon and royal jurisdiction in cases of error.

[1] Hardy, *Charters*, ix. (Feb: 28, 1377).

All other *regalia* are handed over to the Duke. Not only, the grant continues, shall the Duke nominate his own justices ; he shall also choose at the King's mandate two knights of the shire and two burgesses for every borough to sit in Parliament ; he shall choose and appoint collectors of subsidies voted by Parliament.[1]

From February, 1377, for the rest of the Duke's life, there is to be one Court of Chancery at Westminster, and another at Lancaster. Side by side with the King's justices are the justices of the County Palatine, the nominees of the Duke, holding office by and during his pleasure.

To " cut off all ambiguity," and to make general terms clear by special and express terms, a further charter[2] declares that the Count Palatine shall have his Exchequer and Barons of the Exchequer and exercise within the county all manner of jurisdictions, profits, and commodities, which would otherwise have pertained to the King : he is to appoint his justices in eyre for pleas of the forest and all other justices for all manner of other pleas touching the assize of the forest, etc.

These are extensive powers. For the life of the Duke England is dismembered. For all purposes of justice, finance and administration the county of Lancaster is severed from the body politic. Within its limits the King is dethroned ; the Count Palatine is set up in his place.

The grant is for life. Thirteen years later, the same

[1] For the Duke's commissions to his officers to levy taxes voted by Parliament in West Derbyshire, Leylandshire, Amoundernesse, Lonsdale, Blackburnshire and Salfordshire, see *Record Report*, xl. App. (No. 4), 18, 30, 46, 53, 71 ; and for the selection of the Knights of the Shire, see Register *passim*.

In every county except Lancashire the sheriff makes proclamations on the royal mandamus. The sheriff of Lancaster waits for the Duke's mandamus (ibid. 8).

[2] Dated November 10, 2 Richard II (1378) Hardy, *Charters*, xiii. *Rot. Pat.*

powers are entailed with the title of Duke of Lancaster, upon John and his heirs male for ever.[1] So long as the Duke's issue remains the dismemberment of England is to continue. It was unnecessary: Richard II, who makes the grant in fee tail, loses the *regalia* of Lancaster, and with them the realm of England, and Henry, third Duke and Count Palatine of Lancaster, is Henry IV of England.

Such a result was not foreseen by the dying King, whose last political act had been to give his assent to the Charter of February 28 ; nor by those who were present when "on April 17, 1377, at the Savoy, near Westminster, John, King of Castile and Leon, Duke of Lancaster, in the presence of Sir Robert de Swylyngton, Knight, Sir Thomas de Hungerford, Knight, and others of the same King's household, in the chapel built within his mansion there did constitute Thomas de Thelwall, Clerk, his Chancellor within the Duchy and County of Lancaster, and upon his taking the oath, the same King with his own hand delivered to the said Thomas his great seal for the governance of the regality of the County Palatine."[2]

Three days later the new Chancellor set the great seal to the first writ issuing from the Chancery of John of Gaunt—a proclamation notifying to the Sheriff of Lancaster the names of the Duke's justices, fixing the date of the sessions, and ordering the Sheriff to give notice that all and singular persons wishing to prosecute their business before the justices should be present on that day.

The first of the twenty-two years of Duke John's regality had begun.

But the *regalia* of the County Palatine do not exhaust the extraordinary powers enjoyed by John of Gaunt as an

---

[1] Charter dated Feb. 16, 1390. Hardy *Charters*, xiv.
[2] *Record Report*, xxxii. App. (1).

English subject. The Palatine franchises are sharply differentiated from the others ; they are the most important, but they are confined to the territorial limits of the County of Lancaster, and there are other extraordinary liberties and franchises to be considered, for not only in relation to England, but also in relation to the sum total of the Duke's lands, the County Palatine forms an *imperium in imperio.*

The source of these other exceptional liberties is, as before, the King's grace and favour : they are built up by a succession of royal grants.

By charter,[1] dated May 7, 1342, certain exceptional franchises had been granted in tail to Henry, third Earl of Lancaster. Seven years later the grant was reconsidered. Henry, son of the grantee, had no male issue. As the law stood the lands and the franchises which they carried would descend to his daughters and co-heirs, Maude and Blanche. Both were mere children, and no one could foretell the consequence of their marriage. It was not surprising, therefore, that the grant appeared to have been made to the " exceeding damage and excessive disherison " of the Crown. The Earl surrendered the grant-in-tail : it was formally cancelled and annulled, and he received in exchange a similar grant for life only.[2]

A fresh grant [3] bestowed the same franchises on John of Gaunt and Blanche, in respect of their share of the inheritance, actual and prospective, and, further, upon the death of Maude and the re-union of the inheritance the grant was extended to cover her share also.[4]

But the matter was not allowed to rest there. The surrender and cancellation of the charter of May 7, 1342,

---

[1] Hardy, *Charters,* i.
[2] Ibid. ii.
[3] Ibid. iv. dated November 13, 1361.
[4] Ibid. v. May 12, 1362.

was, of course, dictated by the fear of allowing an extensive source of wealth and power to descend to persons unknown, perhaps friends, possibly enemies of the Crown. Now that the actual course of events had placed the lands in the power of a member of the royal family, the danger disappeared.

Hence a new charter,[1] declaring the surrender by Earl Henry, and consequent cancellation of a grant in fee-tail duly passed under the great seal of England, to be null and void, and renewing the grant to John, Duke of Lancaster, in its original form and extent, viz., in fee-tail, and applying to the whole of the lands held by the original grantee, Earl Henry, on May 7, 1342.

A subsequent charter[2] dating, be it noted, from the last days of the dying King, bestowed upon his all-powerful son and minister similar liberties to those thus recovered for the Lancastrian lands, in respect of the fiefs which the Duke had received in exchange for the Honor of Richmond.

Such is the history of the grants ; now for the franchises and liberties themselves.

The golden age of feudal law is, by the middle of the fourteenth century, passing away if it is not past, but still the main characteristic of feudal ideas holds good : jurisdiction and property have not yet become differentiated ; in surrendering the first the king surrenders the second. Edward III adds to his son's sources of income by increasing his jurisdiction ; in giving him new franchises he gives him new revenues.

To name these franchises runs through the gamut of feudal tenure ; their names exhaust the vocabulary of the law books.

The Duke and his men are quit of paviage, passage,

---

[1] Dated July 14, 1364, Hardy, *Charters*, vii.
[2] Dated June 4, 1377. Hardy, *Charters*, x. Cf. *Parl. Petition*, 4679.

payage, lastage, stallage, tallage, carriage, pesage, picage, and groundage. He has the return of all writs and summons of the Exchequer ; attachment of pleas of "withernam" and pleas of the Crown and of all pleas whatever ; he has fines and amercements, fines for licence to agree, chattels of felons, fugitives, and condemned persons ; infangthef and outfangthef, year, day, waste, estrepements and murders, assay and assize of wine and bread, waifs and strays, wreck flotsam and jetsam, deodand, and that most coveted of royal liberties—treasure trove. To deal with these terms which denote rights, some of which have passed away and some of which are with us still, in the concrete—this is what they mean.

If any of the Duke's men or tenants "made fine," or were amerced in any of the royal courts, wheresoever it might be, the fines and amercements went not to the King but to the Duke. Needless to add, the Duke's men and tenants, like the men of other tenants in chief, were being amerced in the King's courts on all possible occasions. If any of the Duke's men were convicted of felony, or fled from justice, "not being willing to stand his trial," or if for any cause he were condemned to lose life, limb, or chattels, those chattels, which, without proof of a claim of franchise, would have gone to the King's exchequer, went in virtue of this grant to the Duke.

It must be remembered here that in the fourteenth century felony was by no means the comparatively rare offence which it has become to later law : convictions of felony are matters of constant occurrence. High and low, layman and cleric, found themselves condemned on a charge of felony ; or else, "not willing to stand their trial," fled from the arm of the law—if they could not reach sanctuary—to the woods. The Duke's register and the patent rolls of the Palatinate under his regality, for the years which they cover, are crowded with instances ; usually the felony was pardoned, and pardon, it goes without saying, meant a consideration to the Duke's exchequer.

Again the Duke and his men and tenants are quit of the oppressive tolls which like many other forms of indirect taxation were more successful in hindering commerce than in benefiting the Exchequer.

Once more : no sheriff, bailiff, or other royal officer could enter the lands and fees of the Duke (within the limits prescribed by the charters) to exact the writs and summonses of the King's exchequer and to make attachment of pleas, this, save in the case of default, being done by the Duke's officers.

So far we have been dealing with the exceptional liberties and franchises, sources of revenue and sources of power, enjoyed by John of Gaunt, including both those confined to the County Palatine of Lancaster and those pertaining to the whole of the lands held by him in chief.

Both these are exceptional in the sense that they were called into existence by specific royal grant ; without such acts of royal favour they would not have existed, at least not for the Duke.

Now let us consider the ordinary sources of revenue and power which the land carried with it. If wealth were merely the power of commanding pleasures and comforts, this would scarcely be worth doing, but in this age wealth and political power were intimately associated with each other, and a survey of the Duke's estates is a survey of his power. It explains an importance which otherwise he would not have possessed, and it shows by the way the extraordinary number of people who in one way or another, directly or indirectly, found their lives and their fortunes bound up with those of the great Duke of Lancaster.

We are now examining the first head in the ducal budget —issues of land in England and Wales.[1]

---

[1] See Appendix iv. p. 447.

These, the ordinary sources of revenue, are three : feudal incidents, ordinary feudal jurisdiction, and the profits issuing from the land itself and the things on it.

John of Gaunt still receives the old feudal profits incident alike to the life of the tenant and to the life of the lord.

When Henry, Earl of Derby, is eleven years old, the Duke levies an aid " for knighting his eldest son." [1] In 1372, when every baron of England is preparing for the military expedition which failed so ignominiously to relieve Thouars, the Duke levies an aid "*pour fille marier*," [2] though at the time Philippa of Lancaster was twelve years old and there was no question of betrothing her.   Again, more than once when the French wars had drained even the Duke's resources to the dregs, and when he had borrowed wherever money was to be raised, the Duke levies a general aid from all his tenants in " relief of his great necessities."   A reasonable aid is asked of the free tenants as an act of grace ; the Duke orders his bondmen to be seized with their chattels until they have satisfied his officers. [3]

Again, on the other hand, every tenant holding of the Duke paid a " relief " on succeeding to his lands ; at his death the wardship of his lands and of his heir or heiress passed to the overlord. This wardship was an asset : it could be farmed for so many marcs down, or it could be used instead of a pension or gift to reward faithful service. The marriage equally had a money value : if passion beguiled a minor into matrimony without the

---

[1] *Record Report,* **xxxii.** App. (1), 16, mandate to the sheriff dated May 20, second year of the regality, i.e. 1378.

[2] Reg. I. f. 51.

[3] In the Duchy of Lancaster bondmen preserved their servile condition longer as a class than in any other part of England. Large numbers were emancipated in the reign of Elizabeth, on payment of an extortionate fine to a royal patentee.

Duke's permission, he must sue for pardon and pay a fine ![1]

With the feudal incidents goes feudal jurisdiction. Wherever among the Duke's innumerable manors the manorial court is held its profits belong to him ; often the jurisdiction of a group of manors has become absorbed in that of the hundred or wapentake : the Duke has hundreds and wapentakes and takes the profits of their courts.

Again we must not forget that the Duke is one of the largest proprietors of ecclesiastical patronage in England : there are plentifully scattered up and down the Duke's lands, abbeys, priories, hospitals and churches, to which the Duke presents, and in such cases the new Prior or Abbot must, unless a charter of immunity can be produced, pay a relief to Lancaster as lord.[2]

Lastly, we come to the land itself

The Duke's interest consists, as usual, in the profits to be derived from the demesne lands, and the right to claim certain services or certain rents or both from tenants free and unfree.

But John of Gaunt's rent roll is not a simple affair : as well as the " free customs and liberties," and in addition to the " manors, hundreds, and wapentakes," there are the issues of " hamlets, meadows, pannage, herbage, fisheries, moors, marshes, turbaries, chaces, parks, woods and warrens, fairs and markets."

The Duke being lord of some hundreds of manors was necessarily an absentee landlord, and it may be of interest to observe the fiscal machinery whereby he was able to receive these complicated " issues of lands in England and Wales."

---

[1] *Record Report*, xl. App. No. 4, 29, 71, etc.
[2] *Sedes vacantes* ought, of course, normally to be *in manu Regis*, but in one of two cases the Duke got the profits, e.g. Hertford. Reg. II. f. 55. Cf. II. f. 30.

I

He might put a bailiff or provost in charge of a manor or a group of manors, and this officer would account directly for its proceeds, or he might lease its profits "at farm" for a money rent. Following the usual practice, the Duke combined both systems as occasion served. He leased the manor in most cases for a money rent, i.e. the lessee paid so much per annum to the Duke and took the ordinary profits; but when the lease expired, or when for one reason or another a lease was inexpedient, he farmed the demesne land through a reeve or bailiff. In both cases, of course, the seignorial perquisites accrued to the Duke, being in normal cases outside the terms of the lease.

This raises the further question, Who were the officers responsible for the administration of the great Lancastrian estates ?

The men of the highest rank in the Duke's service were those who kept his castles and his forests.

More than thirty castles were held by John of Gaunt in fee, and as if these were not enough he had also the ward of three royal castles—Chester, Hereford, and Queenborough.

Down in the South, in the Honor of Eagle, lay the Conqueror's old castle of Pevensey, an important post when year after year privateers from Normandy came over to harry the Sussex coast.

Queenborough,[1] began by Edward III in 1361, was in the Duke's custody.[2] It commanded the entrance to the Thames, and formed one of the strongest naval bases on the Kentish coast.

Hertford was not a strong place; the rebels did what they liked there in 1381. Being primarily residential and not military, the castle had no constable, but was

---

[1] 1361. Rex abundans auro coepit aedificare castrum insigne in insula Shipey. *Cont. Eulog.* 333.
[2] Reg. II. f. 120.

placed under the bailiff who had the management of the Savoy.

With these three exceptions, Pevensey, Queenborough, and Hertford, the Duke's castles lay in the North and West. They fall into three great groups, those of the Welsh border, the Midlands, and the North. Draw a line across England from the mouth of the Severn to the Wash, and to the north of it there are scarcely a score strongholds of importance out of the Duke's hands.

In Monmouthshire, Whitecastle, Monmouth, Skenfrith, and Grosmont form a buttress against the Welsh—the last bound up in more ways than one with the story of the Lancastrian House, for at Grosmont the Good Duke Henry was born, and its Welsh name Rhôslwyn, the castle on the rose-clad hill, first suggested, it is said, the red rose of Lancaster.

These four castles are flanked on the north by Hereford, impregnable in its marshes, another royal castle in the Duke's ward; on the south by the strongholds of Carmarthen and Glamorgan—Kidwelly, Iskennyn, Carreg Cennen, and Ogmore. In the days when Welsh disaffection had been a standing menace to the peace of the realm, the command of these places had been a matter of the first importance; now Wales was pacified, but the Duke always kept a firm grip of them. No sooner has the news of the rising reached him, in June, 1381, than a courier is riding in hot haste to the south to warn the constables of his castles on the Welsh border.

Leaving Hereford, if Lancaster rode round the southern bend of the Malvern hills, where William Langland as a young man had dreamt dreams and seen the vision of Piers the Ploughman, past Evesham, where his great-grandfather had crushed Simon de Montfort; or again, if he rode to the north across Worcestershire by the Shropshire border, he would find himself once more within range of his own strong walls—the second group, the castles of the Midlands stretching out with unbroken continuity to the North.

Tutbury, Newcastle-under-Lyme, Halton, Chester (the third royal castle held in ward), Kenilworth and Leicester, Melbourne and the High Peak, Higham Ferrers, Lincoln and Bolingbroke, Liverpool, Clitheroe, Lancaster and Hornby, Tickhill, Pontefract, Knaresborough, and Pickering—all these were garrisoned by the Duke's men, and held by his officers, and far up in the North his banner waved from the walls of Dunstanburgh in the midst of the Percy country, and Liddell by the Scottish border. This represents a power which no other feudatory of the Crown could rival, and more than once Lancaster was to find his castles a very present help in time of trouble. To each castle he appointed a constable, a knight or esquire who was entitled to the wages of his office, " with twenty shillings for a robe " of the Duke's livery, and two pence a day for a porter. The constable was responsible for the military efficiency of his castle ; he stocked it with artillery and saw that his garrison had bows and sheaves of arrows enough : he superintended the repairs of its walls and the new works planned by his master—the most lavish and inveterate builder of his age. In times of danger he answered for it that no one passed the gates without express mandate under the Duke's privy seal. In time of peace and quiet, too, he might have the ward of civil prisoners, defaulting debtors and other evildoers, until the justices in eyre arrived and assizes claimed their victims.

The ward of castles being a military service ranks first in dignity, but next to the profession of arms venery is the most serious and respected pursuit of the times.

Was there ever a Plantagenet who did not love the deer ? John Plantagenet was no degenerate scion of the race whose passion for hunting is written plain in

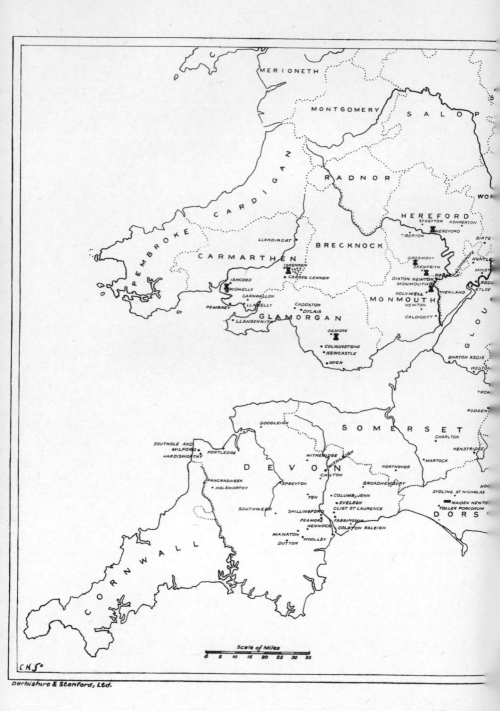

MERIONETH

MONTGOMERY

SALOP

RADNOR

WOR

HEREFORD

STRETTON ASHPERTON
TIBERTON HEREFORD

CARDIGAN

PEMBROKE

LLANDINGAT

BRECKNOCK

BIRTS

GROSMONT HUNTLE
SKENFRITH MINST
DIXTON NEWTON HARDCK ROO
MONMOUTH ETLOE
NEWLAND

CARMARTHEN

ISKENNEN
CARREG CENNEN

ISKCOED
KIDWELLY

CARNWALLON
LLANELLY
PEMBREY LLANELLY

CADOXTON
DYLAIS

MONMOUTH

HOLYWELL
NEWTON

GLAMORGAN

CALDICOTT

GLOU

LLANGENNITH

OSMORE
COLWINSTONE
NEWCASTLE
WICK

BARTON REGIS

WESTON

SOMERSET

TROW

RODDEN

GOODLEIGH

CHARLTON

SOUTHOLE AND
MILFORD
HARDISWORTHY

PORTLEDGE

HENSTRIDGE

DEVON

WITHERIDGE
WITHLEIGH
CHILTON

MARTOCK

NORTHOVER

PANCRASWEEK
HOLSWORTHY

SPREYTON

BROADHEMBURY

SYDLING ST NICHOLAS

SOUTHWEEK

YEN

COLUMB JOHN
EVELEGH
CLIST ST LAURENCE

MAIDEN NEWTO
TOLLER PORCORUM

SHILLINGFORD
PEAMORE
HENNOCK

FARRINGDON
COLATON RALEIGH

DORS

MANATON
DUTTON

WOOLLEY

CORNWALL

Scale of Miles
0   5   10   15   20   25   30   35

C.H.S.

Derbishire & Stanford, Ltd.

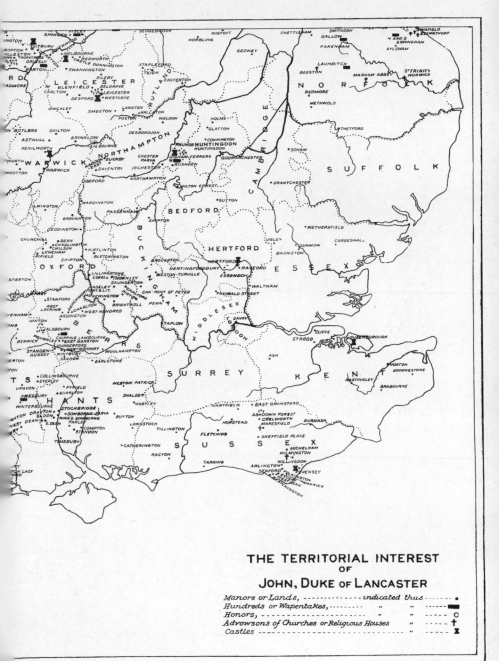

THE TERRITORIAL INTEREST
OF
JOHN, DUKE OF LANCASTER

Manors or Lands,	indicated thus	•
Hundreds or Wapentakes,	"	"	▬
Honors,	"	"	○
Advowsons of Churches or Religious Houses	"	"	✝
Castles	"	"	�

NORTHERN MAP ON FOLLOWING PAGE 5

The Oxford Geographical Inst.

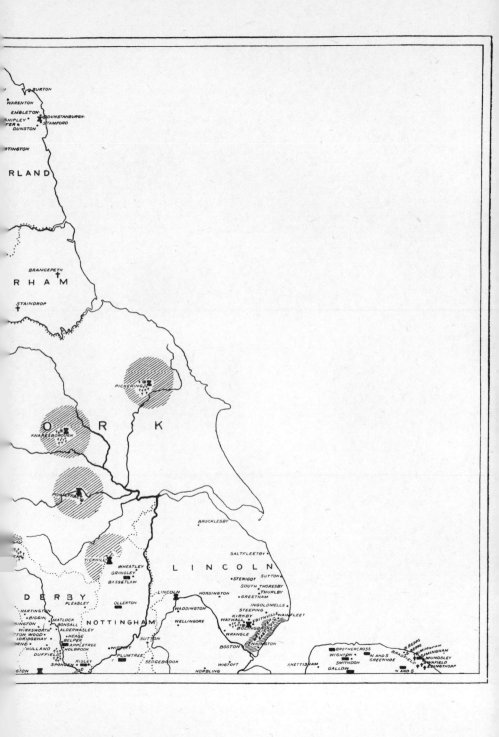

the harsh letter of the English forest law. The Duke has forests, chaces, parks and warrens, north and south and west, from the Chace of Ashdown in the Honor of Eagle, to the forest of Liddell, far away in the North, " called Nichol forest " ;[1] from the woods of Glamorgan to the Chaces of Needwood and the High Peak and the great forests of Yorkshire and Lancashire. To keep them he has in his pay an army of forest officers, knights, esquires, and yeomen (for this is no clerk's work), fighting men one and all, though varying in dignity and degree, from the humble freeman who holds the moiety of the office of parker, through the warden of a chace, to deputy foresters, foresters, and foresters in chief.

At the head of the hierarchy stands that gallant soldier and best of sportsmen, Sir Walter Ursewyk, the man whom Lancaster had made knight on the battle-field of Najera, and whose courage and devotion raised him from the rank of a humble esquire to the highest positions of trust in the Lancastrian household. Sir Walter is justice of the forests in the Duchy and County Palatine of Lancaster ; he is forester in chief of all the chaces in Blackburnshire, Trawden, Pendle, Rossendale, Tottington, and Hoddlesden ; he has letters patent under the Duke's privy seal appointing him master of all the Duke's games, sports, and hunting,[2] and he has jurisdiction over all the forest officers high and low, even over men like Sir John Marmion, a Knight Banneret, who keeps the Chace of Knaresborough. These forest officers have the most varied duties ; they enclose parks and stock them with bucks and does ; they look to the underwood and trees, settle complicated questions of agistment, and doubtless, and do not forget the tithes pan-nage ; at the Duke's mandate they make presents of venison or timber, for, as in the royal economy

[1] Reg. II. f. 119.
[2] Reg. I. 53.

itself, not a buck can be taken from his forests, not an oak or sapling from his woods for timber, not a bundle of brushwood for fuel without a warrant under the privy seal, and even the bream and luce in his fishponds and the conies in his warrens are numbered. Above all, their duty is to see that no " evildoers or sons of iniquity " hunt in the Duke's forests,[1] chaces or parks without his licence ; even to kill a hare without a due permit brings down on the hapless offender the full weight of the ducal displeasure, and a trespass of venison is among the mortal sins.

In the duke's lands there were, it appears, many that left the rule of " Seinte Maure " or " Seint Beneit " to follow St. Hubert—in his unregenerate days—men who

> " Yaf nat of that text a pulled hen,
> That seith, that hunters been not holy men."

At least, they are to be found among those guilty of forest trespass. One at least was forgiven ;[2] for whatever Wycliffe might think, John of Gaunt at least preferred a sporting parson to a political bishop !

Before we leave the army of forest officers, the grooms who kept the Duke's horses, ambling palfreys ridden by Dame Catherine Swynford and her charges, Philippa and Elizabeth, and great destriers for the Duke's own use, and the boys who keep his hounds, the falconers deserve a mention. There was a whole staff of them under Anthony the head falconer, a person of importance, for his yearly wages are £10, as much as the retaining fee of an esquire !

Hunting, coursing, and hawking—for all these the Lancastrian household was well equipped. Men might question the Duke's political principles, but no one could deny that he was a keen sportsman.

His castles and forests provided the Duke with a

---

[1] Reg. I. f. 150.
[2] Reg. II. f. 131.

possible refuge in times of danger, and the means of gratifying a predominant passion : the lands and franchises, which provided the sinews of wars, were administered by officers equally useful if less interesting. They fall into three classes—feoders, stewards and bailiffs, and receivers. It was of course quite possible for one man to hold several offices : the Constable of Liverpool Castle was also a forester and the steward of a wapentake. In an out-of-the-way and self-contained lordship, like that of Dunstanburgh, the same man was steward, receiver, and constable of the castle. But in normal cases there was a receiver, and a steward, and a feoder for each county or group of counties, and the individuals who held these offices were sharply distinguished one from the other ; for while the receiver is almost always a " clerk," the steward and feoder are knights or esquires.

The "issues of lands in England and Wales " are, as we have seen, those arising from extraordinary franchises, from feudal incidents, from seignorial jurisdiction, and from money rents or profits.

A desire for completeness and symmetry would lead us to suppose *a priori* that the feoder or " warden of fees and franchises " would deal with the extraordinary franchises and the incidents of feudal tenure, and the steward and bailiff with the profits of jurisdiction and money rents ; but in point of fact, this distinction cannot be maintained, and in many cases the duties of the first and second are interchangeable.

The feoder and steward distrain for homage on the lands of those who hold of the Duke by knight's service : they supersede distress and deliver seisin of lands at the Duke's warrant, homage done; on a tenant's death they take possession of the heir and his lands and tenements until their master has signified his pleasure as to the wardship of the heir and his lands ; they levy and collect aids, and they are responsible for the franchises granted by royal bounty.

If a ship is wrecked on the coasts of Lincoln or Lancashire they seize the wreck and sell it for their master's profit, unless, as sometimes happens, the owners belong to some powerful trading company having interest at the Savoy, when they restore the wreck to the owner. They collect the profits of the Duke's court in manor, hundred and wapentake, or where these have been farmed, they see that the ferm is handed over with their other moneys to the receiver.

This officer is the centre of the Lancastrian fiscal system. The receipt (a county, or a group of counties) is the unit of the financial administration, and illustrates its great merit, decentralization—devolution of work and responsibility. For the receiver is not merely the channel by which the " issues of lands in England and Wales " reach the Savoy ; he receives with one hand while with the other he defrays the costs of administration. He pays the wages of steward, bailiff and feoder, and of so many knights and esquires of the Duke's retinue. His surplus moneys, less these wages, he surrenders to the Duke's chief financial officer, the Receiver General. Thus the Receiver General's accounts only show a tithe of his income and expenditure, viz., the net proceeds of the Lancastrian estates, less the cost of administration and considerable other payments.

But decentralization is not enough without supervision. Hence the itinerant officers, whose task it is to see that the various local officers do their duty. There are chief stewards—three in number—men of rank, always knights bachelor, who go on circuit and exercise a general supervision. For the purpose of this supervision the Trent is the dividing line ; one works over the Duke's lands south of Trent and in Wales ; one " north of Trent " for the Duchy of Lancaster, Stafford and Derby, one for the other northern lands. Finally, following the same divisions, there are the auditors, clerks of course, who check the accounts of each receiver, examine the warrants which are his vouchers for each item of expenditure, see that no greedy feoder is exacting more than the accustomed wages of his office, and that no unjust steward or bailiff has taken his bill and written fifty marcs where eighty are due.

Finally there is the Duke's Council, a definite and formal body, who help him in the administration of his estates. Under the presidency of the chief of the council (in 1377 Sir John d'Ypres, one of the Duke's retainers), accompanied by the clerk to the Council, they go on progress through the Lancastrian lands, listening to the petitions of aggrieved tenants, settling questions of disputed ownership, respiting demands on a farmer in arrear with his ferm or a minister in arrear with his accounts, acting in short as a final court of appeal, to which all causes may be brought, and thus becoming the custodians of the Duke's good name for clemency and justice. The Duke's councillors too are men of substance ; they go surety for his debts.

Leaving the local and subordinate officers, let us go to headquarters and ask : What did Lancaster do with the great wealth at his command ? This takes us to the Receiver General, the keystone in the arch of Lancaster's financial system. The Receiver General, a highly paid officer who has his own official residence, finds the funds for the three great spending departments—the Household, Wardrobe and Privy Purse. At intervals, by warrant under the privy seal, he pays to the Treasurer of the Household, the Clerk of the Great Wardrobe and the Clerk of Privy Expenses, the sums necessary for their departments, and even these, large as they are, do not exhaust their expenditure, for the issues of certain lands and lordships are " appropriated in aid " of the several departments and paid over direct. The Lancastrian household is unique. No other in England can rival it; it rivals that of the King. The Duke aspired to the command of English armies and the control of foreign relations. He must therefore maintain a state to correspond with his position. Whenever a king or prince visits King Edward's court, the welcome at the Savoy must equal that of Westminster Palace. The sovereignty of Castile must be brought home to Englishman and foreigner. *Émigré* Spanish knights, the Spanish ladies of Queen's Constance court, or Portuguese envoys must realize that they are enjoying the hospitality of one who is not only the first subject of King Edward, but the legitimate heir of Don Pedro. Hence a lavish expenditure upon the household. Like the King, the Duke has his Chamberlain, Steward, and Controller of the Household; all these are men of position. His chief butler and paneter, who has charge of "all things pertaining to the butlery, pantry, ewery and saucery" is an esquire; so is his master cook. Beneath their command they have a force of poulterers, achatours, purveyors, etc. The mere cost of living was enormous. It must not be forgotten that the fourteenth century was an age of *décadence*. Doubtless the influence of the French wars explained much. Human life counted for little, but while men lived it was as though each man said "Let us eat and drink, for to-morrow we die!" Hence the strange and appalling contrasts: a profusion of wealth side by side with the extremes of poverty; a wild luxury side by side with want and misery. *Gula* had long since taken its place beside *accidia* in the official catalogue of monastic sins; but now gluttony invades every rank of society. In vain Parliament enacts that the common people shall not wear furs, and prescribes the legal number of dishes according to each man's degree. Sumptuary laws serve not to alter but to chronicle the vices of their age, and it is significant that in this age the poets go to the kitchen for their metaphors, and borrow from the menu terms to describe the entanglements of the "grande passion."[1] Against extravagances of dress, those bizarre and fantastic devices of fashion, which give to the costumes of the period such a quaint picturesqueness, the puritans of the period lay and clerical protested, but protested in vain. In vain the moral Gower mixed his breath with the popular cry; society turned a deaf ear.[2] Even the Church was divided against itself, for some of the worst offenders of Edward's lavish court were the "religious," who, discarding the seemly dark raiment of their orders, vied with courtiers no more worldly than themselves in the brilliance of their slashed doublets, dyed ruffs and sweeping gowns.

When in the house of a simple franklin it "snowed meat and drink," when mere knights put the rent of a manor into one garment, what wonder that there was luxury and profusion in the household of the greatest magnate of the realm? The possessions of which the Clerk of the Wardrobe had charge were priceless, and the furs and cloth of gold which John of Gaunt gives to the Queen his consort are worth a king's ransom; while for the charge of the pearls, diamonds, rubies, sapphires and emeralds in the Savoy, a whole staff of warders under a yeoman of the jewels is necessary.

But if the Duke spent freely on himself he spent as freely on others. The bulk of the sums handed to him for his secret expenses by the Clerk of the Privy Purse

---

[1] Was never pyk walwed in galuntyne.
As I in love am walwed and y-wounde.
Chaucer. *To Rosemounde,* 17–18.

[2] Gower, On the Corruptions of the Age—" *Contramentis Saevitiam in causa superbiae* " Political poems, i. 350, Cf. the Chronicles *passim.*

went in presents ; he had his Almoner *en titre*, who every Friday disbursed ten shillings, and twelve and sixpence every Saturday to the poor, but this does not exhaust his almsgiving. The Duke is above all things a cheerful giver. He is not guilty of the sins of omission, and the official charity of the Almoner is supplemented by his master in person.

Enough has been said to form a rough estimate of the numbers of the Duke's officers ; the whole army cannot be reviewed. There are many of importance of which a bare mention must suffice ; the legal officers for instance, the ministers in the King's court at Westminster, Attorney General, sergeants, attorneys in Chancery, and Exchequer, King's Bench and Common Pleas, clerk of estreats and apposer, clerk of the marshalsea, and the rest ; there is the Duke's " mire and surgeon," who, like the fighting men, accompanies him to the field and receives in war double his accustomed wages ; there are clarioners, buglers and minstrels, some of whom are incorporate by ducal charter, under the King of the Minstrels. Once at least they forget to be merry, for there is a general strike among the Duke's minstrels and he has to take severe measures to restore order.[1] There is the Master of the Duke's barge, with his crew of eight oars, who row the Duke on the Thames between the Savoy and West-minster, and once stand him in good stead when the London mob is at his heels and he has to fly for safety to Kennington ; and there is Lancaster Herald, a person of international importance, for it will be his task to proclaim through Europe the challenge of Regnault de Roye at the Jousts of St. Ingelvert. There are, too, the officers of the separate establishments of the Queen Consort—for Constance has her own treasurer and clerk of the wardrobe—of the young Earl of Derby and of Katharine of Lancaster, under the charge of Lady

---

[1] Reg. II. f. 117.

de Mohun, and Philippa and Elizabeth under the charge of Dame Katharine Swynford. These we must leave, and pass to the highest dignitary and the most significant members of Lancaster's household—his Chancellor and his Retinue.

The Chancellor is always in orders, sometimes like Ralf de Erghum, Bishop of Salisbury, a man of high ecclesiastical rank. He is the Duke's councillor in chief, the guardian of his secrets and the keeper of his seals. He is altogether superior to the Chancellor of the County Palatine, who holds the " magnum sigillum pro regimine regalitatis." The Duke's Chancellor keeps the " great silver seal with the arms of Spain," while for the privy seal he has under him a Keeper of the Privy Seal specially deputed for that office. Through his hands pass the most important documents that issue from the Savoy, the treaties with foreign powers, to which Lancaster as envoy extraordinary and plenipotentiary or as independent potentate is a signatory.

Lastly we reach the apex of the structure and the crown of the Lancastrian Household. More important than the administrative and financial officers, more important than the ceremonial officials of the Savoy are the knights and esquires of the Duke's Retinue.

John of Gaunt did not sit alone with his family in the banqueting halls of Hertford, Leicester, or Kenilworth, and when he went to the wars the men who followed his banner were not hired troops alone. The " grand seigneur " must have his circle of comrades in arms, his followers and his bodyguard, and, in accordance with the custom of the age, these followers are united to their chieftain by a bond of a special and peculiar nature. More than a hundred knights, banneret or bachelor, and as many esquires, entered into a formal compact with the Duke, swearing to serve him faithfully in peace or war for their lives. They expoused his quarrels (which were not few) at home, and they followed his banner into the field of battle, forming with their attendants the nucleus of the force which he led in his sovereign's service or his own adventures. In return for this service they enjoyed the Duke's favour and protection, and received each one his retaining fee, so much for a simple esquire, more for a knight bachelor or banneret, more still for a baron, the amount varying not only with the rank of the retainer, and the regard which the Duke had for him, but also in proportion to the number of men whom he might bring into the field, from the fee of ten pounds per annum drawn by an esquire to the annuity of five hundred marcs paid to a great north country baron. In time of war the fee was doubled, and in addition to the "regard" the Duke paid for the "restore" of horses killed or captured by the enemy, and advanced in part or wholly the ransom money of a captured retainer. The cost of a permanent establishment on such a scale as this was, of course, enormous; but his political influence, if not his personal safety, depended in no small measure on the power to command the support of armed force at short notice. This formed the material guarantee of his power and dignity—*decus et tutamen in armis*. So soon as the clerks in the Savoy could write copies of the summons, and the Duke's couriers could carry his message, mobilization began, and the Duke's men rode to the rendezvous, equally prepared to fight the foreigner, to follow their master to the Scottish border, or to stand by him during a stormy session at Westminster.

Among the men whom Lancaster gathered about him were many of note both in the arts of peace and war : Sir Robert Knolles, the brave and dashing captain of Edward III, Sir Richard Le Scrope (Lord Le Scrope of Bolton), and Sir Michael de la Pole (afterwards Earl of Suffolk), the faithful minister of Richard II. Lord Neville of Raby, Lord Roos of Hamelak, Lord Dacre, and Lord Welles took the Duke's wages and wore his livery ; the roll of his men contains many a well-known name—Banastre, Marmion, Dymmok, Blount, Ursewyk, Curzon and Foljambe. For the most part the Duke's men were recruited in the great northern lordships, but southerners from Kent and Sussex, and East Anglians, find a place in the ranks, while Cornwall, Wales and Scotland are also represented. Like Duke Henry, Duke John had little insular prejudice, and true to the spirit of chivalry, which inclined to place knighthood above race and nation, John of Gaunt maintained foreigners as well as his own countrymen among his retinue. Jean d'Aubrécicourt the Hainaulter, and Mauburni de Linières the Poitevin fought side by side with their English comrades for the Duke of Lancaster in France and for the King of Castile in Spain ; Spanish knights follow Queen Constance from Bordeaux to the Savoy and enroll themselves in the Lancastrian retinue, while in the " eighties " the chivalry of Portugal is also represented.

Such was the territorial interest and such the household of the most powerful subject of Edward III. and Richard II.

Chapter XI

LANCASTER RETURNS TO POWER

SELDOM has the accession of an English King taken place under more humiliating conditions than those of 1377. While the great feudatories were engrossed in coronation ceremonial, and the capital was holiday making—the shores of the kingdom lay at the mercy of the invader, and England seemed in danger of losing for ever the prestige of her great victories and her position as the first military power of Europe. From June to September the admirals of France and Castile, Jean de Vienne and Ferrand Sanchez de Tovar, swept the Channel and harried the south coast at their pleasure. They overran the Isle of Wight, and put the inhabitants to ransom; they burnt Rye, Hastings and Rottingdean, and carried off the Prior of Lewes, and finally sailed up the Thames and burnt Gravesend. The Government, thoroughly alarmed, had ordered tenants in chief to go back to their lands and hold their retainers in readiness; they ordered Lancaster to strengthen his castles on the Welsh marches, and even bethought them of putting the crumbling walls of Oxford in repair. But such defensive expedients were, of course, useless against an enemy which held the control of the sea; the real danger of England lay not in the weakness of fortifications, but in the absence of a fleet capable of being mobilised at short notice and of clearing the seas of the combined forces of France and Castile. Such half-hearted at-

230

tempts at offensive action as were made were doomed to failure ; a fleet sent to attack the Spaniards at Sluys was first scattered by bad weather, and then rendered useless by lack of combination among the commanders and by mutiny among their crews.

Since 1374 John of Gaunt had taken no part in any military operations ; he still maintained the attitude of reserve adopted immediately after the coronation, and was still trying to avoid responsibility and suspicion together. The retirement of the King's eldest uncle was the opportunity of the youngest ; Thomas of Woodstock at once stepped forward to claim the place yielded by his brother, and for a few months controlled the affairs of the kingdom. Even in the field of diplomacy Lancaster was content to leave the conduct of affairs to others ; there were negotiations with France, but he took no part in them ;[1] the politics of the Peninsula were of the first interest to him, but he declined any share in the negotiations with Aragon,[2] and though he had been appointed commissioner to settle outstanding difficulties with Scotland, when the time came he resigned the task to others.[3] A year's complete self-effacement might have been expected to calm the passions of 1376 and to disarm suspicion ; perhaps the Duke thought so, or perhaps in 1378 he began to feel a genuine alarm at the situation. At any rate, in the summer of that year he abandoned his resolve, and left the deer of the northern forests to accept a military command. The object was to put an end to these continued humiliating descents of the enemy upon the south coast.

When hostilities began England had two allies on French soil, for the Duke of Brittany had espoused

---

[1] *Foed*, VII. 183–5.
[2] Ibid. 200.
[3] The Earl of March, Lord Neville, and Richard le Scrope. *Foed*, VII. 174–5 ; 183.

the English cause, pledging himself to surrender
Brest, and to serve King Richard, while Charles of
Navarre was negotiating to place Cherbourg in English
hands, and, as Charles V believed, planning a blood
alliance with the royal house of England.[1]

In addition to Calais, Bordeaux and Bayonne, therefore, Cherbourg and Brest were, or were soon to be, at
the disposal of England; but the Government had yet
to learn that naval bases do not win battles or secure
the control of the sea. Meanwhile the Castilian fleet
had returned, for Enrique II found enough to do for
the moment in protecting his commerce from Gascon
privateers, and his frontiers from his cousin of Portugal,
to say nothing of his son-in-law of Navarre.

Such was the naval situation when Lancaster, after
long delay caused by contrary winds, put to sea at the
beginning of July to meet the French admiral.[2]

If Jean de Vienne had fought, he would have fought
single-handed without the support of Castile, but his
orders were not to fight, for Charles V was resolved to
carry out at sea also that policy of inaction which had
achieved such signal success in 1373. When, therefore,
Lancaster's fleet, after lying weatherbound at Sandwich, reached the Isle of Wight and thence made for the
Norman coast, there was no enemy to be found, for Jean de
Vienne had crept up the coast to Harfleur and was lying
in the Seine. After searching the Norman coast in vain

---

[1] *Foed*, VII. 174; 190–5; 196–7. The proposal for a marriage
between Katherine of Lancaster and Pierre, second son of Charles
of Navarre, was said to have been found in the secret correspondence captured with Navarre's agent, Jacques de Rue. *Chr. Val.*
265. Froissart K. de L. 55.

[2] Letters of protection for Lancaster's suite, dated March 4,
1378; *Foed*, VII. 186; orders to impress mariners dated May 20
and May 24, ibid. 195; letters of attorney for members of his
suite, dated June 18, ibid. 199–200; letters of protection, dated
June 16, ibid. *Record Report*, xxxii. App. (i.) 17. Froissart,
K. de L. 54-93. *Chr. Angl.* 194, 204. Wals. i. 367, 373-5.

the Duke was compelled to abandon his main object. Operations on land had formed no part of his plans, and he had embarked no horses, but to return without striking a blow, as the great fleet had returned in 1372 after the failure to reach La Rochelle, would be to play into the hands of the critics at Westminster, so Lancaster, finding the wind favourable for St. Malo, determined to land there and besiege the strongest port on the northern coast yet remaining in French hands. The idea was an afterthought ; it took the enemy by surprise. They had just time to throw a couple of hundred lances into the town before the siege began. It was difficult for Charles V to relieve St. Malo without departing from his defensive policy, but he sent du Guesclin to give the town all assistance compatible with the standing orders to avoid an engagement. While the French and English forces faced each other, and skirmished at low tide across the tidal river which separated their camps, the siege went on. Lancaster kept his batteries busy on the walls, and delivered assaults, but now, as at the siege of Limoges, he relied on his miners to carry the town. The work was well advanced, when one night early in August the Earl of Arundel was in charge of the mine ; the Earl had proved himself an energetic and able commander at sea, but on this occasion his conduct left much to be desired. A sortie from St. Malo took him completely by surprise, and succeeded, under cover of the confusion of a night attack, in completely wrecking the mine.

As a council of war, which censured Arundel for his carelessness, decided that it was useless to begin the work again, the siege was raised, and the Duke's force returned to England. Arundel was in disgrace, but responsibility for the failure was, naturally enough, laid at the door of the commander-in-chief ; a new count had been added to the indictment against the unpopular Duke.[1]

[1] For the naval expedition and the siege of St. Malo, see

It was unfortunate that the Duke's first military expedition since his retirement should have ended as it did ; still more unfortunate that this military failure should be followed by another quarrel with the Bishops. This new conflict with the powers of the Church was the result of an act of violence done during Lancaster's absence, the story of which takes us back to the Spanish campaign of 1367.

Among the foreign volunteers who came to the help of Enrique of Trastamare in 1366 was Alfonso, Count of Ribagorza and Denia, son of the Infante Don Pedro, and grandson of the King of Aragon Don Jayme II.[1]

Enrique rewarded his adherence by a grant of lands on the frontier of Castile and the title of Marquess of Villena,[2] and sixteen years later created him Constable of Castile.[3]

Froissart, *K. de L.* ix. 54–5, 60, 64–5, 67–71, 79–83. *Chr. Val.* 274. *Chr. Angl.* 194–197, 201, 204–6 ; and Wals. i. 367, 371, 373–5 (an untrustworthy account).

[1] Ayala, i. 397, and ii. 235 ; besides the passages quoted below, see Ayala ii. 661 (*Adiçiones a las Notas*) and Fernan Perez de Guzman, *Generaçiones de los Reyes*, pp. 597–8.

Jayme II. King of Aragon
(1291–1327)
|
Don Pedro, Infante of Aragon
|
Don Alfonso, Count of Ribagorza
and Denia Marquess of Villena,
Duke of Gandiá, Constable of   Enrique II. = Doña Elvira
Castile   Iñiguez

Don Alfonso   Don Pedro   = Doña Juan
hostage of Hauley and Shakyl) (hostage of the
                               Count of Foix),
                               d. 1385
                                                 Don Enrique de Villena

[2] E dió á Don Alfonso Conde de Denia del Regno de Aragon, que venia con él la tierra que fuera de Don Juan fijo del Infante Don Manuel . . . é mando que le llamasen Marques de Villena. Ayala, i. 408.

[3] Ayala, ii. 157.

HAULEY AND SHAKYL

Alfonso fought in the cavalry division of the usurper's army at Najera, where he was captured[1] by two squires, Robert Hauley and John Shakyl. By the ordinary rules of warfare the captive, being of the blood royal, remained at the disposal of Prince Edward, who was bound to compensate the captors with a suitable reward. The Marquess of Villena, or to give him his more familiar title, Count of Denia, was allowed to go on parole, giving as hostages his two sons, Alfonso and Pedro. The younger, Pedro, was handed over to the Count of Foix, a friend of the Denia family, who made himself responsible for his ransom; the elder, Alfonso, was assigned to the squires, who returned to England with their prize and the prospect of a substantial ransom.

Unfortunately for all concerned, the asset was hard to realize. With the double object of rewarding his supporter and disposing of the hands of two illegitimate daughters, Enrique II agreed to advance 60,000 florins towards the ransom, on the understanding that Alfonso should marry one daughter, Leonor, and Pedro should marry the second, Juana, the advance being considered as the joint dowry of the two.

So far as the younger son is concerned this arrangement was carried out; Pedro married Juana, and continued to serve the House of Trastamare until 1385, when he was killed at Aljubarrota.[2] Alfonso, however, flatly declined to accept the hand of a lady of Leonor's reputation, and her father in consequence demanded back 30,000 florins, i.e. half the dowry advanced as ransom.

So much is necessary to explain, firstly the importance of the Count of Denia in international politics, and secondly, the long delay in ransoming the English hostage.

[1] Ayala, i. 457 ; Wals. i. 304 ; *Chr. Angl.* 59.
[2] Fern o Lopes, *Chronica d'el Rey D. Joao* I, iv. 182.   Higd. ix. 66.   Wals. ii. 135.   Cf. Ayala, II. 110–11 and note.

For in 1377, ten years after the windfall which had come to them at Najera, the squires were still cherishing their hopes and their security. Their troubles began when in the autumn of that year the Count of Denia sent representatives to England with a portion of his son's ransom and instructions to negotiate terms for his release.[1]

Being a cadet of the Royal House of Aragon, Denia was able to induce the Court of Aragon to move in the matter.[2] It was an opportune moment, for negotiations between the two countries were just beginning.[3]

The Government requested Hauley and Shakyl to produce their hostage, but the squires, fearing the loss of their ransom money, refused. A writ ordering the Count of Denia to be produced before the King and Council in Parliament[4] succeeded no better, for the Count could not be found; finally the captors, by the order of Parliament, were committed to the Tower for contumacy and for keeping a "private prison" in their own house.[5] A plea that their case might be referred to a committee of the King's Council,[6] proved of no avail; the Government remained obdurate, and the squires remained contumacious.

This situation lasted from November, 1377, to August, 1378. Then the squires escaped from the Tower and took sanctuary at Westminster. The Constable of the

---

[1] Safe conduct, dated August 4, 1377. *Foed*, VII. 171.

[2] *Cont. Eulog.* iii. 342—an important point which has been overlooked, as also has the fact that Denia was Aragonese, not Castilian.

[3] Powers to two commissioners to treat with Aragon, dated October 30, 1377. *Foed*, VII. 179.

[4] Dated October 28, 1377. *Foed*, VII. 178.

[5] *Rot. Parl.* iii. 10 a. Sir William Faringdon was also committed to the Tower in connexion with the Count's disappearance; he was released and handed over to the Earl of Northumberland, who undertook to be surety for him. Warrant dated December 5, 1377. *Foed*, VII. 179–80.

[6] *'Rot. Parl.* iii. 50a. The Count of Denia's was not the only case: there was trouble about Flemish prisoners too.

Tower, Sir Alan Buxhill, who was responsible for their safe custody, determined to get them back. Accompanied by Sir Ralf Ferrers and a body of armed men, he went to the Abbey and soon succeeded in getting Shakyl out of the precincts by a ruse. Hauley was less fortunate. A heated argument ensued, the Constable charging him with contumacy in resisting the King's commands, the squire charging the King's councillors with injustice and avarice. Finding argument useless, the Constable ordered his guard to drag the man from the Abbey. Mass was being celebrated at the time, and the priest had just reached the words " If the Master of the house had known at what hour," etc., when the Abbey became the scene of wild confusion, the hunted man breaking in among the monks in the chancel, with a body of armed guards at his heels. It was useless to try to protect the fugitive ; the monks were driven back at the sword's point, and one, a sacristan, bolder than the rest, was cut down. Hauley himself was caught and despatched on the very steps of the altar.

Blood had been shed in the sacred building, and not only had sanctuary been violated, but the Abbey miraculously consecrated by Saint Peter himself had been desecrated by murder ! For a while the clergy hesitated between desire for vengeance and fear of the secular power. The murderers were the King's officers : Was it wise to defy the Government and challenge the strong anti-clerical feeling of the day, when the King's mother was notorious for her Lollard sympathies, when the King's uncle was protecting Wycliffe, and the reformer's ideas were gaining every day a stronger hold on the court and people ? Bold counsels prevailed : the Bishop of London, with five suffragans, proceeded to St. Paul's and solemnly excommunicated Sir Alan Buxhill and Sir Ralf Ferrers and all directly or indirectly responsible for the outrage.

JOHN OF GAUNT

It was in vain that the King wrote to the Bishop requesting him not to publish, or at least to postpone the sentence. The Bishop ignored the royal letters, and repeated his curses three days a week at St. Paul's. It is true that the names of Richard himself, the Princess Joan and the Duke of Lancaster were specifically excepted from the sentence of excommunication, but this exception, insinuating a responsibility which could not be openly maintained, only served to irritate the Government more. The King's officers had violated a privilege of the Church, and the Church had declared war on the Government.

Such was the situation when John of Gaunt returned from his ill-fated expedition to St. Malo. In the outrage of August 11 the Duke can have had no share direct or indirect, for he had been at sea for more than a month when the crime took place. He has been held responsible, however, for the events which led to it, for the attempt, that is, to get possession of the Count of Denia, on the word of the Monk of St. Albans, evidence which would prove the Duke guilty of all possible crimes and treasons from his first appearance in public life to the year 1388, when the "Scandalous Chronicle" ceases. The St. Albans chronicler says that the attempt to secure Denia's person was made to please the Duke of Lancaster, giving the statement on the strength of a popular rumour,[1] producing a confession of guilt on the same authority,[2] but making the mistake of coupling with this explanation another equally unconvincing, to the effect that the attempt was made not by the Duke at all, but by the King's advisers, who wanted to marry the Count of Denia to the King's half-sister, Matilda Courtenay.

A priori it is difficult to see how the possession of the

---

[1] Ut quibusdam placet. *Chr. Angl.* 210.
[2] Ut quidam dicunt. *Chr. Angl.* 210.

person of the young Alfonso could help Lancaster's Castilian ambitions, seeing that the Count himself, a noble of Aragon, was definitely committed to the cause of Trastamare. But in this case there is something more than antecedent probabilities or the reverse to go upon. The writ ordering the production of the hostage, and the committal of his captors, was issued not by the Lancastrian Parliament of January, 1377, but by the Parliament of October, 1377,[1] led by Sir Peter de la Mare, recruited from the veterans of 1376, a house, we are told, which if not anti-Lancastrian, was the most independent of all the assemblies of the reign.[2]

To overcome the improbability that such a Parliament would go out of its way to perpetrate an act of injustice to please John of Gaunt requires evidence rather more satisfactory than one of two inconsistent explanations offered, on the strength of idle rumour, by the St. Albans chronicle. There is no reason to reject the plain and natural explanation, that the Count of Denia wanted to get his son back, that he got his own court to back his request, and that Richard's Government, anxious as they showed themselves to conciliate both the King of Aragon and the Count of Foix, were prepared to do what they could. The rest is explained by the natural fears of the captives and the violence of the King's officers, and to look for the traces of a deep political conspiracy, or to cast an air of mystery about the incident, is gratuitous.[3]

Lancaster then had no share in the crime of August 11,

---

[1] *Rot. Parl.* iii. 10a.

[2] Stubbs, *Const. Hist.* ii. 463.

[3] Higden, viii. 397, says explicitly that the act was done by "*scelerati de familia regis.*"

See *Chr. Angl.* 207–8, 241 ; Wals. i. 376–8, 411 ; *Eulog.* iii. 342 ; *Record Report*, xlv. App. x. 308. Delpit *Collection*, p. 205. *Foed*, VII. 275, 287, and 312.

In the end the King agreed that in exchange for the captive Shakyl should have lands worth 100 marcs p.a., and promised or in the circumstances which led up to it ; the wise course, the course which ten years later he would certainly have adopted, was to stand aside and leave the Bishop of London and the monks of Westminster to fight their quarrel out with the King's Council. But instead of doing this the Duke repeated his mistake of 1376 ; and threw himself into a quarrel which was none of his making. The Bishop of London had been summoned to a meeting of the Council at Windsor, and had refused to attend. Irritated by another example of the arrogance of the chiefs of the hierarchy, the Duke offered to ride to St. Paul's and drag the Bishop to Windsor " in spite of the ribald knaves of London." [1]

Once more a rash threat aroused popular passion. Once more suspicion was aroused, taking, as usual, the form of exaggeration and invention. The failure at St. Malo must be the result of corruption : the Duke had got into his hands the taxes voted by Parliament, and was using them for his own ends! He was plotting the destruction of the Church : wholesale abolition of privilege and confiscation of property were the main features of a scheme of disestablishment to be propounded to the forthcoming Parliament!

to found a chantry for the souls of those killed by his officers. Lancaster's only appearance in the case is as arbiter in a quarrel twelve years later between Hauley's heir and Shakyl (*Rot. Pat.* Oct. 20, 1390) as to the division of the spoil.

The account of Mr. Shirley (*Fasc. Ziz.* Introduction, xxxv.) is most misleading. Denia was a "*relation of the reigning house*" of Aragon, not "*of Castile.*" Sir Ralf Ferrers was not "*one of the Duke's retainers.*" Lancaster did not, and could not "*follow the squires to sanctuary.*" Where is the evidence that he "*offered the squires a price for the prisoner*" ? Or that he "*put forward claims, we scarcely know what, on the part of the Crown*" ?

The *scandalosa mendacia* of Lancaster's "deeper scheme of revenge" are refuted by the events which followed, and by the passage from the *De Ecclesia* which Mr. Shirley quotes (*Fasc. Ziz.* Introduction, xxxvi.–xxxvii.).

[1] *Chr. Angl.* 210.

THE GLOUCESTER PARLIAMENT

Parliament met at Gloucester, out of the reach of the " ribald knaves of London," [1] and opened with every sign of an uncomfortable session. The Lords refused to follow the precedent of the last three Parliaments by allowing a number of themselves to be selected to confer with the Commons ; the Commons, on their part, showed a disposition to grumble at everything, and a strong reluctance to vote taxes.

Lancaster's chief object was to clear his own name and to place it beyond question that the subsidies had been spent on the purposes for which they had been voted. Knowing his position and foreseeing suspicion, he had taken care to name Walworth and Philipot, the Parliamentary Treasurers, among the commissioners of array appointed to supervise the preparations for the naval expedition of the summer.[2] When, therefore, Richard le Scrope declared in the King's name that every penny of the taxes had been spent on the war, the Treasurers were compelled to support the statement. But the Commons were not satisfied even by the words of their own officers ; they demanded that the accounts should be produced. There was a strong feeling among the Council against making a concession which might become an inconvenient precedent, but Lancaster insisted, and the accounts were produced. A scrutiny justified the statements of Richard le Scrope, Walworth and Philipot. It was proved that all the money had been spent on the war, and the Commons had to content themselves with grumbling that it was not proper to charge to voted moneys the expense of maintaining Cherbourg, Brest, Calais, Bordeaux, and Bayonne, ports which, as the ministers reminded them, were not only " beles et nobles

---

[1] Summoned by writ dated September 3, 2 Rich. II, to meet on Wednesday after St. Luke (Dugdale, *Summons, 297*), it sat from October 20 to November 16, 1378. *Rot. Parl.* iii. 32–54.
[2] *Foed*, VII. 199.

entrees et Portz pur grever noz enemys," but also the "barbicans" of the Kingdom.

As for the threatened spoliation of the Church, the charge had to go the way of the other equally fanciful charge of corruption.

Common sense and justice alike demanded that a limit should be placed on the abuse of sanctuary, and that a time-honoured privilege of the Church should not be employed to protect the person and property of a fraudulent debtor. Such a limitation of a long-standing grievance Lancaster supported :[1] it represented the extreme limit of his "revolutionary policy;"[2] and that others besides Wycliffe supported his view appears from the fact that a year later the reform was embodied in a statute.[3]

It was seven years since John of Gaunt had married the heiress of Castile. He had never laid aside his continental ambitions or abandoned his resolve to win a place among the kings of Europe. In spite of difficulties the work of preparation went on. Of those negotiations with the Peninsular powers which led to the expedition of the Earl of Cambridge in the summer of 1381 more will be said later. While circumstances made it impossible to carry out the scheme, the Duke found occupation in a political problem nearer home, and now for the first time began to play a prominent part in the relations between England and her northern neighbour.

The condition of the Border was a constant source of anxiety to Parliament. Since 1369 there had been, in theory at least, a truce between England and Scotland, but

---

[1] *Fasc. Ziz.* Introduction, xxxvi.–xxxvii.
[2] The Monk of St. Albans is amusing : " [Dux] se in lucis angelum transformavit, *nihil pro tunc omnium quae decreverat temptaturus,* sed universa facturus quae ipse archiepiscopus et suffraganei pro tunc decernerent vel juberent. *Chr. Angl.* 211 . Cf. Wals. i. 380.
[3] In the Parliament which sat at Westminster from 25 April to 27 May, 1379. *Rot. Parl.* iii. 55-70.

the period was one of constant fighting and disorder. Berwick was taken and retaken with a wearisome regularity; again and again the Earls of March and Douglas and Archibald Douglas, Lord of Galloway, swept over the border and harried the northern counties; as often Percy, Greystock and Neville led their border riders to ravage the Lowands. It is useless to attempt to distinguish aggression from retaliation, or to say who began a quarrel which in point of fact never ended. This anarchy was tempered by the institution of March days, on which commissioners from either Government met at some Border village to discuss infractions of the truce and to make redress.

The Scottish king was prepared to accept peace but powerless to control his subjects; both Governments had grounds for the belief that the turbulent border families were largely responsible for a state of disorder which, ruinous at any time, might prove fatal to England in a critical period of foreign relations.

One of the political convictions of the Duke of Lancaster was the possibility and desirability of cultivating better relations with Scotland. He was led to form this conclusion both by political considerations and personal prepossessions. Obviously, while the French war lasted it was necessary to secure the northern frontier against invasion; to remove the threat of such invasion was equally necessary to the prosecution of the expedition to Castile. Not only so, but the Duke was strongly prejudiced in favour of the Scots. There were Scottish knights among his retinue, and Scottish lances had fought under his banner in the war, while the Duke could breathe more freely in a political atmosphere where few institutions flourished to check the power of the great feudatories. The Duke had formed a definite Scottish policy; in the autumn of 1380, for the first time, he prepared to carry it into effect. Not, however, without opposition. The

Earl of Northumberland did not share Lancaster's Scottish sympathies, and regarded border politics as part of the Percy inheritance. Given an irregular dictatorship in the North, the control of the Marches, and a free hand to harry the Lowlands when he thought fit, Percy would have been willing enough to leave Government and opposition, Lollard and Churchman to fight out their pitiful quarrels at Westminster without interference. Unlike his brother, Sir Thomas Percy, Henry, Earl of Northumberland, was no politician and no courtier. He was happy fighting, especially fighting on the border, and his ambition was to convert into a permanent arrangement the position which he had first held in 1368, when the custody of both the Eastern and Western Marches had been placed in his hands.

It happened that in the summer of 1380 there was an unusually flagrant breach of the truce. The men of Hull and Newcastle captured a Scottish ship with a rich cargo : by way of revenge, the Scots invaded the northern counties in force, surprised Penrith during the fair, and carried away with them their loot and their prisoners.[1] This was enough to rouse the Lord of Alnwick and light the border firebrands. The Percy lands had suffered, and the Earl called out his moss-troopers and prepared to strike back.

But in the midst of his preparations he was stopped by a mandate from Westminster, and, riding to London to ask the reason for this inexplicable order, the Earl learnt that a March day had already been arranged, and there must be no hostilities.[2]

Percy was out of humour when he reached London ; it did not calm him to hear that at the head of the

---

[1] *Scotichronicon*, xiv. 43.
[2] *Chr. Angl.* 267–270.

border commission the King had placed his uncle the Duke of Lancaster. [1]

The Duke went to the Border prepared for war ; [2] but, met in a conciliatory spirit, difficulties soon disappeared, and after a week's preliminary discussion at Liliotcross, the Scottish Commissioners (the Earl of Douglas, the Bishop of Glasgow, the Chancellor) met the Duke in person at Berwick, and agreed to prolong the truce until November 30, 1381. [3]

After naming deputies and wardens of the marches, [4] Lancaster turned south to report his success to the Parliament which had been sitting for the last three weeks at Northampton, busy as usual with financial problems, and trying to get at the facts of the supposed treasonable correspondence with the enemy on the part of Sir Ralf Ferrers. [5]

The Commons had feared an expensive compaign as the result of the Scottish incursion of the summer,

[1] Lancaster's commission is dated September 6, 1380 (*Foed*, VII. 268–9) ; see also notification of his appointment (ibid. 269–70) ; writ *de intendendo*, dated October 2 (ibid. 274) ; memo. of copies of documents relating to Scotland to be sent to Monseigneur d'Espaigne (ibid., 273–4).

[2] Warrants, dated Tutbury, August 14, 1380, to the Receivers of Lancashire and Yorkshire, to call out the most serviceable knights and squires of his retinue to go with him against Scotland ; appointment of John de Norfolk to be Treasurer of the " expedition of war " against the Marches of Scotland, etc. Reg. II. 46, etc.

[3] Safe conduct for the Scottish Commissioners dated Bamborough, October 28, 1380. Reg. II. 46. The truce was struck November 1, and orders were given for it to be proclaimed December 2. *Foed*. VII. 277–8, 278–9.

[4] Warrants dated Newcastle, November 8, 1380. Reg. II. 147.

[5] Parliament had been summoned by writ dated August 26, 4 Ric. II, to meet at Northampton on the Monday after All Saints Dugdale, *Summons*, 304. It sat from November 5 to December 6, 1380. *Rot. Parl.* iii. 88–98. Cf. warrant to the Receiver in Lincolnshire to pay for purveyances made for the household at Northampton, dated Knaresborough, October 2,1380. Reg. II. 38 ; *Chr. Angl.* 280 ; Wals. i. 449.

and the Duke's successful dealings amounted to a pleasant surprise. Froissart says that no envoy was able to secure such good terms from Scotland as John of Gaunt. One reason for this lay in the Duke's readiness to hear both sides. His idea of international relations was that there should be " peace in time of peace, and war in war."[1] If a definite infraction of the truce could be proved, he was willing to give judgment against his own side, punish the offender, and make redress.[2]

Success made the Duke acceptable to the Government, and in the spring of the following year he received his second commission,[3] the second instance, as Henry Percy thought, of vexatious interference in the affairs of the Border.

Little did John of Gaunt think as he rode out of the Savoy on May 12 that he had lived his last day in the stately palace of the Earls of Lancaster, the treasure-house of their precious possessions, or that within a few months he would find in the place of the Savoy a heap of charred ruins! Little did he think, as he rode with his retinue through Hertford, Bedford and North-ampton to his castles of Leicester and Knaresborough, that beneath the calm surface of English life forces were at work which in a few weeks were to break out, threaten-ing to overwhelm the whole structure of society. Yet,

[1] Froissart, K. de. L. viii. 326.

[2] For instances, see Warrant dated December 6, 4 Rich. II, to the Chief Baron of the Exchequer and Steward of Lancaster to make redress for the injuries done (1) to the Castle of Old Rox-burgh ; (2) to the Earl of Douglas in the last expedition against Scotland to the amount of £505. Reg. II. 41 : Mandate to the Sheriff of Lancaster to distrain on certain persons . . . for casks of wine taken contrary to the truce with Scotland, and to pay 10 marcs for each cask. Dated March 20, sixth year of the Regality (1382). *Record Report*, xxxi. App. No. 54.

[3] Dated May 1, 1381. *Foed*, VII. 288-9 : his colleagues were the Bishop of Hereford and the Earl of Stafford. Note of money paid to the Duke by the hands of his clerk, John Norfolk, £1,000 and £1,333. 6s. 8d. Issue *Roll*, May 10, 1381.

though no signs of the coming revolution met Lancaster's eye, perhaps among the peasants who stared at his cavalcade, among the friars or russet-gowned Lollard preachers who met him on the road, there may have been agents of the "Central Committee," emissaries of the discontented, organizers of revolution. The calm which for the most part lay over England was the calm before the storm. This is not the place to tell the story of the Peasants' Rebellion, or to sketch the causes and results of an upheaval unique in English history. It is a familiar story how the burden of villein service, weighing all the more heavily since the ravages of the Black Death and repressive legislation;—the unpopular poll-tax of 1380, which brought home to every household, however humble, the cost of the war;—the abuse of purveyance, and the general weakness of the administration;—how these grievances, leavened here and there by the preaching of theoretical socialism, drove the peasants to rise against the established order.[1]

Equally familiar is the stirring history of the march of the men of Kent and Essex to London : how they entered the City and murdered the Primate-Chancellor and the Treasurer.

The first act of the rebels after reaching London was to make for the Savoy. There, with the help of the London mob, they wrecked the palace built by Boniface of Savoy and the good Duke Henry, the building which, by all contemporary account, had no equal in England for beauty and magnificence. They tore to pieces cloth of gold and silver and rich tapestries, broke up the rich furniture, crushed the Duke's plate, and ground his jewels and precious stones under foot. All that could not be destroyed was cast into the river, and when the

---

[1] *Chr. Angl.* 285–326 ; Wals. i. 453–484, ii. 1–41. Higd. ix. 1–10 ; Kn. ii. 131–143 ; *Eulog.* iii. 351–4. *Memorials of London Life,* p. 449.

work of destruction was over the Savoy lay a smouldering ruin.

Nothing is more striking in the whole story of the rebellion than the eagerness of the rebels to prove their single-minded hatred of the Duke of Lancaster. " We are no thieves," they cried, when one of their number tried to make off with a piece of the Duke's plate, and cast the wretch with his plunder into the flames. No indignity that could be invented was spared : a "jack" of the Duke was set up on a spear riddled with arrows, taken down, and hacked to pieces. The rebels hated the Duke as the most prominent man in England, as the type of the administration responsible for their troubles. They hated his assumption of royal dignity ; they would have " no King named John." Failing to satisfy their lust for vengeance, they wreaked it on the humblest victims. To be connected with the Duke in any way was to be in peril ; to be in his service was to be marked out for certain destruction. A certain Minorite Friar, the Duke's physician, was murdered for no other reason than the Duke's friendship for him,[1] but, by some strange fatality, while his servants were being murdered in London and in the Eastern counties, the Duke's eldest son, Henry of Bolingbroke, who was in the Tower with the King, escaped notice.

So great was the terror inspired by the rebels' hatred for John of Gaunt that no one dared to harbour his property. At Hertford no effort was made to defend the castle : the rebels entered and caroused in the Duke's cellars as they had done at the Savoy, where more than thirty had perished in the ruins.[2]

[1] Knighton (ii. 133) calls him " Johannes de ordine Minorum in armis bellicis strenuus, in physica peritissimus, domino Johanni duci Lancastriae familiarissimus." Cf. Froissart, K. de L. ix. 400 ; 404. His name was William de Appleton, and he was retained by the Duke at 40 marcs p.a. for life. Reg. I. f. 128. Cf. Anglo-French Chronicle (*Hist. Rev.* 1898), p. 517.

[2] Warrant to the Treasurer of the Household to allow in the accounts of William de Overbury, Esquire, chief butler, for

THE PEASANTS' RISING

The attack on the Savoy had taken every one by surprise : Leicester, on the other hand, was warned in time. When a courier arrived with the news that the rebels were marching north to wreck the castle and burn all the Duke's property, the keeper of the Duke's wardrobe packed his treasures and drove them to the Abbey. The Abbot refused to admit them ; to harbour the goods of the patron of Leicester was to court destruction, and as no one seemed anxious for martyrdom in the cause, the Duke's property found no asylum save in the precincts of St. Mary's Church.

Still more extraordinary is the story of the Duchess Constance and her flight. When the rebels entered London the Duchess was probably at Hertford, her usual residence, but on the first warning of the outbreak she hastened north with the intention of joining the Duke on the Border.[1] But Constance reached Pontefract only to find its gates shut in her face. The craven who held the castle for the Duke dared not admit his lady, and from Pontefract she rode on, the same night, to Knaresbrough by torchlight.

That the pious Duke should be beyond the reach of the rebels' fury appeared to the Canon of Leicester at least a manifest dispensation of Providence.[2]

When the peasants were gathering for the march on

two pipes of wine lost and destroyed at the Savoy by the common rebels in time of the great rumour, and for one pipe of wine destroyed by the rebels at Hertford, dated London, February 20, 1382. Reg. II. 58. Warrant to the Auditors to allow in the accounts of the Treasurer of the Household the prices of several articles destroyed at the Savoy, etc., dated Pontefract, September 8, 1381. Reg. II. 67. Cf. *Rot. Pat.* April 24, 1382.

[1] Warrant to the Receiver of Lancashire to send all the money in his hands to him by his Queen, dated Roxburgh, June 23, 1386. Reg. II. 47.

[2] For Lancaster on the Border and in Scotland, his return and quarrel with Northumberland, see *Chr. Angl.* 327–30 ; Wals. ii. 414–5 ; Kn. 143–149 ; *Cronykil of Scotland*, iii. iv.16 ; *Scotichronicon*, xiv. 46 ; Froissart, *K de. L.* ix. 383–6 ; 397–8 ; 417–27.

London, Lancaster was safe within the castle walls of Knaresbrough ; two days' discussion with the Scottish marchers had already taken place at Coldingham and Abchester when the mob was wrecking the Savoy.[1]

But ill news flies fast, and before an understanding had been arrived at, it had reached the Border. The truth was terrible enough, but in the form in which the news reached Lancaster panic had exaggerated the danger. He was told that his castles in the south were lying in ruins, that everywhere his property had been destroyed, and that now two bodies of rebels, each ten thousand strong, were marching north, sworn to make him share the fate of the slaughtered Primate and Treasurer.

John of Gaunt was a true Plantagenet ; no sign of fear betrayed his secret to the Scottish envoys. While his couriers were riding with orders to the constables of his castles in Yorkshire and on the Welsh marches to garrison them for a siege and admit no one without letters under his seal,[2] the Duke quietly went on with the negotiations, and by the offer of liberal terms persuaded the Scots to prolong the truce.[3]

Not till the compact was sealed did the Scots learn that they had lost the golden opportunity of attacking England in the hour of weakness. Too loyal to repudiate their engagement, but unwilling to lose the chance of fighting, the Scottish Earls offered Lancaster an army to lead against the insurgents. To this strange offer, doubtless made in good faith, the Duke's answer was firm. Remembering that he was the representative of his country,

[1] £597 14s. 9d. was paid for the expenses of the negotiations between the Earl of Carrick and the Duke of Lancaster. *Exchequer Rolls of Scotland*, iii. 81.

[2] Warrants to the Constables of Whitecastle, Grosmont, Skenfrith, Tutbury and Tickhill, dated Berwick, June 19. Reg. II. 46–7.

[3] Payment of the balance of King David's ransom was postponed : the truce (to last till February 2, 1383) is dated Berwick, June 19, 1381. *Foed*, VII. 312–315.

and that his country's honour was at stake, he told the Scots that if their forces entered England, rebellion or no rebellion, they would find fighting enough before ever they reached York.

On leaving the Border he turned south, intending to march to the help of the King.[1]

At Bamborough he found reason to change his plans. It was not surprising that the rebels should be crying out for his life ; as the most prominent man among the ruling class he might expect to have to bear the brunt of revolutionary fury. But not only were the people against him ; the Government whom he was serving had, it seemed, declared him a traitor. The wildest rumours were repeated and believed ; one story said that he was marching South with an army of twenty thousand Scots to seize the kingdom ; according to another, he had freed all his bondmen, and they had sworn to make him King.[2] The man for whose head the Kent and Essex peasants had been clamouring found himself the centre of an imaginary conspiracy, the subject of wild and conflicting rumours, in which only one thing appeared probable, that he would be sacrificed to the fury of the insurgents and the hatred of his enemies. There was a general belief that the King had placed him beyond the protection of the law ; some of his men began to desert, his

---

[1] Lancaster's itinerary here becomes interesting : May 12, the Savoy ; 19 and 20, Leicester ; 26, 28, 31, Knaresboro' ; June 1 and 2, Knaresboro' ; 11 to 20, Berwick and Abchester (near Ayton) and Coldingham ; 20 and 21, Bamborough ; 23, Roxburgh ; 24, Melrose ; 25, 29, and 30, Edinburgh ; July 1 and 10, Edinburgh ; 13, Berwick ; 14, Bamborough ; 16, Newcastle ; 17, Durham ; 19, Northallerton ; 20 and 21, Boroughbridge ; 21 to 25, Pontefract ; 28, Leicester ; August 1 to 4, Leicester ; 7, Sunning ; 10, Reading ; 13, Southam ; 18, Brackley ; September 6, Pontefract, etc. (Reg.)

[2] Cf. *Rot. Pat.* Feb. 14 and April 14, 1383. Isolated cases of manumission and remission of dues on the part of Lancaster may have been talked of and exaggerated. Cf. Reg. II. f. 38, etc.

friends wavered, and his enemies declared themselves,[1] among the number Henry Percy. At length, the Earl thought, the time had come for getting rid of a rival on the Border, for Percy believed the Duke ruined, and the wish was father to the thought. Before the crisis he had invited the Duke to dine with him and stay for a night on the journey south. On leaving Berwick on June 20 the Duke received a curt message to the effect that he could not receive him or admit him to any castle in his charge without the King's licence. This threat was made good at Bamborough[2] by the Earl's order. Sir Matthew Redmayne, the Captain, shut its gates in the Duke's face, and even prevented the removal of the Duke's transport wagons, which had been left there during the negotiations at Berwick.

Betrayed by his friends, sacrificed, as he believed, by the Government, Lancaster turned back to the north and threw himself upon the protection of the Scots. The Earls of Carrick and Douglas had protested their friendship ; he put their professions to the test and was not disappointed. In answer to a letter asking for permission to visit Scotland, the Duke received an eager welcome. He might stay in Scotland at his pleasure and travel at his will ; his messengers were to be free to come and go and his armed retinue might accompany him.[3]

The Duke's late adversaries exhausted every possible courtesy in their welcome ; they met him at the Border, escorted him to the capital and lodged him in the Abbey of Holyrood, where, from June 25 to July 10, he re-

[1] Here the Monk of St. Albans inserts the usual repentance. *Chr. Angl.* 328. Kn. i . 147–8.

[2] Froissart says Newcastle.

[3] The letters of safe conduct for the Duke and for a hundred attendants (later two hundred) are dated Melrose June 22, and Scone, June 28, 1381. Reg. II. 147. See also warrants to the Receiver of Yorkshire to pay for sending archers from Knaresboro' to Berwick, dated Edinburgh, June 29 ; Berwick, July 13, and Pontefract, October 10. Reg. II. 48, 55.

mained the guest of the Scottish nation. It was an extraordinary situation; the greatest feudatory unable to return to his own country, the King's representative disowned, as it seemed, by the Government from which he was accredited, relying on the protection of a foreign power.

Obviously such a situation could not last, and it was natural that Lancaster should write to demand an explanation. He had been sent to the Border on the King's service, and had loyally carried out his instructions. He had been refused entrance to the King's castles, and had been given to understand that he was an outlaw and a traitor. If this had been done with the King's sanction, and if it were the King's pleasure, he was ready to turn his back on England and go into exile. Or, if his presence were required, he was willing to return without his retinue, with only a single knight, a squire and a servant to attend him.

The reply proved that the Earl of Northumberland and his party had misjudged the situation. The absurd stories of complicity in the rebellion, which his enemies had been willing to believe or at least to circulate, were never seriously entertained by those in authority. On the day that Lancaster entered Scotland the King had placed him at the head of a commission to quell disorder in the North.[1]

Richard requested his uncle to return, bringing with him a sufficient armed force. A writ commanded the sheriffs to protect him on the journey, and a proclamation denied the defamatory reports in circulation, declared the Duke's zeal for the King's service, and commanded all loyal subjects to render him due obedience,[2]

[1] The other Commissioners were the Earl of Northumberland, Lords Roos, Neville, Clifford, the Baron of Greystock, and Richard le Scrope. Dated Waltham, June 23, 1381. Reg. II. 150.
[2] Writs dated July 2 and 3. *Foed*, VII. 318-19. *Rot. Pat.*

while the Earl of Northumberland and Lord Neville were specially commissioned to escort the Duke through Northumberland, Yorkshire and Nottingham to the King's presence.

On July 10 John of Gaunt said farewell[1] to the city which had given him so royal a welcome, and which was soon to receive a signal proof of his gratitude.

He set out for the South, but not alone. Along the road from Edinburgh, through Haddington to Berwick, by which many a troop of English borderers had ridden back with the spoils of the Lothians, the Duke was escorted by his Scottish hosts, the Earls of Carrick and Douglas, the Lord of Galloway, and the principal barons of Scotland, with a guard of honour of eight hundred lances, to English territory, where Lord Neville, one of his retinue, met him with a body of men-at-arms, the escort of the Earl of Northumberland, present by the King's order, being dismissed.

Before the events of June could be forgotten there was more than one score to settle. The first was wiped out when the Duke reached Pontefract and laid on the goods and chattels of Sir Matthew Redmayne a fine amounting to half the damages due to Lord Archibald Douglas for trespasses done in Annandale in violation of the truce[2] But Sir Matthew was only a second; the duel with the principal was to be fought later. After five days' halt at Pontefract, Lancaster rode on through Leicester to the King at Reading, the sheriff of every county on the line of march turning out with his levies to swell the Duke's escort.

Expressions of good will, words and gifts[3] were all very well, but the Duke's honour had been touched, and

[1] Warrant to the Treasurer of the Household to send gold and silver cups to Scotland for presents, dated Edinburgh, July 10, 1381. Reg. II. 48.

[2] Warrant dated Pontefract July 23, 1381. Reg. II. 51.

[3] The Duke was promised the wardship of the first heiress

he intended to have satisfaction. Far more heinous in his judgment than the plot of the rebels against his life was the insolence of the Earl of Northumberland. Henry Percy was his kinsman,[1] had been his friend ; to him he owed his Earldom and the Marshal's staff. John of Gaunt regarded his conduct, therefore, as ingratitude and disloyalty, as well as gross disobedience and contempt of the King's representative. His complaint, laid before the King at Reading, was considered at an extraordinary meeting of the Council at Berkhamstead,[2] but Lancaster's demand for satisfaction only drew angry retorts from Northumberland, who, disappointed at the failure of his plan, was in no mood for conciliation. Threats and recriminations were exchanged until the King commanded both disputants to be silent. The Duke was wise enough to obey, but the Earl, losing control of himself, burst out into violent abuse of his rival, and ended by throwing down his gage of battle in the King's presence, for which he was placed under arrest until the

---

worth less than 1,000 marcs in the King's gift. *Rot. Pat.* (Carte) 208, 12.

[1] They were third cousins.

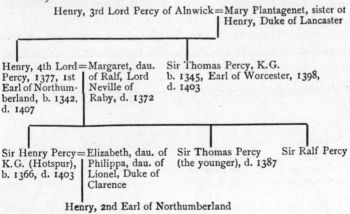

Henry, 3rd Lord Percy of Alnwick=Mary Plantagenet, sister of Henry, Duke of Lancaster

Henry, 4th Lord=Margaret, dau. Percy, 1377, 1st of Ralf, Lord Earl of Northumberland, b. 1342, Raby, d. 1372 d. 1407

Sir Thomas Percy, K.G. b. 1345, Earl of Worcester, 1398, d. 1403

Sir Henry Percy=Elizabeth, dau. of K.G. (Hotspur), Philippa, dau. of b. 1366, d. 1403 Lionel, Duke of Clarence

Sir Thomas Percy (the younger), d. 1387

Sir Ralf Percy

Henry, 2nd Earl of Northumberland

[2] *Higd.* ix. 10–11.

Earls of Warwick and Suffolk [1] went surety for his appearance at the forthcoming session of Parliament.

Sure of a backing from the Londoners in a quarrel with their great enemy, Percy forthwith enrolled himself as a citizen of London, and quartered troops of borderers in the City. But if it were to come to fighting the Duke could hold his own, as he showed when at the end of October he rode out of Leicester Castle with five hundred men at his back. As the session of Parliament approached London began to look like a city in a state of siege ; barricades were thrown up, and guards were set at the gates in case the Duke's men attempted to enter, —an unnecessary precaution, for Lancaster quartered his men at Fulham, and gave the City a wide berth.

When the session began at Westminster on November 3,[2] nothing could be done; the quarrel prevented any pretence of transacting public business ; the Peers all came armed and chose sides, and things looked like civil war. In the end the Earl of Northumberland had to submit. It was not only a gross outrage to shut the Duke out of Bamborough, but disobedience of orders, for the Duke held the King's commission. Again at Berkhamstead Lancaster's bearing had been correct, while Percy, by his violence, had placed himself hopelessly in the wrong. The sympathies of Parliament, too, were on the Duke's side, as appeared from the fact that the Commons named him among the committee of consultative peers, and that he was placed at the head of a committee appointed to reform the royal household.[3] The result

[1] William Ufford, who died a few weeks later. Higd. ix. ii.
[2] Parliament was summoned for the day after All Saints by writ dated August 22, 5 Rich. II. (Dugdale, *Summons*, 308). *Rot. Parl.* iii. 98–113. The first session lasted till December 13 ; the adjourned session from January 27 to February 25, 1382. *Rot. Parl.* iii. 113-122.
[3] The name of the Earl of Northumberland does not appear among the Triers of Petitions.

was an unconditional surrender on the part of the Earl. His apology, ample enough to satisfy the King's offended dignity and the Duke's honour, unlike that made by the Earl of Arundel four years later, was not entered upon the Rolls of Parliament, but Lancaster took care to have it enrolled in his private records.

Addressing the King the Earl said :—" My honoured liege Lord, in that in your high and honourable presence at Berkhamstead, I, in my ignorance, offended you by answering without leave or licence my Lord of Spain here present otherwise than I ought in reason to have done, and by throwing down my gage of battle before him, I submit myself to your grace and will, and pray you pardon my offence."

Then turning to the Duke :—" My Lord of Spain, in that in the presence of my redoubted Lord the King at Berkhamstead I answered, in my ignorance, otherwise than I ought to have done to you, my Lord, who are son to my redoubted Lord the King, whom God pardon, and uncle to my redoubted Lord the King here present, and so high a person and of such noble royalty of blood, and the greatest Lord and most high person of this realm after my liege Lord the King here present, who is of your blood and kindred, and also in that I cast down my gage of battle before you in the presence of my Lord the King, I beseech your honourable Lordship's pardon." Once more addressing Richard, the Earl said :—" My Liege Lord, as for the disobedience done to you, God knows that never was it my will or intent to disobey in any wise your Royal Majesty. And if through ignorance any disobedience were done, I submit me to your gracious will."

Finally turning to the Duke :—" My Lord of Spain, if any disobedience were done to you, in ignorance or otherwise, such was not my intent, and I pray you pardon me and forego your anger. And as for the disloyalty charged against me, I am not always so wise or well advised as to do always what is best ; and insomuch as I have failed to do my duty as fully and naturally to your Lordship as I might have done and as I was bound to do, I beseech you have me excused of your good lordship, which I desire with all my heart." [1]

After this apology had cleared the air it became possible to proceed to business—the business of restoring

---

[1] Apres les replications Monseignur Despaigne sanz responce del Conte de Northumbreland ce fust la submission du dit Conte en pleine Parlement.

Mon treshonore Seignur Liege quant a ce que en vostre honorable et haute presence a Berkhampstede sanz congie et license de vous monseignur liege par ma ignorance Je vous desplesa respoignant Monseignur D'Espaigne qi si est autrement que je ne devoi de réson faire et en mettant mon gage devers lui je me sumet en votre grace et ordonance et vous prie de pardonner de ma desplesance.

Et Monseignur d'Espaigne quant a ce que en presence mon tres redoute Seignur le Roi a Berkhamstede je vous respondue par ma ignorance autrement que je ne devoy faire a vous Monseignur qui estez filz a mon tresredoute Seignur liege le Roi qui Dieux assoille et Uncle a mon tresredoute Seigneur le Roy liege qi si est, et si haute persone et de si tresnoble regalite de sang come vous estez Monseignur et auxint a vous Monseignur qui estez le plus grant seignur et plus haute persone del Roialme apres mon Seignur liege le Roi qi si est, et est de votre sang et alliance mettant mon gage devers vous en presence Monseignur liege le Roy qi si est Je vous prie pardon de votre honourable seignurie.

Monseignur lige quant a la desobeissance envers vous dieux sait que unque n'estoit ma volentee ne entente a desobeir aucunement a votre Roiale Mageste. Et si aucune y estoit par ignorance Je me en souzmett a votre gracieuse ordenance.

Monseignur d'Espaigne si aucune desobeisance estoit fait a vous par ignorance ou autrement ce n'estoit mye ma entencion en suppliant que vous me veullez pardonner votre maltalent.

Et quant a l'autre matire touchante disnaturesse a moy surmise Je ne fu mye si sages ne avisez de faire toutdys le meilliour et en ce que je n'ay faite si naturelment ne si pleinement mon devoir devers votre seignurie come je pourroy avoir fait ou come je fuy tenuz il m'en poise fortment et vous supplie de votre bone seignurie la quele je desire de tout mon cuer.

(Register, II. f. 153 *intergo*.)

order and confidence in the country after the upheaval of the summer.

On one point all parties were agreed—cordial support of the King's action in cancelling the charters of manumission. The Commons assumed responsibility for the act and gave it their sanction. For the rest, they contented themselves with abusing the administration and indulging in an academic analysis of some of the social evils of the times. Their reflections,[1] which are interesting but innocent of much practical result, were cut short by the news of the arrival of Anne of Bohemia, the chosen bride of Richard II,[2] and the session was adjourned for the royal marriage[3] and the coronation of the young Queen.

[1] Higd. ix. ii.   [2] *Cont. Eulog.* ii. 355.
   [3] Kn. ii. 150.   *Chr. Angl.* 331.

Chapter XII

PARLIAMENT AND THE KING OF CASTILE

WHEN Parliament met again after the King's marriage, for the adjourned session, it must have marked the strange tenacity of purpose shown by John of Gaunt in the pursuit of the object which for ten years had been uppermost in his mind—the conquest of Castile. It was a perfectly definite proposal which the Duke laid before Parliament at the end of January, 1382. He asked for 60,000 pounds to be advanced to him to pay two thousand men-at-arms and two thousand archers for six months for operations in Portugal and Castile, offering as security the Lancastrian estates, and undertaking, if he were neither killed nor captured, to repay the debt within a period of three years, either in money or service, at the King's choice.[1]

It was unfortunate for the Duke that the proposal came at a time when the condition of England was so unsettled, and when his opponents could urge the danger of withdrawing a considerable body of fighting men from the country. This consideration had weight with the Commons, and while voting supplies for the next few years for national defence and for "resisting the malice of the King's enemies," they declined to express any opinion on the question whether Lancaster's proposal would or would not be the best means of achieving that object. Going further, they expressly protested that their action must not be interpreted directly or indirectly as sanctioning the scheme.[1] Discussion on the policy involved had been heated, and the conclusion bears all the marks of compromise. It was understood that while the Commons were lukewarm, a majority of the Peers favoured the scheme. To pour out English blood and treasure in the dynastic quarrel of a single member of the royal family might, to the clearer and cooler heads, appear unjustifiable; but England had grown used to dynastic quarrels. The ambitions of Edward III were as personal as those of his son, and it was only a succession of great victories which had made his private quarrel a national cause. To enlist popular sympathy for the present undertaking Lancaster did not fail to dwell on the effects of the Franco-Castilian alliance.[2] Two years before, a French and Castilian fleet had sailed up the Thames and burnt Gravesend. The damage done to English shipping made it easy to represent the expedition as a matter of public policy, and to urge that if England were smarting under the loss of the control of the seas, the country had only to support the Portuguese alliance to restore the disturbed balance of naval power.

But the strongest argument that the supporters of the scheme could urge was that public faith was already

[1] Faisantz nientmains lour protestation expressement, qe l'entention de la Commune d'Engleterre n'est mye de leur obliger parmy aucunes paroles devant ditz a la querele, conquest, ou la guerre del Roialme d'Espaigne en especial par aucune voie, einz soulement en general, al defens du Roialme d'Engleterre et resistance des ditz enemys (*Rot. Parl.* iii. 114).

[2] Within a few days of his accession Juan had despatched eight galleys to the assistance of Charles V. The next year (1380), at Seville, " fizo armar veinte galeas, las quales envió con Don Ferrand Sanchez de Tovar su Almirante, en ayuda del Rey de Francia ; pero el Rey de Francia pagó lo que costaron armar las diez galeas, segund los tratos que eran entre ellos. Las quales ficieron grand guerra este año á los Ingleses por la mar ; é entraron por el rio de Artamisa fasta cerca de la cibdad de Londres, á dó galeas de enemigos nunca entraron." Ayala, ii. 130.

pledged, and that it was imperative to support the English army then in Portugal under the command of the Earl of Cambridge. To understand Lancaster's position it is necessary to make a brief retrospect of the politics of the Spanish peninsula, and his share in them, during the period between the proposal to Parliament of January, 1382, and those first treaties with Portugal ten years earlier, the effect of which was frustrated by the great failure of 1373.

The throne of Portugal in 1382 was still occupied by Fernando and his consort Leonor. Their most powerful minister was João Fernando d'Andeiro, Count of Ourem, Master of the Order of St. James of Portugal, and, unless Leonor of Portugal has been deeply wronged, the lover of the Queen.

In 1380 Andeiro was at Richard's court, engaged in procuring a renewal of the former treaties between England and Portugal and in particular the treaty between his master and the claimant of the Castilian throne.[1] For the moment the main object of his mission was unattainable, for the condition of domestic politics kept Lancaster at home ; but the Count concluded an agreement by which the Earl of Cambridge was to be sent to Portugal with a thousand lances and as many archers, to make a combined attack with Fernando upon Juan I of Castile,[2]

[1] Commission from Richard II dated Westminster, May 23, 1380. Andeiro was in England at the time, acting as intermediary between the two courts. *Foed*, VII. 253–4.

[2] See in *Foed*. VII. 262–5, three instruments of the King and Queen of Portugal dated Estremos, July 15, 1380 (in the era of Portugal, 1418).

(1) Renewal in favour of Richard II as King of England and France of the previous alliance with Edward III, concluded by Juan Fernandez and Vasco Dominguez, Canon of Braganza. (Confirmed by Richard II, May 14, 1381. *Foed*, VII. 307).

(2) Renewal of the alliance with John of Gaunt as King of Castile, concluded by the same envoys. (See Ch. V. p. 101 and note.)

who had succeeded his father Enrique the Bastard in 1379.[1]

Juan had inherited the kingdom, but little of that dashing courage which, in spite of disaster, had set up the House of Trastamare. With his last words Enrique II had urged his heir to continue the French alliance ; the first act of Juan I was to renew that alliance and send a fleet to the help of Charles V.[2] A blind reliance on France supplied the place of a policy with the Bastard's degenerate son ; equally distrustful, with perhaps equal justice, of himself and his subjects, the young king looked to France to maintain the power which France had created.

From the day of his accession Juan was haunted by the spectre of the Lancastrian claim. While John of Gaunt lived Juan could know no peace. In renewing the old alliances with the power north of the Pyrenees, he was careful to stipulate that if ever the Duke of Lancaster were captured in any operations of the allied armies, the prisoner should be handed over to him to be dealt with at his pleasure.[3]

But John of Gaunt was not destined to languish in a Castilian dungeon. While the Duke was detained in England by Border politics his brother, the Earl of Cambridge, for the time took his place, and in 1381 led an English army to fight the battles of Portugal and Lancaster against their common enemy.[4]

Leaving England in June, 1381, Cambridge dropped

(3) Undertaking (also contained in 2) to support Cambridge's force in the campaign against Castile and to marry the Infanta Beatrix to his son Edward.

[1] Enrique II died Monday, May 30, 1379. Ayala, ii. 123 (and note).

[2] Ayala, ii. 138–9 ; 125.

[3] Treaty concluded Bicètre, April 22, 1381. *Pièces Inédites*, i. 15.

[4] Orders to impress ships for the Earl of Cambridge, dated May 12, 1381. *Foed*, VII. 305. Juan had intelligence of the preparations. Ayala, ii. 151–2.

anchor in the Lisbon roads just at the time when the Essex peasants were wrecking the Savoy and the Spanish admiral, Tovar, after routing a Portuguese fleet, was landing his prisoners at Seville.[1]

The first part of the engagements concluded by the Count of Ourem was soon fulfilled. Fernando of Portugal had no heir. His little daughter Beatrix, born to him by Leonor Telles de Meneses (whose husband João Lourenço da Cunha he had driven into exile), was recognized as heiress of the kingdom, and the Pope, to reward the support of his firmest ally in the peninsula, had covered by a Bull of legitimation her more than doubtful birth.

Immediately after Cambridge and his men had reached Lisbon this child was married to Edward Plantagenet, the Earl's son. Then the English marched to the frontier and waited for the campaign to begin.

They waited in vain. The result of the mission of the Count of Ourem had been a blow to his master's hopes. Instead of Lancaster at the head of a field army, determined to prosecute his quarrel with Castile to the end, Cambridge, a man of no energy and little experience, had been sent to Portugal with a force which by his own admission was only strong enough for a reconnaissance. While Fernando waited[2] for Lancaster and the bulk of the invading army which he had been led to expect, Cambridge's force, quartered between Estremos and Villaviciosa, on the right bank of the Guadiana, almost within sight of the Spanish outposts, grew daily more discontented.

Their orders were precise. There was to be no attack. But the dull routine of garrison duty in Alemtejo soon

---

[1] Ferrand Sanchez de Tovar, Admiral of Castile, defeated the Portuguese Admiral Juan Alfonso Tello, brother of Leonor, the Queen, on June 17. Cambridge landed about the same time at Lisbon. Ayala, ii. 153.

[2] One difficulty which the King of Portugal had to face was that of mounting the English force, a treaty obligation. Cambridge brought no horses. Ayala, ii. 155.

exhausted their patience. Ignoring their orders and the remonstrances of their general, the Earl's men crossed the river and sacked a few of the enemy's towns out of sheer *ennui*. Disobedience of orders was made a pretext for withholding pay—the worst grievance that soldiers of fortune could suffer. The result was a mutiny. In this expedition the Earl of Cambridge counted for nothing. He could neither manage his troops nor his ally. While he remained on the spot, feebly protesting, a deputation went to the King at Lisbon with the threat that if he did not begin fighting they would begin without him, and that if he would not fulfil his treaty obligations by paying their wages they would help themselves.

The argument was convincing ; the troops were paid and Fernando promised to open the campaign in June. In spite of renewed representations to the English court,[1] there was still no sign of Lancaster's arrival. From the first the Portuguese king had been playing a double game, for, a couple of months after the offensive alliance with Richard II and the Duke of Lancaster against Castile, he had entered into absolutely incompatible engagements with the supposed enemy.[2] With no intentions of fighting, Fernando marched to Elvas in the summer while the enemy advanced to Badajóz. The Guadiana alone separated the two armies, but nothing happened except negotiation.[3]

It was useless for Lancaster to plead the cause of his brother and his ally in Council and Parliament. First

---

[1] Venerunt . . . quidem episcopus et quidem miles cancellarius regis Portugaliae duci Lancastriae missi quatinus dirigeret auxilium fratri suo comiti Cantabrigiae. Sed dum ista fierent concordati sunt reges. Higd. ix. 15.

Lourenço Fogaça, the Chancellor, was on the point of leaving England for Portugal on July 5, 1382. *Foed*, VII. 361.

[2] The Infanta Beatrix of Portugal was to marry the Infante Enrique of Castile and the two kingdoms were to be ultimately united. Ayala, ii. 132.

[3] Ayala, ii. 156–7.

one and then another obstacle was thrown in his way. The Parliament which sat at Westminster in May, 1382,[1] had refused to discuss anything but a proposal, constantly debated but never seriously entertained, for the King to go in person to France.

In October[2] the Duke seemed to have made a little progress, for one of the first subjects put forward for discussion was the " socours de les nobles gentz esteantz en Portugal, illocques esteanz en grant peril." He had lost one ally, for his friend, Richard le Scrope, had been forced to surrender the seal in July[3] for a sturdy opposition to Richard's reckless alienation of crown lands, but the Bishop of Hereford supported the Duke's policy, and, addressing Parliament in the King's name, in a pessimistic account of foreign relations, assured the House that the shortest way to the goal of the wars was a vigorous support of the Portuguese undertaking.

The kingdom, he told the House, had never been in greater danger : its very existence was at stake. But the Chancellor's hopes for the future were as bright as his view of the present was gloomy. It was an attractive picture that he sketched for the Commons. For the paltry sum of £43,000 (it had been estimated at £60,000 before) in wages for the Duke's army the Commons would get a speedy and sure return. In six months Lancaster, with the help of Heaven, would be King of Spain, and England would have seen the last of the war and war budgets.

This was promising : still more so was the attitude of the Commons in naming not only Lancaster but Lords

---

[1] Parliament sat from May 6 to 22 at Westminster ; the Duke as usual was among the Triers of Petitions. *Rot. Parl.* iii. 122–131.

[2] Parliament met at Westminster on October 6, 1382. *Rot. Parl.* iii. 132–143).

[3] Higd. ix. 14; Wals. ii, 68-70; *Chr. Angl.* 353-4.

Neville and Richard le Scrope among the Peers to confer with them on the proposal. The result was a victory for the cause. The Commons declared the scheme of invasion to be "honourable and profitable for the realm," remarking somewhat pertinently that an army of two thousand men seemed scarcely adequate for the conquest of Castile. At length the scheme was sanctioned : but too late ! For the King of Portugal at last had made up his mind, chosen his side and made terms with the enemy. There was a strong party in Castile which had no desire to see Lancaster on their frontiers reinforcing a Portuguese army, and a *modus vivendi* had been reached. Quietly ignoring the engagements just entered into, Fernando promised the hand of his daughter Beatrix to the second son of the King of Castile, and made peace with his enemy without consulting his ally.[1]

Fernando pleaded that he had not been treated in good faith. He had been led to expect Lancaster and Lancaster had not come. Cambridge could only protest and withdraw. Taking Prince Edward with him he returned to England, out of temper with the Government which had failed to support him, his army which had mutinied, and his ally who had made peace behind his back. To complete his humiliation he was brought home in a Castilian fleet, for Juan, only anxious to be rid of English interference in the politics of the peninsula, had placed ships at the disposal of his new ally to replace the fleet captured by his admiral in 1381.[2]

---

[1] Ayala, ii. 158–9. The Infanta Beatrix had already been betrothed three times. (1) to Don Fadrique, brother of Juan I of Castile ; (2) to Enrique (III), Infante of Castile ; (3) to Edward Plantagenet, and now (4) to Don Fernando, brother of the Infante Enrique. For (1) and (2) see Ayala, ii. 131.

[2] Ayala, ii. 159–60. Higd. ix. 14–15. Cambridge returned to England about Christmas, 1382. He sat in the Parliament which met on February 23, 1383. *Rot. Parl.* iii. 145a.

At the close of 1382 the golden opportunity seemed lost beyond hope. So sure had Lancaster felt of succeeding that before the end of the October Parliament he had called out his retinue and made preparations for the expedition.[1]

Then came the news of the humiliating fiasco. To the end the Duke never forgave the blundering half-measures of the Government and his brother's incompetence, and seventeen years later in his will he expressly disclaimed any responsibility for the cost of Cambridge's expedition.

His disappointment at the result of his brother's achievements in Portugal was shared by others also. It was quite clear that the money spent on the expedition was so much waste, and the undertaking itself one of those costly half-measures that could satisfy no one. Its uselessness was certainly realized by the Parliament which sat at Westminster in February and March, 1383,[2] a session decidedly hostile to Lancastrian influences. The Commons showed their hostility first by omitting the Duke's name from the list of advisory Peers, and secondly, by actively opposing his wishes.

Departing from their usual attitude of reserve in relation to foreign policy, the Commons, alarmed at the attitude of the Scots, entreated the King neither to leave England himself in the existing condition of foreign affairs, nor to allow his uncles to withdraw from the country, which needed their protection.[3] They went further, and petitioned Richard to listen to the proposals of his Gascon vassal, the Sieur de Lesparre, who professed to have

---

[1] Warrant dated November 20, 1382. Reg. II. f. 65.

[2] Parliament was summoned for Monday in the third week of Lent by writ dated January 7, 1383 (Dugdale, *Summons*, 315.) *Rot. Parl.* iii. 144–8).

[3] Semble a la Commune avaunt dite, que vous notre Seigneur lige, ne nul de voz trois Uncles, de Lancastre, de Cantebr', et de Bukyngham, purra quant au present estre desportez hors de votre Roialme (*Rot. Parl.* iii. 145 b).

found a convincing solution of the Spanish problem, showing thereby an unmistakable unwillingness to be drawn further into the vortex of Lancastrian dynastic ambitions.[1]

This recommendation had weight : John of Gaunt could not ignore it. Probably the dispatches of his trusted councillor Juan Guttierez, now Bishop of Dax, who was in Spain at the time, contained matter for serious reflection. At any rate, as there seemed no prospect of succeeding by force, the Duke was persuaded to try other means. The inheritance of Don Pedro was still an asset, and though difficult to realize, something could be raised on it. War being for the time out of the question, the Duke raised no objection to diplomacy. The duel was not to be foregone, but he would change the broadsword for the foil. In April, 1383, he acquiesced in the appointment of commissioners to find a pacific settlement of the differences between England, himself, and Castile,[2] and

[1] Item, la Commune prierent a notre Seignur le Roi, qu'il vousist doner ascout et audience al Seignur de la Sparre, qi novelment s'estoit venuz del Roialme d'Espaigne, lequiel Seignur dit, et il se face fort, que a l'aide notre Seignur de Roi, si vous notre Seignur lige vorrez a ce encliner de votre grace, qu'il vous monstrera diverses bones et honorables voies, par lesquelles vous pourrez bien honorablement venir a la Paix avec le dit Roialme d'Espaigne ; laquelle Paix si vous notre Seignur Lige purrez avoir, votre honor salvez, pur Dieux le vorrez rescevier et prendre, pour grant profit de vous et de votre Roilame, et quiete de vos subgitz.

A quoy feust responduz de par le Roi de son commandment, Qe le Roi s'adviseroit avec les seignurs de son roiaume, et sur ce par lour advis ent ferroit ce qe lui sembleroit a faire en le cas, son honor salve (*Rot. Parl.* iii. 148 b).

[2] Dated April 1, 1383. They are also accredited to the courts of Aragon and Navarre, and empowered to make terms with the King's rebellious Gascon vassal, the Count of Armagnac. *Foed*, VII. 386–90. Warrant dated April 19, 1383, to the Treasurer of the Household to pay £40 to the Bishop of Dax for his journey to Spain. Reg. II. f. 72. The departure from England of Alfonso Ruys, Knight of Cordova, envoy from Portugal, closes the

the diversion of the martial enthusiasm of his countrymen into a different channel.

When the Parliament of the autumn of 1382 had
approved of the project of invading Castile, it had at the
same time given a still more pronounced opinion in
favour of another proposal—an expedition to Flanders
to support Ghent against Bruges, and the popular party
of Flanders against the Count and French influence.
The Count was a Clementist, and his suzerain Charles,
King of France, was the strongest supporter of the
Anti-pope. Therefore Urban had urged the invasion
of Flanders and had consecrated the expedition with the
sanctity of a crusade. This crusade was the pet project
of Henry le Spencer, Bishop of Norwich. The Bishop
was one of those prelates who were particularly obnoxious
to the Duke of Lancaster. Like William Courtenay, he
had strong family influence, great energy and ambition
of a pronounced secular flavour. He represented the
system denounced by Wycliffe in the interests of apostolic
purity and detested by John of Gaunt in the interests of
feudal power. The Bishop's hobby was fighting. His
exploits in this direction won him the favour of the Pope,
the nickname " Pugil Ecclesie " and, later, a place among
Capgrave's portraits of the " Illustrious Henries." [1] In
his youth he had fought the enemies of the Church in the
service of Urban V. His reward was the Bishopric of
Norwich, granted by Papal provision in 1370 Then, for ten
years the unfortunate prelate had been condemned to
the dull routine of diocesan work. His opportunity came
again in 1381, when in the universal panic of the Peasants'
Rebellion, the Bishop had scored some successes over
the insurgents in East Anglia, and had duly confessed

negotiation with Don Fernando. See Letters of Protection,
dated June 9, 1383. *Foed*, VII. 396.

[1] In robore juventutis sola bella sitire visus est. Capgrave,
De Illustribus Henricis, 170.

and hanged the ringleaders of the revolt. A little success is a dangerous thing. Flushed with his triumph over a disorderly mob of half-armed peasants, the Bishop aspired to lead armies against the enemies of the faith and to win the fame of a Crusader.

To the disgust of Lancaster and the Peers, in 1383 he was allowed to lead an expedition to Flanders in fulfilment of the Pope's commission.[1]

Devout ladies, fascinated by the dashing piety of this hero of the Church Militant, contributed gold and jewels, and the doctrines of purgatorial torment denounced by Wycliffe's preaching were exploited to their full value to fill the Bishop's war-chest.

Landing in Flanders, he took Gravelines and marched into Dunkirk without much difficulty, commemorating his victories over the peaceful Flemings, who were as good subjects of Urban as himself, by the pompous title of " Conqueror of West Flanders." There his short career of victory ended. There was no discipline among his mob of armed priests, sham regulars and sanctified adventurers. His captains got out of hand, and some of them were suspected of negotiating with the enemy. The Bishop, having undertaken the siege of Ypres to please Ghent, was compelled to withdraw on the advance of a French army, and to shut himself up in Gravelines. After an ignominious failure he was released by the good offices of the Duke of Brittany and allowed to return to England. The Bishop, who had set out " en establisment de seint Esglyse," beyond slaughtering a few thousand faithful subjects of the canonical Pope, had done nothing. He had thrown away the forces which Lancaster wanted to lead against Castile, and on his return he was punished with the loss of his temporalities, while to complete his humiliation he was made to pay for masses for the souls of those whom he had destroyed !

[1] *Chr. Angl.* 355 ; Wals. ii. 71-82, 88-104 ; *Eulog.* 357.

JOHN OF GAUNT

" Benedictus Deus qui confundit insolentes "—such is the comment of the continuator of the *Eulogium.*

Another failure was registered in the account of the executive. Little wonder that the Commons began to weary of the constant proposals for war. In the summer of 1383 the Duke had concluded a truce with the Scots. That was so much to the good, for the country was growing daily more anxious for peace. But instead of building " castles in Spain " the Duke had to undertake yet further diplomatic duties, for when Parliament met at Westminster in October,[1] foreign relations were once more the burning question of the hour. The great seal was now in the hands of the Duke's friend Sir Michael de la Pole, and the Chancellor, in declaring the causes of the summons of Parliament, laid stress, undue stress it might seem, on the dangers of the kingdom.

On all sides, France, Spain and Flanders, England was encompassed by enemies. Unless God of His grace should provide a remedy, and the faithful Commons do their part, the greatest mischief might ensue. The result was that John of Gaunt was sent to France, where in the following January he concluded a short truce.

All this had done nothing directly towards the achievement of the great quest. In the autumn of 1383 the dynastic claim seemed to have merely an academic interest for politics. Mismanagement and misfortune had combined to ruin the chances of invading Castile with the help of Portugal.

Suddenly a gleam of hope broke across the darkness of the situation. When the Earl of Cambridge left Portugal at the end of 1382, taking Edward Plantagenet away from his child-bride the Infanta Beatrix, who for a while the pivot of Peninsula politics, her hand had just been pledged by his fickle ally to the second son of the King of Castile.

[1] *Rot Parl.* iii. 149-65.

JOHN I OF PORTUGAL

After four successive betrothals the Infanta at length found a husband, for in 1382 the Queen of Castile died, and the next year Juan I, supplanting his son, married the heiress of the kingdom of Portugal himself. Solemn oaths bound the nobles of both kingdoms to accept the ultimate union of their crowns. By the marriage treaty it was provided that on the death of Don Fernando, Leonor his widow should be regent until the child to be born of the union of Juan and Beatrix reached the age of fourteen ; then the heir to Castile should become sovereign of Portugal, and Portugal and Castile should become one.

Fernando had agreed with his adversary in haste ; his subjects were left to repent at leisure. To the forces of disunion, difference of race and language, blood and tradition, must be added the bitter hatred bred by long feuds on the border, for in the fourteenth century Portuguese hated Castilian as the Scot hated his southern neighbour.

These passions, instinct of race and a fierce love of independence, Fernando had chosen to defy. When the time came it is not surprising that two-thirds of those who had sworn to the marriage treaty of Badajóz in 1382, broke their oaths, and would have none of the foreign dynasty. The day of reckoning came soon, for in October, 1383, Fernando died, and the question of the succession was opened at once. Leonor his widow ought by the terms of the treaty to have become Regent, but Juan of Castile at once assumed the royal style of Portugal and prepared to enforce his claim by arms. A possible pretender, João, half-brother of the late king by Inez de Castro, was seized and imprisoned in Castile. But there was another João, also half-brother of the late king, who was to prove a more formidable rival, and he, as fate would have it, had been left out of the reckoning.

João, afterwards surnamed " de Boa Memoria," the hero of Portuguese independence, whose fortunes now

273

find a place in the Lancastrian story, was the son of
Pedro I and Theresa Lourenço, and Grand Master of
one of the four great orders of chivalry in Portugal,
the Cistercian Order of Avis.

Within two months of Dom Fernando's death the cities
of Portugal elected him Regent.

Being a man of action, his first step was to kill the
Count of Ourem, a veteran intriguer who had negotiated
the hated marriage of the Infanta Beatrix to the
Castilian king, and who, with the help of his paramour,
the Queen, was trying to sell his country into bondage.

The Count disposed of, Queen Leonor was dismissed
to repent in a cloister. At first the Portuguese tried to
reconcile the Infanta's claims with national independence.
To acknowledge Beatrix as Queen in theory and to vest the
royal power in the Regent was the first solution attempted.
But no peaceful solution was possible, for the enemy were
overrunning the country, and Leonor, to avenge her
lover's death, had transferred her treaty rights as Regent
to the invader. Juan advanced through the heart of
Portugal, occupied Santarem and shut up Dom João in
Lisbon. For four months the siege dragged on, until
the plague threatened to annihilate the army of Castile
and forced Don Juan to withdraw.

Meanwhile the Regent had sent to England for help.
Once more a Portuguese ruler was in difficulties, the
enemy being a prince of the House of Trastamare, and
once more it was to England that Portugal turned for
help.[1] The new Master of the Order of St. James, Dom

[1] Acordaram de enviar pedir a el rei de Inglaterra que lhe
prouvesse dar lugar e licença aos do seu reino, que por soldo e
a sua vontade viessem ajudar contra seus inimigos (Fernão Lopes,
i. 141). The envoys left Lisbon at the end of March, 1384 (ibid.
v. 80), landed at Plymouth on April 10 and did not return until
1386, when they landed at Coruña on July 5. Lopes makes a
mistake of a year when he says (v. 110): " Os quaes duraram fóra
do reino do dia que partiram de Lisboa até que chegaram á

ENGLISH RECRUITS FOR PORTUGAL

Fernando Affonso de Albuquerque and Lourenço Annes Fogaça, Chancellor of Portugal, were despatched to recruit in the dominions of Portugal's traditional ally.[1]

In spite of Dom Fernando's treatment of the last English army which had come to the Peninsula, the envoys found no difficulty in raising a strong body of men. A stream of volunteers, archers and men-at-arms flowed from England to Portugal, and their help in the great crisis of Portuguese history was never forgotten, for the English contingent had no small part in the victories of the campaign which followed.

Such support, however, was purely voluntary and unofficial; the ambassadors hoped for something more. Their credentials were addressed not only to Richard II, but to the " King of Castile," and they were charged with the duty of renewing the proposals made by Fernando before the fiasco of 1381-2 for joint operations against Juan of Trastamare.

Once more John of Gaunt began the task of importuning King and Parliament for men and money to fight his battles.

For the next few years the chief interest of his life and the key to his position in domestic politics, is to be found in his foreign relations, in his efforts to overcome the

Corunha *trez* annos e trez mezes e vinte e cinco dias. *Trez* should be *dois*, viz. March 3,[1]1384 (1383, old style, which probably explains the error) to July 5, 1386.

[1] For recruiting in England by the Master of St. James and Chancellor of Portugal, see licence dated July 28, 1384. (*Foed* VII, 436); letters of protection for thirty recruits dated December 1st, 1384 ; (ibid. 450-1) ; for fifty-five more dated January 16, 1385 (ibid. 454) ; orders to arrest ships for their passage to Portugal dated January 8, 1385 (ibid. 453) ; orders to arrest all Portuguese ships in English ports and to hand them over to the Chancellor and Grand Master, dated January 23 (ibid. 455), and May 26, 1385 (ibid. 472-3) ; appointment of commissioners of array, February 16, 1385 (ibid., 462-3) ; letters of protection for the Portuguese envoys for a further period of six months, dated October 20, 1385 (ibid. 479).

obstacles successively placed in his path, until at length the very jealousy and suspicion which had thwarted his designs overreached itself and conceded him his desire.

It was obvious that so long as the Commons continued to feel the nervousness on the score of foreign relations which they had displayed in recent Parliaments, the Duke would never induce them to vote supplies for an army to invade Castile. His task therefore was to remove apprehension by improving the relations between England and her enemies, and this, with the attempt to keep the peace among the factions at home, fully occupied him for the next few years. In December, 1383, and the January following he was at Calais, debating terms with the Dukes of Berri and Brittany for the renewal of the truce ; the result was the Truce of Lelinghen,[1] the half-way house between Calais and Boulogne, where so many French and English envoys met, by which peace was assured until September 29, 1384. If the period were short, and seemed a poor result for two months' negotiations carried on as usual at ruinous expense, it was at least a diplomatic victory for Lancaster, for he had secured one concession all-important for his object—the Scots were to be free to come within the provisions of the agreement.

To induce the allies of Charles VI to profit by this condition was another matter.

The truce with Scotland ran out on February 2. The Scots lost no time ; on the 5th Archibald Douglas, Lord of Galloway, that dark spare big-boned hero of the

---

[1] For the negotiations of December, 1383, and January, 1384, ending with the truce of Lelinghen, concluded January 26, 1384, see *Religieux de St. Denys*, i. 299, and *Partie Inédite des Grandes Chroniques de France* (Pierre d'Orgemont), p. 44 ; Lancaster's powers, dated September 8, 1383 (*Foed*, VII, 407-8), notification of the appointment of the envoys, dated September 12 and November 4 (ibid. 408-410) ; letters of safe conduct for the French envoys dated November and December (ibid. 412-8).

Scotichronicon, who with eighty men could rout an army of two thousand and take five hundred prisoners, surprised Lochmaben Castle, and a little later the Baron of Greystock, while on his way to Roxburgh, was captured by the Earl of March, who carried him off to Dunbar, and set before him a feast served from his own plate in a hall hung with his own tapestries. Meanwhile, envoys to Scotland were in England commissioned to lay the terms before the Scots.[1]

On Lancaster's return the English Government, annoyed by the reverse in Annandale, schemed for revenge by means which can only be described as sharp practice.[2]

The French envoys were entertained with unnecessary cordiality, and every inducement was held out to them to prolong their stay in the south, for the Government intended to strike a blow before the Scots could come within the provisions of the truce. Unfortunately they were hampered in their choice of a general. Any military command went as a matter of course to the Duke of Lancaster, and the Duke was therefore sent north with orders to ravage the Lowlands and avenge the loss of Annandale. John of Gaunt had his private reasons for wishing well to his late hosts, but apart from personal motives, he had made it his settled policy to cultivate good relations with the northern neighbours. But further, to invade Scotland at the present moment was to stultify the whole of the negotiations just concluded at Lelinghen and to throw away the whole result of his labours. Lancaster was not a man to set aside the policy of years at the bidding of the King's Council. Regarding the invasion as a flagrant act of bad faith, but being unable to prevent it, he determined to carry out his instruc-

---

[1] Letters of safe-conduct, dated February 13, 1384. *Foed*, VII. 423.
[2] *Exchequer Rolls of Scotland*, Vol. III. lxiii (Introduction).

tions in such a way as to inflict as little damage as possible.

The rendezvous was Newcastle on March 24,[1] and the Duke entered Scotland on April 4, and following the east coast route viâ Haddington, Berwick, Dunbar and Preston, marched on Edinburgh.[2] A flotilla of store ships followed the army from the Humber, as before during the invasion of Edward III in 1355. A couple of ships were surprised at Queensferry—the only loss in action during the whole military promenade, for the Scots, true to their usual policy, avoided the enemy and withdrew to the north of the Firth. Arriving within striking distance of Edinburgh the Duke called a halt, and refused to leave his camp until the citizens had had time to remove their property. When the army entered, the city was deserted. All movables had been carried away; looting was impossible, and wrecking was forbidden by the most stringent orders. Holyrood Abbey, where the Duke had stayed in the troubled days of 1381, and the city itself were saved from the flames. Was there no fair châtelaine to entreat the general to spare Edinburgh as the Countess of Douglas had entreated Edward III thirty years before? Or must the more prosaic story of a ransom[3] be accepted? The fact remains,

---

[1] Mandate dated March 17 to the Sheriff of Lancaster to meet the Duke with all men-at-arms and archers arrayed within the Duchy at Newcastle on March 24. *Record Report*, xl. Ap. (4), No. 35. Cf. ibid. No. 36, 37.

[2] For the demonstration in Scotland, April 3–18, 1384, see *Cronykil of Scotland*, Ch. V. § 2, p. 20; *Scotichronicon*, xiv. 48; Hig. ix. 32; Kn. ii. 203; Wals. ii. 111–112; *Chr. Angl.* 358–9; *Ypod. Neust.* 339; *Mon. Eve*, 50.

[3] Bot thai that dwelt into the towne
Gert it be sawffyt for ransowne.
—*Cronykil of Scotland*.

Sed propter Scotorum curialitatem sibi per prius exhibitam quanto minus potuit malum eis ingessit burgenses favorabili summa pecuniae promissa et postea soluta villam redimerunt *Scotichronicon* ibid). Malverne has the same story.

that the Duke, out of gratitude to his Scottish hosts, and in pursuance of his policy, refused to allow a single house to be burned.

By April 23 he was back at Durham. His demonstration had only lasted a fortnight, and beyond burning a few villages on the march and destroying some of the woods of the Lothians, he had done nothing ; but the spring had been exceptionally severe, and the army had suffered accordingly.

Before leaving the North the Duke, in consultation with his friend and recent enemy, Henry Percy, drew up an agreement as to the defence of the border.[1] Percy was to have his wish ; the command of the whole border from Carlisle to Berwick was placed in his hands, but the Duke took care that with this power the Earl should accept full responsibility for the safety of the northern counties, and had the agreement, which reads like a treaty between two hostile powers, ratified by the King in Parliament.

It might have been expected that Parliament, which had been summoned[2] to meet at Salisbury on April 29, would show signs of resentment at the Duke's inaction in the North. This, however, was not the case. After the Chancellor, Sir Michael de la Pole, had declared the causes of summons, the House was at once adjourned till the following Wednesday, to await the arrival of Monseigneur d'Espaigne and his suite, who were still on the border. The Duke had not arrived on Monday, May 9, when the Commons named their committee of advisors, but so soon as he reached Salisbury they added his name to the list.

The most important subject for discussion was the

---

[1] Dated Durham, April 23, 1384. (*Foed*, VII. 425) ; ratified in the Salisbury Parliament, May 16, 1384 (*Foed*, VII. 427).
[2] By writ dated March 3, 1384 (Dugdale, *Summons*, 320). It sat from April 29 to May 27. (*Rot. Parl.* iii. 166–183.)

policy to be adopted with regard to the war. With due safeguards to the King's prerogative the Commons were invited to give their opinion. They had not yet aspired to control foreign relations, and their reply recognized that foreign policy was properly a matter for the King and Council. But their attitude was clear; it amounted to an unmistakable approval of the Duke's policy so far as France was concerned. If " peace with honour " could be had, the Commons would welcome it and with it a relief from war taxation, and were content to leave questions of detail to the King and his advisers.[1]

Unhappily, discussion of policy was hampered by violent personal quarrels.[2] Peers quarrelled with one another and with the King. The Earl of Arundel, the strongest man among the opposition and the most determined enemy of the King and the young Court party, chose the moment to launch a wholesale denunciation of the government and ministers, telling the King that his advisers were at fault, the administration was incapable and the country was going to destruction.

Richard flew into a passion. White with fury, he gave the Earl the lie. " If you say that I am at fault," the King shouted, " you lie in your throat ; go to the devil."[3] This was unparliamentary language. The Lords of the Council and his intimates knew Richard's temper and were not to be surprised at such unseemly outbursts, but Parliament was astounded at this public affront to a man of Arundel's position. There was an uncomfortable

---

[1] *Rot. Parl.* iii. 168a. Cf. 170a : la dite Paix, si pleut a Dieu de l'ottroier tielle que feust honorable et profitable a lour dit seigneur lige et son Roialme, si lour serroit la pluis noble et graciouse eide et confort que homme purroit en monde deviser.

[2] For the quarrels in the Salisbury Parliament see Higd. ix. 32-33. Sed dux Lancastriae superveniens eas in multa verborum faccundia minas intermiscens pacificavit.

[3] Higd. ix. 33.

feeling in the House until Lancaster, who since his arrival had been doing his best to keep the peace, after a long silence, rose and tried to pacify the King and explain the Earl's words away.

The Salisbury Parliament marks a climax in the relation of the Duke to party politics. In 1376 Lancaster was the best hated man in England : of that there can be no question. But during the last eight years a fundamental change had taken place in party politics. The Duke's retirement and correct bearing at the critical period of the accession had done something to efface his unpopularity. Still more had been done by Richard's favourites, for side by side with the waning jealousy of Lancastrian influence there was growing up a hearty distrust of the new court party.

Richard was now in his eighteenth year, and was beginning to assert himself. His favour was monopolized by a small coterie of friends and courtiers, the most conspicuous being the young Earl of Nottingham, Thomas Mowbray, and Robert de Vere Earl of Oxford, who held the first place in his affections. Besides the court, three other parties have to be taken into account in an analysis of the political situation of the year 1384. On the other extreme the Earl of Arundel, who had the support of the Earl of Warwick and the sympathy, at present somewhat suppressed, of Thomas of Woodstock, the King's youngest uncle, an able if violent and unscrupulous politician. Between these two extremes, the royal favourites on the one hand, and the irreconcilables of the opposition on the other, come the moderate constitutional party and the Lancastrian party. It is true that Scrope and de la Pole, the leaders of the moderates, were also retainers of the Duke and always attached to his interests, but these two parties, though now working together are distinct, and a dozen years later draw apart. The position of the Lancastrian party was peculiar.

JOHN OF GAUNT

During the last few years of his father's reign John of Gaunt had been the acknowledged leader of the court, but his nephew's accession completely changed his position. His sympathies were throughout with the Crown, but he found himself alienated from the party of " prerogative " by rivals who had monopolised Richard's favour, while to throw himself into opposition would be to court misrepresentation and suspicion, and perhaps to provoke civil war. Had he given his whole thought to English politics his position would have been extraordinarily strong; for as yet Arundel was his friend, while in addition to his vast territorial influence he could rely on the ministerial experience of Scrope and de la Pole[1] and enjoy the moral influence of their support. As it was, the Duke chose to stand aloof from internal politics, detached from ordinary interest by his private and dynastic ambitions.

That his power was still dreaded is proved by the sequel, for the Salisbury Parliament, which had opened with an onslaught by the opposition on the court, closed with an attack by the leaders of the court party on Lancaster. Vere had now displaced the Duke as the centre of national distrust. He must have known his unpopularity, but he also knew his influence with the King, and determined to measure it against the Lancastrian power. The defence or apology for Arundel coming hard upon the Duke's doubtful dealings with the Scots may have given him his cue. At any rate, he made a reckless attempt to get rid of his rival.

[1] In face of the conclusive evidence of the Register it is impossible to accept the views of Bishop Stubb that Michael de la Pole was a " powerful enemy to Lancaster influence." (*Const. Hist.* ii. 489). Both Richard le Scrope, who as Stubbs admits (ibid.) was " the Duke's friend and honest adviser," and Michael de la Pole were moderates and retainers and friends of John of Gaunt. This, I submit, must greatly modify the accepted view of the Duke's position.

LANCASTER CHARGED WITH TREASON

The means chosen, if discreditable, were ingenious and all but successful. One day, during the session of Parliament, the King was in the chamber of the Earl of Oxford, when suddenly a Carmelite Friar, who had just been celebrating mass, came forward with a story of a conspiracy against the King's life. The friar was of Irish birth ; his name was John Latemar, and he was a Bachelor of Theology. His story was that a widespread conspiracy was afloat, in which the citizens of London and Coventry and other cities were implicated, but which was organized and controlled by the Duke of Lancaster.

Richard, as usual giving way to his first impulse, ordered his uncle to be seized and killed forthwith. That was doubtless the consummation hoped for by the Earl of Oxford, but happily there were cooler heads who prevailed upon the King to listen to reason. Sir John Clanvowe, Prior of the Hospital of St. John of Jerusalem, an eye-witness from whom a most detailed account is derived, gave a graphic description of the scene which followed.[1] Richard, nervous and highly strung at all times, now completely lost self-control. He behaved like a madman, took off his hat and shoes and threw them out of the window.

When he became calmer he was induced to order the informer to write down the story, giving the names of his witnesses. At this turn of events the friar's face fell ; Vere and the accomplices had reckoned on some such hasty act as Richard had ordered on the impulse of the moment, and were unprepared for a calm sifting of evidence.

It happened that on the day of this *affaire* arrangements had been made for a solemn procession to be made to

[1] See the account of Malverne, who got his facts from Sir John Clanvowe, Higd. ix. 33–40 ; *Mon. Eve,* 50–52 ; Wals. ii. 112–5 ; *Chr. Angl.* 359 ; Ypod. *Neusk,* 339. Both Malverne and the Monk of Evesham think the friar *dementiâ instigatus ; stimulo fatuitatis adductus.*

the cathedral, King, Lords and Commons taking part, where mass was to be celebrated and intercession made for the safety, honour and welfare of the Church and realm. The clergy had taken their places in the cathedral precincts and every one was waiting for the King's arrival. As he did not appear Lancaster went to find out the reason. So soon as the Duke entered Vere's chamber, where the King was, the friar shouted : " There is the villain ! Seize him and put him to death, or he will kill you in the end." The Duke's astonishment can well be imagined. When the plot was explained to him, he indignantly denied all knowledge of it, and offered to prove his innocence by wager of battle. Richard, completely swayed by his emotions, in a sudden revulsion of feeling, convinced by his uncle's bearing, turned his fury on the informant and ordered him to be put to death. That Lancaster prevented. Failing the success of their manoeuvre the friar's death was the next best thing for those who had hatched the plot. Dead men tell no tales, but the Duke's anxiety was that the tale should be told. The Carmelite was obviously a mere tool, and Lancaster wanted to expose his enemy.

The friar was told to repeat his story, and did so, naming Lord la Zouche as a witness. The witness denied all knowledge of the story, and, like Lancaster, offered to defend his honour with his life. A second witness named by the friar was equally ignorant. The friar was then removed in the custody of John Holland, and the solution of the mystery was as far off as ever.

What would have happened had the proposed judicial inquiry been held is a matter for conjecture, for it never was held.

Sir John Montague, the King's Seneschal, and the Chamberlain, Sir Simon Burley, led the prisoner away, intending to take him to Salisbury Castle. At the door of the King's lodging they were met by Sir John Holland

and four other knights. Their names are important. They were Sir Peter Courtenay, Sir Henry Grene, Sir William Elmham and Sir Thomas Morieux. Sir Peter Courtenay, the Beau Brummel of Richard's court,[1] was a son of the Earl of Devon, and, like the rest of the Courtenay family, had little love for Lancaster, and had led the opposition in 1382 to the Castilian expedition. Holland himself was the King's half-brother and not yet a partizan of the Duke. Elmham and Morieux were royal officers. Morieux was a favourite of both the King and of Lancaster ; he had married an illegitimate daughter of the Duke and was entirely devoted to his interests. Thus of these five one was an enemy of the Duke ; one was a partizan, and all were friends of the King, but none were members of the faction of the Earl of Oxford.

Acting as they thought in the King's interest they determined to get at the truth. A mortal feud between Richard and his uncle was clearly not for the interests of King or nation.

Unhappily the means employed were only too characteristic of the age. In the presence of the King's Chamberlain and Seneschal they proceeded to torture the friar with a brutality too foul to be described, in order to make him disclose the real movers in the plot. All the devices of a devilish ingenuity failed. The victim had fortitude enough to preserve silence and incriminate no one.

Mutilated and dying, he was handed over to the Warden of Salisbury Castle. When the King heard what had been done he wept for pity. Neither he nor Lancaster had known of the torture : callous cruelty was not part of the nature of either. The dying man had made one last request—to be allowed a secret interview with Lord la Zouche. The interview was granted, but not in secret. Six of the King's knights, three of Lancaster's and three from the Commons, were present. But the mystery was

[1] *Scotichronicon*, xv. 6.

not cleared up. Asked if he knew anything against Lord la Zouche, the friar replied that he knew him to be a brave and true gentleman. Then words failed him, and after lingering for a few days, he died without making any further statement.

Whatever the interest in which Latemar had spoken, it was certainly not that of the Carmelite Order. The usual attempt was started to make capital out of the man's death. Miracles were invented; it was said that the dead wood of the crate on which his body had been dragged through the streets put forth leaves, that a blind man had got back his sight by touching it, and that a light had been seen shining over the martyr's grave. But the Carmelites knew their friend and refused to sanction the fraud; when a month later a Carmelite of Oxford tried to preach inflammatory sermons on the subject he was promptly suppressed by orders from the Provincial. The solidarity of the mendicant orders is notorious, and it is a striking proof of the Duke's influence with the Carmelites that they should thus readily support him against one of the brotherhood.

There can be little doubt as to the real instigator of the plot. It was revealed in Vere's chambers. It could scarcely have been opened without his knowledge and permission, and the state of party politics makes the presumption practically certain. The details had been clumsily concocted, for a conspiracy in which Lancaster was leagued with the Londoners is little short of ludicrous, and the conspirators ought to have been prepared for either event, and to have had a supply of plausible witnesses forthcoming at short notice.

No one believed the charge, but while all agreed in attempting to calm the King and appease the Duke, the loudest championship of his brother's innocence came from the Earl of Buckingham. Thomas of Woodstock was no violent partizan of Lancaster. The Duke had thwarted his cherished scheme of absorbing the whole Bohun inheritance, by rescuing Mary de Bohun from the cloister and marrying her to his son Henry. Buckingham too was strongly opposed to the peace policy, and jealous of his brother's predominant influence. Yet when this monstrous charge was put forward he drew his sword in the King's presence and swore that he would kill any one who charged his brother with treason.

The friar was dead, but the effect of his words did not die with him. The poison of suspicion worked in the King's sensitive nature. He could neither believe nor entirely forget. The scene had made a lasting impression upon him, and for the next half-dozen years it was always easy for mischief-makers to work upon his fears and revive the dormant suspicion.

For a while Vere was defeated, but he did not abandon his object. The conspiracy scare was not allowed to interfere with Lancaster's diplomatic labours. In the summer negotiations were resumed at the old rendezvous between Calais and Boulogne. Considering the number of interests involved, the proceedings were singularly ineffective, and the result was altogether disproportionate to the cost.[1]

Not only England and France, but Castile, Scotland, Flanders and Navarre were represented directly or indirectly, England by Lancaster, France by the four Dukes of Berri, Burgundy, Bourbon and Brittany ; Castile by Pero Lopez de Ayala, now Lord of Salvatierra and Seneschal of Guipuzcoa (who, however, has not thought it worth while to record his doings in the *Cronicas*), Scot-

---

[1] For the negotiations in France between July and October, 1384, see Higd. ix. 44 ; *Chr. Angl.* 360 ; Wals. ii. 115. Lancaster's commission is dated Salisbury, May 27, 1384, (*Foed*,VII. 428-9 and 429-431); safe-conduct for the French envoys, *Foed*, VII. 431- and 433-4. The Duke was named Lieutenant of the King in France, June 15, (*Foed*, VII. 432). The truce was concluded September 14. (*Foed*, VII. 438-443.)

land by her Chancellor and the Bishop of Glasgow, Navarre and Flanders by one or other of the principal envoys.

The position of John of Gaunt as pretender to the throne of Castile was a standing source of difficulty, and presented one of those problems where etiquette merges in policy. It was obviously impossible for the French, as allies of Don Juan, to concede him the style of King of Castile ; " Duke of Lancaster " is the only title of which the French envoys were officially cognisant. At the same time for practical purposes he was recognized to be acting in a double capacity, not only as an envoy of the King of England, but as a principal.[1]

The Duke strained every effort to attain some solid result. The social aspect of diplomatic intercourse was not neglected ; he entertained lavishly, and is said to have spent as much as fifty thousand marcs in the short period of the meeting.[2] But his hopes of a substantial result were defeated ; he could get no better terms than a short extension of the existing truce, viz. till May 1, 1385.

England and her representative were equally disappointed. Another war budget seemed inevitable, and the prospects of a clear field for the great event were not favourable.

There was no disguising the fact that English diplomacy had sustained a reverse, and when Parliament met in November the fact was faced.[3] The truce, such as it was, was duly ratified and published, but, two days after its proclamation, the King, in a letter addressed to the

---

[1] *Tanque a luy appartient en chief. Foed*, VII. 446.

[2] *Chr. Angl.* 360 ; Wals. ii. 118 ; Higd. ix. 44.

[3] Parliament was summoned, by writ dated Sept. 28, to meet at Westminster Nov. 12. It sat from Nov. 12 to Dec. 24. *Rot. Parl.* iii. 184–202. Mandate to the Sheriff, dated Oct. 20, 1384 *Foed*, VII. 444.

Archbishops,[1] commented on the untrustworthy attitude of the French and exhorted the country to renewed efforts. He had already received a substantial vote from the Commons for national defence.

Lancaster's failure to get better terms disappointed himself, the Commons, and every one but his enemies. To them it was welcome, for it might give them a chance of attack. Nothing daunted by his failure during the Salisbury Parliament, the Earl of Oxford again took up the forlorn hope of crushing the Duke of Lancaster.[2] A good hater, he was a poor general in the campaign of political intrigue. Somehow or other his forces never concentrated their attack to time, and so the enemy was always able to get away. Above all he had little imagination, and his only expedient was that of assassination. These defects exclude him from the front rank of political intriguers, but in persistence he was second to none.

Shortly after the rising of Parliament and the Christmas festival, the King held tournaments on two successive days at Westminster, and in the entertainments which followed his boon companions were of course with him. Vere was easily the first in the King's favour, but Thomas Mowbray, Earl of Nottingham, and the Earl of Salisbury, an older man, were among the number. The favourites now hatched a further plot to get rid of the Duke of Lancaster.

---

[1] Letter to the Primate dated Oct. 22, 1384. *Foed*, VII. 444.

[2] For the plot against the Duke's life see Higd. ix. 55–9 ; *Mon. Eve*, 60 ; *Chr. Angl.* 364 ; Wals. ii. 126 ; Ypod. *Neustr*, 340–1. The plot was admittedy hatched " *instructu juvenum qui cum rege nutriti fuere.*" This description fits two men and two only— Robert de Vere, Earl of Oxford and Thomas Mowbray, Earl of Nottingham.

There may be more than meets the eye in the dispute between Oxford and one Walter Sibille, which came up before the Parliament of Nov. 1384. Lancaster appears to have acted as arbiter. *Rot. Parl.* iii. 184, 299.

The legacy of the murdered Carmelite was still an asset ; it was bearing interest in an accumulating fund of suspicion. The plot was briefly this. A meeting of the Council was to be held at Waltham. The Duke, as the King's principal adviser, would of course be summoned to attend. On his appearance he was to be seized. This time appearances were to be preserved ; a complaisant bench of judges had already prepared a verdict of guilty on a charge of treason. The Duke would be executed ; the ghost of the Lancastrian power would be exorcised, and Vere and the King's favourites would then have a free hand. How far Richard knew of the plot must remain uncertain ; the details were probably left to the conspirators, but it is scarcely probable that the King was left in entire ignorance of the main idea, even assuming that it was originated by others.

Once more there was a weak link in the chain. On the King's Council there were men of different parties ; moderate men like Michael de la Pole, who was honestly devoted both to Lancaster and his nephew, and others who were the Duke's men. The conspiracy leaked out ; the Duke was warned, and instead of attending the council made excuses. His excuses were not accepted. The King's command must be obeyed. If John of Gaunt throughout his public life had acted with the same boldness as he did on this occasion, some of his earlier trouble might have been avoided. It was a critical situation, and the Duke kept his head. Ten days after the plot was hatched, February 24, Richard was at Sheen. Taking a strong escort, the Duke went to the royal palace. Reaching the river, he left most of his men to be ready at a summons. Another body was left to guard the barge in which he crossed. The rest went with him to the palace and halted at the entrance, with strict orders to prevent any one from going in or coming out. Accompanied by a few friends, the Duke, who had taken the precaution of wearing chain armour under his clothes, entered, and in Richard's chamber spoke his mind.

Without charging the King with complicity in the plot the Duke denounced the would-be murderers, declared that while the King surrounded himself with men who were plotting against his life he would not come to the council, and concluded with a warning against his nephew's choice of advisers.

Whether Richard knew that he was helpless, or whether he had once more changed his mind about his uncle, he listened to this explanation with astonishing calmness, and even promised to act on the advice.

Having simply stated the course he intended to pursue the Duke left, and the same night withdrew to Tottenham and soon after to Hertford Castle.

Every one except Vere and his friends knew that the best thing for the country was an understanding between the King and his uncles, and that a serious quarrel might mean civil war. Princess Joan saw the situation as clearly as most people, and feared for the issue more than any. The Lancastrian power was great enough to disturb the balance of public life ; and had John of Gaunt been a man of the temper of Thomas of Woodstock, Richard would probably have felt the result of playing with edged tools. Happily for the King, his mother still lived, and her influence with her brother-in-law was considerable.

Once more the Fair Maid of Kent came forward in the guise of a peacemaker. On March 6 she brought Lancaster and his nephew together at Westminster, and a reconciliation took place between the Duke and his would-be assassins, at which he declared himself reconciled with the ring-leaders, the Earls of Oxford, Nottingham and Salisbury.

So far as the Duke's position went this abortive conspiracy had done little harm. For some time the clouds had been gathering ; now the storm had come and had cleared the air, and Lancaster's unpopularity had almost entirely disappeared. Vere had taken the burden from his shoulders. Even old enemies like Courtenay the Primate had completely transferred their hatred to the King's favourites. Indeed Courtenay and a number of Peers openly reproached the King for his reckless conduct, and warned him of the consequences of countenancing a reign of terror in which assassination was to be the fate of all who provoked the jealousy or dislike of a small coterie of unprincipled favourites. The Primate's plain speaking exposed him to a furious outburst on the part of Richard, and only Buckingham's interference prevented the King from killing him with his own hand. But before very long the wisdom of his advice was proved by the event.

After this quarrel and hollow reconciliation John of Gaunt withdrew to his northern kingdom, garrisoned Pontefract Castle for a siege, and shut himself up in it. From the walls of that impregnable fortress, his favourite northern dwelling, upon which he had spent lavishly in building, the Duke could see the spot where two generations ago his predecessor, Earl Thomas of Lancaster, had been murdered to avenge a royal favourite. History was repeating itself, telling over again in 1385 the story of 1322. Duke John was standing in the same perilous position as that of Earl Thomas, while Robert de Vere, like Piers Gaveston, in plotting the ruin of those whom he hated was in truth leading his friend to the fate of the second Edward.

But John of Gaunt was not a man of the temper of Thomas of Lancaster, or Thomas of Woodstock, or indeed of Henry of Bolingbroke. He never attempted to avenge himself upon his nephew. Strong enough to defy open violence, he was too loyal to meet treachery with treason, and chose to bow before the storm and

to repeat the policy of 1377—a policy of self-effacement.

Negotiation with France, the result of his own initiative,
was abandoned to others ;[1] when the King's Council met
in June at Reading the great Duke of Lancaster was
absent.[2]

Perhaps the policy of retirement which had overcome
unpopularity in 1377 might have disarmed suspicion
in 1385, but events precluded the Duke from carrying it
into effect for long.   Though Richard, until schooled
by adversity, never trusted his over-powerful uncle, he
could not do without him, as the events of the summer
proved.   For in 1385 Charles VI, young and ambitious
of fame, had devised the boldest scheme of offensive
action that France had as yet attempted.   This was
nothing less than to carry war into the enemy's country
by a combined attack upon the south coast and the
northern border simultaneously.

A powerful fleet assembled at Sluys intended to transport an army to invade England.   Meanwhile Jean de
Vienne had been sent to the North, and in May had
landed with a force of French lances at Dunbar and Leith
to join Charles' Scottish allies and to harry the northern
counties.

At the last moment the combination failed, for the
army which had mustered at Sluys was diverted from its
objective by affairs in the Low Countries.

It was left to the Government to deal with the northern
force in detail and to concentrate the whole strength of the
kingdom on the Scottish border.[3]   At last, men thought,

---

[1] Item xxiii° die Martii tractatores pacis ex parte nostra
omnes excepto duce Lancastriae Calesiam transierunt qui circa
finem mensis Aprilis redierunt absque pacis effectu.   Higd. ix. 59.
[2] Higd. ix. 60.
[3] For Jean de Vienne in Scotland and the invasion August,
1385, see Froissart, K. de L. x. 376-405 ; Wals. ii. 131-2 ; *Chr.
Angl.* 364 ; Kn. ii. 204-6 ; *Eulog.* 358 ; Higd. ix. 63-5.

the son of the Black Prince and grandson of Edward III would show the martial spirit of his race, and would display against an alien and an enemy the courage which for a moment had cowed the rebels at Smithfield. Summoning his levies to meet him at Newcastle on July 14, Richard prepared to invade Scotland in force.

Even before he reached the rendezvous the King's troubles began. Near York, in a brawl between retainers of Sir John Holland and the Earl of Stafford, a favourite squire of Holland was killed. As the murderers took sanctuary and Richard refused to let them be dragged out, Holland took the law into his own hands. Riding from Bishopthorpe to York he met the son of the Earl of Stafford. It was easy to provoke a quarrel, and Holland, a man of great strength and a master of his weapon, struck Stafford dead with one blow. The murdered man, like Mowbray and Vere, was of the King's age, and had been brought up with him, and had been one of the knights of the Queen's retinue.

Richard received the news with extravagant grief, and though Holland was his own half-brother, swore that he should be treated as a common murderer. It was in vain that Princess Joan interceded for one son to the other ; her prayers were useless, and wearied with the hopeless task of mediating in the quarrels of the royal family, Princess Joan a few days later died broken-hearted.

On July 20 the King reached Durham and found the Duke of Lancaster with his levies, awaiting him. Once more the farce of reconciliation was gone through, and the Duke agreed to forget the quarrel with the Earls of Oxford, Nottingham, and Salisbury. A more practical task was to array the army for the coming invasion.[1] The forces which Richard was leading against Scotland,

---

[1] See the " Army Order " issued by Richard II, the Duke of Lancaster, the Constable and Marshal, at Durham, July 27. Brit. Mus. Cotton Nero, D. vi. f. 91.

unlike the armies which invaded France, were feudal levies : the great feudatories brought their retainers.

The "ordinances of war made at Durham"[1] form therefore a measure of the comparative fighting force of the nobles of England in 1385.

The army consisted of 13,734 men, i.e. 4,590 men-at-arms and 9,144 archers. Of this total the Duke of Lancaster alone contributed almost a third, for he led 4,000 men, 1,000 men-at-arms and 3,000 archers. The proportion of archers to men-at-arms in the Duke's contingent is striking : the old campaigner had learnt the lesson of the French wars. But still more striking is the disproportion between the Duke's forces and those of all the rest. His men number nearly half as many again as the King's own levies ; more than three times as many as those of his brother the Earl of Buckingham, and just five times as many as those of the Earl of Northumberland, the next most powerful feudatory.

It is also worth noting that five hundred men were brought by Lord Neville of Raby, and Neville was, like Lord Roos who brought fifty and Michael de la Pole who brought 140, a retainer of Lancaster. As usual, the formation of "three battles" was adopted : vaward, centre with two wings, and rearguard, Lancaster, with the Constable and Marshal commanding the van, the King the centre and the Earl of Northumberland the rear. To prevent the factions of politics being carried into the field, friends were separated, and enemies thrown together ; Lancaster marched with the Earl Marshal, and Lord Neville, the Duke's retainer, was with the Earl of Northumberland. The King consented to have the Earl of Arundel in the centre, but he would not be parted from his favourite Vere, a fact which had a great influence on the conduct of the campaign.

[1] See Appendix ii. p. 437 (Cotton Nero, D. vi. f. 92).

JOHN OF GAUNT

On August 6 the King entered Scottish territory and signalized the occasion by the bestowal of dignities. The Earl of Cambridge was created Duke of York, the Earl of Buckingham became Duke of Gloucester : Michael de la Pole's faithful service was rewarded by the Earldom of Suffolk, which had become extinct at the death of William Ufford three years before.

Pursuing their usual tactics the Scots retreated before the invader, and even the enthusiasm of Jean de Vienne cooled when he saw the imposing army which Richard was leading against his allies. On the northward march therefore the English found no enemy to attack ; the few stray prisoners, Scots and Frenchmen, who fell into their hands were killed in cold blood, and the adherence of Scotland to the anti-pope was made the excuse for burning the monasteries, which Lancaster had always spared. The Abbeys of Melrose and Newbattle were destroyed, and Holyrood itself was only saved at the Duke's entreaty.

On reaching Edinburgh the young commander was faced with a difficulty. One body of the enemy had fled to the north, but it was hopeless to attempt a pursuit into " sauvage Ecosse." Another body, stiffened by Jean de Vienne's French lances, had made a counter move into England, marching westwards as the English army advanced north, burning Penrith and attacking Carlisle. Lancaster's advice was to turn to the west and cut off their retreat.

A council of war accepted the proposal, but on the eve of the march the plan was suddenly abandoned. Robert de Vere, the evil genius of the young King, was bent once more on making mischief. It was an easy task to fan into flame the king's smouldering jealousy, and the end was probably achieved by some such words as Froissart[1] puts

[1] Froissart K. de L. x. 395. This is the advice of " *li ccntes d'Asquesuffort, qui estoit pour che tamps tous li coers et li consaulx*

into his mouth. : " Ha ! monsigneur, à quoi pensés-vous, qui volés faire che chemin que vostre oncle vous conseillent à faire ? Sachiés, que se vous le faites ne allés aucune- ment jamais n'en retournerés, ne li dus de Lancastre ne tire ne tent à autre cose que il sois rois, et que vous soyés mors." Richard was in command, and it was open to him to accept or reject his uncle's advice, but with his usual maladroitness he displayed his suspicion and, reversing the policy agreed upon, took the occasion to heap insults on his most powerful subject. He cast the Duke's own military failures in his face, and told him that he was a traitor and that he might march whither he would with his own men, but the rest would return to England.

Once more, as at the famous quarrel with Percy four years before, Lancaster, who had learnt the lesson of caution and self-restraint with years, kept his head. There was a certain dignity in his reply, that the King had no more faithful subject than himself and he would follow wherever his sovereign should lead.[1] The intervention of the Peers brought about the usual reconciliation ; the retreat took place, and by August 20 this short military parade, Richard's most pretentious effort in arms, was over, and the army was back at Newcastle.

At last John of Gaunt was nearing the goal of his ambitions. The situation of domestic politics was not one which could last. Quarrels, conspiracies and sham reconciliations could not go on for ever, and in the

dou roy." Asquesuffort is of course Oxford not Suffolk, but Mr. G. M. Trevelyan ("England in the Age of Wycliffe," p. 286) ascribes the speech to Michael de la Pole Earl of Suffolk, the Duke's friend. This mistranslation by Johnes involves an entire misunderstanding of the relation between the party leaders, but apart from this the words above quoted could in 1385 apply to no one but Robert de Vere.

[1] The king and his uncle were better friends again about the end of the year, if borrowing money is any test. Lancaster lent him £100. *Rot. Pat.* Nov. 16, 1385.

autumn of 1385 it became clear that there was no room for both the Earl of Oxford and the Duke of Lancaster in English politics. There was one obvious solution to the difficulty, one which pleased all parties—the Spanish expedition.

For eighteen months the Portuguese envoys, the Grand Master of St. James and the Chancellor of Portugal had been in England, working hard at recruiting and waiting for the turn of the tide which should carry Lancaster and his army to Portugal. Meanwhile fortune had strengthened their hand, for João, Master of Avis and Regent, was now João I, King of Portugal : the deliverer of the nation had been chosen by his people to succeed to the throne of Dom Fernando, and had abundantly justified the choice. While Richard II was quarrelling with his uncle at Edinburgh, João I, with the help of English archers, had on August 14, won the crushing victory of Aljubarrota, which established Portuguese independence for good and crippled the military power of Castile for a generation. Instead of the friendship of a weakling like Fernando, who never knew his own mind, the Portuguese envoys could offer the active support of a tried soldier, the favourite of his people, a general commanding all the prestige of a momentous victory. A combined attack upon Castile would solve the domestic difficulty and the problem of the Lancastrian claim. Once more the Council and Parliament[1] debated the Duke's proposal. His friends and enemies were agreed. De Vere, if he could not ruin his rival, would gladly be rid of him : his jealousy played into the enemy's hand. The project was approved, and the Commons voted the necessary supplies.[2]

[1] This Parliament was summoned by writ dated Sept. 3, 1385, for Friday after the feast of St. Luke. It sat from Friday, Oct. 20, to Thursday, Dec. 6. *Rot. Parl.* iii 203–14.
[2] Et sciendum quod dictum viagium dicti Regis Castelli in

PARLIAMENT CONVERTED AT LAST

From their lodging at the *Falcon Inn*, in Gracechurch Street, the Master of St. James and the Chancellor were summoned to the presence of the King and Queen of Castile to hear the welcome news that their mission had succeeded, and that a Lancastrian army would soon be fighting side by side with the forces of their master against the usurper of Castile !

Ispanniam concordatum fuit et concessum per dominum regem, prelatos, proceres magnates et communitates predictes in pleno Parliamento. *Rot. Pat.* iii. 204b.

For the Spanish expedition, the safe custody of the sea and the Scottish border and for the relief of Ghent the Commons voted a tenth and fifteenth and half a tenth and fifteenth, the first to be paid by Feb. 2, 1386, and the second by June 24 following. *Rot. Parl.* iii. 204 *a*.

III. CASTILE AND LEON

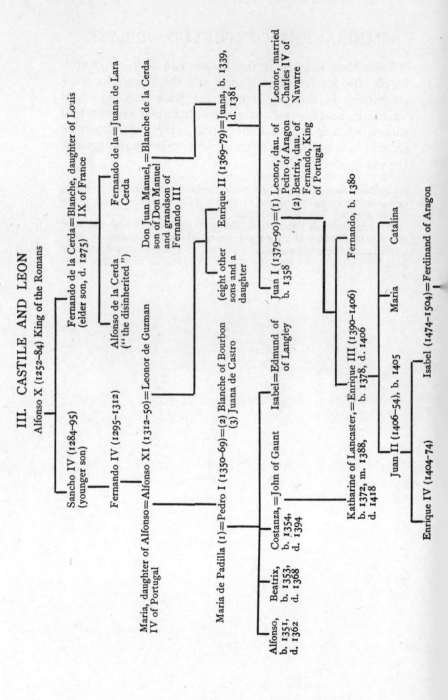

Alfonso X (1252–84) King of the Romans

Chapter XIII

THE SECOND INVASION OF CASTILE

IN the *Chronica d'El Rei D. João I* there is a striking scene, depicting the passionate longing of the exiled daughter of Don Pedro to recover her fatherland and her father's throne. The time is the autumn of 1385, when England was ringing with the news of the great victory of Aljubarrota ; the place, the Duke's chamber ; and the actors are Lancaster himself, his consort, and the Portuguese ambassadors. The Master of St. James has just been urging the Duke to attack Castile in the hour of weakness, and to accept the proposed alliance of the victorious Portuguese King. His arguments are reinforced by the prayers of Constance of Castile.

Leading her daughter Katherine by the hand and falling upon her knees before her husband, the Duchess entreats him with tears to champion her right and avenge the murder of her father.[1]

Tears and entreaties indeed were scarcely necessary, and Lancaster's ambition needed no spur. For sixteen years " Monseigneur d'Espaigne " had claimed and used the royal style. Edinburgh, Paris, Bruges and Lisbon knew as well as Westminster the maker of treaties and alliances, " Roy de Castell et de Leon, Duc de Lancastre." At last, it seemed, his infant fortune had come to years ; the day-dream was to become a waking reality, and he was to cease building " castles in Spain " to begin the more practical task of capturing them.

[1] Fernão Lopes, *Chronica de El Rei D. João I*, v. 83–4.

The Duke was now in his forty-sixth year, well past middle age as the fourteenth century understood it. His career had not been one of uninterrupted success ; yet neither age nor experience had blunted the edge of his ambition. In 1386 his hopes were higher than ever. That before long the throne of Castile would be won, either by arms or by treaty, he for one had little doubt. He knew the demoralization of the enemy ; the anticipation (abundantly justified by the event) that his adversary would hasten to agree with him by the way, can be read between the lines of his contract with Richard II, made on the eve of the enterprise. It is assumed as a matter of course that Juan I will cower at the advance of the rightful king. Richard's only solicitude is to prevent the interests of England being sacrificed by the inevitable capitulation.[1]

In treating as an independent sovereign with his nephew " of France and England," John of Gaunt promises to Richard the friendship of the kingdom yet to be won, and binds together Castile and England in an indissoluble alliance by the concord of Plantaganet kings as yet unborn.[2]

[1] John of Gaunt undertakes (i) that he will make no agreement with his adversary of Castile until Richard II is satisfied in respect of 200,000 *doubles d'or*, representing the damage done to English shipping by Castile ; (ii) that any alliance he may make with Juan I shall be without prejudice to his engagements to Richard ; and (iii) that he will repay as soon as possible, and within three years at the outside, the 20,000 marcs advanced to him by Richard.

(Dated Feb. 7, 1386, and cancelled May 26, 1390.) *Foed.* VII, 495.

[2] The alliance between John, King of Castile, Leon, Toledo, Galicia, Seville, Cordova, Murcia, Jaen, Algarve and Algeciras, Duke of Lancaster and Lord of Molina on the one part, and Richard II, King of France and England on the other, was concluded by their plenipotentiaries (Sir John Marmion with William Ashton, the Duke's Chancellor, and Sir Richard Atterbury with Sir John Clanvowe) at Westminster, April 28, 1386. (Powers for the Duke's proctors are dated Kingston Lacy, April 8.) Lan-

THE SECOND INVASION OF CASTILE

The Portuguese alliance, the Duke's own creation, was conceived on a grand scale. It bound England and Portugal together in a league offensive and defensive against all Europe, saving only Pope, Emperor, and the legitimate King of Castile.[1]

Was it only anxiety to be rid of the nightmare of Lancastrian domination, that shadow ever lying across the throne, that worked in the mind of the young king ? Or was Richard II also, impulsive, impressionable, easily led by a stronger hand, deceived by the delusive promise of his uncle's fancies ? Perhaps he was for a moment convinced, and came to see John of Gaunt, as the Duke saw himself, the creator of a great Peninsular alliance, which should raise again the fallen barrier of the Pyrenees, restore to England the command of the seas, and hem France in north and south between confederate kingdoms.

Whatever his motives, it is impossible to doubt the sincerity of Richard's support, for he lent money to his uncle for the purpose.[2] Financial help came too from

caster confirmed the alliance at Plympton, June 20. (*Foed*, VII: 510–15, and 525–26) : Richard II on June 1 (*Rot. Franc.* ii. 152 1 and 2.)

[1] The offensive and defensive alliance of Richard II and João I (against all powers save Pope, Emperor, and John of Gaunt) was concluded by Fernando, Master of St. James with Lourenço, Chancellor of Portugal, and Sir Richard Atterbury and Sir John Clanvowe, May 9 (Windsor), and May 17 (Westminster), 1386. The Portuguese envoys' powers are dated April 15, 1385. *Foed*, VII. 518–24; Fernão Lopes, v. 87–89. It was confirmed by João I at Coimbra, August 12, 1387. *Foed*, VII. 561, 562. Cf. Safe conduct for two ambassadors of the King of Portugal, the Bishop of Elvas, and Gonsalvo Gomes da Silva, dated Westminster, April 3, 1386. *Foed*, VII. 508–9.

[2] The King commands that the sum of 1,000 marcs advanced to his uncle by the Treasurer of the Royal Chamber shall be refunded from the first instalment of the Parliamentary grant. *Rot. Pat.* May 14, 1386. Richard had to borrow from Lombard merchants for the purpose ; see bond dated May 22, 1386. *Rot. Pat.*

another source besides the coffers of the Lombard bankers with whom the King was pledging his credit.

The Castilian quarrel can be viewed from various standpoints. It is a piece in the puzzle of dynastic history. It is a side current in the stream of the Hundred Years War. It is also a scene in the drama of the Great Schism, an interlude in the struggle of the rival popes.

Castile was for Clement,[1] Portugal for Urban, and John of Gaunt was a *persona gratissima* at the court of Urban VI. It was three years since the Pope had conferred on the patron of Wycliffe the title of " Standard Bearer of the Cross for the Pope and the Roman Church," naming him Captain and Standard Bearer against Juan of Castile.[2] Just at the moment when encouragement was most needed, when the Earl of Cambridge had made a fool of himself in Portugal and Dom Fernando had gone over to the enemy, came the apostolic exhortation to this faithful son of the Church to " merit the rewards to be gained by diligently and faithfully carrying out the office entrusted to him." At the same time plenary pardon had been granted to all who, fortified by the sign of the Cross, should embark in Lancaster's company on the intended expedition, and die truly penitent and confessed,[3] while at the Duke's petition his army received the promise of all those privileges and indulgences which the Crusaders had received by the constitution of Innocent III published in the Fourth General Lateran Council.[4] For three years these powers had lain dormant. Now

[1] Enrique II was neutral, but Juan I took the schism seriously, and after some hesitation declared for Clement VII in 1381. (Ayala, ii. 130, 140–1 ; 142–150.) This was the result of French influence.

[2] Dated Rome, 12 Kal. Apr. (5 Urban VI), 1383: *Papal Letters*, iv. 264.

[3] Dated Rome, 12 Kal. Apr. (5 Urban VI), 1383. *Papal Letters*, iv 265.

[4] April 6 (5 Urban VI), 1383. *Papal Letters*, iv. 265.

they were called out of abeyance and enlarged. Four Bulls were issued in Lancaster's favour.[1] Choosing as his agents the Bishop of Hereford (the prelate who had urged the Spanish expedition on Parliament in 1382), the Bishops of Llandaff and Dax, and Walter Dysse, the Duke's confessor, the Pope empowered them to restore all churches and cemeteries, however polluted, in England and Spain ; to create fifty Papal chaplains from persons of good repute, regular or secular, and fifty notaries public, even married clerks being eligible ; and fourthly to remove the barrier of illegitimate birth for persons wishing to be ordained to the priesthood.

The ecclesiastical campaign began on February 18, when the standard of the Cross was raised in St. Paul's, and the first sermon was preached in favour of the Crusade.[2] The secular arm seconded the efforts of the Church, and in every county of England the sheriffs, by royal mandate,[3] published the Bull promising absolution to all who directly or indirectly should further the expedition of the Duke for the succour, help and comfort of the Holy Mother Church against the schismatic usurper of Castile.

Wycliffe must surely have turned in his grave when the Bishops of Llandaff and Hereford went on progress through England, selling Papal indulgences to finance a dynastic quarrel. But though Wycliffe was dead there were many who from various motives were ready to raise a protest against the Crusade. Unhappily for Lancaster, the novelty of the thing had been spoilt by the Bishop of Norwich three years before, but there was still a brisk market for the papal wares. As a papal

---

[1] *Fasc. Ziz.* 508. See Baronius, *Annales Ecclesiastici* (Ed. Theiner), vol. xxii. p. 466.

[2] Higd. ix. 81–2.

[3] Mandate to the sheriffs to cause the Bull to be published, dated April 11, 1386. *Foed.* VII. 507–8.

M

chaplaincy removed its possessor from the control of his ecclesiastical superiors, regulars and seculars, black monks and white, canons, rectors, vicars and friars rushed for the bait.

The Abbot of St. Albans, always at his best in disciplinary matters, took strong measures to repress the movement among his brethren. Every Benedictine who bought a papal chaplaincy (except one old man whose years and past service saved him) was turned out of his house.[1] But on other grounds than those of discipline the Crusade encountered vigorous opposition. Sermons were preached against it, and it became necessary for the secular power to intervene.[2] The strongest support, however, came from the friars. Once more Lancaster reaped a solid benefit from his alliance with the Carmelites. Dysse the Carmelite was one of the Pope's commissioners. The Duke was the Carmelites' friend. That was enough : the whole order made his quarrel their own. The sort of argument advanced in support of this last sham crusade may be gathered from a fragment still extant of a sermon, doubtless one of many, preached by a Carmelite friar at the time.[3] The faithful are invited to ponder on the wickedness of that monster Robert of Geneva, calling himself Clement VII, who is indeed no true shepherd, but a thief, a robber, a wolf who devours the lambs of the Church, a deceiver who has led astray many, including Juan, calling himself King of Castile. To bring back this erring sheep to the true fold, the Pope has called not once, but many times, at first softly, then angrily, but always in vain. At length he has commissioned the true King of Castile to drive him back by force. It is vain to say, as some do, that the Spaniards

[1] *Gest. Abb. Sc. Alban*, ii. 417.
[2] Orders to three sergeants-at-arms to arrest John Elys, of Stowmarket, Chaplain, who had preached against the Spanish Crusade, dated February 12, 1387. *Rot. Pat.*
[3] *Fasc. Ziz.* 506–11.

are as good Christians as ourselves, and that it is a sin to shed their blood. Not so. They are guilty of the sin of schism, a sin against the whole body of the Church. Faith without works is vain ; the faithful will show their devotion by supporting the Pope and his minister, John of Gaunt. Equally vain is it to argue that the sale of indulgences amounts to simony. Distinguish between obtaining things *for* money and *through* money. These indulgences are obtained through money, it is true, for money is necessary to pay for the soldiers who are to fight in the good cause. But they are bestowed not for money but for the spiritual ends of restoring Spain to the true fold, and promoting the unity of the Catholic Church. Such contributions are therefore an acceptable oblation. " *Date eleemosynam et omnia munda vobis* "—an elastic, if not convincing formula, and one which the friars knew well.

The results were eminently satisfactory, for the contributions of the faithful were considerable.

On March 25, the date fixed for the ceremony of farewell, King John and Queen Constance, after receiving crowns of gold from Richard II, took leave of the court and began their royal progress through the southern counties to Plymouth, the port of embarkation.[1] Lancaster had to wait for more than two months in the west country while the ships and vessels impressed for the expedition assembled.[2] It is difficult, as usual, to

[1] Kn. ii. 207. Higd. ix: 82.

[2] Mandate to impress 20 ships of 70 casks burden and upwards within the Northern Command, to be at Plymouth by Palm Sunday, dated March 15, 1386. *Foed*, VII. 501-2. Cf. (ibid. 504) orders to impress mariners for the *Marie of London*, the *Margaret of London*, and the *Maudelyn of London*, dated March 26. Orders to impress 24 "mineatores" from the Forest of Dean and carpenters from the western counties, dated March 24. *Foed*, VII. 503-4. Orders to hasten the ships impressed, dated April 20 and 23. *Foed*, VII. 509. One roll gives the names of 57 ships, which with 20 more from the Northern Command gave a total tonnage of nearly 10,000 *dol*. (*Exchequer Accts*. Q.R. Bundle 42, No. 18, Army).

IV. PORTUGAL

ALFONSO IV. (1325–57)=Beatrice, daughter of Sancho IV of Castile

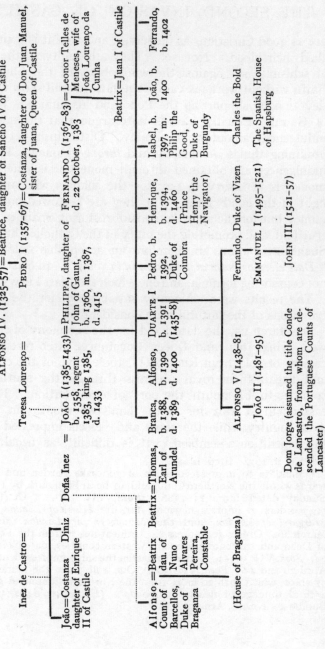

PEDRO I (1357–67)=Costanza, daughter of Don Juan Manuel, sister of Juana, Queen of Castile

Inez de Castro=

Teresa Lourenço=

Doña Inez =

FERNANDO I (1367–83)=Leonor Telles de Meneses, wife of João Lourenço da Cunha
d. 22 October, 1383

Beatrix=Juan I of Castile

João I (1385–1433) = PHILIPPA, daughter of John of Gaunt, b. 1358, regent 1383, king 1385, b. 1360, m. 1387, d. 1433 d. 1415

Branca, b. 1388, d. 1389

Alfonso, b. 1390, d. 1400

DUARTE I, b. 1391 (1435–8)

Pedro, b. 1392, Duke of Coimbra

Henrique, b. 1394, d. 1460 (Prince Henry the Navigator)

Isabel, b. 1397, m. Philip the Good, Duke of Burgundy

João, b. 1400

Ferrando, b. 1402

Charles the Bold

The Spanish House of Hapsburg

Fernando, Duke of Vizen

EMMANUEL I (1495–1521)

JOHN III (1521–57)

ALFONSO V (1438–81)

João II (1481–95)

João=Costanza, daughter of Enrique II of Castile

Diniz

Beatrix=Thomas, Earl of Arundel

Alfonso, =Beatrix, dau. of Nuno Alvares Pereira, Constable
Count of Barcellos, Duke of Braganza

(House of Braganza)

Dom Jorge (assumed the title Conde de Lancastro, from whom are descended the Portuguese Counts of Lancaster)

speak with anything like certainty of the numbers of the army. Knighton's guess, twenty thousand men, must be a wild exaggeration. On the other hand, the Duke certainly had more than the 1,500 men-at-arms and 1,500 archers who, according to Ayala, followed him to Castile.[1]

He had led 4,000 men-at-arms and archers in the Scottish promenade, and with the lesson of Cambridge's expedition in his mind, and the warning of Parliament, he would certainly raise more for the object for which he was straining every nerve. Probably the Portuguese chronicles are near the mark when they put the numbers at 2,000 lances and 3,000 archers, or some 10,000 men in all. At any rate the force was large enough to make transport a matter of some difficulty, and it appears that the greater part of the English marine was engaged in the Duke's service.[2] This, in view of the attitude of the French, constituted a grave danger. One of the engagements entered into by the Portuguese envoys was to place a naval force at the disposal of England in the autumn,[3] but in addition to this Dom João volunteered naval assistance to his ally.[4] On June 30 his admiral, Affonso Furtado, reached Plymouth with a flotilla of transports for Lancaster's use, ten fine galleys, and half a dozen smaller ships.

At length all preparations were complete. Lancaster and his knights had given their evidence at Plymouth in

[1] Kn. ii. 207 ; Ayala, ii. 249 ; Fernão Lopes, v. 91. Many names of the knights and esquires of the Duke's retinue appear in the lists of those who obtained letters of protection (dated January 7 and March 6, 1386 ; *Foed*, VII. 490-1, and 499-501), and letters of attorney (dated April 12, ibid. 508).

[2] See commission to Lancaster to provide for the safe return of the fleet, and appointment of two sergeants-at-arms to bring it home, dated June 1, 1386. *Foed*, VII. 524-5.

[3] *Foed*, VII. 521-3.

[4] Kn. ii. 207. Fernão Lopes, v. 39, 40 ; 86, and 90. According to Lopes the whole flotilla numbered 130 sail, v. 91.

the *cause célèbre* Scrope *v.* Grosvenor ;[1] the great officers of the army were named.

The Constable was Sir John Holland. After a few months' disgrace Holland had emerged from sanctuary at Beverley to be restored to favour and to give another proof of the violence of his passions. Impetuous alike in love and hate, Holland, after a rough wooing, had won the heart of Elizabeth of Lancaster. Elizabeth had been betrothed in childhood to the Earl of Pembroke ; this was annulled, and Holland, who had forestalled a legal union, saved appearances by a hasty marriage.[2]

Sir Thomas Morieux, husband of another daughter of the Duke, the mysterious Lady Blanche, with Sir Richard Burley, acted as Marshal. Sir Thomas Percy was Admiral. Where there was fighting to be had, the Percies were always to the fore; and the old quarrel was forgotten, for besides his brother the Admiral, the Earl of Northumberland had a son, Sir Thomas Percy the younger, in the Duke's army. The Courtenay feud too was now over also, for on the eve of his departure Lancaster, protesting his " entire affection " and confidence in the Earl of Devonshire, names him lieutenant of his fees and franchises in Devonshire.[3]

All the Duke's children accompanied the expedition save one : the omission is significant. Henry, Earl of Derby, was left to watch over his father's interests, and to act as Lieutenant of the County Palatine [4]—a very necessary precaution—but the Duke took with him his two unmarried daughters, Philippa of Lancaster, and Katharine her half-sister, as well as Constance and Elizabeth.

On Sunday, July 7, a fair wind sprang up. The Earl

[1] *Scrope-Grosvenor*, i. 49.
[2] Higd. ix. 96-7. See Appendix, viii. p. 458.
[3] Brit. Mus. Ad. Ch. 13910.
[4] This appears from the Patent Rolls of the Palatinate.

THE RELIEF OF BREST.

of Derby said his last farewells and returned to the shore, and in the afternoon the fleet hoisted sail.[1]

With an object as definite as the invasion of Castile, and a kingdom for the prize, it might have been thought that Lancaster would steer a straight course for the shores of Spain. Such was not the spirit of adventure. There is a certain knight-errantry in the Duke's adventures which touches them with romance, and lends to them an interest which perhaps might not be felt in the fortunes of a more practical character. As the fleet doubled Cape Ushant news came that the Duke of Brittany, to prove his new-born loyalty to France, was beleaguering the English garrison of Brest.[2] The besieged were hard pressed, and in particular they were harassed by two forts, one nicknamed the "Dovehouse," built by the besiegers uncomfortably near the walls of the town. John of Gaunt landed his men, and allowed Lord Fitzwalter to storm the forts. The effort cost some valuable lives, but it should never be said that a Duke of Lancaster left a besieged English garrison to its fate.

Putting to sea again, the Duke and his council debated the question where the landing should be effected. The Portuguese admiral offered his master's ports, but Lancaster, sensible of the moral effect of landing on Castilian soil, ordered his pilots to make for the coast of Galicia.[3]

On July 25 the fleet dropped anchor in the harbour of

[1] Kn. ii. 207.
[2] For the relief of Brest see Knighton's inspired account, ii. 208–10 ; Froissart, K. de L. xi. 331-7 ; *Religieux de St. Denys*, i. 433–49, whose narrative is not very helpful ; Wals. ii. 143 ; *Chr. Angl.* 368-9 ; Fernão Lopes, v. 90–1.
[3] For what follows the authorities of the first value are Ayala and Fernão Lopes. Duarte Nunes do Liam, in the *Cronicas del Rey Dom João I*, adds nothing of importance to the narrative of Lopes. The events of 1386-7 are treated with the greatest brevity in the *Chronicle of the Constable* (*Chronica do Condestabre de Portugal Dom Nunalvarez Pereyra*, Lisbon, 1623, pp. 51, 52).

Coruña ; it was a happy omen that the King of Castile should first set foot in his kingdom on the day of St. James, the patron saint of Spain and the eponymous hero of the Galician capital, and the capture of a squadron of Don Juan's ships at Betanzos on the same day seemed to confirm this augury of success.[1]

The captain of Coruña, Ferrand Perez de Andrade, not being strong enough to offer resistance, and not knowing which way things would go, elected to temporize. Lancaster accepted his professions without putting them to the test, and pushed on without staying to occupy the town, to the capital of Galicia, Saint James of Compostella.[2]

In the troubled days of 1366 the Gallegos had been the last to abandon the cause of Don Pedro, and even now the sentiment of loyalty to his line lingered among the hidalgos of the Northern Province. Events justified Lancaster's choice of the port of disembarkation, for Santiago opened her gates at the first summons ; a procession of clergy met the Duke and conducted him to the shrine of St. James, and nobles and gentlemen from Galicia and Castile came in to kiss the hand of Queen Constance and to do homage to the rightful king.[3] Lancaster's first act after entering the city was to turn out the Clementist archbishop, Don Juan Garcia Manrique,[4] and to put in his place an adherent of the canonical Pope. Then the " Captain and Standard Bearer of the Cross " forgot all about the Crusade, and began business by announcing his arrival to the Kings of Portugal and Castile. Sealed with the royal arms of Castile, and bearing the

---

[1] Fernão Lopes, v. 91–2; Ayala, ii. 249 ; Froissart, K. de L. xi. 338–44.

[2] Lopes, v. 108–9 ; Ayala (ii. 249) differs ; Froissart, K. de L. xi. 344–9.

[3] Ayala, ii. 250.

[4] The Duke killed two birds with one stone, for the archbishop was also Don Juan's Chancellor. Ayala, ii. 635.

THE SECOND INVASION OF CASTILE

proud signature NOS EL REY, his letters conveyed a message of friendship to the first and a challenge to the second.[1]

Don Juan had for long been familiar with his rival's plans; the challenge only confirmed the fears which had haunted him from the day of his accession. After Aljubarrota he had made an abject appeal to France for help,[2] to which Charles VI had replied in a sympathetic letter containing commonplaces on providence and the mutability of fortune, accompanied by the more welcome promise of men and money. Less practically useful, the Court of Avignon was equally sympathetic. To console Don Juan in the hour of defeat Clement had sent him a homily on the text " Whom God loveth He chasteneth," and with graceful allusions to the sufferings of Saul and Jonathan at the hand of the Philistines, had entreated him not to despair.[3]

In spite of the promises of the first and the consolation of the second Juan did despair. Only the political and military condition of Castile can explain Lancaster's confidence, and the large measure of success which in the end attended his rash adventure.

At Aljubarrota the Castilian army had been ruined; all Castile was in mourning, and king and kingdom were utterly demoralized. Nothing is more significant of the utter collapse of the power which a generation earlier had almost driven the Moors out of the Peninsula than the eagerness of the de facto king to make terms with the

[1] Lopes, v. 107–8 ; 93 ; Ayala, ii. 250, 253.
[2] Relig. St. Denys, i. 438, etc. ; Ayala, ii. 243–5 ; Froissart, K. de L. xi. 375-7.
[3] Ayala, ii. 246–7 ; Chr. Reg. Franc. iii. 85. Guillaume de Naillac and Gaucher de Passac undertook for 100,000 francs to lead 2,000 men-at-arms to the help of Juan (agreement dated Paris, Feb. 5, 1387, Pièces Inédites, i. 77, See also Brit. Mus. Add. Ch. 3358, 6759, 1360–62, 11368).

313

pretender. Before Lancaster had been a month in Galicia an embassy arrived to negotiate.[1]

Don Juan Serrano, Prior of Guadelupe and Chancellor of the Privy Seal, Diego Lopez de Medrano, Knight, and Alvar Martinez de Villareal, Doctor of Laws, carried the King's reply to his adversary's challenge. They found the Duke at Orense in August, and there, in the presence of his council, each in turn delivered his message.

The Prior, in the most solemn manner, protested that the true right of succession lay with his master, and conjured Lancaster by God and Saint James not to invade the kingdom in an unrighteous cause. To the Duke's challenge of battle the Knight replied with a counter challenge in the usual form. In order to avoid the shedding of Christian blood his master was ready to meet John of Gaunt man to man, ten against ten, or a hundred against a hundred—a conventional reply which of course meant nothing. The man of law then argued the question of hereditary right at length. It is noticeable that the legality of Don Pedro's marriage with Maria de Padilla was never called in question. The son of Enrique the Bastard could scarcely stand upon the punctilio of legitimate birth. Neither was it convenient to urge the objection which in later years decided that ardent Lancastrian jurist, Sir John Fortescue, to condemn the Lancastrian claim ; [2] it was scarcely open to Juan of Castile, who laid claim to Portugal in the right of his wife Beatrix, to condemn the transmission of hereditary right through females. The lawyer took a very different line and tried to establish the position of Don Juan as the heir, through his mother Juana, of the House of la Cerda, the elder line of descent from Alfonso X, dispossessed ever

[1] For the negotiations at Orense see Lopes, v. 94–104 ; Ayala, i. 253–261. Froissart has nothing.
[2] Fortescue, *Works,* p. 497.

since Sancho IV set aside his nephew Alfonso de la Cerda the " disinherited," and usurped the throne.[1]

After this argument, which lasted long, the envoys were courteously entertained by the Duke. The next day they had their answer. Juan Guttierez, Bishop of Dax, as spokesman for the Duke, answered each in turn. It was rather absurd to support the strong claim of Constance as elder surviving child of Don Pedro by a far-fetched claim of John of Gaunt himself as great-grandson of Edward I and Eleanor of Castile, but any argument was good enough in a case of hereditary right. The Bishop was on stronger ground when to the claim of the House of la Cerda he opposed their formal renunciation and the homage actually done by Enrique the Bastard to his brother.

But the interest of the conference at Orense does not lie in this academic discussion of title. Don Juan's real motive was betrayed when at the close of the second day's palaver the Prior of Guadelupe disclosed to the Duke that he was the bearer of secret instructions.[2] He was empowered to propose a compromise of the dynastic quarrel by the marriage of the heir of Don Juan with the heiress of Queen Constance, Katharine of Lancaster!

If Lancaster had realized his true position he would have closed with this offer forthwith. It was the natural

---

[1] The House of La Cerda could not establish any such right for (i) the *Siete Partidas* which first recognised the modern rule of succession had not, at the time of Sancho's " usurpation," been accepted by the Cortes, and (ii) any claim which the descendants of Alfonso " the disinherited " might have had been renounced, in exchange for a grant of lands, by the Treaty of Camillo (1305).

[2] The " Secret Treaty " is established beyond a doubt by a document in the French archives. On September 11, 1386, Charles VI empowered Jean Sire de Foleville to represent him in the negotiations with Lancaster, and the commission recites that *terms had already been discussed*. (*Pièces Inédites*, i. 74–6.) See also Lopes, v. 104, and the convincing account of Ayala, ii. 255, 261.

and obvious solution of the dynastic problem. But to accept a compromise at the outset would have placed him in difficulties. The Duke could not reckon without his ally ; he had already contracted definite obligations to the King of Portugal. The invasion of Castile was presupposed by all the elaborate negotiations which had been taking place between himself, Richard II and Dom João. He may of course have suspected the good faith of his adversary and regarded the whole proposal as a ruse invented to gain time, and to break up the Anglo-Portuguese federation. These considerations had weight, but there was something further.

The truth is that John of Gaunt never realized the hopelessness of his position. The fundamental folly of the Plantagenet claim to France and of the Lancastrian claim to Castile was the same—the attempt to force an alien dynasty on a high spirited people keenly sensible of their national honour. Don Pedro died in 1369 ; Enrique in 1379 ; since then Don Juan had held the sceptre without challenge. The House of Trastamare had established a prescriptive right.

Lancaster, misled by the support of a few Galician gentlemen who still cherished a sentimental affection for the line of Don Pedro, and a few malcontents from Castile and Leon, imagined that one striking success would throw the whole people into his arms. He forgot that such a success, which could only be achieved by the united forces of England and Portugal, could not help the dynastic cause. A king who carved his way to the throne by Portuguese swords would never rule long in Castile.

Miscalculation of political forces, loyalty to his ally and personal pride, all urged him in the same direction. He chose to go through with the adventure and play the

---

[1] Juan's protestations of faith in his subjects' loyalty make one suspect that the number of Castilians who were sitting on the fence was considerable. Ayala, ii. 303.

JOÃO I OF PORTUGAL ENTERTAINING JOHN OF GAUNT.

game. To the proposal of the Prior of Guadelupe he returned an evasive answer. Neither rejecting the offer outright nor accepting it, he sent Sir Thomas Percy, the best head in the army, to hear what Don Juan had to say, and then proceeded to commit himself still further to hostilities.

For, on the heels of the departing envoys from Castile came a second embassy.[1] The *Falcon Inn* in Gracechurch Street knew the Chancellor of Portugal no longer ; after more than three years' service in England, Lourenço Annes Fogaça had returned to Portugal, and now headed a deputation sent by Dom João to bear words of welcome and presents to the Duke of Lancaster. The Chancellor and his colleague, Vasco Martins de Mello, were also charged to arrange a conference between their master and his ally at a place on the northern frontier of the two kingdoms, Ponte do Mouro, on the river Minho, between Melgaço and Monção. The offer was accepted, and by the end of October John of Gaunt with his court was at the Benedictine Monastery of Cellanova near Milmanda, a few miles from the meeting place, waiting for the approach of the King of Portugal.[2] It was on November 1 that for the first time the two kings met ; John of Gaunt, surrounded by an imposing retinue of English, Galician, and Castilian knights; Dom João and his knights in the white robes of the Cistercian order, with the crimson cross of St. George, emblem of the Knights of Avis.

While the chivalry of England and Portugal were fraternizing, the councils of the allies met in the royal pavilion of Castile, a trophy of Aljubarrota, to concert measures against the enemy.

---

[1] Lopes, v. 109, 112–3 ; Ayala, ii. 250.
[2] For the meeting at Ponte do Mouro see Lopes, v. 115–119. There are several inaccuracies in Ayala's account of the treaty (ii. 251–2) Froissart, K. de L. xi. 403–410.

JOHN OF GAUNT

It was at Ponte do Mouro that Portugal repaid her debt to England. For the last three years volunteers had been pouring from the island kingdom to fight in the battles against Castile. As a soldier the Master of Avis knew the value of English archers and men-at-arms ; as a statesman he knew the moral force of the acknowledged sympathy of the first military power of the day. But for the events of the last few years, the terms of the present treaty would be inexplicable ; it would appear the most one-sided of political bargains. The first article disposed of Sir Thomas Percy's mission for good, for the allies bound themselves together in an offensive alliance against the usurper of Castile. By the second João undertook to lead an army of 5,000 men to help Lancaster from January 1 to the end of August at his own cost. If after the expiration of eight months John of Gaunt still needed Portuguese support he was to pay the cost of further operations, but the allies evidently considered eight months enough to dispose of Don Juan.

Lancaster on his side agreed that after the conquest of Castile a line of towns on the Portuguese frontier, from Ledesma in the north to Fregenal in the south, should be ceded to his ally,[1] such cession being obviously contingent on the success of the expedition.

The last article united Lancaster and Portugal by a blood alliance. The Duke, as we have seen, had brought both his unmarried daughters to Spain, Philippa his eldest child and Katharine. It says much for the political wisdom of Dom João that he chose the hand of Philippa. Katharine, as the only surviving child of Queen Constance, would ultimately become the heiress of Don Pedro's claim, and her rights vested in a Queen of Portugal might at any time re-open the vexed question

[1] Ledesma, Matilla, Monleon, Plasencia, Grimaldo, Cañaveral, Alconeta, Carceres, Alcuéscar, Merida, Fuente del Maestre, Zafra Fregenal.

of political union between the two kingdoms, the principle against which the Portuguese king had successfully protested. João, whose policy was not aggressive, chose the elder daughter, and the hand of Katharine remained at her father's disposal.

On Novermber 11, Lancaster at Cellanova ratified the Treaty of Ponte do Mouro, and João went south to prepare for the coming invasion. Philippa was entrusted to the care of the Archbishop of Braga and lodged in the Franciscan Abbey at Oporto.[1] One difficulty yet remained, before effect could be given to the treaty obligations. João of Avis was still bound by his priestly vows. Immediately on his election as king he had despatched envoys to the Pope to secure his release, and though dispensation had been promised, formalities were not completed. In January the King was still a suitor; Lent, the close season for marriages, was approaching, and the campaign was soon to open; yet João and Philippa were still exchanging presents, but not the vows which should make Philippa Queen of Portugal and definitely seal the Lancastrian alliance.

It was clear that a hitch had occurred in the negotiations at the Papal court. This *contretemps* has given an opening to the gossips of the ancient and modern world. Froissart would have us believe that Lancaster, who had staked everything on the Portuguese alliance, hesitated at a blood alliance with one whom his enemies described as a bastard, and renegade monk, and that João on the other hand, alarmed by the preparations of the French to invade England, began to repent of the alliance,[2] while a modern writer has assured us that Philippa was not beautiful and that the King found among his subjects ladies who were both charming and complaisant.[3]

[1] Lopes, v. 121.
[2] Froissart, K. de L. xii. 77–79.
[3] Count Villa Franca in *Joao I e a Alliança Ingleze*.

Like so many pieces of court scandal, the tale is without foundation. What really happened was this. Lancaster, who constantly had dealings with the Papal court, had there in 1386 an agent who, like many of his master's partizans, possessed more zeal than discretion. A little knowledge proved, as usual, a dangerous thing. The agent knew that John of Gaunt claimed the kingdom of Castile, and knew also that the *de facto* King of Castile claimed Portugal as well. Of the relations between Lancaster and his ally he appears to have been ignorant, and when Dom João's envoys pressed for the issue of the Bull of dispensation they encountered opposition in the most unexpected quarter, the Duke's agent protesting that Dom João was a usurper, and that Lancaster was the legitimate king. When the circumstances were laid before him the Duke was naturally indignant, denied all knowledge of the affair, and offered to send his own Chancellor to the Pope to explain. All this took time, and João determined to wait no longer.[1] On February 2, 1387, João of Avis and Philippa of Lancaster received the blessing of the Church in the Cathedral of Oporto. In a manifesto addressed to his subjects the King explained the situation.[2] The Bull had been already granted; only formalities remained. In a few days Lent would begin and the campaign would open. He declared his intention of beginning his married life on February 14, and invited his subjects to welcome their

---

[1] After considerable delay the Bull was finally issued by Boniface IX (dated Rome, February 5, 2 Boniface IX). It recites the circumstances, absolves João from the penalty of excommunication for marrying, dispenses him from his vows, and legitimates the marriage and offspring.

It was read from the pulpit of the Cathedral at Lisbon on July 1, 1391. Soares da Silva, *Collecção dos Documentos para as memorias del Rey. D.* João I, Vol. iv p. 50, Nos. ix. and x. and Fernão Lopes, vi. 9–28. *Papal Letters* iv. 367.

[2] Lopes, v. 122–128 ; Froissart, K. de L. xii. 90–95.

THE MARRIAGE OF JOÃO I AND PHILIPPA OF LANCASTER.

new Queen with appropriate rejoicings. Portugal responded with enthusiasm, and for fifteen days the marriage which was to inaugurate the new dynasty was celebrated throughout the kingdom.

In postponing the military history of this enterprise to the story of diplomatic intercourse, the narrative has only followed Lancaster's own procedure, for the first place in his mind was occupied by negotiations, the threads of which he kept in his own hand while leaving the fighting to his officers.

The military operations of 1386–7 fall into two parts, the reduction of Galicia, and the invasion of Castile.

The first task was accomplished by the Duke's Marshals, Sir Thomas Morieux and Sir Richard Burley, and was fairly complete before the joint invasion of Castile by the Portuguese and English armies. The campaign, so far as it deserves that name, was one of sieges; there was no battle, for there was no enemy. From Santiago the Marshals rode to town after town summoning the inhabitants, who for the most part were perfectly indifferent to the dynastic quarrel, to accept their lawful sovereign Queen Constance and King John.[1] Where resistance was offered it was because the burgesses feared pillage at the hands of the army, or dreaded that surrender to King John would be punished sooner or later by King Juan. Now and then, where the *de facto* king's garrisons were stiffened by Breton or French soldiers of fortune, there was some stubborn fighting. It is impossible to follow the course of events with any sort

[1] Froissart's account of the Galician campaign is simply hopeless. Chronology and topography are nothing to him. The Marshal takes a town in the heart of Leon, and goes back to Santiago to dinner! It is curious that Froissart should have made such a muddle of it, for he was in Foix in 1388, where there were eye-witnesses to question, and João Fernandes Pacheco, who told him about it at Middelburgh a few years later, was in a position to know.

of precision, for the accounts that have survived are either meagre or hopelessly confused, but the main features of the operations are fairly intelligible. At first Santiago was the headquarters, but very soon the army appears in the south of Galicia, and the Duke seems to have been in possession of Orense in August. Then, from Betanzos and Ferrol in the north to the river Minho, which forms the southern boundary of Galicia, the English army got possession by force or by composition of the most important towns and strongholds, until by the spring of 1387 they had got a grip of the whole northern province.[1]

Pontevedra surrendered after a day's siege, and a Galician knight of the retinue of Queen Constance replaced Don Juan's captain.[2] Vigo followed suit, and Bayona surrendered at the first assault. Ribadave formed an exception to the indifference of the Gallegos and made a stout defence. The town was built on a strong position, assailable on one side only, but neither the natural strength of the position, nor the courage of the besieged, saved it. The English army stormed the walls, sacked the town, and captured a certain amount of treasure.

From a strategical point of view the conquest of Galicia was useless. It was not even necessary to hold Coruña as a base, for no supplies or reinforcements were expected from England or Gascony, and the fleet had been dismissed. The excellent port of Vigo in the south would serve the purposes of re-embarkation, and after the treaty of Ponte do Mouro the harbours of Portugal were at the disposal of the English, and in the end, as will be seen,

---

[1] Lancaster's successes in Galicia were reported in England, where his dynastic policy was followed with interest. Higd. ix. 96–7.

[2] For Pontevedra see Froissart K. de L. xi. 410–17 ; Vigo, 417–420 ; Bayona, 420–5 ; Ribadave, 425–90 ; xii. 79–87 ; Orense, 185–202 ; Ferrol, 205–215.

THE SIEGE OF BAYONA.

the army sailed from Oporto. Not only were the operations in the northern province useless for any military purpose, they were actually harmful, for the casualties [1] which resulted from the unimportant fighting and marching in a poor country, where supplies were difficult to get, together with the locking up of valuable forces in garrisons damaged the army as an effective fighting force.

From a political point of view, however, there was a certain justification for the Duke's policy. With his banner flying from the walls of the Galician strongholds the pretender was in a better position to make terms with his adversary on the one hand and his ally on the other. Failing the possibility of immediate decisive action by the English and Portuguese armies acting together, which was the proper course, the Duke may have held with some show of reason that the occupation of the northern province strengthened his hand and gave him a certain prestige.

The real military interest of the story begins with the joint invasion of March, 1387.[2] The allies met near Braganza,[3] at the end of March : this was later than the date contemplated by the Treaty of Ponte do Mouro, but Dom João's excuses were readily accepted, for the fault lay solely with the busybody at the Papal Court who had delayed the marriage. To clear up any possible misunderstanding on this score John and Constance formally renounced and transferred to their ally any right which they had or could have in the Kingdom of Portugal.[4]

[1] For the English losses by disease in Galicia see Ayala, ii. 251.
[2] For the invasion see Lopes, v. 130-171 ; Ayala, ii. 263-6 ; Froissart, K. de L. xii. 295-308.
[3] It was at Braganza that the duel was fought by Sir John Holland and Sir Regnault de Roie. See safe conduct, undated (? end of March, 1387). Delpit Collection, No. ccxciii. p. 206 ; Froissart, K. de L. xii. 115-124.
[4] The donation is dated Babé (near Braganza), March 26, 1425, A.D. 1387, Sousa Provas de Historia Genealogica, i. 354; Soares da Silva, Colleccão dos Documentos, iv. No. xi.

Then, when the last Portuguese levies had come from the south, Philippa returned to Oporto and the march began.

Disease and garrison duty had reduced Lancaster's available force to something like six hundred men-at-arms and six hundred archers ; João, however, put about ten thousand men in the field, an army nearly twice as large as that stipulated for by the treaty. In spite of this disproportion of force the King of Portugal made no claim to direct operations ; indeed the deference which he showed to his father-in-law throughout the campaign appeared to his own subjects extravagant, and only the instances of Nuno Alvares Pereira, the Constable, prevented him from conceding to Lancaster the post of honour which he held in the campaign of 1367, the command of the van.

The plan was to march north-east into Leon ; once established there, Lancaster expected his adherents to declare themselves and to flock to his standard. By March 30 the combined armies had passed Alcañices and entered Don Juan's territories ; by Easter they were at Benavente, in the heart of the old kingdom of Leon.

Meanwhile Don Juan was moving about in a helpless way on the line of the Douro between Tordesillas Toro and Zamora. How far he had relied on negotiations to stave off invasion must remain uncertain,[1] but, the invasion once a fact, the King's plan was clear. He had no intention of risking battle, and was committed to a wholly defensive policy. Though the large reinforcements promised by Charles VI had not yet arrived, there were numbers of French volunteers in Juan's service, and their advice was accepted [2]—to clear the country so far

[1] Ayala admits that Juan was afraid to fight : " temia mucho la guerra, por quanto avia grand mengua de gentes de armas en el su regno, ca los mas é mejores capitanes avia perdido en la guerra de Portogal de pestilencia, é de batallas (ii. 252).
[2] For the advice of the French volunteers, see Froissart, K. de L. xi. 350–6.

as possible before the invaders, garrison the strong places and abandon the weak, and while leaving no vulnerable point for attack, to wear out the enemy by fatigue, starvation and disease. Juan was taking a leaf out of the book of Charles V, but the policy of inaction accepted in France was new to Castile, and required justification.[1] Could a more convincing argument be conceived than that afforded by the great march from Calais to Bordeaux ? The King reminds his subjects of Lancaster's failure in 1373, and proposes to defeat him by the same means in 1387.[2] Once more the policy of inaction was fully justified by its results. Lancaster's archers and João's lancers never had the chance of winning another Aljubarrota. For all practical purposes the invasion ended at Benavente. It was hopeless to attempt a siege of the town, which was held in force by Alvar Perez de Osorio, a noble of Leon ; and though individual Castilians were quite willing to break a lance with English or Portuguese knights, there was no chance of bringing on an engagement. João Fernandes Pacheco, who in later years told the story of the campaign to Froissart, marched north threatening Astorga, but the demonstration produced no appreciable effects. Other attacks were delivered

---

[1] In a circular letter to the cities of the kingdom Juan gives his reasons for not fighting a pitched battle. (1) His forces are scattered on the frontiers of the kingdom ; (2) *the English may go away without fighting* ; (3) the precedents of Alfonso and the Moors, Charles V and the English, point the other way ; (4) Bourbon and the 2,000 French lances have not yet arrived. Ayala, ii. 634–7 (note).

[2] Otrosi el Rey de Francia, quando el Príncipe entró en su regno, é quando el Duque de Alencastre nuestro enemigo pasó á Francia agora há diez años con el poder mayor que jamás salió de Inglaterra, que eran fasta quarenta é quatro mil de á caballo, los entretuvo en tal manera, que salieron muy perdidos de su regno, especialmente el dicho Duque, que non tornaron con él á Burdeos mas que tres mil lanzas ; por lo qual fasta agora nunca los dichos Ingleses han podido facer otro ningun pasage : tanta pérdida é mal rescibieron. Ayala, ii. 636 (note).

east and south of Benavente, but a fortnight's desultory fighting and the capture of some half-dozen towns, Matilla, Roales, Santillan, Valdéras and Villalobos,[1] left Lancaster no nearer to the goal of his ambitions. Meanwhile a deadlier enemy than French or Castilian had been fighting the English army. Froissart says that the English archers drank the strong wines of the country till they were useless for fighting. Whether it was intemperance, or short rations, and hard marching in an unaccustomed climate, dysentery broke out ; and dysentery was succeeded by an outbreak of the plague.[2] Lancaster himself is said to have sickened, but his great physical strength pulled him through. Among his followers the mortality was fearful. According to one estimate three hundred knights and esquires died besides a great number of archers. After the deadly summer of 1387 many a well-known name falls out of the roll-call of the Lancastrian retinue. More fortunate than their comrades, the gallant Poitevin Sir Mauburni de Linières and Sir John Falconer died with arms in their hands ; disease accounted for Lord Poynings, Lord Fitzwalter, Lord Scales, both the Marshals, Sir Thomas Morieux and Sir Richard Burley, Sir John Marmion, Sir Hugh Hastings, Sir Thomas Symond and Sir Thomas Fychet. A Percy too was among the victims, Thomas the younger brother of " Hotspur." [3]

It was clear that as a fighting force Lancaster's army was useless. Dom João put the issue to him clearly : either he must get together another force from England, or he must accept the compromise offered at Orense. The enemy believed that the first alternative would be chosen, and already the rumour had got about that Lancaster

---

[1] For Roales and Villalobos see Froissart, K. de L. xi. 377–87.
[2] For the plague and the break up of the English army, see Froissart, K. de L. xii. 308–11, 311–26.
[3] Here Walsingham inserts the usual repentance. The Duke weeps for his past life, etc. etc. ii. 193–4.

had sent home to recruit a second army.[1] There were the Portuguese forces moreover to be reckoned with, for the plague had not touched them. On both grounds therefore Don Juan was willing to resume negotiations. When the French auxiliaries under the Duke of Bourbon began to arrive the campaign was already over. There was little* to choose so far as the cities of Castile were concerned, whether they should be plundered by Breton free lances or English archers, and the King was as much afraid of his friends as of his enemies. It was an expensive matter to maintain a large body of foreign mercenaries, so the Frenchmen were thanked, paid, and dismissed.[2]

The plague-stricken army was disbanded; some received letters of safe conduct from Don Juan to return through his territory to Gascony; others followed the Duke to the friendly soil of Portugal. Turning south from the neighbourhood of Benavente, between Zamora and Toro, Lancaster and his ally marched to Ciudad Rodrigo, and thence over the frontier to Almeida. At Trancoso[3] the Duke was overtaken by Juan's envoys, who offered once more the terms of the secret treaty of Orense as the price of renunciation of rights which could not be enforced—generous terms to a foiled if not defeated foe. This time they were accepted, and after agreeing to a compromise on the lines suggested, to be ratified at Bayonne as soon as convenient, Lancaster withdrew to Coimbra.

The allies had passed unscathed through the campaign only to encounter more formidable dangers at its close, for in July the King of Portugal fell dangerously ill and the " King and Queen of Castile " narrowly escaped being poisoned by a Castilian conspirator. However, João recovered, and the plot against his father-in-law was dis-

---

[1] *Eulog.* iii. 367.
[2] Ayala, ii. 266–8.
[3] For the negotiations at Trancoso see Ayala, ii. 268–9.

covered in time, and in October John of Gaunt said farewell
to his ally and left Oporto for Bayonne.[1] There, where the
body of the first Earl of Lancaster rested, Edmund " King
of Sicily and Apulia," the " King of Castile and Leon "
waited for the embassy from his rival, and prepared to lay
down his royal state. But while day after day passed, no
embassy arrived. Once more the Duke, whose experience
had taught him what faith was to be put in princes, began
to entertain the old suspicion—that Don Juan was playing
him false and, once rid of the invading army, would repudiate his undertakings.

If he could not win the crown of Castile for himself
John of Gaunt was at least resolved that it should be
worn by his daughter. Force being out of the question,
he had recourse to other means, and proceeded to teach
his contemporaries a short lesson in the art of statecraft.

Relations between the Courts of France and Castile
for the moment were somewhat strained. The Duke of
Bourbon and the French auxiliaries had been dismissed
with scant ceremony, and Charles VI considered that
Juan had not behaved with proper deference to the para-
mount power. Lancaster, understanding the situation,
and being, as Froissart tells us, " *sage et imaginatif*," used
the jealousy of Charles VI to produce the very result
which Charles feared. The courtly author of the *Chronicles* assures us that Katharine of Lancaster was beautiful. The Duke of Berri was a widower, and, according
to the same authority, a man of confirmed domestic

---

[1] Letters of general attorney of John, King of Castile, " qui in
partibus transmarinis moratur." *Foed*, VII. 564. Notification of
the appointment of Lancaster as the King's Lieutenant in the
Duchy of Aquitaine, dated May 26, 1388. *Foed*, VII. 585–6.
Lancaster's arrival caused some alarm at the French court.
See mandate of Charles VI to the receivers of Bayeux for the
levying of an aid dated Compiègne, Dec. 19, 1387. *Pièces Inédites*,
i. 83 (Brit. Mus. Add. Ch., 3360).

habits. It was one of Berri's maxims that "*un hotel d'un seignenr ne vaut rien sans dame, ni un homme sans femme!*" When, therefore, his wise councillors suggested that Juan might very well be thrown overboard, and the hand and heritage of Katharine won for a French prince, Berri was charmed with the idea. He proposed himself for the match, and forthwith despatched Helion de Lignac, his right-hand man, to Lancaster's court on this delicate mission.[1]

There is a time to speak one's whole mind, and a time to be silent. John of Gaunt thought the case was one for reserve, and without committing himself encouraged the suit, and contrived to make the visit of Helion de Lignac to Bordeaux particularly agreeable. The next step was to bring Berri's suit to the ears of the King of Castile. What more natural than that the Duke should mention it to his friend the Count of Foix? For the purposes of gossip Foix was particularly well placed. Soldiers of fortune bound for Spain, pilgrims bound for Santiago, every one in fact bound for the south knew the hospitality of Gaston Phœbus, and felt sure of a welcome at the Court of Orthez, where a few months later that paragon of gossips, Sirc Jean Froissart himself, puzzling over the intricacies of the Spanish campaign, learnt the news of this startling development.

From Foix the tale of Berri's courtship spread to Navarre, and from his brother-in-law of Navarre it reached the ears of Don Juan himself. There is no reason to doubt Juan's good faith; financial difficulties were probably responsible for the delay, but when the report of Berri's *démarche* reached him Juan took alarm. Before many days his envoys were on the way to Bayonne to claim the fulfilment of the conditions proposed at Trancoso.

[1] For Berri's courtship see Froissart, K. de L. xiii. 110–116, 132–4. Ayala says nothing about it.

Lancaster had won the game ; and while the wits of Charles' court were making merry over the short and ill-fated courtship of the Duke of Berri, John of Gaunt was sealing the compact with his adversary which promised Katharine to the Infante, and put an end once and for all to the Lancastrian claim.

The Castilian embassy consisted of Brother Fernando de Illescas, the King's confessor, and a couple of trusted lawyers. An edifying discourse on the blessings of peace was preached before the Duke and Duchess in their chapel by the chief envoy, but as Lancaster had never learned Spanish the point of the homily was rather lost upon him. When it came to business, however, the Duke made himself understood and showed that he could drive a hard bargain.

A few articles of the Treaty [1] concluded in the spring of 1388 are of general interest ; the first, for instance, in which the two contracting parties professed their anxiety to heal the schism in the Church, and which could not amount to much more than a pious hope while both remained committed to opposite sides. By the second they bound themselves to promote better relations between England and France, an engagement in which the Duke was certainly sincere, though he failed to induce his adversary to abandon his existing obligations to Charles VI. After this preamble the treaty is perfectly definite, and astounding in the generosity of its concessions to Lancaster's claims.

On the one hand John and Constance undertook to swear upon the holy gospels (an oath from which under pain of excommunication they were never to seek release) to renounce and transfer to Juan I any right which they had or might have in the kingdoms of Castile, Leon,

---

[1] For the Treaty see Ayala, ii. 271–8 ; Higd. ix. 97. It was ratified by Enrique III in 1391. Ayala, ii. 387.

Toledo, Galicia, Seville, Cordova, Murcia, Jaen, Algarve,[1] and Algeciras, and the lordships of Lara, Biscay and Molina.

On the other hand the *de facto* King agreed to terms of compensation so important as to constitute an implicit acknowledgment of the legality of his rival's claim.

The foundation of the compromise was the ultimate fusion of the claims of Trastamare and Burgundy. Within two months of the ratification of the treaty Katharine of Lancaster was to be married to Enrique, eldest son of Juan I. The Prince and Princess of the Asturias (such was to be their new title) were to be presented to the Cortes at the earliest moment and recognized as heir and heiress to the throne, while to support their dignity a sufficient appanage was to be assigned to them—the towns of Soria, Almazán, Atienza, Deza and Molina, the large fief formerly granted by Enrique the Magnificent to Bertrand du Guesclin.

In 1388 Enrique the Infante was only in his tenth year,[2] while Katharine was fourteen. To guard against any possible danger that Katharine might lose her right, it was provided that Juan's second son, Don Fernando, should remain unmarried until the union had been consummated, and that should Enrique die before that date, he should take his brother's place.

So much for the ultimate succession. It remained for Don Juan to satisfy the immediate claims of the heirs of the dispossessed House. This he agreed to do in the most ample manner. The cession of the revenues and government of three important towns, Guadalajara, Medina del Campo and Olmedo, saving only the direct suzerainty, to "Queen" Constance was perhaps only claimed by

---

[1] Portuguese Algarve had been already ceded to João I by the donation of March 26, 1387. See above, p. 323 note.

[2] Enrique (III) was born in Burgos, October 4, 1379. Ayala, ii. 128.

sentiment, but the other articles were practical, and sufficiently serious for Castile.

For the lifetime of the Duke and Duchess, and for the
lifetime of the survivor, Juan undertook to pay an annuity
of forty thousand francs of gold, and the unhappy King,
who had already been compelled to pay his allies, was
now compelled to indemnify his enemy for the costs of
the campaign. John of Gaunt was to receive the enormous sum of six hundred thousand francs of gold, to be
paid at Bayonne by equal instalments within the next
three years. For both payments hostages, nobles and
burgesses of Castile, were to be given.

Even now Juan's concessions were not exhausted. It
was necessary to contemplate the ultimate failure of the
royal line. The agreement fixed the succession first in
the issue of Katharine and Enrique ; if Katharine died
without issue, in Enrique and his line ; if both died without issue, in Don Fernando and his line, and finally
in any other issue, of Don Juan. But in case all these
claims became extinct the right to the throne was to
revert to Constance of Castile and her husband and their
issue. In any case the act of renunciation was to become
void if payment of the annuity fell three years in arrear.

On these conditions Juan I and John of Gaunt, no longer
" King of Castile," consented to be true friends and allies ;
onerous as they were, they were for the most part loyally
fulfilled.[1] Few will be found to quarrel with the judg-

---

[1] The indemnity was paid, though it produced a financial crisis.
The general tax proposed at the Cortes of Briviesca had to be
abandoned, for the nobles and clergy succeeded in asserting their
privileges (Ayala, ii. 272 and 279). Safe conduct for the hostages
dated Aug. 26, 1388 (*Foed*, VII. 603). Knighton says that it took
47 mules to carry the second instalments (ii. 208). The annuity
seems to have been paid almost up to the end of Lancaster's life. See general safe conduct for Juan's agents
dated July 13, 1391 (*Foed*, VII. 704). In 1393 it was two years in
arrear ; Lancaster sent envoys to Enrique III, excusing payment of interest in honour of Queen Katharine, but claiming the

ment of that disinterested spectator, the Count of Foix, who, expressing himself in terms far from complimentary to Juan I, added of Lancaster : " Par ma foi, il y a ung sage homme au duc de Lancastre, et vaillamment et sagement il s'est porté en ceste guerre ! " [1]

The great adventure, which had cost so many years of labour and scheming to prepare, and so many gallant lives to achieve, ended with the sound of marriage bells. In September at Fuentarrabia on the Guipuzcoan frontier, a cortege of prelates, knights, and ladies of Castile received Katharine of Lancaster from her English escort and conducted her with the honour due to the heiress apparent to Palencia. There in the Church of St. Antolin she was married by the Archbishop of Seville to the Infante.[2]

There were two powers who found the settlement of the Lancastrian claim far from satisfactory—France and the Papacy.

There was no disguising the fact that so far as the Church was concerned the Crusade had been a failure. Urban VI showed his displeasure by revoking the powers granted to Brother Walter Dysse and the Bishops of Hereford, Llandaff and Dax, and citing them to appear before him in person to explain their conduct in continuing to raise money by the sale of indulgences, long after the cause for which they had been granted had ceased to be operative.[3]

The King of France, too, affected to see in the protracted negotiations which Lancaster set on foot after the Treaty

principal (Ayala, ii. 480). For payment in 1394 see Appendix IV. Balance Sheet. There is a safe conduct for the King's agents dated January 12, 1397 (Foed, VII. 849), three years after the death of Constance. In 1399 there were arrears. (Appendix I. p. 429–430).

[1] Froissart, K. de L. xiii. 297.

[2] Ayala, ii. 278–80.

[3] Mandate to the Archbishop of Bordeaux dated 17 Kal. Feb. 1389 (11 Urban VI). *Papal Letters*, iv. 270–1.

of 1388 [1] a deliberate attempt to detach Castile from the French alliance. Apart from the fact that the Duke was now firmly committed to a policy of international peace and had no aggressive intentions, there was a certain justification for this view, and it was natural to look for a political motive for the long visit paid by the Duchess of Lancaster to her cousin of Castile in 1388–9.[2]

But the meeting which had been arranged between John of Gaunt and Juan of Castile on the frontier never took place. The cause, or as Lancaster thought the pretext, was the King's ill-health, and Constance had other interests besides those of policy for her stay in Castile. There was a sacred duty to be fulfilled. Going to the place near the battlefield of Montiel, where nineteen years ago Don Pedro had been murdered by his half-brother, Constance reverently caused the remains of the last monarch of the House of Burgundy to be gathered up and laid in the burial place of his ancestors.

For the rest, the only political significance of her visit was to promote better relations between Lancaster and Castile,[3] and to strengthen the position of the Princess of the Asturias.

The dynastic quarrel was forgotten in the interchange

---

[1] Notification of the appointment of Lancaster by Richard II to treat with his adversary of Castile, dated June 1, 1388. (*Foed*, VII. 587–8). Ratification by Juan I of the alliance between Enrique II and Charles V, dated Segovia, Nov. 23, 1386. (*Foed*, VII. 550–1.) On Jan. 3, 1390, at the instance of John of Gaunt, envoys were appointed to conclude a treaty of alliance, or peace, or truce with Castile (*Foed*, VII. 680–2). This was followed by a confirmation by Enrique III of the French alliance (dated May 27, 1391. *Foed*, VII. 700–1). The same story is repeated three years later. On April 17, 1393, envoys are appointed to treat with Castile (*Foed*, VII. 739–40); a few months later Enrique again confirms the alliance with France. *Foed*, VII. 763.

[2] For the visit of the Duchess of Lancaster to Castile see Ayala, ii. 281 ; Froissart, K. de L. xiii. 302–4.

[3] E de cada dia se enviaban sus joyas, é sus dones, é muy buenas cartas, é crescia grand amor entre ellos. Ayala, ii. 281.

of courtesies between the Castilians and their former enemies. To the King's presents of Spanish mules and horses Lancaster replied by sending to his rival the golden crown which he had brought from England for his own coronation. *Dis aliter visum.* The Duke's ambition was realized in the person of his daughter.

Between Katharine of Lancaster and her half-sister the Queen of Portugal the contrast is as striking as that which tradition draws between their husbands, Enrique surnamed El Dolente, a grave and austere man of few words, but, so far as his colourless disposition shows him, of good intentions, and João, soldier, statesman, man of affairs, a man of vast strength with a full measure of virile activity.

Katharine, to judge by the portrait in the fascinating gallery of Fernan Perez de Guzman,[1] was tall, fair, a Plantagenet in build and feature, stately, and with something of her father's haughtiness, never forgetful of her royal ancestry, as is shown by her defiant signature " Yo sin ventura reyna."[2]

The worst that scandal could whisper of the Queen of Castile was a fondness for wine and a readiness to listen to favourites. If the first failing was responsible for the troubles of her later years (she died of paralysis), the second may be excused by her early difficulties,[3] for after

---

[1] Fué esta Reyna (Doña Catalina) alta de cuerpo, mucho gruesa, blanca é colorada é rubia, y en el talle y meneo del cuerpo tanto parecia hombre como muger : fué muy honesta é guardada en su persona é fama, é liberal é magnifica, pero muy sometida á privados é regida dellos. . . .

No era bien regida en su persona [*Fertur quod temulenta erat mulier*]. Ovo una gran dolencia de perlesía de la qual no quedó bien suelta de la lengua ni libre del cuerpo. She died June 12, 1418, and was buried at Toledo. *Generaciones semblanzas é obras de los reyes de España :* Fernan Perez de Guzman, Valencia, 1779, pp. 582-4. The author was Ayala's nephew.

[2] M. A. E. Wood, *Royal Letters*, p. 85.

[3] It would be interesting to trace the influence of Katharine, a firm adherent of the canonical Pope, on the relations of Castile

a reign of six years Enrique III died and left to his consort the cares of a minority and the guardianship of their child Juan II, the first of a long line of Castilian monarchs who could trace their ancestry to John of Gaunt.

Devotion was the feature which impressed her contemporaries most in the character of the Queen of Portugal,[1] devotion to the Church and the daily duties of religion, to the subjects whose love she won, above all to the large family of sons and daughters whom she bore to the King. The lesson learnt at the Savoy was remembered at Lisbon, and Philippa's sons were taught to add to the practice of arms a love of more humane pursuits. For two hundred years the descendants of the daughter of John of Gaunt ruled Portugal ;[2] the Lancastrian alliance, which had synchronised with the brilliant opening of a new chapter of national life, was never forgotten, and the dynastic union produced others besides Prince Henry the Navigator to continue the Lancastrian tradition of adventure.

to the Papacy. See the story in *Ann. Ric. II* (p. 162-4), of an attempt to detach her from the cause, and the mandate to Juan Guttierez, Bishop of Dax (Lancaster's old agent), to dispense Enrique III and Katharine being related in the third degree, to contract marriage anew on returning to obedience of the Roman Church, dated 8 Kal. Oct., 2 Boniface IX, 1391. *Papal Letters,* iv. xxii.

Cf. Raynaldi, *Annales Ecclesiastici* (sub anno 1391).

[1] Foy a Rainha D. Filippa dotada de formosura discrição, e de muita piedade, e singular modestia de sorte que o seu ordinario modo de andar era com os olhos baixos, e o rostro cuberto de hum natural pejo.

Philippa died of the plague, July 18, 1415. Sousa, *Historia Genealogica da Casa Real Portuguesa.* Cf. Lopes, v. 128–130.

[2] In the British Museum there is a series of vellum tables (sixteenth century) elaborately illuminated, showing the descent of the royal houses of Castile and Portugal from John of Gaunt, Ad. MS. 12, 531 (x. and xi.).

Chapter XIV

JOHN OF GAUNT THE PEACEMAKER

"ONCE upon a time the rats and mice, persecuted incessantly by their enemy the cat, met together in parliament, and resolved that it was expedient that a bell and a collar should be bought and hung round the cat's neck to signal the approach of danger. The bell and chain were procured, but when the time came no one of them was bold enough to carry out the plan."

Langland did not invent the fable of the mice who would bell the cat,[1] but in the Vision concerning Piers the Plowman he adds a touch of his own, for in his version of the tale a certain wise mouse points out that a cat is an inevitable and indeed salutary feature of the constitution : if the cat were killed another would take its place, and better an old cat able to keep the rest in order than a kitten, for " *There the catte is a kittoun the courte is ful elyng.*"

This allegory, which the poet probably meant for the events of 1376, though he says that he dare not explain himself, fits the circumstances of 1386 equally well.[2] The Lancastrian power, which Richard regarded with suspicion and Robert de Vere with hatred, had at least imposed a check on the forces of disorder and of rival ambitions ; so soon as the check was removed, the struggle for power began, and Richard learnt to his cost the dif-

[1] B. Prologue, 145–191.
[2] See M. Jusserand's essay *L'Épopée Mystique de W. Langland,* pp. 37-46.

ference in character between his eldest and youngest uncle.

Thomas of Woodstock, now Duke of Gloucester, was resolved to fill the place left vacant by his elder brother; that was much, but Gloucester's ambition went farther. Lancaster's position was merely that of an acknowledged primacy exhibited mainly in the fields of war and diplomacy; it had clashed with no legal or constitutional principle, and at least in the last few years it had been exercised with due restraint. Gloucester however aimed at nothing less than an absolute dictatorship, which would reduce the position of the King to that of a mere figurehead, and to gain his end he had courted popularity and rallied all the forces of discontent, social, political and religious.

Four great names are associated for a while with his, those of Warwick, Arundel, Derby and Nottingham. The Earls of Warwick and Arundel were the natural leaders of the old baronial party; united by the hatred of royal favourites, bitter enemies not only of Robert de Vere but also of Richard himself, they had long been the centre of opposition. The position of Henry, Earl of Derby, was different. During the next three years he is found acting with Gloucester in opposition to Vere and his party, but never going to extremes, never like his uncle committing himself hopelessly and beyond recall. He is among the leaders of the opposition, but he is ready to leave them, and is not prepared to be made the tool of another man's ambition. It must not be forgotten that in spite of their temporary alliance, Derby and Gloucester were in a sense rivals, and that it was the marriage of Henry and Mary de Bohun which defeated Gloucester's cherished ambition of absorbing the whole Bohun inheritance. Thomas Mowbray, Earl of Nottingham, the fifth of the opposition leaders, was a man of no principle, political or other, a shifty time-server ready to ally himself with any party for the interest of the moment. In 1384 and 1385 he is found in the ranks of the King's favourites; in 1386 he joins the opposition, but is ready to accept a bribe to revert to his old allegiance.

In October, 1386, Richard made the favourite Robert de Vere, already Marquess of Dublin, Duke of Ireland. This was the signal for hostilities. Gloucester declared war and opened with an attack on the King's friends and ministers. The Chancellor, Michael de la Pole, Earl of Suffolk, and the Treasurer, were removed from office; then following the precedent of the " Good " Parliament, a baseless charge of malversation was brought forward to ruin one of the King's ablest ministers. It was in vain that Suffolk disproved the charges laid against him, and that another of the moderate or Lancastrian party, Richard le Scrope, pleaded on his behalf. Judgment was given against him : his property was confiscated and he was condemned to be imprisoned pending payment of an exorbitant fine. His path now cleared, Gloucester extorted from the King a commission of regency with himself at its head, and at the age of twenty-one Richard found himself once more a child in tutelage, with less freedom than the poorest of his peers. It is not surprising that he rebelled ; he released the Earl of Suffolk from prison, gathered his friends about him, compelled the judges to declare the commission illegal, and prepared to use force. An unsuccessful attempt to arrest the Earl of Arundel brought about the crisis, and in November, 1387, civil war seemed inevitable. Once more Robert de Vere proved to be Richard's evil genius. With the hated favourite at his side the King could command no support and proved powerless to protect his friends. Michael de la Pole fled to France and died there a year later ; Robert de Vere, after seeing the forces which he had raised routed by the Earl of Derby, followed him into exile.

In February, 1388, the "Merciless" Parliament began its

bloody work. Of the five victims arraigned by the Lords Appellant and condemned as guilty of treason, four, Vere, de la Pole, Neville Archbishop of York and the Chief Justice Tresilian were beyond their reach. Nicholas Brambre was hanged, but one death could not satisfy Gloucester's hatred. In spite of the protests of the Earl of Derby he hanged Sir John Beauchamp, Sir James Berners and Sir John Salisbury, and in an evil hour for himself refused to spare Sir Simon Burley who had been the King's tutor and was one of his dearest friends.

For a year Gloucester retained his position, but the *coup d'état* by which he rose to power was not more sudden than his downfall. On May 3, 1389, Richard declared himself of age, dismissed the Chancellor and Treasurer, removed the Lords Appellant, and in a manifesto to the country declared his intention of ruling. Gloucester, whose violence and cruelty had alienated all moderate men, taken completely by surprise, was compelled to submit. How long he would have acquiesced in political annihilation is another matter, but Richard by his next step forestalled the possibility of another council of regency and sealed Gloucester's political fate for good, for he recalled the Duke of Lancaster.

Preparations for the Duke's return began in August ;[1] but delay only increased the King's impatience, and on October 30 a formal summons to return either by sea or land was despatched to the Duke at Bordeaux. A courier reported to the Privy Council that weighty matters touching the custody of Aquitaine had prevented the Duke from returning as he had hoped to do at the beginning of November. As it was, he proposed to come back at the beginning of February ; if, however, the King required his presence earlier he would obey forthwith, but to guard himself against suspicion

[1] Mandate to sergeant-at-arms to collect freightships, *cum omni festinatione possibili*, dated August 11, 1389. *Foed*, VII. 641.

and the malice of enemies he requested formal sanction for travelling if necessary overland.

But Richard, fearing some act of violence from Gloucester, refused to wait until February ; and on November 19, 1389, John of Gaunt landed at Plymouth.[1]

On December 10 there was to be a meeting of the Council at Reading : [2] as Lancaster rode thither he was met two miles from the town by the King. Three years and their bitter experiences had worked a change in Richard's estimate of parties and their leaders : the man whose departure in 1386 he had welcomed with ill-concealed satisfaction he now hailed as a deliverer.

The Duke's arrival marks the beginning of a new era in the reign, the period of orderly constitutional government, which like the *quinquennium Neronis* precedes the troubles of the last years. It also marks a new era in the Duke's life. Henceforth, the man round whom the darkest suspicions had gathered, and the fiercest party fights had raged, appears in the guise of a peacemaker. His first act is symbolical of the part which he was about to play : to the King and to each of his suite John of Gaunt gave the kiss of peace, declaring the old quarrels forgotten.[3]

Lancaster's presence worked wonders. On the Council faction suddenly became silent. In Kent and Essex the royal justices had been guilty of injustice and oppression under colour of a Court of Trailbaston. On the Duke's arrival, we are told by an authority with a pronounced anti-Lancastrian bias, they desisted.

The Church and the City showed that past bitterness was now forgotten, for when the Duke, escorted by peers and courtiers, rode to Westminster, he found the Mayor and Sheriffs vying with the Abbot and Monks of West-

---

[1] Higd. ix. 218. *Rot. Pat.* 22 Ric. II, part ii.
[2] Privy Council, i. 14 c. Delpit *Collection*, ccxcii.
[3] Higd. ix. 218 sqq.

minster to do him honour. A procession of the clergy conducted him to the Abbey, and chanting the response *Honor virtus* led him to the high altar. The Abbot preached, and the Duke made his offering, and then went away to repeat the same ceremony at St. Paul's.

The same spirit of compromise and moderation marked the conduct of all parties in the Parliament [1] which met at Westminster in January, 1390.

The Chancellor and Treasurer voluntarily resigned and demanded a scrutiny of their tenure of office, but when Lancaster the next day in the King's name demanded the opinion of the Commons, the reply amounted to an unhesitating vote of confidence, and both ministers were restored to office. Richard himself set an example of moderation and forbearance. He discharged his Council and reappointed the members, with the addition of two names, those of Lancaster and Gloucester. [2] Assured of the support of his eldest uncle, the King had no fear of the Lords Appellant, and to purchase that support he was prepared to pay lavishly. On February 16 the County Palatine of Lancaster with the title of Duke, which John of Gaunt, like Duke Henry, held for life only, was granted to him and his heirs male in tail. [3]

On the last day of the session another equally striking proof of royal favour was given. Prominence had been given in the Chancellor's opening speech to the dangerous position of Aquitaine, and at the Council of Reading [4] the same subject had been discussed. Despatches had then

---

[1] Summoned by writ dated December 6, 13 Ric. II, for Monday after St. Hilary ; it sat from January 17 to March 2. *Rot. Parl.* iii. 257–76.

[2] Lancaster (with York, Gloucester and the Chancellor) was placed a little later on the committee appointed to restrain Richard's lavish grants. Privy Council, March 8, 13 Ric. II, 1390.

[3] Hardy, *Charters*, xiv.

[4] Privy Council, i, 17.

been sent to the south, notifying Lancaster's return and sanctioning the provisional measures proposed by him for the safety of the King's dominions. At the same time the promise had been given that in the forthcoming Parliament measures would be taken " for the governance of Aquitaine, the comfort of the King's subjects there and the honour and profit of the Duchy." What these measures were now became clear, for on March 2, by the advice and with the assent of Peers and Commons in Parliament assembled, the King created John of Gaunt Duke of Aquitaine for life.[1]

Had the grant of the Duchy of Aquitaine been made half a dozen years earlier, it might legitimately have been interpreted as evidence of the King's anxiety to be rid of his uncle. But in 1390 John of Gaunt was necessary to Richard's peace of mind, and four years were to elapse before he could be spared to rule his new dominions. Those four years were devoted to the realization of his cardinal policy, the policy of peace with France. The *rapprochement* which a decade before the Duke had desired as a necessary condition of prosecuting the dynastic quarrel in Spain, he now desired as a consequence of the settlement. If, as he had reminded Parliament at the accession, he had interests in England second in importance to those of no other subject of the Crown, interests which would assuredly be imperilled by internal troubles, it was equally true that in continental Europe he had given pledges to fortune, which might be forfeit in a general disturbance of the peace. Sensible as he was of the necessity of peace to England, it was inevitable that Lancaster should find his views on foreign policy coloured

---

[1] *Foed,* VII. 659–63. *Rot. Parl.* iii. 263. a. For other marks of Richard's favour see (1) a grant of exemption from payment of fees in Chancery dated February 8, 1391, *Foed,* VII. 695 ; (2) grant of exemption from import duty on wine, dated May 30, 1392, *Foed* VII. 721.

by his own dynastic interests. Public and private motives therefore combined to lead him to devote the last vigorous years of his life to the work of pacification ; and he may fairly claim the credit for setting on foot and leading to a successful conclusion those negotiations which led first to a considerable truce and finally to the *entente cordiale* of 1396, when the King of England married a daughter of France and the Hundred Years War was adjourned *sine die*.

In the Parliament of November, 1391,[1] the Commons, assuming an unusual degree of initiative, gave an unhesitating expression to their approval of the peace policy and their preference for the Duke as ambassador, and for once at least John of Gaunt found himself singled out as a popular and trusted minister. " If," said the Commons, " there should be negotiations for a peace or a truce between our Lord the King and his adversary of France, it seemed expedient and necessary, if it pleased the King, that Monseigneur de Guyenne (the title of Monseigneur d'Espaigne was obsolete) should proceed to such negotiations, he being the most sufficient person of the realm," and when the King had concurred, and asked the Duke if he were willing to go, Monseigneur de Guyenne replied that " he would very willingly undertake the work, and labour for the honour and profit of the King and kingdom."

Peculiar qualifications fitted Lancaster for the duty of representing England at foreign Courts. That grand manner, which to some of his fellow countrymen passed for haughtiness, made a favourable impression abroad : it covered a thorough knowledge of international relations resulting from a long and varied experience. In 1392, when negotiations began, the Duke of Lancaster was a

---

[1] *Rot. Parl.* iii. 284-99. Parliament was summoned by writ dated September 7, 15 Ric. II, for the day after All Saints, and sat from November 3 to December 2, 1391.

THE JOUSTS OF St. INGELVERT.

personage of international importance. One son-in-law was King of Portugal ; another was King of Castile. The Duke felt the power given him by his family alliances, a power which a generation later was to prove invaluable to his son, Cardinal Beaufort, in his capacity of foreign minister. He knew and was personally known to nearly all the potentates of Western Europe ; the Dukes of Berri and Burgundy, the King of Navarre, the Duke of Brittany and the Count of Foix, the Scottish Earls and the princes of the Low Countries—all at one time or another had met him in battle or diplomacy. In an age when the personal character of rulers was a matter of the first importance in determining policy, John of Gaunt, unlike his untravelled nephew, had the power which comes from knowing men ; in an age when chivalry, hardening into caste, was tending to override with its own distinctions those of race and nation, Lancaster was the best known citizen of the world of chivalry, and it was Lancaster Herald who proclaimed the jousts of St. Ingelvert, where Sir Regnault de Roye and the Marshal Boucicault threw down their challenge to Europe and where the Earl of Derby and Sir John Beaufort maintained the honour of England and the Lancastrian name.[1]

When, therefore, Lancaster took up again in 1392 the task of negotiation which as a younger son of Edward III he had first attempted in 1364, his own position was vastly different ; the conditions of politics had undergone a change equally decisive.

The peace policy had first appeared at Bruges in 1374, after five years' continuous fighting and on the morrow of a disastrous campaign, when England, disappointed of victory, considered herself defrauded of that which she had a right to expect. In 1392 most men, though not all, had outgrown the illusions of the war, and Parliament

[1] *Livre des faits de Jean Bouciquaut*, I. xvi. ; Pierre d'Orgemont, 73 ; *Chr. Reg. Franc*, iii. 97.

was ready to welcome a definite settlement. In France, too, the obstacles to peace had been one after another removed. While Lancaster threatened the dynastic policy of the Duke of Burgundy, first by attempting to secure the hand of the Duchess Margaret for Edmund of Langley, later by proposing the hand of Philippa of Lancaster for William Count of Ostrevant, heir of Albert of Wittelsbach, Philip the Bold had remained committed to hostilities with England. But now the Burgundian alliances with the princes of Southern Germany and the Low Countries were complete, and for the moment at least the Burgundian supremacy was in abeyance.

When therefore Lancaster landed at Calais in March, 1392, there was every prospect of arriving at an understanding.[1] He had taken care that his colleagues should be, like himself, chosen from the peace party; they were the Duke of York, the Earls of Derby and Huntingdon, and Sir Thomas Percy. There was no dissentient like the Duke of Gloucester, who tried to wreck the success of the later negotiations. The French had expected Richard II to come over in person; but after accompanying the envoys to Dover, the King returned to Westminster. No welcome, however, could have been more royal than that accorded to John of Gaunt, for the French king treated him with marked deference, and showed every possible courtesy to his suite.[2]

---

[1] For the negotiations at Amiens see *Relig. St. Denys*, i. 735 ; *Chr. Reg. Franc.* iii. 102–4 ; Wals. ii. 205–6 ; Higd. ix. 265 ; Kn., ii. 318 ; *Ypod. Neust.* 392 ; *Cronykil of Scotland*, ii. 56 ; Froissart, K. de L. xv. 79–82, etc. Lancaster landed at Calais on March 11, 1392, and returned between April 8 and 22. The truce was signed at Amiens on April 8. Brit. Mus. Add. Ch. 11, 310. Lancaster's powers are dated February 22, *Foed*, VII. 710–11 and the prolongation of the truce was confirmed May 5. *Foed*, VII. 714–22.

[2] Ipse rex (Charles VI) venit ei obviam, salutans eum et praenominans dignissimam personam militae totius christianitatis regali dignitate inuncta solummodo excepta. (Kn. ii. 318.)

JOHN OF GAUNT THE PEACEMAKER

Throughout their visit the envoys were treated as guests of the French nation, and their entertainment cost as much as a campaign. On reaching Amiens every knight of the Duke's retinue found his arms painted on the door of his lodging, that he might have no difficulty in finding it. No innkeeper was allowed to take money from any of the Duke's suite. Every precaution that could be devised was put into effect to prevent unpleasantness. Brawling was forbidden on pain of death : no French gentleman was allowed to go out at night without lights, and the streets of the town were patrolled by a body of 4,000 watchmen, while the King's forethought even went the length of improvising a fire-brigade.

From the day the Duke left English territory the attentions began. From Calais [1] the Count of St. Pol escorted Lancaster and his suite, which numbered a thousand horsemen, through the lands which he had harried in days gone by, to St. Riquier and Doullens. On Monday, March 25, Charles, with a stately retinue, lords spiritual and temporal, knights and men-at-arms, made his entry into Amiens ; simultaneously Lancaster rode into the city from Doullens under the escort of the " Princes des fleurs de lys."

When his hosts offered to lead him to his lodging the Duke refused, insisting on being taken immediately to the King. Charles received him in the Archbishop's palace, and the interview over, Lancaster was conducted to Malmaison,[2] where he was to stay. The next day at a state banquet the Duke found himself seated at the King's right hand, and served by the Dukes of Orleans

Cuius adventui Rex Franciae non minora parari fecit quam pro adventu imperatoris cujusque maximi providisset. Wals. ii. 205.

[1] It was then that the Duke built Lancaster's new tower at Calais. *Archaeologia*, iii. 250 note.

[2] For Malmaison in the fourteenth century, see *Chr. Reg. Franc.* ii. 12 (note).

and Bourbon. So far as ceremonial could smooth the way to peace, the path was clear.

But when business began it became clear that the political situation was not yet ripe for a permanent peace. Both sides opened discussion with extravagant and unpractical proposals. The French demanded that Calais should be evacuated and its fortifications razed to the ground, a proposal to which Lancaster returned a curt *non possumus*. On the other hand Lancaster put forward the claim, out of date in 1384, but absurd in 1392, to the balance of King John's ransom, and a reversion to the *status quo* of Brétigni. All this was, perhaps, a matter of form, for envoys were bound by the diplomatic traditions of the age. But, on the English side, there were reasons of policy for haggling. Though Parliament was weary if not of the war at least of a succession of war budgets, there was a formidable party who did not want to see the doors of France and campaigning closed for good. Lancaster in Amiens had Westminster in mind ; it was necessary to go warily ahead and not to give colour to the charge actually preferred later, that by unduly favourable terms he was sacrificing the rights of the Crown and the interests of England. Apart however from the large question of peace there was no difficulty. Both sides readily agreed to a truce and consented that the existing truce should hold good for twelve months more. A year had been won in which to work for the end of peace, and the Duke had made a great impression.

He returned to England in the middle of April and a month later laid the results of his embassy before an extraordinary meeting of the Council at Stamford, to which a number of peers and representatives of the counties and boroughs had been summoned. This little parliament approved the Duke's policy, and the King formally ratified the truce.[1] In the spring of 1393 the

[1] Kn. ii. 318–9. Higd. ix. 265–7.

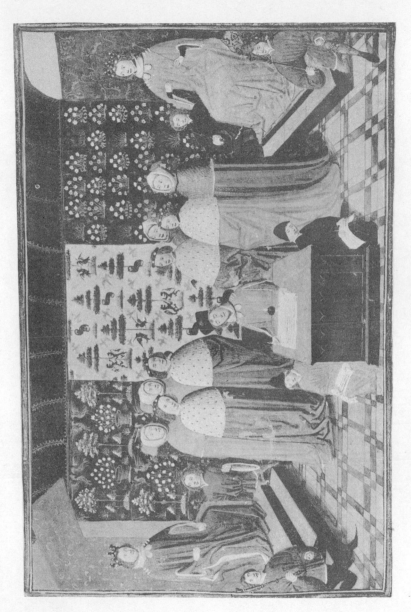

AMBASSADORS CONCLUDING A TRUCE.

same story was repeated, the scene of negotiations being moved to the old rendezvous, Lelinghen, whither the French Commissioners repaired from Boulogne and the English from Calais.[1] Again the envoys had to content themselves with a prolongation of the truce :[2] any consideration of the larger issue was postponed by the King's illness, for in August of the previous year Charles had lost his reason, and for the rest of his reign he was liable to intermittent fits of madness which effectually hindered the treatment of serious affairs.

To Lancaster this interruption was a disappointment,[3] but he stuck to the work, and when he met the French envoys at Lelinghen in the spring of 1394 the end was well in sight.[4] The first thing was to remove sources of misunderstanding, one of which lay in the difficulty of language. It is scarcely surprising that the official language which passed for French in formal documents puzzled the French ambassadors, while the English complained of not being able to follow discussion in what was fast becoming a foreign tongue. To clear the path towards mutual understanding, it was agreed that all proposals should be written down and presented in the form of a verbal note. A more serious stumbling-block was found in the presence of the Cardinal of Luna, a

---

[1] It was in April, 1393, at Boulogne that the Duke of Burgundy gave the Duke of Lancaster some tapestry hangings pourtraying the history of Clovis. *Itineraires de Philippe le Hardi*, 547 (note).

[2] For the second period of negotiation see Higd. ix. 280 ; Kn. ii. 321 ; Wals. ii 213 ; *Ann. Ric. II*, 157 ; Froissart, K. de L. xv. 108–12, 116–9, 123–4 ; *Cont. Eulog.* 369 ; *Foed*, VII. 737–9, 741, 748–9. On April 28 the truce was prolonged till September 29, 1394. Lancaster and Gloucester received further powers September 12, 1393. Ibid. 752–3.

[3] Froissart, K. de L. xvii. 52.

[4] For the final negotiations see Wals. ii. 214 ; Kn. ii. 321 ; Higd. ix. 282 ; *Ann. Ric. ii.* 168.
Lancaster's powers are dated March 10, 1394 ; he left for France soon after and returned about June 24. Peace was signed at Lelinghen May 24, 1394. *Foed*, VII. 775 ; *Rot. Franc.* ii. 170.

truculent Spaniard who had taken upon himself the task
of representing Clement VII, and was trying to extort
recognition of his master from the English Commissioners.

On the papal question John of Gaunt was sound. He
would not palter with the claims of the canonical Pope,
and refused to begin negotiations until the Cardinal was
removed. After that all went well. A fortnight's discussion brought the envoys within reach of an understanding and they separated to communicate with their
Governments. Meanwhile the terms were not divulged ;
even Froissart, who was present, failed to discover their
exact import, though in spite of official reticence he
had got enough information to persuade him of the
existence of a secret treaty. When the envoys met
again they found themselves in agreement ; on May 27
a truce for four years was concluded between France and
England. At length the great war seemed at an end, for
before the expiration of the truce of Lelinghen England
had drawn still closer to France, Richard had married
the daughter of his adversary, and the struggle of Valois
and Plantagenet for the crown of the *fleurs-de-lys* was
forgotten for a generation.

More difficult however than the task of reconciling
Richard II with his adversary of France, was that of
maintaining peace and order among the King's subjects.
The interludes between negotiations in France were spent
by the Duke in attempting to compose political factions,
personal quarrels and popular discontent.

For half a dozen years successive Parliaments had
called attention to the dangerous state of anarchy prevailing in many parts of England. It was an almost
daily occurrence for leaders of armed bands to dispossess
tenants of their property, carry off and put to ransom
their wives and heirs, and forcibly marry their heiresses.
It is significant of the general disorder, which was, however, worst in the north, that one of Lancaster's first

proclamations as Count Palatine had been to prohibit the gathering of armed men to hinder the sessions of the justices in Lancaster.

This state of anarchy, the result of weak administration rather than of unwise laws, long since chronic in England, had become acute in the summer of 1393.

An insurrection, which threatened to become formidable, broke out in the northern counties in the spring of that year.[1] Beginning in Chester it spread across the County Palatine to Yorkshire, and assumed such dangerous proportions that, according to popular belief, there were at one time as many as twenty thousand malcontents under arms.

The objects and the origins of the discontent are confused and obscure. Once more political issues are mixed up with personal feuds. The men of the royal palatinate of Chester, the most disorderly county in England, were led to believe that their liberties were being threatened. Some said that the Dukes of Lancaster and Gloucester were attempting to deprive the King of his right to France and to dispossess him of the Palatinate. In Yorkshire disorder turned on a local feud between Sir Robert Rokeby and William Beckwith, who, having slain his enemy, fled from justice, and, like the "tough-belted outlaw" of Sherwood Forest, gathering his friends about him in the forests, bid defiance to the law. It is clear that in some quarters the intention was to kill Lancaster and Derby, but the relation of Gloucester and Arundel, whose names were mentioned in connexion with the disturbance, to the rebels and their plans must remain a mystery. There was a rumour that Arundel had

---

[1] For the Cheshire rising and the "*famosa discordia*" of Lancaster and Arundel with which it is connected see *Rot. Parl.* iii. 309–23; *Ann. Ric. II*, 159–62, 166 (a strongly Lancastrian account); Wals. ii. 214; Higd., ix. 239–40, 265, 281. Malverne is usually most accurate in dates, but here he seems to be wrong.

organized the disorder and that Gloucester was secretly aiding his designs ; it is probable, though the evidence is insufficient to prove the case. On the other hand, when the day of reckoning came Gloucester and Lancaster are found side by side, and Arundel was never formally charged with complicity. The distribution of inflammatory placards denouncing Lancaster, which were posted on the doors of every parish church in the disaffected districts, proves that the disturbance was carefully organized by certain mischief-makers who were bent on fishing for themselves or their party in troubled waters. So far as can be seen, these mischief-makers belonged to the war party, who were infuriated by Lancaster's foreign policy, and the old opposition of 1386.

As usual, a political *motif* allowed the development of other sub-plots in the drama. Political or social grievances were made the colour for a general disturbance, in which private hatreds and greed of plunder had free play.

It was to meet this situation that Lancaster hastily left the French Commissioners in the summer of 1393, for the King, who had allowed the evil to grow unchecked in his absence, had placed his uncle at the head of a special commission of royal justices.

Lancaster went first to Yorkshire, where the disorder had grown round the outlaw Beckwith and his adherents, and contrary to the expectations of his enemies, set himself to work cautiously and in a moderate spirit. Having succeeded in dispelling suspicions as to his own conduct, he restored order in the districts where his territorial power lay, and then turned westwards toward the dangerous palatinate of Chester. For once at least the Duke seized the leading feature of a political situation. Social and economic causes were largely responsible for the unrest. Since the era of truces with France there were a large number of disbanded soldiers in England, men without means of subsistence and unfitted for civil employment. The Duke enrolled them for service in Aquitaine, whither he intended soon to proceed. A few ringleaders were arrested for trial. Most were suffered to go. The disorder collapsed, and Lancaster returned to the south with the news that his mission had accomplished its end and that order was restored.

The relation of Arundel to the episode had not been cleared up. Arundel and Lancaster, friends in the seventies, had long since drifted apart. The Earl despised the peace policy and was jealous of the Duke's influence with the King. He feared too, and as it proved not without reason, that Richard had never forgiven him for his part in the events of 1386.

When Parliament opened in January, 1394, Arundel determined to forestall an attack. He had watched the young King's temper, and knew his fickleness of character. If he could succeed in doing what Robert de Vere had only just failed to do at the Salisbury Parliament ten years before, and destroy the confidence of the King in his uncle, there might be another deal in the game, and his own hand might be stronger. Political annihilation was little to his taste ; however, if he were going to be brought to book for the events of the summer it might go hard with him. So he chose the bold course and struck the first blow.

So soon as the Chancellor had declared the causes of the summons of Parliament and the usual business of appointing receivers and triers of petitions had been got through, the Earl rose and declared that there were certain matters touching the honour and profit of King and kingdom so nearly that his conscience did not suffer him to be silent. His indictment of Lancaster and his policy, was comprised in six articles. It was contrary to the King's honour, firstly, that his uncle the Duke of Guyenne and Lancaster should be seen constantly walking hand in hand and arm in arm with the King ;

secondly, that the King should wear round his neck the Duke's "livery"; thirdly, that the King's retainers should wear the same livery; fourthly, the Duke in Council and in Parliament was in the habit of using such " rough and bitter words," that he, the Earl, and others, often dare not fully declare their intent; fifthly, it was greatly to the King's disadvantage that he had granted to his uncle the Duchy of Aquitaine; sixthly, the King had squandered the resources of the kingdom on his uncle's crusade against Castile.

The challenge was made and the Earl hopelessly compromised. He expected considerable support among Peers and Commons; as it proved he was disappointed, for no one followed up the attack.

The first three articles were calculated to catch popular favour, and revive the old cry against " livery and maintenance." But things had changed since the days of the " Good" Parliament, when the Duke's retainers had been glad to hide their livery from the London mob, and the political war cries of 1376 did not fit the circumstances of 1394. Again, in the hot days of Lancaster's youth the charge contained in the fourth article might have struck home. Had not John of Gaunt cursed Bishop Courtenay in Saint Paul's, and offered to ride to London and drag the Bishop to Windsor in spite of the " ribald knaves " of London ? But that, too, belonged to the past, and years had calmed the Duke's passions and taught him the lesson of restraint and caution. The fifth article was a skilful attack. The grant of the Duchy of Aquitaine was unpopular, as will be seen, in the duchy itself, and there was a large party in England also who feared the results of the grant on Gascon loyalty and viewed with the utmost jealousy any further alienation of lands and honours by the Crown.

But Arundel had saved his strongest point till the end. The invasion of Castile had wrecked an English army, without appreciably altering the political situation. The Commons cared very little whether or not Philippa of Lancaster were Queen of Portugal, or whether Katharine secured the reversion of Don Pedro's throne. If the Duke chose to prosecute his dynastic ambitions, at least he might be made to pay for them, and the party for economy might well hold that the treasure which was being poured over the Pyrenees into the Duke's coffers at Bordeaux ought to be called on to pay the cost of the Spanish crusade.

There was, doubtless, still a party in the Commons and a smaller one in the Lords who, for personal or political reasons, retained the old jealousy of Lancastrian influence, but Arundel had miscalculated the strength of political forces. Lancaster had outlived his unpopularity. The old anti-Wycliffe feeling among clergy and laity was useless in 1394 to the enemies of the Lancastrian power. The country, too, was tired of the Lords Appellant, and since Richard's assumption of power had welcomed a period of orderly government. Consequently the Earl's manifesto fell flat ; he failed to fan into flame the embers of the King's jealousy or to touch his pride by this skilful attempt to represent him as still in the tutelage of his uncle.

In reply to the indictment, the King presented a formal answer, taking the Earl's points one by one.

If the King walked arm in arm with the Duke of Lancaster, that was only what he did habitually in the case of his other uncles. As for the livery, in point of fact on Lancaster's return from Spain he had himself taken the collar from his uncle's neck, and worn it " *en signe de bon amour d'entier cor entre eux*," and if his retainers did the same it was by the royal command. He denied that Lancaster had ever overborne any member of the Council in his hearing ; it was open to the Earl as to the rest to speak their will.

The grant of the Duchy of Guyenne had been made with the assent of the estates in Parliament assembled. Of the cost of the army in Spain, 200,000 marcs had been voted freely by the Commons ; the other half was a loan for which the Duke acknowledged his liability and which he had offered to repay ; in consideration, however, of the relief of Brest and other expeditions in the King's service for which he had not received payment in full, this sum, with the consent of Parliament, had been remitted.

As for the negotiations with France, Lancaster, like the other envoys, had merely carried out his instructions. He had laid the result before the Council ; Council and Parliament had been free to accept or reject the terms, and it had been open to Arundel with the rest to criticise the policy.

The indictment and the King's reply were examined by Parliament. Opinion was unanimous that Lancaster was free and quit of any blame.

The vote of censure was defeated. Asked if he had anything further to say, the Earl replied in the negative. Thereupon the King, with the assent of Parliament, ordered the Earl to apologize. There was no choice but to obey. Addressing the Duke of Lancaster, Arundel repeated these words : " Sire, sith that hit semeth to the Kyng and to the other lordes, and eke that yhe ben so mychel greved and displeisid be my wordes, hit forthynketh me, and byseche yowe of your gode lordship to remyt me your mautalent." [1] Whether or no John of Gaunt carried the duty of forgiveness to the extent of " remitting his mautalent" entirely may be questioned in the light of events which happened two years later. Nothing had been said officially of Arundel's share in the northern rising ; and the matter was allowed to drop. Arundel retired from the Council for a time, and the Duke, having quieted the rising in the north and won a victory

[1] *Rot. Parl. III*, 314 a.

over the opposition, went back to France to finish the business of peace-making.

It was at the time of his departure for the final negotiations in France that John of Gaunt lost his second wife. Constance of Castile died on March 24, 1394.[1]

By a strange fatality Lancaster, the King and the Earl of Derby all became widowers in the same year, for within a few weeks of the death of the Duchess of Lancaster, Queen Anne and Mary Countess of Derby passed away. Of the two daughters of Pedro the Cruel contemporary annalists have little to say; only enough to point a contrast between Constance, a pattern of orderly and devout living, and her worldly and *legère* sister, the Duchess of York,[2] who did not pass unscathed among the ladies of Richard's luxurious Court.

The silence of the chronicles is not broken by Chaucer's verse. A threnody on Constance of Castile could not have breathed the same evident sincerity as the lament for Blanche of Lancaster ; the tie which bound John of Gaunt to his second wife was too obviously the result of political convenience, and when death loosed it, the poet had no graceful and touching memorial to raise to the second Duchess of Lancaster. Half her life, a life of exile, had been spent in England, but she had never identified herself with the country of her adoption and left no impress upon the life of the Court. From the first she had had a rival ; it must have been difficult for her, even allowing for a different standard of taste in such matters, to do the honours of the Lancastrian household, while every one paid court to the Duke's mistress, and Katharine Swynford's position was openly acknow-

[1] A fairly certain inference from the date of the obit. See Will. p. 429 ; Higd. ix. 283, who says March 25. Kn. ii. 321 *Ann. Ric. II*, 168 ; Wals. ii. 214.

[2] Isabella died in 1392 (Higd. ix. 278), not 1394, as most of the chronicles have it. Her will was proved January 6, 1392. *Test. Vet.* 135.

o

ledged not only at the Savoy or Hertford, but at the State ceremonies of Westminster and Windsor.[1]

Constance remained Castilian at heart ; her strongest feelings were those of attachment to the memory of her father, her happiest days those of the autumn of 1386, when the Galician nobles came to do homage to their Queen, or of 1388 and 1389, when, the last honours paid to the memory of Pedro the Just, Constance saw his right acknowledged in the person of her daughter, Katharine of Lancaster, Princess of the Asturias.

One of her letters, an autograph, has survived.[2] It is addressed to the Chancellor of the University of Oxford, entreating him to commend a friar, Brother Alvarez, one of her own subjects, to the Prior of the Oxford Dominicans, evidence perhaps of her care for the poor and her regard for learning.

Her son, " John of Gaunt," had died in infancy ; after the marriage of her daughter in 1388, Constance seems to have lived apart, with a Court of her own, a few gentlemen of Castile and a train of ladies who followed her into exile in 1366 and came with her from Bordeaux at her marriage. She was buried with great magnificence in St. Mary's, Leicester, where every year on the anniversary of her death Lancaster caused an obit to be celebrated for her soul.[3]

[1] Robes were provided for Katharine Swynford at the feast of the Garter, St. George's Day, 1387. Beltz, *Memorials of the Garter*, p. 250. For her influence see Bateson, *Records of the Borough of Leicester* : Mayor's account, 1375–6 : 16s. for wine sent to the Lady Katharine Swynford (ii. 155) ; 1377–9, £3 6s. 8d. for a horse given to the Lady Katharine Swynford ; £2 0s. 6d. for a pan of iron given to the said Katharine for "expediting business touching the tenement in Stretton, and for other business for which a certain lord besought the aforesaid Katharine . . . so successfully that the aforesaid town was pardoned the lending of silver to the King in that year" (ii. 171).

[2] M. A. E. Wood, *Royal Letters*, i. 66.

[3] For the enormous expense of the burial see balance sheet (Appendix, p. 449) ; for the obit, see Will (Appendix, p. 429).

THE QUESTION OF THE SUCCESSION

Her death had no effect on the relations between Lancaster and the Castilian Government. The yearly tribute continued to be paid, and no attempt was made to repudiate the obligations of the treaty of 1388. Only an outbreak of the war would have been likely to jeopardise the Duke's position, but with the notable successes achieved by his policy in May, 1394, such a contingency was now more remote than ever. He might rest content, his hopes realized and with the assurance of success.

Yet, according to one authority, there was still an anxiety weighing on the Duke's mind ; he could not, we are told, leave England with any peace of mind until he had secured the recognition of his son, Henry Earl of Derby, as heir apparent !

The writer who continued the *Eulogium* is responsible for the statement that Lancaster asked Parliament (meaning that of January, 1394, though the chronology of the passage is hopelessly confused) to reopen the question of the succession, which he elsewhere states to have been definitely settled nine years earlier by the proclamation of the Earl of March as the lineal heir to the throne.[1]

The story (of which it is needless to say that the Rolls of Parliament and the records of the Privy Council know nothing) briefly is this : that Lancaster asked that his son should be recognized as heir to the throne ; that the Earl of March rebutted the claim and urged his own right (which was indisputable), and that the Duke thereupon came forward with an absurd story to the effect that Edmund Crouchback, great-grandfather of Blanche of Lancaster, was really the elder brother of Edward I, but that owing to a personal deformity (the origin of his name), he had been set aside in favour of the younger brother, on the understanding that this deviation from the right

---

[1] *Cont. Eulog.* iii. 361, 369–70.

line of descent should not prejudice the rights of his children.

The myth was capable of expansion ; to read it in its completed form we must turn to the pages of John Hardyng's chronicle.[1] Hardyng improves on the simple absurdity of the original, first by making John of Gaunt, who was thirty-seven years older than Richard II, claim himself to be recognized as his nephew's heir ; secondly, by adding his famous embellishment—the story of the forged pedigree and chronicle. Hardyng states that John of Gaunt " among the Lords in Council and in Parliaments and in the Common House among the knights chosen for the Commons asked by bill to be admit heir apparent to King Richard, considering how the King was like to have no issue of his body." To this he adds, " the Lords spiritual and temporal and the Commons in the Common House by whole advice said that the Earl of March, Roger Mortimer, was his next heir to the crown of full descent of blood, and they would have none other, and asked a question upon it, who durst disable the King of issue, he being young and able to have issue." Foiled in his first intent, the wicked Duke puts forward the story about Edmund Crouchback, and " feigns an untrue chronicle " to support it, "which chronicle so forged the Duke did put into divers Abbeys and in Friaries for to be kept for the inheritance of his son to the crown." Hardyng then goes on to relate how Henry IV, in 1399, having got Richard II securely in the Tower, made use of this forged chronicle to prove his hereditary right to the throne.[2]

It is unnecessary to go into the sequel, for this part of the story has already been disposed of : [3] all that concerns the history of John of Gaunt is the first part, his share in

[1] *Archaeologia*, vol. xvi. pp. 139 sqq.
[2] See also *Scotichronicon*, xv. 7.
[3] Stubbs, *Constitutional History*, iii. 11 and 12 (notes).

this supposed childish attempt to delude England and alter the line of succession.

In the absence of any decent evidence, it may be sufficient to point out the inherent absurdities of the whole story. The tale about Edmund of Lancaster, who was known to have been " one of the seemliest persons in England," would of course have deceived no one, and, if ever it had been put forward, would have been refuted by common notoriety; yet there is no hint in official records or trustworthy contemporary annals of any such plea being produced, and had it been produced it would certainly have awakened Richard's former jealousies and fears and wrecked his new-born confidence in his eldest uncle. The Duke's " bills " and the forgeries themselves have never been seen,[1] and supposing the insuperable difficulties overcome of executing a fraud which would convince no one, the task of foisting copies of the forged chronicle upon " divers abbeys and friaries " would have baffled all ingenuity. How much influence Lancaster had upon the writing of history even in abbeys which claimed him as a benefactor, appears from the existence of the " scandalous chronicle " of St. Albans.

Hardyng gives his account on the authority of certain conversations which took place at different times between himself and his patron, Henry Percy, and it bears all the marks of an invention produced to explain previous events.

Cross-examination being impossible, it may be material to say something of the character and antecedents of the witness.[2]

---

[1] Henricus . . . vendicavit sibi coronam, primo ex propinquitate sanguinis, quam probavit ex antiquis quidem gestis, quorum veras copias necdum vidi. Capgrave, *de Illust. Henricis*, 106.

[2] See article " Hardyng " in *Dict. Nat. Biog.* and Sir F. Palgrave's introduction to *Documents and Records illustrating the History of Scotland.* (Record Commission, 1837.)

JOHN OF GAUNT

Born in 1378, Hardyng was brought up in the household of Henry Percy the younger (" Hotspur "), and was devoted to the family of Northumberland. He had two passions, a love of antiquities and a hatred of the Scots, and he was fortunate in finding a vocation which gratified both together. This was to collect documents concerning the relation between England and Scotland with a view to proving the fact of English suzerainty over the northern kingdom. Failing to find proofs, Hardyng forged them, and the fruits of his labours, a series of spurious charters, were sold by him to the English Government for a consideration, and duly deposited among the records of the Exchequer in a box labelled " *Scotia Hardyng.*" The tale of the forged chronicle deserved a place in that box. It amounts to gossip between the Percies, bitter enemies of the Lancastrian dynasty who lost their lives in rebellion against it, reported by a convicted swindler, who, himself an expert, under-rated the difficulties of the profession of forgery.

If the story proves anything at all, it may be taken as evidence of the anxiety felt by the nation as to the succession, ever since Richard's marriage with Anne of Bohemia had proved sterile, and of the interest felt in the position of the House of Lancaster in relation to the dynastic problem.[1]

---

[1] For another instance of this feeling see the detailed account of the family of Lancaster and Clarence, Higd. ix. 96–7.

Chapter XV

THE DUCHY OF AQUITAINE

IN September, 1394, the King left for Ireland, and soon after the Duke sailed for the south.[1]

Almost a generation of Gascon liegemen had passed away since the Duke of Aquitaine had first seen the land which he now came to rule ; but since the parliament at Bayonnne of 1366, when Don Pedro had boasted of the hoarded treasures of Castile, since the return to Bordeaux while the laurels of Najera were still fresh, John of Gaunt had lived many months among the sunny vineyards of the Garonne and Dordogne. Six months' experience as Lieutenant for the Prince his brother, in 1371, had taught him something of the difficulties military, political and financial, which beset the King's representative in the Gascon dependency. In Gascon territory he had married Constance of Castile ; to Bordeaux he had led the remnants of the shattered army which followed him through France in 1373, and in 1388 during a third Lieutenancy in the south the Duke had won the diplomatic victory over the courts of Castile and France, which secured a throne for Katharine of Lancaster.

More than three years spent in Aquitaine, and three successive terms of supreme military command must

---

[1] Froissart, K. de L. xv. 136, 139. Order to collect ships for the voyage to Ireland " exceptis dumtaxat navibus et aliis vasis de partibus borealibus pro passagio carissimi Avunculi nostri Johannis etc. . . versus partes Aquitaniae . . . ordinatis." September 13, 1394. *Foed*, VII. 789.

have made him familiar with the men whom he was now to rule. Baron and burgess were known to him alike, the turbulence of the one and the stubborn pride of the other. Hot-headed courage and impulsiveness have made the name of the Gascon noble a by-word: to the proud independence of the burgesses of the great cities, Bordeaux, Bayonne and Dax, the Italian republics or the great towns of Flanders can alone supply a parallel.[1]

Gascon differed from Frenchman as much in political conditions as in race, language and sentiment. The administrative system of Aquitaine was complete and self-contained. At its head stood the " Seneschal of Gascony," the chief executive officer military and civil. The " Constable of Bordeaux," at first a military officer, had been forced by time and circumstance to the head of the financial system. These two great officials, together with the " Chancellor of Aquitaine," acting with the advice of the royal council, formed the executive government of Aquitaine.

The King's Lieutenant stands outside the ordinary governmental system. He is Commander-in-Chief of the forces, charged with the defence of the King's dominions. During the Hundred Years War the force of circumstances converted into a permanent office what had been in its origin a temporary military command, called into existence to meet special and extraordinary conditions. So, throughout the reigns of Edward III and Richard II the government of the dependency is never left for long without the protection of the King's special representative, though, of course, when the " Duke " or the " Prince " of Aquitaine is present, the special office of King's Lieutenant is merged in the higher dignity.

---

[1] The provision excluding nobles from the Corporation of Bordeaux was suppressed by Lancaster at the request of the city 28 Oct. 1392. *Livre des Bouillons,* 291.

THE DUCHY OF AQUITAINE

Two features stand out clearly in the picture of four-teenth-century Aquitaine ; the extreme independence of Gascony under English rule, and the loyalty of the Gascons to their alien suzerain.[1]

The situation was unnatural : it was doomed to fall with the growth of a national sentiment, of a French patriotism. As yet that sentiment scarcely existed. It must not be forgotten that the Gascon dialect marked off the men of the south as a distinct race, and that the Gascon still looked upon the man from the north much in the same way as the Provençal had regarded Mont-fort and the northern invaders in the Albigensian crusades of the thirteenth century. Froissart can still speak of Gascons in distinction to Frenchmen and Burgundians, Picards and Normans.

Meanwhile policy had maintained in equilibrium a balance of forces that could not in the nature of things be permanent, for while the Kings of France had made it their settled policy to crush municipal independence, English sovereigns had for more than a century done everything in their power to foster local liberty.

When John of Gaunt arrived in Aquitaine the French monarchy had already won a barren victory over its own subjects ; the French communes had entered upon the period of their decline. In Gascony municipal liberty had reached its zenith.

The judicial system of Aquitaine, allowing appeal to the suzerain, but virtually self-centred, preserved justice between Gascon and Englishman. A fiscal system far less burdensome than that of France offered advantages which the cities were not slow to appreciate. English rule meant a large measure of self-government, and considerable commercial privilege.

Bordeaux, the emporium of the great wine trade, and the entrepôt of the scarcely less important carrying trade

[1] See M. Brissaud's valuable essay *Les Anglais en Guyenne*.

in pilgrims (who flocked from the north, from England, France and the Low Countries, to the shrine of St. James of Compostella) had for a century basked in the sunshine of royal favour; indeed, on more than one occasion Edward II had supported the interests of his Gascon capital against those of London itself, and since 1272 the city had enjoyed the privilege of electing its own mayor.

Bordeaux therefore was identified with the English supremacy.

But the loyalty of Aquitaine must not be overstated. Resting solely on self-interest, it lacked what is perhaps the strongest of all bases, the sentiment of common race and blood, language and tradition, and such bonds of union as did exist, were from their nature stronger with the cities than with the feudal classes.

The English, it has been remarked,[1] never succeeded in producing a Gascon-English patriotism. If the Gascon was not French, neither was he English. Gascons remained a race apart, subject to alien rule, and to them the wine trade and local liberty were more than the English leopards or the lilies of France. The bond, therefore, which united this dependency to the English crown remained material, not racial or sentimental, and under a strain it would snap.

Such a strain had been brought to bear upon it by the taxation of the Black Prince in 1368.

In spite of Prince Edward's personal charm, a prestige without rival in the lands of chivalry, a court without parallel for its brilliance in Western Europe,[2] his eight years' government (1362–1370) had ended in disaster and ruin. The Prince had alienated the nobles; he had thrown the powerful House of Albret and its following among the noblesse into the arms of France. He had

---

[1] *Les Anglais en Guyenne*, p. 115.
[2] For Prince Edward's court at Bordeaux and Angoulême, see Chandos Herald 1607–1637 and Froissart.

weakened instead of strengthening the hold of England over the Principality: his government recalled the memories of the fatal " fouage," the appeal to France and the rebellion.

The difficulties which in 1395 were awaiting the new Duke of Aquitaine were part of Prince Edward's legacy. Once more the fortunes of the younger brother are shaped by the stronger hand of the elder. Prince Edward's example had fired John of Gaunt with the martial spirit ; his precept had trained the young soldier to arms. The Spanish campaign produced the Spanish marriage : the mistakes of the Black Prince in 1368 are visited after a generation upon his brother in the suspicion and mistrust of a disaffected baronage and jealous people.

To strengthen the grip of England on the Gascon dependency, after years of uninterrupted military failure had damaged her prestige and pushed back her frontiers, might seem difficult ; to succeed where the Black Prince had failed might well seem impossible. The new Duke of Aquitaine was called to a task requiring in a rare degree tact both personal and political, and firmness. Strangely enough, the chroniclers from whom such an assurance is least expected, say that he had almost overcome his difficulties when the task was taken from his hands.

The four and a half years between the formal investiture and the departure for the south were full of ominous signs. The charter [1] which granted to him the Duchy of

---

[1] See in *Foed*, VII. 659–663 five instruments all dated March 2, 1390 (i.) The Charter (ii.) Letters addressed to the three estates commanding obedience. (iii.) Letters addressed to the officials of the duchy commanding them to produce their accounts to the Duke's officers. (iv.) Letters revoking concessions and grants. (v.) Letters enjoining obedience, specially addressed to the Seigneur de Castelnau, the Sieur de Le-sparre and Arnald Giliam de Marsen.

Aquitaine made over to the Duke "all cities castles towns places lands communes and provinces within it, to be held of King Richard and his heirs *as Kings of France* by homage liege for life." The grant included " all islands adjacent, homages, fealty, honour and obedience, all vassals, questals, fees, reversions, services, jurisdictions and rights, justice, advowsons of religious houses, and all revenue, emoluments and regalia, as fully, wholly and perfectly as the King possessed them, in spite of any grants previously made to the contrary," but the King adds, " saving to us as Kings of France and to our heirs as Kings of France the direct lordship, suzerainty and reversion of the Duchy." It is expressly provided that on the Duke's death the Duchy shall revert intact to the Crown.

The known susceptibilities of the Gascons had been spared, so it seemed, in the letters patent (bearing the same date), reciting the grant and commanding obedience, addressed to the prelates, nobles, officers and citizens of Aquitaine. Existing privileges might indeed appear to receive sufficient guarantee in the clause " Sauvez toutdis a vous vos privileges franchises et libertees et a nous et a noz heirs le directe seignurie soverainetee et resort de la dite Duchee et des pais et subgitz de notre seignurie d'Aquitaigne."

Only the entourage of Bordeaux and Bayonne, with the littoral between the mouth of the Garonne and the Pyrenees remained at this time under effective English rule. With shrunken territory, therefore, and a depleted income the King had thought it necessary to revoke such concessions as had alienated sources of revenue.

Hence a third instrument (bearing the same date), which runs : " Inasmuch as the country is so heavily charged by certain donations made by us and by our predecessors . . . that the Duke cannot have aid or comfort for the sustenance and support of his officers, all such concessions and grants are hereby revoked in order that the profits and revenues may be applied to and expended on the good government and safeguard of the country."

This act of resumption was unfortunate. It is clear from the Duke's language in Parliament at the time of his investiture [1] that he expected considerable financial embarrassment on taking up his new duties. That was nothing new. He had felt the same difficulty in 1371. Anything like wholesale expropriation was certainly not contemplated, but the letters seemed of dangerous import. They were interpreted as an attack on vested interests. It is always impolitic to disturb prescriptive rights, and so it proved in this case, for those who feared for their own interests were not slow to raise the cry that Gascon liberties were threatened and the constitution was in danger. Before the end of the year a deputation from Aquitaine had laid a remonstrance before the King, who, with a protest against misrepresentation, caused the objectionable instrument to be revoked, while Lancaster with his own hand tore up the letters patent of revocation. [2]

But his difficulties were not over : they were only just beginning.

To the Gascon it seemed that the palladium of his freedom was the direct and immediate connexion of Aquitaine with the English crown.

---

[1] *Rot. Parl.* III. 263 b 264 a. Cf. ibid. II. 311 and Appendix IV. p. 447.

[2] After reciting the letters of revocation dated March 2, the instrument goes on : " Ascuns disans autrement que a point, et mal gratiousement, que non seulement dessons avoir revoque les donations suisdites, mes les privileges francheisies et libertes a mesme les paiis et subgiz . . . ottroies, come par le teneur des dites lettres revocatoires aparoit du tout le contraire."

The letters of revocation are then cancelled, without prejudice to the grant of the duchy. Nov. 30, 1390. *Foed*, VIII. 687–8.

This is what Malverne has got hold of and twisted. Higd. ix. 263–4.

JOHN OF GAUNT

So strong was this feeling that Edward III, on assuming the royal style of France, had thought it politic to place on record, in the most formal manner, that the suzerainty of Aquitaine belonged to him and to his heirs as Kings of England and not as Kings of France.[1]

The grant of March 2 had sinned against this principle in two ways. In the first place, it had been made by Richard II as King of France, and in this capacity homage was claimed. With no semblance of probability that the crown of the Valois would now be won by the Plantagenets, this might pass as a constitutional point of merely academic interest. But, in the second place, it was argued that to create as Duke of Aquitaine any one save the heir to the throne of England, was a violation of the Gascon constitution. The Gascons protested against a mesne lord being thrust between them and their suzerain. They would "hold of the King of England or of themselves."

This opposition, however unexpected, was met in a spirit of conciliation. In letters patent (dated November 23, 1390)[2] the King replied to the objectors. He had no intention of cancelling the liberties of Aquitaine, least of all that which united the Duchy irrevocably to the English crown, but merely of suspending this privilege for the lifetime of the present Duke.

"Inasmuch as it is a privilege of the said Duchy that it may not be withdrawn, separated, or bestowed away from the royal hand and crown of England . . . we declare that it was not and is not our intention to derogate from or prejudice by the said donation, the said privilege for the future, but merely to suspend it for the lifetime of our uncle, for the good of our country and subjects, and for just and reasonable cause moving us thereto."

[1] Dated June 4, 1342. *Mélanges Historiques*, ii. 170.
[2] *Livre des Bouillons*, i. 233.

THE DUCHY OF AQUITAINE

The reservation of suzerainty and reversion to the crown are again repeated.

By admitting expressly that the Duchy could not be alienated, and by implication that the grant to Lancaster was in this sense an alienation (which is disputable), Richard had virtually conceded the whole position. A privilege that could be suspended for one life could be suspended for a second, for a succession of lives—in fact, indefinitely. The direct suzerainty of the crown of England, and its immediate connexion with Aquitaine recede into remote distance.

A grant "saving all privileges," coupled with the admission that the inalienable character of that which is granted is one of those privileges, is indeed an elaborate contradiction, hard even for the subtlety of constitutional law to explain away.

But the legal contradiction was not of course the vital point at issue.

It was a mediaeval habit of thought to cloak a practical issue in legal garb. The burgesses of Bordeaux were men of business, and what touched them nearly was the prospect of a resident governor instead of an absentee suzerain. Hitherto, with the exception of the last few years of Prince Edward's government, the balance of Gascon liberties and English claims had been nicely preserved. The presence of a Duke of the blood royal, whose pride was known and whose ambition was notorious, might disturb that balance. Another "fouage" would assuredly lead to another rebellion, and revolutions are not good for commerce. "Laissez-faire," said the Gascons, "and we will be loyal." There was no motive to be otherwise. But would the new Duke leave things as they were?

The period between the grant of the duchy and the Duke's departure for the south saw repeated attempts at conciliation. Sir William le Scrope, who was Seneschal of Aquitaine, had confirmed in the Duke's name all existing privileges. Lancaster was careful to publish his ratification of this act. He claimed the nomination of public officers; for the rest he left things as they were.[1]

To put people's minds at ease, the royal charters stating the inalienable nature of the duchy were reissued and proclaimed anew.[2]

A batch of new privileges followed the confirmation of the old,[3] and a politic effort was made to humour Bordeaux in its jealousy of its neighbour and rival, Dax.[4]

This was not without effect, for by July, 1392, most of the prelates, barons and commons had taken the oath of allegiance—with reservations.

But consciences were tender, and there yet remained a scruple to remove. Had the grant been made of the King's free will, and was it still his intention that it should take effect?

The Gascons pretended to have their doubts. The King could only repeat, in words as explicit as words can be, that the grant had been made of his free will in full Parliament, by the advice and with the assent of

[1] Instrument dated September 4, 1391. *Livre des Bouillons*, i. 293–4.

[2] Notarial instrument dated November 13, 1391. *Record Report*, xlv. Appendix, ix. Box ii. No. 295. Cf. instrument dated Winchester, Jan. 24, 1393. *Livre des Bouillons*, i. 298–9.

[3] Orders to the Duke's officers to respect a grant to the Mayor and Jurats of Bordeaux of the right to compel merchants whose ships anchor before the town to land provisions carried by them. *Livre des Bouillons*, i. 246.

Grant to the Mayor and Jurats of power to compel the payment of accustomed "péages" which some people had tried to avoid, dated July 24, 1392. Ibid. 248.

Declaration that no privileges which have been or shall be granted to towns or persons in the duchy shall prejudice the existing privileges of Bordeaux (same date).

Grant of building rights dated October 28, 1392. Ibid. i. 249.

[4] Ibid. i. 298-9.

the Privy Council and both Estates of the Realm; that it had been and still was his will, purpose and intention that it should take effect.[1] The document appears convincing, but the Gascons remained of the same opinion still, and when in the next year Harry " Hotspur " went south as the Duke's lieutenant, Bordeaux refused to receive him except as the representative of the King.[2]

By the spring of 1394 a deputation was on its way from the unwilling subjects of John of Gaunt to the English court. The Sieur de Lesparre, the Vicomte de Dort and the Seigneur de Castelnau, three of the leading magnates of Aquitaine, were charged to speak with the King " on certain weighty matters touching the King and the state of Aquitaine." [3]

If the minutes of the Privy Council meetings for these years survived, it would be interesting to hear the Gascon doubts and scruples from the lips of the Lord of Castlenau. But the result of the mission is clear. A fresh declaration was issued by the King. The grant had been made of his entire free will, and he was determined to make it good.

The Gascons are reminded that an oath of obedience " with reservations " is contrary to the tenour of the King's commands. Idle rumours to the effect that in making his uncle Duke of Aquitaine the King had not acted as a free agent are to be ignored. So also is the offending oath; the proper oath must be taken, and homage and obedience rendered in due form.[4]

Fortified with this instrument, the Duke and his

---

[1] Dated July 7, 1392. *Rot. Gasc.* i. 178 (4).
[2] Henry Percy was sent out in 1393. *Ypod. Neust.* 368, *Ann. Ric. II*, 158. He was still acting as Lieutenant in March, 1394. *Livre des Bouillons*, 484.
[3] Letters of protection, dated April 8, 1394. *Foed*, VII. 767.
[4] Mandate, dated Cardiff, September 10, 1394. *Livre des Bouillons*, i. 228. For the Gascon oath see *Record Report*, xlv, App. Box ii. Nos. 313, 318, and 325.

retinue set sail from English shores. The passage was
stormy, and heavy gales were blowing in the " Bay." [1]
It was ominous of what remained in store.

At length the Duke of Aquitaine reached his dominions,
and disembarked at Libourne on the Dordogne. From
Libourne he sent messengers to announce his arrival
to the prelates, nobles and cities of the Duchy. Everywhere the envoys were received with respect, but without
enthusiasm. The Council of Bordeaux declined to
recognize his authority unless Bayonne and Dax did
the same.

The same answer was received from the other cities.
As the King's representative, Lancaster was welcome.
That was all. It was obvious that the greatest caution
must be exercised. A false step at the start might
offend susceptibilities and render the difficulties of
the Duke's position insuperable. The imposing retinue
of men-at-arms and archers was in itself a danger : no
one must be allowed to represent this force as a menace.
The Duke intended to achieve his object by fair means
and fair words.

Libourne is hard by Lormont, and from Lormont on
the right bank of the Garonne it is only a step to Bordeaux. Lancaster took up his residence at Lormont and
prepared to face the initial difficulty of entering his
capital.

At Bordeaux the council debated. To shut their gates
on a Prince of the blood would scarcely be regarded in
England as a convincing proof of their boasted loyalty
to the crown. Lancaster held the King's commission,
and Duke or not Duke, he was the King's representative. He had lived among them, and had led their

---

[1] *Ann. Ric. II*, 169. This may explain the liberal annuity
granted by Lancaster on his arrival to John Brambre, mariner,
" for good and agreeable service," dated Libourne, Dec. 1, 1394.
Duchy of Lancs. Accts. Bundle xxxii, No. 22.

armies and protected their territories. An extreme course would put them hopelessly in the wrong. Moreover it might be dangerous. The burgesses of Bordeaux were men of peace, and Lancaster had an army.

On the other hand, to receive him *sans phrase* might appear to concede the whole position, and prejudge the issue.

Lancaster cut the knot by issuing letters patent in which he declared that by passing through Bordeaux " at the request of the good people of the city " on his way to Saint Seurin, where he intended to spend the next few months, he was acting without prejudice to any right or privilege which might be involved. He added that no damage should be done to the city, and that no one should suffer in body or estate.[1]

The first step had been taken. The Duke reached Saint Seurin.

Three days later a politic manifesto appeared in which, after reference to the losses suffered by the Gascons in the wars, and their steady loyalty to the English cause, the Duke, in view of the good and true obedience which he expected of them, confirmed all existing rights, liberties and privileges, to those who had recognized his authority or would do so before February 2 next following.[2]

Meanwhile there had been parleyings with the lords spiritual and temporal, and a " modus vivendi " had been reached. The Duke was to be received in Bordeaux provisionally ; but he agreed not to perform any act of sovereignty without the concurrence of the municipal government.[3] The real issue was deferred.

---

[1] *Livre des Bouillons*, i. 253 and 257, dated Lormont, January 9, and Saint Seurin, March 13, 1395.

[2] *Livre des Bouillons*, i. 244, dated Saint Seurin, January 12, 1395.

[3] *Livre des Bouillons*, i. 257. See also confirmation of a number of concessions dated March 20, ibid. 269, and *Record Report*, xlv. App. (Dip. Doc.) Box ii. No. 324.

JOHN OF GAUNT

This was made the subject of a formal treaty between representatives of the three estates, the Archbishop of Bordeaux with some of the leading clergy, Archambaud de Graily and the leading barons, and the Mayor and Jurats of the city.[1] This document, the Magna Carta of Aquitaine, opens with general considerations. The terms which follow are to be submitted to the King for his approval (Article I). There is to be a general amnesty for the past; the contumacy of the Duke's unwilling subjects is not to be visited by fine, amercement or imprisonment (Articles II and III). The Duke will respect the franchises and liberties granted to Aquitaine by his predecessors and by his own officers; he renews and confirms all grants hitherto made (Articles IV, V and VIII).

The body of the treaty itself (for it is virtually a treaty between two independent contracting powers) reflects, as might be expected, the separate interests of the three estates. It is possible to distinguish between the shares of the nobles, the clergy and the commons respectively.

In Aquitaine as in England the clergy were the estate most easily conciliated. The clergy of Bordeaux had no fears of a dangerous enemy to ecclesiastical possessions or accepted doctrine. To them Lancaster was the friend of the Church,[2] and what was for the moment equally important, the friend of the Pope. Their demands, which the Duke at once concedes, go farther than those of nobles or commons. They raise the cry which Aquitaine under English rule never dared to raise: "Gascony for the Gascons." They ask (and

[1] Dated March 22, 1395. *Livre des Bouillons*, i. 259-267.
[2] It is perhaps significant that Lancaster's decision in a suit between the Canons of St. Andrew and St. Seurin and the clergy of Bordeaux generally on the one hand, and the corporation on the other, about the privilege of selling wine in the Bordeaux taverns, was given in favour of the clergy (dated Oct. 22, 1389). *Registre des Jurades*, iv. 160. Cf. *Livre des Bouillons*, i. 289, 290.

the Duke grants) that their lord will so use his influence with the Papal court that the benefices of the duchy shall be given to ecclesiastics native to the duchy ; if possible to those who are friendly to the English cause (Article XXVII). In other words, the clergy place Gascon birth first and loyalty to the crown second among the qualifications for a benefice, and the Duke tacitly accepts their position. It was perhaps necessary ; certainly it was a politic concession. It cost him nothing, and it secured a powerful ally. Henceforth the lords spiritual and their levies, that is, one third of the estates and one half of the upper classes, would be on his side in the coming struggle.

What benefices were to the clergy, feudal jurisdiction was to the noblesse. Even before the formal treaty the Duke had done something to conciliate the most power-ful of his subjects and the most staunch of his opponents, Archambaud de Graily, by guaranteeing him immunity from interference with his seignorial rights.[1] What he had granted by a separate charter to the Sieur de Graily he now granted to the whole Gascon baronage. He undertakes not to step in between the seigneur and his "serfs questiaux"—between the lord and his justiciables (Article XI). Feudal jurisdiction *haute moyenne et basse* is to be left untouched. One further concession is made clearly in the hope of conciliating the Gascon gentlemen ; the Duke promises that any lands which may be recovered from the French shall be restored to their former tenants (Article XVIII). Anything like a campaign of restoration was of course out of the question, but the frontier even in the quietest times was by no means a fixed and immovable boundary. It fluctuated ; if it receded at the expense of the French, the former lord should regain his lands on payment of a reasonable "fine" by way of contribution towards

[1] Dated March 14, 1395. *Variétés Bordeloises*, iii. 297.

military expenses. Again a politic concession. It cost nothing ; it held out an incentive to adventurous knights whose lands lay in the debatable zone, and it bound up the interests of the dispossessed with the Duke's rule.

The concessions clearly granted in the interest of the commercial classes are neither so important as the foregoing, nor so easy to distinguish from those which are general in their scope and application.[1] On the one hand, Lancaster doubtless cared less for the friendship—or enmity—of the burgess than for that of baron or churchman ; on the other, the privileges for which the commercial classes were anxious naturally affected the interests of all classes of society.

On one point the burgesses of Bordeaux received a distinct rebuff. Knowing, as a commercial community might be expected to know, how much the prosperity of Bordeaux depended on a stable currency, they had tried to make Lancaster pledge himself to make no innovation in the coinage. The Duke turned their own argument against them. They were standing on the time-honoured inalienable privileges of Aquitaine. The weapon was double-edged. The Duke took his stand on the same ground, and refused to depart from the privileges which by royal charter his predecessors had enjoyed. The regality of coinage in England was enjoyed by no subject of the crown, not even by a Count Palatine. Lancaster had no intention of giving up any portion of his rights.

---

[1] During his tenure of office as Lieutenant Lancaster had been careful to conciliate the commercial classes ; e.g. his intervention brought about an agreement between the cloth merchants of London and Bordeaux who were quarrelling about the length of the measure (*Livre des Bouillons*, i. 374, letters dated Jan. 31, 1374). He had supported a claim of Bordeaux to pontage as against Corbiac (ibid. 297, letters dated Oct. 23, 1389) ; and had granted the burgesses a *boucherie* outside the Médoc gate (Oct. 25, 1389, ibid. i. 300).

To Article XIV, therefore, he returned a refusal, at the same time promising redress to a practical inconvenience, the insufficient number of money-changers.

Yet the commercial classes did not go away empty-handed. Next to the wine-trade the most lucrative industry of Bordeaux was the transport of pilgrims. When Saint James chose a local habitation in Galicia, and gave his name to Compostella, he conferred a boon of the first value upon the great port of Aquitaine; for it was at Bordeaux that the flocks of pilgrims met to be shipped viâ San Sebastian and Coruña to the Galician shrine.[1] A prohibitive tariff might deprive the Spanish saint and the Gascon dealers of a considerable revenue. To commerce and devotion alike it would be calamitous. Article XXIV promises that in this matter only the customary dues shall be exacted by the officers of the port.

The other financial articles are of general application. Confiscated property of rebels shall be devoted in the first instance to discharging the royal liabilities (Article XXV). Persons who have an assignment on the revenues of the Castle of Bordeaux shall receive due payment (Article XXI). The Duke will not disturb old tariffs like that of the Chateau de l'Ombrière (Article XV). Letters " of chancery and seals " shall be taxed according to a preconcerted scale, so that every one may know beforehand what he has to pay (Article VI). Had the Gascons heard of the capricious extortion which the Duke's father-in-law of Castile had practised in the matter of chancery fees? The hated right of purveyance shall not be exercised in the capital (Article X); no issue of fraudulent " *lettres d'état* " shall deprive creditors of

---

[1] See Early Naval Ballads, No. 1 (*Ed.* J. O. Halliwell, Percy Society: London, 1841), for the discomforts of the sea voyage, which in the fourteenth century was usually broken at one of the Gascon ports.

their due under colour of fictitious debts to the sovereign (Article XII). Lastly, no new imposition or tax shall be established without the consent of the Estates (Article IX).

Next in importance to finance comes the administration of justice. To this four Articles are devoted. No one shall be liable to confiscation until his cause has been duly heard (Article XIII); no one shall be hanged or tortured without a sentence of the courts (Article XIX); no one who has the right to be tried at Bordeaux shall be transferred to any other court [1] (Article XX); finally, the appellate jurisdiction of the royal courts in England is to be duly respected.[2]

As to the general conduct of the administration, the Gascons confine themselves to moderate and sensible demands. Froissart's testimony may be accepted without suspicion when he tells us that under Prince Edward's rule the chief practical Gascon grievance was the monopoly of official position by Englishmen, and the pride and arrogance of the official class. The Gascon commons do not ask Lancaster for concessions so large as those demanded by the clergy; they do not raise questions of blood and race. They merely pray that the Duke will choose capable and honest administrators from men who know the country (Article VI), and will only lease

[1] For Gascon susceptibilities on this point see *Livre des Bouillons*, i 295. When Lancaster removed a prisoner to England for trial he issued letters patent at the request of the Mayor and Jurats of Bordeaux declaring that the transfer was made at the prisoner's own request, and without prejudice to the privileges of the city (dated Oct. 23, 1389).

[2] For instance, during Lancaster's lieutenancy a question arose as to the jurisdiction of the Abbot of Holy Cross, Bordeaux, and others, over six members of the parish of St. Seurin, whom they claimed as *questales*. A judgment of the courts of Bordeaux in favour of the defendants (with costs) was reversed on appeal to Lancaster as the King's Lieutenant. The defendants in the original action appealed to the King's courts at Westminster. *Foed*, VII. 653-4.

or farm offices to men of good repute (Article XXIII).
In other words, Aquitaine must not be exploited by a
class of needy and unscrupulous adventurers.

The treaty concluded, the high contracting parties
sat down to wait for the royal approval and a better
understanding of one another. In later days, when the
son of the Duke of Aquitaine became King of England
and suzerain of the duchy, the Gascons remembered
the events of the year with some alarm. Things had
gone too far, and they evinced some anxiety on the score
of a possible retribution.[1]

But though relations had for a while been strained,
the treaty had cleared the air, and John of Gaunt did
his best to remove misapprehension and distrust. That
a large measure of success attended his policy of conciliation may be accepted as a fact, for all the chronicles,
hostile or otherwise, attest it.

And the secret of this success is not hard to find. For
while the Black Prince had looked on his principality, as
King Edward looked on his kingdom, merely as a source
of revenue and a recruiting ground for soldiers to fight
his battles, Lancaster came not to tax but to spend.[2]
The tribute of Castile and the rent rolls of the Lancastrian lands were exhausted in lavish expenditure—a sure
way to conciliate merchant and burgess. Nor was the
Gascon noblesse insensible to the attractions of a
luxurious and stately court such as the Duke maintained.

---

[1] Henry IV, by letters patent dated May 10, 1401, pardons
the officers of Bordeaux "omnem rancorem omne odium et
omnes excessus et transgressiones . . . contra nos et progenitores,
ac contra carissimum dominum et patrem nostrum nuper Ducem
Aquitainie et Lancastrie . . . usurpando dominium nostrum,
vel dominiis privilegiis franchesiis et statutis suis abutendo
(*Livre des Bouillons*, i. 309 and 315).

[2] "Cum jam inaestimabilem summam thesauri profudisset
in illis partibus pro adipiscenda patriotarum benevolentia,
subito per mandatum revocatur. *Ann. Ric. II*, 188. Cf.
Ypod. Neust. 370 and Wals. ii. 219.

So the work of restoring confidence in Aquitaine progressed. Meanwhile others besides the Gascons had been troubled by the Duke's arrival : Paris as well as Bordeaux had taken alarm. By 1395 it must have been clear to those who understood politics that Lancaster's influence had been thrown into the scale of peace. Since the great meeting of Amiens, if not before, the " Princes des fleurs de lys " must have known that peace was the keynote of his policy, and statesmen like Burgundy had no longer any fears as to aggression on the part of the Duke of Lancaster. Their enemy was Gloucester, and they knew it. Still the presence of John of Gaunt had caused some uneasiness, for hard on the news of his arrival came word of fighting in the " debatable land," and the capture of a couple of towns in Saintonge and Angoulême. Nervous politicians began to fear the reopening of the old quarrel ; their fancy saw a Gascon and English army spreading desolation in the south as Prince Edward had done on the famous march to Carcassonne a quarter of a century before.

To sound Lancaster's intentions Jean Boucicaut, now Marshal of France, was sent to the South. From Agen the Marshal announced his arrival, and the Duke advanced to his old Gascon lordship of Bergerac to meet the French envoy.[1] The breach of the Truce in Saintonge and Angoulême was disowned and restitution promised, and all fears of aggression were removed ; indeed, it was easier to disarm the suspicion of enemies than of subjects. His mission accomplished, the Marshal was in no hurry to go ; a certain stately hospitality was part of the Lancastrian tradition, and the Duke was never more ready to display it than to his " adversaries of France." Boucicaut, mirror of the latter day chivalry, a "*chevalier sans peur et sans reproche*," stayed to talk with the veteran campaigner of " arms and the deeds of knighthood."

[1] *Livre des faits de Jean Boucicaut,* i. xx.

Doubtless to such a willing listener the Duke "fought his battles o'er again"; there were many things to talk of—the campaign of '70; the glorious day of Najera, and the invasion of Leon when the Marshal had been found in the ranks of his enemies, or again the famous joust at St. Ingelvert, where Boucicaut had thrown down his gage to the chivalry of Europe, and Henry of Bolingbroke and John Beaufort had borne themselves with honour. When the Marshal left it was to report that alarm was needless.[1]

With this twofold reconciliation accomplished, the French reassured and the Gascons pacified, John of Gaunt might have looked forward to a period of quiet rule in Aquitaine, but it was not to be. Six months after the famous treaty of Bordeaux came a royal mandate summoning him back to England. To understand the King's latest move it is necessary to leave Gascony for a while, and follow the envoys charged to submit the "Treaty of Bordeaux" for the royal approval. Hitherto the case for plaintiffs and defendant has been followed on unimpeachable evidence, state papers and the municipal records of Bordeaux. When the legal tangle is carried to the court of appeal the nature of the evidence changes. Formal documents fail, for the minutes of the Privy Council before which the envoys went to lay their "draft agreement" have not survived. But in their silence is heard a voice more eloquent, if less certain. A new witness enters, and with him sunlight and the breath of the open air burst into the court close with the dust of legal records.[2]

For soon after the Gascon envoys arrived in England, on July 12 there landed at Dover "Sire Jean Froissart,

---

[1] Lancaster was also visited by envoys from Hungary escorted to Bordeaux by officers of the Duke of Anjou. Brit. Mus. Add. Ch. 3371-7.
[2] Froissart, K. de L. xv. 140-168.

treasurer for that time and Canon of Chimay in the county of Hainault and the diocese of Liége," who, after twenty-seven years' absence, was returning to visit the English court. Fortified with letters from the Princes of the Low Countries, Froissart had come to pay court to the grandson of his earliest patroness, that "noble lady Philippa," of whom he cannot speak without gratitude and affection. The times had changed since Froissart's first visit to England. The little child whom he had seen last at the font in the Cathedral of Bordeaux on the eve of the great march across the Pyrenees was now King, and as Froissart made his offering at the shrine of St. Thomas at Canterbury he saw the tomb of King Richard's father, the hero of Najera. A generation had changed the players on the stage of English society. The " goodly fellowship of famous knights " who met at Windsor for the first festival of King Edward's table round, was all unsoldered. Sir John Chandos, Sir Walter Manny and the great captains of the old days had passed away, and in their place a generation had arisen that knew not the favourite of Queen Philippa. A sense of loneliness came over him when, his " great longing and affection " satisfied, he stood once more on English soil.

At length, however, he found a friend. Lancaster's councillor, Sir Thomas Percy, received him courteously and promised to bring him to the King. As Froissart rode along the highway from Canterbury to Ospringe, where the Wife of Bath had told the joys of marriage, and mine host with unfailing good humour had kept the peace among the strange company who rode to Canterbury from the *Tabard Inn* in the spring of the year, and the dawn of English poetry, he listened the while to Sir William de Lisle fresh from Donegal and full of tales of St. Patrick's purgatory.

At Leeds, half way between Ospringe and Rochester,

the chronicler had his desire. He was presented to the
King. More potent talisman to conjure royal favour
than letters from the Count of Hainault, Froissart had
brought with him a book wherein, with the bright
illumination, which still delights the lover of manuscripts, were written " all the matters touching morality
and love which for the last four and thirty years by the
favour of God and of Love he had indited and composed."

The treasured volume, with its rich binding of crimson
velvet studded with silver nails, was not yet to be presented, for weighty matters lay on the King's mind.

The ambassadors sent to France to demand the hand
of Isabella, and the Gascon envoys were both awaiting
audience.

Riding from Rochester through Dartford to Eltham,
where the King's Council was to meet, Froissart learnt the
news of Aquitaine from Jean de Graily, bastard of the
great Captal de Buch, whose heir Archambaud de Graily
had led the Gascon noblesse in their opposition to the
new Duke of Aquitaine.

At Eltham by good fortune Froissart found another
friend, Sir Richard Stury, now in disgrace for a too
vigorous support of Lollard doctrine, and as they
walked about the gardens of the royal palace at Eltham,
Sir Richard, undeterred by any " Official Secrets Act,"
told Froissart what happened at the Council.

First the envoys from Bordeaux, Bayonne and Dax
and the Gascon noblesse had been introduced ; then Lancaster's two knights, Sir Peter Clifton and Sir William
Perrers.

Then the Council, dismissing them, discussed the position of affairs in the Duchy.

Opinion was divided. Some sympathized with the
Gascons, and some with the Duke. But one voice
dominated the Council. The Duke of Gloucester,

secure of power while Lancaster was absent, but reduced to insignificance with his brother's return, was determined that the Duke of Aquitaine should be kept away from England. He stood on punctilio. The King's honour demanded that the grant should be made good and the royal commands obeyed. The Earl of Derby for different motives supported his uncle in his father's cause.

The agreement between the Duke of Aquitaine and his subjects was duly recorded among the archives of the exchequer, and the King went on to discuss the affair which he had more at heart.

With characteristic impulsiveness Richard had resolved to marry the French king's daughter. The marriage would definitely seal the policy of peace with France. Though Gloucester had failed to prevent negotiations he had not failed to obstruct, and with the violent and overbearing manner which made his nephew detest his presence as much as his interference, he endeavoured to thwart the King's favourite scheme. Like all the King's decisions, this last was sudden and unexpected.

That Richard feared disaffection in Aquitaine as a result of his uncle's further stay is unlikely, for the fight was over, and the combatants were ready to make peace. But the King was thinking of England, not of Aquitaine.

The summons was inconvenient but it was obeyed ; Lancaster returned at once. Knighton, or the pseudo-Knighton, usually well informed in all that concerns the Duke's life, says that he came back through France.[1] It is not improbable, though for a few months his movements cannot be traced. There would be no difficulty about a safe-conduct from the French king, and the return through France had been contemplated six years

---

[1] Kn. ii. 322. Et post Natale Domini sequens dominus Johannes Dux Lancastriae rediit in Angliam de Vasconia et venit per Franciam. Froissart, K. de L. xv. 181, 182, 189.

before. When next the Duke can be traced he is in Brittany, where on November 25 he made a treaty of alliance with England's inconstant ally, the Duke of Brittany.[1] This was something more than a mere treaty of friendship and alliance, for John of Gaunt, an inveterate matchmaker, after disposing of his daughters and his son in marriage, had bethought him of his grandson Henry, afterwards Fifth of England. A marriage between Brittany's daughter Mary and the son of Henry, Earl of Derby, was to confirm the old alliance of the Montforts with the royal house of England. But Montfort changed his mind, and in June following, when the wedding should have taken place, Mary of Brittany married the Count d'Alençon and " Prince Hal " found another bride.

Lancaster's abortive marriage treaty was his last act before setting foot on English soil. He had left his Gascon fief behind him ; he was never to see it again. Had he remained, there would have been little to do. While the peace held, as Lancaster intended it should hold, the Gascon frontier could not be pushed back again. The Gascon governmental system was complete and needed no interference. What tact and forbearance could do the Duke had done. Had he shown in 1376 the same astuteness in the face of opposition, our reading of an obscure page of English history must have been

[1] Mr. Williams in the Preface to his edition of the *Chronicque de la Traïson et Mort de Richart Deux Roy d'Engleterre* (London, 1846), says that this treaty of alliance was made without any reservation as to allegiance to Richard II (p. xix.), and that the King was so displeased with the conduct of the parties in this affair " either with the Duke of Brittany or with the Duke of Lancaster or as is most probable with both," that it required all the efforts of the King of France to reconcile them. But in the first place reservation of allegiance is made, and that in the most express terms ; and in the second place Richard confirmed the treaty. See the text given in full in Lobineau's *Histoire de Bretaigne*, ii. 791, quoting from the Chronicle of Nantes. Cf. Pierre Cochon *Chronique Normande*, 196.

changed and history might perhaps have registered a different verdict on John of Gaunt. The Duke of Aquitaine returned to England leaving the Duchy as he had found it. If the Gascons had trembled for their liberties and the French for their frontiers they had trembled at a shadow. The menace of feudal tyranny proved as vain as the threat of a war of aggression. His short tenure of power left no permanent results but the Treaty of March 22, 1395.

Recalled after ten months' government, he left no impress on the province. Once more, like the "King of Castile," the "Duke of Guyenne" had perforce to content himself with the semblance rather than the reality of power: once more history is deceived by the "boast of heraldry the pomp of power." A century and a half later an ambassador of Henry VIII found the "armories of the Duke of Lancaster" still entire in a glass window in the church of the Friars Preachers at Bordeaux.[1] For history, the only abiding traces of the last Duke of Aquitaine are to be found in the vigorous protests of municipal independence written on the pages of the *Livre des Bouillons* and the *Registre des Jurades*, and for the Duke's life the ten months' rule has its interest mainly in the great change which years and their experience had wrought in the character of the man once so "jealous of honour, sudden and quick in quarrel."

---

[1] Speed, *Great Britain*, 618. For the Duke's acts after his recall, see *Livre des Bouillons*, i. 214, 251, 255, 256, 268; and *Rot. Gasc.* i. 180 (1).

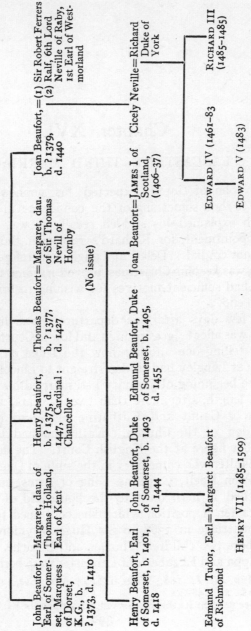

V. THE BEAUFORTS

JOHN OF GAUNT=Katharine Swynford, b. 1350,
m. 1396, d. 1405

John Beaufort, =Margaret, dau. of
Earl of Somer- Thomas Holland,
set, Marquess Earl of Kent
of Dorset,
K.G., b.
? 1373, d. 1410

Henry Beaufort,
b. ? 1375, d.
1447, Cardinal:
Chancellor

Thomas Beaufort=Margaret, dau.
b. ? 1377, of Sir Thomas
d. 1427 Nevill of Hornby

(No issue)

Joan Beaufort, =(1) Sir Robert Ferrers
b. ? 1379, (2) Ralf, 6th Lord
d. 1440 Neville of Raby,
1st Earl of West-
morland

Henry Beaufort, Earl
of Somerset, b. 1401,
d. 1418

John Beaufort, Duke
of Somerset, b. 1403

Edmund Beaufort, Duke
of Somerset, b. 1405,
d. 1455

Joan Beaufort=JAMES I of
Scotland,
(1406–37)

Cicely Neville=Richard
Duke of
York

John Beaufort, Duke
of Somerset, b. 1444,
d. 1444

EDWARD IV (1461–83)

RICHARD III
(1485–1485)

EDWARD V (1483)

Edmund Tudor, Earl=Margaret Beaufort
of Richmond

HENRY VII (1485–1509)

P

Chapter XVI

LANCASTER'S THIRD MARRIAGE

IF John of Gaunt expected his nephew's welcome to show something of the confidence in his support which explained his sudden recall, he was destined to disappointment, for Richard's reception, though correct, was not cordial. Delay at Langley, therefore, where the King was keeping Christmas, proved irksome to the Duke, who had sufficient motives for wishing to bring his visit to an end.

A few days after his departure a startling piece of news was afloat : gossips high and low in Court and cottage were telling one another how the Duke on leaving the court at Langley had ridden straight to Lincoln, and there at the beginning of January had married his mistress.[1]

At length, after more than twenty years,[2] the union of John of Gaunt and Katharine Swynford received the sanction of the Church. Katharine had long been a familiar figure at the English Court. The daughter of a Hainaulter who came over in the suite of Queen Philippa, Sir Paon Roelt, Guyenne King of Arms, she had been attached in her youth to the household of Blanche of Lancaster, a position which she continued to hold after her marriage in 1368 to Sir Hugh Swynford, to whom she bore two children, Thomas and Blanche. Then, when Philippa and Elizabeth of Lancaster were born, Katharine

[1] *Ann. Ric. II.* 188 ; Wals. ii. 219 ; *Mon. Eve,* 128. Froissart, K. de L. xv. 238–40.

[2] See note on Katharine Swynford, Appendix VI. p. 461.

became their guardian, and as the elder of the children was only in her ninth year when the Duchess Blanche died, the guardian found herself in the position of a foster-mother to Lancaster's little daughters. If tradition can be trusted Katharine was beautiful, and the Duke's " visits to the nursery " allowed an intimacy to ripen which soon after the death of his first wife, but while Sir Hugh Swynford still lived, resulted in the Duke becoming her lover. In 1372 Sir Hugh died fighting in Aquitaine ; henceforth " Queen " Constance had to bear a rival near her throne, and Dame Katharine took her place as the Duke's mistress *en titre*.

When, ten years later, she ceased to be guardian to the Duke's daughters, retiring from the Lancastrian household to the estates in Lincolnshire and Nottingham given her by her lover, Katharine was the mother of four children, John, Henry, Thomas, and Joan, surnamed " Beaufort," or, as the wits of Richard's Court preferred to have it, " Faerborn," with a jesting allusion to the open secret of their birth.[1]

In spite of law social and canonical, the Beauforts took a place with their legitimate half-brother and sisters in the front rank of public life ; the Lancastrian love of arms, and a certain administrative capacity, were conspicuous in the eldest, John, while Henry, the future Cardinal and Chancellor of England, was laying at Oxford the foundations of his reputation as a jurist and a scholar. One disability alone attached to their position, the defect of illegitimate birth, and it was partly with a view to smoothing the way to remove it, that in 1396 John of Gaunt, then in his fifty-sixth year, married Katharine, who was herself only ten years younger. Negotiations had already been set on foot at the Papal Court, and in September Boniface IX issued a bull con-

---

[1] See Appendix VI. (Percy MS. 78), p. 463.

firming the Duke's third marriage, and declaring the offspring past and future legitimate.[1]

When, therefore, in the following February, the King in Parliament granted to the Beauforts letters patent of legitimation,[2] their position was established so far as law ecclesiastical or civil could establish it, and one of Lancaster's most cherished wishes was fulfilled.

The third marriage, easily explicable on a calm examination of the Duke's motives, proved, however, a stumbling-block to those who had hitherto regarded him as the type of unqualified ambition. No one had expected that John of Gaunt, now an old man according to the standard of the age, would marry again : had such a possibility been forecast the quidnuncs of the day would certainly have chosen as the third Duchess of Lancaster an heiress who would bring another roll of lands and honours to swell the Lancastrian inheritance. It was natural that some should point the contrast between Blanche, a princess of the blood royal, and Constance the " Queen " of Castile, on the one hand, and the *gouvernante* of the Duke's daughters on the other. It was inevitable that others should moralize on the *liaison* which, however, was of a kind too prevalent to shock or surprise the Court of Richard II. The *Scandalous Chronicle* has, it is true, chosen to describe the Duke's mistress in offensive language; but the mortal sin in which Lancaster lived is too obviously his connexion not with Katharine Swynford, but with John Wycliffe, and the best answer to detractors who, like the Monk of St. Albans, attempted to class Katharine with adventuresses like Alice Perrers, is furnished by his new Duchess of Lancaster herself.

[1] Dated Rome, Kal. Sept. 1396 (7 Boniface IX), *Papal Letters*, iv. 545.

[2] Dated Feb. 9, 1397, *Rot. Parl.* iii. 343. *Foed.* VII. 849–50. *Rot. Pat.* 213, ch. 6 (Carte). Cf. *Ann. Ric. II.* 195 ; Wals. ii. 222. The interpolation *excepta dignitate regali* was made by Henry IV when he had begun to be jealous of his half-brothers.

Froissart, a witness by no means indifferent to questions of rank and precedence, only states the fact when he describes her as *une dame qui sçavoit moult de toutes honneurs ;* and when placed in the first position of English society Katharine behaved with a quiet diginity which silenced comment, and forced the high-born dames who had expressed horror at the *mésalliance* to reconcile themselves to the idea of yielding precedence to the daughter of a plain Hainault knight.

The legitimation of the Beauforts, however, though the most obvious, is by no means the only proof of the King's anxiety to conciliate the man whose influence was still so important a factor in the balance of party power. Signs of the same disposition recur constantly from the Duke's return until his death.

The circumstances under which, in 1398, the venerable Bishop of Lincoln was turned out of his see to make room for Henry Beaufort, then a mere boy, amounted to a grave scandal, but the episode proved that, if Boniface IX was ready to gratify a faithful son of the Church, Richard II was equally willing to reward a staunch supporter of the Crown, by sanctioning the bull of provision which raised the third son of Katharine Swynford to the ranks of the Lords Spiritual.[1] With less questionable justice, but with equally transparent intention, Richard appointed John Beaufort, now Earl of Somerset, to the office of Admiral [2] in 1397, while with the same object, in 1398, he confirmed and enlarged for John of Gaunt and his heirs male in perpetuity the powers which since the days of Edward III the Duke had held as Constable and Steward of the royal Palatinate—now Principality—of Chester.[3]

[1] Ob Ducis reverentiam et honorem. *Ann. Ric. II.* 226–7. Wals. ii. 228.

[2] *Rot. Parl.* iii. 343, 368.

[3] Letters Patent dated Holt Castle, August 8, 1398. *Record Report*, xxxi. App. p. 41. Cf. *Record Report*, xxix. App. p. 49 ,

From any explanation of these marks of royal favour one motive at least must be excluded. Richard had no sort of affection for the man at whose attempted assassination he had connived in 1384, and whose last trust he betrayed in 1399; he was willing, however, to pay the price, not an extravagant one, for the support of the Lancastrian party.

Sir John Fortescue, discoursing on "the perils that may come to the King by over mighty subjects," writes : "Certainly there may be no greater peril grow to a prince than to have a subject equipollent to himself, . . . and it may not be eschewed but that the great lords of the land by reason of new descents falling unto them, by reason also of marriages, purchases, and other titles, shall oftentimes grow up to be greater than they are now, and peradventure some of them to be of livelihood and power like a King, which shall be right good for the land while they aspire to none higher estate."[1]

And when the great Lancastrian jurist, who finds everything for the best in the history of the best of all possible dynasties, proceeds to add : "For such was the Duke of Lancaster that warred the King of Spain one of the mightiest Kings of Christendom in his own realm" —the opinion was one in which Richard II, with certain qualifications, might now have acquiesced.

Whether he would have classed the heir of Lancaster also with those who "aspire to none higher estate" is another question, but to one man assuredly the words could not apply—Thomas of Woodstock, Duke of Gloucester and Constable of England.

Time, instead of abating the King's resentment against

appointment by the Duke of Sir T. Sotheworth as his deputy, dated August 5, 1377, and also *Record Report*, xxxvi. App. (*Recognizance Rolls of Chester.*)

[1] *The Governance of England*, p. 130. Ed. C. Plummer, Oxford, 1885.

the authors of the commission of government, had accentuated his hatred, and during recent years Gloucester by his opposition to the King's French policy had added a count to the indictment already severe enough. Therefore Richard found it convenient to humour his uncle of Lancaster until he had avenged himself on his uncle of Gloucester; then, perhaps, time would help him to rid himself of his cousin of Derby.

The result was that John of Gaunt, in 1396–99, found himself once more, as in 1382–6, in a middle position. If he had failed to learn any sympathy for the constitutional party, and had not drawn any closer to the opposition, he was still as widely divided as ever from the real Court party; he stood opposed to the King's upstart favourites, Bussy, Bagot, and Grene, in the nineties, as he had stood opposed to Robert de Vere, who had steered the King's party to shipwreck in the eighties, for while prepared to go a long way in supporting his nephew, the Duke would not go the whole course.

The first step, indeed, was easy and agreeable. All the preliminaries had now been concluded for the marriage of Richard II and Isabella of France, and with feelings of unmixed satisfaction Lancaster left England, in October, 1396, to arrange the formalities of that meeting [1] between the two Kings which was to inaugurate a new period of peace, and unite the Houses of Valois and Plantagenet by the bonds of a blood alliance.

According to a doubtful though possible tradition reported by Froissart,[2] the Duke, fourteen years earlier, had proposed the hand of Philippa for his nephew; fortune, however, had ruled that the name of the eldest daughter of Lancaster should be associated with the brilliant sunrise of the new Portuguese dynasty rather

---

[1] *Mon. Eve,* 128–9; *Relig. St. Denys,* ii. 450–475.
[2] Froissart, K. de L. ix. 212.

than the fast fading light of the Plantagenets. So far as could be forecast in 1396, no alliance could have been better fitted than that now proposed to secure an effective result for the Lancastrian policy.

There was, indeed, every excuse for believing in the definite and permanent triumph of that policy, as expressed in the Articles of the twenty-eight years' truce, when at the end of October John of Gaunt, after finding himself the honoured guest of Charles VI, and watching the new Duchess of Lancaster do the honours of England to the French Court, accompanied the two Kings on Friday, October 26, from their meeting-place between Guines and Ardres to a spot not fifty miles from Crécy, or thirty from Agincourt, where they vowed to build conjointly a chapel to " Our Lady of Peace," and when in the evening of the same day he saw Richard receive Isabella from the hands of her father, thanking him for " so gracious and honourable a gift " ; when, too, in the Church of St. Nicholas at Calais, on Saturday, November 4, the Archbishop of Canterbury married the King of England to the daughter of his hereditary adversary, the war party appeared to have no alternative but to acquiesce in complete political defeat, and the Duke might view with legitimate satisfaction the results of his diplomacy upon the Great Powers, Portugal, Castile, France, and England, their differences laid aside, and their dynasties united by common kinship with the House of Lancaster.

Yet, in fact, nothing could be more illusory than the hopes built upon the French marriage. It failed to perpetuate peace between the two countries ; it failed inevitably to settle the question of the succession ; and in relation to home affairs, it served not to inaugurate a golden age of peace, but to mark the beginning of a fatal period of disorder and misgovernment.

The few short years of the King's constitutional rule

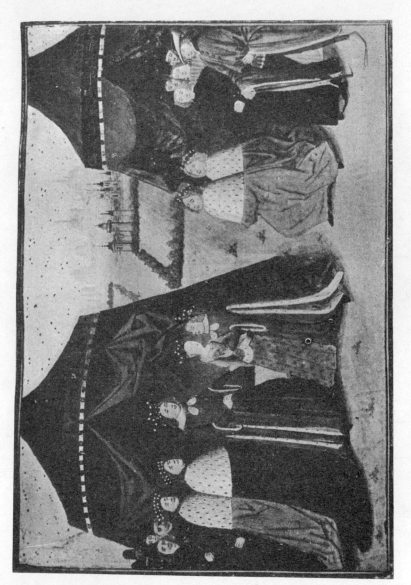

Richard II. receives Isabella of France from Charles VI.

lay behind : before him the attempt at absolutism and its disastrous failure.

Perhaps, as has been suggested, the extravagant pomp and meaningless ceremonial with which Charles VI surrounded himself may have inspired Richard with the hope of transplanting to English soil the growth of continental despotism ; if so, the example was no less lamentable than its imitation was calamitous. It was always easy to flatter the King's vanity, and now his ambition was excited by the prospect of succeeding Wenceslaus of Bohemia on the Imperial throne. Everything conspired to bring upon him " judicial blindness," the pride which goes before destruction. Reckless extravagance involved him in debt, and to meet debt his only expedient was to levy oppressive and iniquitous forced loans, unsound finance proving, as usual, a precipitating cause of revolution. The King, too, forgetting the lesson which the moral Gower would teach, that the only security of princes lies in the affection of their subjects, chose to surround himself with a bodyguard of Cheshire archers, and the royal progresses were followed by the curses of the people oppressed and pillaged by these lawless pretorians.

The causes of discontent were various, nor was it difficult for the Duke of Gloucester to exploit them to their full political value. Brest and Cherbourg were to be restored to Brittany and Navarre, the logical corollary of the peace ; but what more easy than to represent such restoration as a treason to England, the folly of a spendthrift King squandering a royal patrimony ? The Duke of Lancaster was reported to have said that " Calais grieved more England and did more hurt thereto than profit for the great expenses about the keeping thereof." [1] Let the Duke, therefore, as the King's chief adviser and

[1] *An English Chronicle*, 1377–1461, p. 7 (*Ed.* J. S. Davies, Camden Soc. 1856).

the exponent of this glorious peace policy, explain to the faithful citizens of London why war taxation was to be continued in peace. The Duke attempted to do so, probably with less success than Froissart would have us believe.[1]

In the summer of 1397 the crisis came. Richard believed that he had discovered a treasonable plot in which the leaders were the Duke of Gloucester, the Earls of Arundel and Warwick, and the Abbot of Westminster [2] ; he believed, too, that the time was ripe for revenge, and with the cunning natural to the weakling and the craven, the King caressed with the hand that was ready to strike.

Arundel, whose brother had just been raised to the primacy, Warwick, and Gloucester were invited to a royal banquet. Warwick complied and found himself arrested ; Arundel hesitated to place himself in the King's power, but, relying on a treacherous promise of safety, surrendered; but Gloucester, urging the plea of ill health, a plea which was soon to prove invaluable to the King's designs, refused, and the most dangerous of the King's enemies was still at large. The situation required prompt and cautious action, and Richard showed himself able to deal with it. Of late the Dukes of Lancaster and York had taken no active part in affairs. Lancaster, it is true, could be counted upon to support the King against the party of Arundel, just as in the Haxey Case he had shown himself ready to act as the spokesman of the prerogative cause against Parliamentary criticism.[3] He was aware, too, of Gloucester's attitude, and was opposed to his whole policy, but declined to regard it as a serious menace to the peace of the realm. But the Duke would certainly discriminate between Gloucester and Arundel : he might

---

[1] Froissart, K. de L. xvi. 9–12.
[2] Froissart, xvi. 1–29 ; 71–79. *Ann. Ric. II*, 201–2. Wals. ii. 223–6. *Eulog.* 371–6. *Mon. Eve*, 129–30.
[3] *Rot. Parl.* iii. 339a.

acquiesce in a condemnation of his old political enemy ; he would never sacrifice his brother to his nephew's hatred. Therefore Gloucester must be got out of the way and dealt with alone. So reasoned the King as on the night of July 8 he rode from London to Pleshey with the two Hollands, Rutland his cousin, and Nottingham, and a force of armed men. Gloucester, taken by surprise, was seized without difficulty ; a ship was lying ready in the Thames, and the Earl of Nottingham conveyed his prisoner forthwith to Calais.

The proclamation notifying the arrest declared that new treasons had been discovered in the prisoners, and that they had not been arrested for their share in the events of 1387 ; but the promise that these new treasons should be investigated in the forthcoming Parliament was never kept : before the session began Gloucester was dead, and to charge the prisoners with complicity in the newly discovered conspiracy (which was probably a fact) would not help men to believe that its instigator had died a natural death. Though the secret of Gloucester's end was well kept at the time, it is easy enough to read now, and history, however unwillingly, must now accept it as a fact that when Parliament opened Richard II and his instrument, Thomas Mowbray, Earl of Nottingham, had the blood of a murdered man upon their hands.[1]

The great difficulty thus surmounted, the King found no obstacle in the path of his vengeance : indeed, the obsequiousness of the Parliament which began to sit at Westminster on Monday; September 17, might have been forecast from the first day's proceedings, for an opening address taking the form of a sermon on the prerogative, and the choice of Sir John Bussy, the King's minion, as Speaker, augured well for Richard's designs. The principal

[1] This has been placed beyond any reasonable doubt by Mr. Tait in his essay, *Did Richard II murder the Duke of Gloucester ?* (Owens College Historical Essays, No. vii. London, 1902.)

victims were Gloucester, Warwick, Arundel, and Arundel's brother, the primate. In answer to the summons to produce the Duke of Gloucester for trial, the Captain of Calais certified his death, but sentence was passed nevertheless, and Thomas of Woodstock was attainted as guilty of treason. The primate was impeached and soon after suffered the penalty of banishment. The greatest interest, however, centred round the trial of Richard, Earl of Arundel. Had the verdict been a matter of doubt, Arundel's attitude to the prosecution would have been foolhardy ; but knowing himself a doomed man, he preferred to answer interrogations with insult and to defy his enemies, rather than to defend himself. It was useless to plead the royal pardon condoning his action in 1387, for the first act of the session had been to revoke the pardons. "Traitor," said the Duke of Lancaster, presiding in his capacity as Seneschal, "that pardon is recalled." Arundel gave the Duke the lie. "Truly thou liest ! Never was I traitor ! " "Wherefore then didst thou get the pardon ? " asked Lancaster, to which Arundel answered, "To close the mouths of mine enemies, of whom thou art one. And in truth as for treasons, thou needest pardon more than I." [1]

Then by the mouth of the Duke of Lancaster the House passed the terrible sentence sanctioned by English law for the crime of treason, a crime now for the first time clearly defined : "Richard, I, Seneschal of England, do adjudge thee traitor, and I do by sentence and judgment condemn thee to be drawn, hanged, beheaded, and quartered, and thy lands entailed and unentailed to be forfeit." By the King's clemency the more barbarous details were omitted, but Arundel was hurried off to execution the same day, and at length, after ten years, the blood of the murdered Simon Burley was avenged.

A less rigorous punishment was meted out to the

[1] *Adam of Usk*, 118.

THE LANCASTRIAN PARTY

Earl of Warwick. Throwing himself on the King's mercy and getting the Earl of Salisbury to plead on his behalf, he escaped with his life, and a sentence of perpetual imprisonment.

So ended the King's vengeance ; such was the answer to the " Merciless " Parliament. The initiative in all this had come from Richard himself, but no party had ventured to oppose. The Lancastrian party, like the rest, had acquiesced ; the Earl of Derby had taken a prominent part in the attack upon Arundel ; Sir Thomas Percy, who since the invasion of Castile must be reckoned as a Lancastrian partisan, had sat at the trial as proctor for clergy, and John Beaufort had figured amongst the appellants ; while the Duke himself had presided at the trial as Seneschal of England.

This support did not go unrewarded. Though the bulk of the honours conferred by Richard to signalize his triumph went to his own personal adherents—the two Hollands and Rutland, who became Dukes of Surrey, Exeter and Aumâle, William le Scrope, who became Earl of Wiltshire, and the Earl of Nottingham, who received the Dukedom of Norfolk as the price of blood—the Duke's party had their share. Two of Lancaster's sons were advanced in the peerage, the Earl of Derby being created Duke of Hereford, and John Beaufort, Earl of Somerset, being made Marquess of Dorset ; the Earldom of Worcester rewarded Sir Thomas Percy, and Lord Neville of Raby, the husband of Joan Beaufort, was created Earl of Westmorland.

With this, Parliament, after a fortnight's session, was adjourned to meet at Shrewsbury on January 28.[1]

This is not the place to tell the story of the strange session in which the great national assembly abdicated in four days the powers which it had taken a century of statesmanship to build up ; or to describe the fatal sub-

[1] *Rot. Parl.* iii. 356–73.

servience of the Parliament which, by voting the King a subsidy for life, placed the royal power beyond their control, and by delegating its powers to a Committee of members struck at the root of representative government; or again to decide whether this consummation was achieved by sudden impulse or deliberate calculation. So far as John of Gaunt is concerned these problems, fascinating as they are, demand no answer. It is true that the name of the Duke, like that of York his brother, Dorset his son, and Worcester his intimate friend, stands on the roll of the Committee of Members to exercise the powers of Parliament, but no more can be argued from this fact than from his titular presidency over the trial of the previous year. Slowly but surely the personal influence of the great Duke of Lancaster had been waning: he is still to be found on the field where the forces of rival political principles and personal ambitions meet in conflict, but he is no longer in the thick of the fight; the hardest blows are dealt by younger arms, and it is by other combatants that the vital issues are decided.

Already the Lancastrian party, though faithful to their old leader, were beginning to group themselves around another, and it is that other—Henry of Bolingbroke, now by the King's grace and favour Duke of Hereford —who henceforth is the real centre of interest in political history.

It was in December, 1397, after the King's revenge, that, while the new Dukes of Hereford and Norfolk were riding side by side between Brentford and London, the conversation took place which from its results has ever been memorable in the dynastic history of England.

What Norfolk's real words and intentions were will never now be known; but according to the version which Henry repeated to Lancaster and Lancaster, as one chronicler has it, to the King, the version which was laid

THE QUARREL OF THE DUKES OF HEREFORD AND NORFOLK.

officially before Parliament, Mowbray talked wildly of
a plot hatched by the King's friends against Lancaster,
Hereford, and himself, declared that Richard could not
be trusted on his oath, and asked Hereford for counsel.[1]

An anti-Lancastrian plot was scarcely enough to alarm
a tried soldier and man of affairs like Henry of Bolingbroke, but Norfolk's words gave him the chance of
picking a quarrel with the man who had murdered his
uncle, and he took it, formally impeaching the Duke of
Norfolk of treason before the Shrewsbury Parliament.

On February 23, at Oswestry, appellant and defendant appeared before the King, and again at Bristol
on March 19, when the cause was referred to a Court of
Chivalry which sat at Windsor on April 28 and 29. It
was with evident reluctance that, after repeated efforts
to reconcile the Dukes had failed, the King appointed a
day for trial by combat. The place chosen was Coventry ; the day September 16, the very day when by
popular tradition Gloucester had been murdered the year
before ; but the duel which would prove either the King's
cousin or his friend and kinsman traitor was not to be
held. Trial by battle would, it is true, rid him either
of the man who knew his secret or of the man whose
power and popularity he feared and hated : better to be
rid of both together. So at least Richard thought, and
when the lists were prepared and the champions had
taken their places, and at the signal Hereford had started
to charge his enemy, he threw his warder down and
stopped the duel.

Like all Richard's acts, his sentence on the Dukes of
Hereford and Norfolk is a puzzle. Hereford's was the
popular cause, and Hereford too was a tried fighter and
a skilful lance. No pains had been spared to win over
Thomas Mowbray to the Court party, and Mowbray had
proved his devotion. Why therefore the disproportion-

---

[1] *Rot. Parl.* iii. 382.

ate sentences, ten years' exile for Hereford, and for Norfolk banishment for life ?

If the ten years were, at Lancaster's entreaty, reduced to six, the difference was immaterial: in less than six years John of Gaunt would be dead and the King would be free.

Whatever its motive, the sentence was obeyed : Norfolk left England to die within a year at Venice ; Hereford, with the tears and regrets of half England, was compelled to betake himself, as Lancaster also had done in 1381, to the hospitality of a foreign Court.[1]

The results of the sentence passed on Hereford, and of the last fatal act of injustice which followed it, concern the larger issues of the history of England, for in truth they decided the fate of Richard and of his dynasty, and when in the lists at Coventry

> The King did throw his warder down,
> His own life hung upon the staff he threw ;
> Then threw he down himself.

The effect of the decision upon John of Gaunt might easily have been foretold. In 1397 the Duke's long and adventurous career was crowned with prosperity. His policy had triumphed at home and abroad ; he had placed his daughters upon the thrones of Castile and Portugal ; he had ended the French War ; he had won his nephew from suspicion to confidence, and the Crown leaned on his support and that of his sons. All at once the keystone of the arch had been destroyed, and the stately fabric of the Lancastrian power was shaken to its foundations. All that the Duke had lived for seemed lost ; the strongest instinct of the man, his attachment to those of his own blood, had received an irreparable injury ; the sentence of exile to the son was a sentence

---

[1] *Chronicque de la Traïson et Mort*, 11–23 ; Wals. ii. 227–8 ; *Eulog.* 379. *Ann. Ric. II*, 225–6. Froissart, K. de L. xvi. 89–116. *Rot. Parl.* iii. 382–385. *Mon. Eve*, 146 ; *Relig. de St. Denys*, ii. 673.

THE BANISHMENT OF THE DUKES OF HEREFORD AND NORFOLK.

of death to the father. John of Gaunt had outlived most of his contemporaries ; his sixty-eight years represented a much fuller measure of life than was accorded to most men of the fourteenth century. For some time he had felt his strength failing, and it was this feeling, perhaps, which led him on February 2 to make his will. In this testament, by far the most elaborate of the documents of its kind which have come down to us from the Middle Ages, the feelings of the Duke as he looked back upon his long life, his regrets, his hopes and his fears, are clearly reflected.

Not only does he display an evident reluctance to part with the great possessions which it had been the work of a lifetime to amass, but his minute and elaborate dispositions, his cautious and laboured repetitions and safeguards, betray an ill-concealed solicitude—the fear that, after all, his last wishes may not be respected. As though he could foresee the act of confiscation which was to convert Henry of Bolingbroke from an injured subject to a usurping King, he shows himself anxious to conciliate his nephew. Even greater, however, is his anxiety to propitiate the powers of the other world, for the Duke, though among those who set great store by corruptible things, does not forget, at least, after the manner of the age, to lay up treasure in heaven.

Hence, before all mention of the great inheritance which, the Duke fondly hoped, would pass by the common law of England to the *droits heirs de Lancastre*, before all provision for his family, absent and present, wife, sons, daughters, and grandsons, precedence is given to the claims of religion and the needs of the Church.

How characteristic of the feeling of the age is the quaint symbolism of the ceremonial prescribed by the testator for his exequies—the ten tapers standing for the ten commandments which he has broken, seven for the seven works of charity which he has neglected, and the

seven deadly sins which lie upon his conscience, five
again in honour of the five principal wounds of Christ,
and the five senses which, like an unprofitable servant,
he has spent to no purpose, and finally the three tapers in
honour of the Blessed Trinity !

And how would Wycliffe, with his Puritanism, his
intellectual detachment from the foibles and super-
stitions of the age, have scorned these poor attempts to
pacify the offended powers of righteousness ; how would
he have condemned the " blabbering with the lips " of
those chantry priests who were to sing masses continually
for the souls of the Duke and his wives, as though men
could buy with money the merits of the saints, and
barter the things of this world for the inestimable gifts
of the Spirit !

But the Church, especially the " religious," must have
found convincing proof, if any further proof were needed,
of that type of devotion which they prized most highly,
in the Duke's bequests to ecclesiastical societies—to St.
Paul's, the monasteries of Bury St. Edmunds and Lincoln,
and to the favourite Lancastrian foundation of Leicester.
Among the friars, no order of whom is forgotten, the
Carmelites as usual are singled out for especial favour ;
hermit, lazar, and prisoner all find a place in his thoughts ;
and when all bequests, public and private, are made, the
Duke's soul becomes the residuary legatee.

Then, a month after his will was sealed, the Duke
carried out his last commission. While the quarrel of
Hereford and Norfolk was still pending, the Duke, true
to the policy which he had formulated nearly twenty
years before, went for the last time, at the request of the
Scottish King, to hold a March Day and to appoint the
Deputies for the Marches.[1]

[1] The meeting had been arranged in October,'1397 (*Foed*, VIII.
17). Lancaster's commission is dated February 5, 1398 (ibid.
32–3) ; the negotiations took place at Hawdenstank, March 11 to

LANCASTER'S DEATH

After that he took no further part in public affairs : the last mission of the enemy of the " Good " Parliament had been one of peace.

Alarming reports of Lancaster's health were brought back to Hereford in Paris by Sir John Dymmok, and these, perhaps, as much as his father's advice, restrained him from taking part in the more ambitious military adventures to which he was being tempted.[1] Nor were these reports exaggerated. The Duke fell into an illness that could only have one end. In December he had reached his favourite castle of Leicester ; he was not to leave it again alive.

The quaint words of a Scottish chronicle describe the last moments of the great Duke : how as he lay worn out by heaviness of age and of heart he was visited by the King—

> Nevyrtheless upon a day,
> In til his sekeness quhen he lay,
> The King com til hym bodely
> And til hym spake rycht curtasly,
> And gaive hym consale of dysporte,
> Wytht plesaund wordis of confort,
> Nevyrtheless he gert be layd
> Upon his bed, as sum men said,
> Prevé billis : thare tenoure
> Amesyt na thing his langoure.[2]

The only " privy bills " capable of bringing consolation would have been letters recalling Henry of Bolingbroke, and that course the King's jealousy and fear forbade.

Exactly a year after making his will John of Gaunt breathed his last at Leicester Castle.[3]

16, 1398 (ibid. 35–6), and the Duke's acts were confirmed by the King September 22 (ibid. 45). *Cronykil of Scotland*, Ch. xviii. ; *Cal. Scot. Doc.* iv. 493.   See letter dated Melrose, March 17, *Record Report*, xxxi. App. li.

[1] Froissart, K. de L. xvi. 131–2 ; 136–7.
[2] *Cronykil of Scotland*, Ch. xix. p. 68–9.
[3] De gravi languore moritur, *Eulog.* 381. See App. VIII. p. 463.

JOHN OF GAUNT

In accordance with his wishes, his body was carried to the Carmelites in Fleet Street, to remain there until the day of burial. As the procession passed from Leicester to London, the body of the Duke rested for one night, as thirty years before the body of the Duchess Blanche[1] had rested, at St. Albans, where Henry Beaufort, now Bishop of Lincoln, celebrated a requiem for the dead. With a strange and unseemly persistence the enmities which had beset the living man followed his body to the grave. The Abbey of St. Albans lay within the diocese of Lincoln but outside the jurisdiction of the Bishop, and it required all Bishop Beaufort's tact to calm the susceptibilities of the great Benedictine foundation.[2] History has a strange love of irony: the walls of St. Albans, within which the "Scandalous Chronicle" was written, were the last to offer their hospitality to the dead Duke.

John of Gaunt was buried, as he had desired, in St. Paul's Cathedral near the principal altar, by the side of Blanche the Duchess, and at the funeral all his peers were present, foremost among them the King, even then plotting how to slay the son, that the inheritance might be his.

At the end, then, of this story of a long life, a story reconstructed from material so ample and so various, let us stop to examine how far the problem of personality has been solved.

Doubtless the impression made by John Plantagenet upon the men of his age differed with the differences of individual temperament and predisposition. For safety,

---

If the Duke had died at Ely House, Holborn, as some of the chronicles state, it would not have been necessary for his body to pass through St. Albans on the way to Fleet Street. The true tradition has been preserved by Higden (viii. 506) and Otterbourne, 197. Cf. Froissart, K. de L. xvi. 137–141.

[1] *Ann. Ric. II*, 434.
[2] *Gest. Abb. Sc. Alb*, iii. 438, 274–7, 472–4.

as usual, a middle path must be chosen, midway between the grotesque caricature of the Monk of St. Albans and the uncritical encomium of Chandos Herald. Chaucer was already a friend when in the hour of mourning he spoke in that forest of dreamland with the " wonder wel-faringe knight " and found him

> so tretable
> Right wonder skilful and resonable.

With less of the prepossessions of friendship, Jean Froissart, who, if he was somewhat over-ready to put his trust in princes and to find merit in the great ones of the earth, still was a man of the world who knew men—Froissart styles him "sage et imaginatif," and forthwith the Duke takes his place with Sir Walter Manny, Lord Audeley, Sir John Chandos, King Edward and the Black Prince among the immortals of the chronicles.

Fernâo Lopes, preserving the tradition of the years 1386–7, draws the picture of a tall spare man, well knit and erect as a soldier should be, prematurely aged doubtless by constant action and much exposure, a man whose conversation was reserved and had something of what with an enemy would pass for haughtiness and with a friend for dignity.[1]

The men of the court and of the camp are agreed : from the cloister little help can be got ; not indeed from the Monk of St. Albans, who sees Lancaster playing Beelzebub to Wycliffe's Lucifer ; not from the Canon of Leicester, who sees in the " pious Duke " the model of piety, wisdom and virtue ; not from the compiler of *Wycliffe's Tares*, who with the same breath wherewith he curses Wycliffe blesses Wycliffe's patron, and finds in John of

---

[1] Este D. João, duque de Alencastro, era homem de bem feitos membros, comprido e direito, e não de tantas carnes como requeria a grandeza do seu corpo, e seria de edade de sessenta annos, de poucas cãs, segundo taes dias, e de boa palavra, não muito trigosa, misurado e de boas condições. (Fernão Lopes, V. lxxxix.)

JOHN OF GAUNT

Gaunt a pillar of Church and State ;[1] nor yet from Capgrave, the fifteenth-century Vicar of Bray, who, impartially sycophantic to York and Lancaster, hands down an attenuated tradition of wisdom and greatness.[2] A sympathetic judgment will adopt the criterion of the age : the age was one of chivalry. In the last days of Richard II, when humiliation and suffering had broken his spirit, shattered his highly strung nerves, and almost unhinged his mind, again and again the King repeated, with a passionate regret that seemed to strive to convince himself as well as his hearers, that he had never forfeited his knighthood. " *Je suis loyal chevalier et oncques ne forfiz chevalerie !* "[3]

The boast repeated by the murderer of Thomas of Woodstock might with more truth have been uttered by the Duke of Lancaster.

For he had remained true to the ethical standard of society as he knew it : he had been loyal to Edward III, to his brother the Black Prince, and, at what cost of personal pride has been seen, to his nephew Richard.

With loyalty goes courage, and here, to his courage and love of adventure and sport, Lancaster found a sympathetic echo in the hearts of his fellow subjects. A certain sturdy love of fair play too marked his character—witness the Monk of St. Albans himself. In 1380 Sir John Annesley fought a judicial duel with Thomas Katrington. The knight, husband of Elizabeth Chandos, daughter and heir of the great Sir John, had accused the squire of selling the Castle of St. Sauveur, part of Chandos' inheritance, to the French, a charge that dated from the day when Lord Latimer was impeached in the " Good " Par-

---

[1] Illustris princips (*Fasc. Ziz.* 3), nobilis dominus dux egregius et miles strenuus, sapiensque consiliarius Dux Lancastriae, Sacrae ecclesiae filius fidelis (ibid. 114).

[2] Prudentissimus vir et nobilissimus dominus. Cap. *De Illust. Hen.* 94.

[3] *Chronicque de la Traïson et Mort*, 76. Cf. 67 and 55.

liament. The Duke was strongly suspected of exercising undue influence in favour of Katrington.[1] But when on the day of the duel Katrington began to hang back and take exception to the conditions of battle which he had previously accepted, the Duke swore that unless he fought in accordance with the laws of arms he would have him hanged as a traitor. The result was an immediate revulsion of popular feeling, for, as the "Scandalous Chronicle" reluctantly admits, the decision was greeted with loud applause.[2] For the last time the testimony of this *advocatus diaboli* has been heard. *Redeat in infernum!*

In truth the Duke loved more to preside over the lists than the council, for he held the laws of chivalry more sacred than those of Parliament. Seven years after the Annesley-Katrington duel we find him presiding over another and less bloody encounter. It was in March, 1387, and the English and Portuguese forces were lying round Braganza on the eve of the great invasion. Suddenly a herald appeared bearing a challenge to Sir John Holland from Regnault de Roye, who six years earlier had fought William de Windsor when the Earl of Cambridge was in Portugal.

Lancaster at once granted a safe conduct for Sir Regnault and his escort,[3] and set his carpenters to work to put up lists, and a platform for the ladies to view the spectacle.

The encounter proved indecisive, but the French knight, by wearing his helmet loosely laced, won some advantage, for Holland, though he struck his aim each time, could

---

[1] Here it may be remarked that Lancaster, doubtless out of gratitude to Sir John Chandos, had exempted the lands of Elizabeth Chandos from payment of an aid. Warrant dated March 23, 46 Edward III. Reg. I. f. 145.

[2] Quo facto dux multorum sibi conciliavit gratiam, et partem infamiae suae antiquae detersit. *Chr. Angl.* 263.

[3] Reg. II. f. 152.

not unhorse his opponent. Murmurs from the onlookers greeted Regnault's ruse, but Lancaster turned a deaf ear to their complaints.

So long as a combatant did not break the laws of arms, he was free to take what advantage he could, and the Duke was loud in his praises of the Frenchman's skill.[1]

But when a knight sinned against the commandments of chivalry and struck a foul blow, the Duke's anger was at once roused. This happened at Bordeaux in 1389, when an Anglo-Gascon killed the horse of a French knight with whom he was jousting, and Froissart, who had ridden all the way from Orthez to see the tournament, remembers Lancaster's indignation, recording how he compelled compensation to be made.[2]

The love of seeing or hearing of "*grandes appertises d'armes*," indeed, was one of the many points of sympathy between Lancaster and the historian of chivalry, and the pages of the chronicles furnish many an example. How the Duke must have envied those soldiers of fortune who led the few hundreds of English soldiers at Aljubarrota ! Though absent himself from the great battle, the Duke learns all about it from the Portuguese envoys. Lourenço Annes Fogaça speaks French fluently, and finds in his host a ready listener. He talks, it is true, at unconscionable length, but the Duke will not let him stop. "I will not let you go," says the Duke, if Froissart is to be trusted, "until you have told me all the story : *car je oy moult voulentiers parler d'armes quoyque je ne soie pas bon chevallier*,"[3] a fine touch of knightly modesty in the mouth of the man who had fought hand to hand with Jean de Villemur at Limoges, who, on the day when the two vawards were facing each other at Najera, said to Sir William Beauchamp : "*Guillaume, velà nos ennemis ; mès, foy que*

---

[1] Froissart, K. de L. xii. 115-124.
[2] Froissart, K. de L. xiii. 301-2.   Cf. Kn. II. 204.
[3] Froissart, K. de L. xi. 318.

je doi à Dieu, vous me verès hui bon chevalier, ou je demorray en le place. Avant! avant bannière, ou nom de Dieu et de Saint George, et face chacuns son devoir." [1]

If Chaucer had not shared the patronage of John of Gaunt with Wycliffe, how different the reputation of the patron might have been! Against the *odium theologicum* has been set the love of letters, and in some measure at least protection of the poet has atoned for protection of the heresiarch; for though the sins of John of Gaunt have been visited upon the name he left behind him far beyond the third or fourth generation, yet posterity has never forgotten the debt owed by Chaucer and English literature to the Duke of Lancaster. In this the Duke has got no more than his due; he was no indiscriminate patron, and if he knew when to give, he knew also when to withhold.

Among those who wrote about the Spanish campaign of 1367 there was one Walter of Peterborough, a monk of Revesby Abbey in Lincolnshire, a foundation not unknown to Lancastrian bounty. Walter wrote a poem on the expedition,[2] with a fulsome dedication to the Duke, an affected piece of doggerel in quite the worst style of the age. Knowing the Duke's treasurer, the author hoped that the merits of his effusion backed by influence might win him a suitable reward either in the Church or in the ducal household. He was disappointed. John of Gaunt, as it seemed, preferred the style of the *Canterbury Tales*, and the author went away empty-handed to regret

---

[1] Froissart, K. de L. vii. 200, who is repeating Chandos Heralds' words—

> Veiez, fist-il, nos enemys;
> Mais, si m'aïde Jesus Cris,
> Huy me verrez bon chivaler,
> Si mort ne me fait encombrer.
>
> (3195–8.)

[2] *Political Poems and Songs*, vol. i. 97–122.

his lost labour and his folly in casting pearls before swine ![1]

A feeling for the value of learning and literature might have been expected to show itself in a liberal support of the Universities. One college at least counted John of Gaunt as a patron—Corpus Christi at Cambridge—and in the troubles of 1381 looked to him for protection.[2]

The Duke was not insensible of the value of academic life, for he maintained several " clerks " at the University, and both Henry Beaufort[3] and the Duke's grandson, Henry V, resided at Queen's College without any fear of contamination from a lingering Lollard tradition in the college where a generation earlier Wycliffe himself had lived.

The Duke too frequently presented petitions to the Papal court on behalf of individual scholars of Oxford and Cambridge ;[4] but on the whole the evidence of a strong interest in the life and work of the Universities is conspicuously small. In the middle of the fourteenth century the collegiate idea was still young at the Univer-

---

[1] Sed margarita nunquam fuit ulla cupita
Porco plus placita stercora dentur ita.
Political Poems and Songs, vol. i. 97–122.

[2] There was a great " town and gown " row in 1381 : the Mayor raided the college and burnt some of its property, and the Master and scholars presented a petition for redress to the Parliament of May, 1382. The college is there described as *de la patronage mon tres honoure Seigneur de Lancastre.* Rot. Parl. iii. 128–9. The draft petition has the word *fundacion* instead of *patronage* (Hist. MSS. Com. I. 65). Neither Duke Henry nor Duke John were, strictly speaking, benefactors, but they used their influence with the King in favour of the college, e.g. by procuring licences for alienation in mortmain, etc. Cf. Reg. II. f. 20, 71.

[3] There is an entry in the College Account, " xxx solidi pro vino Duci Lancastrie," on the occasion of one of the visits paid by the Duke to Henry Beaufort, and there are several references in the Receiver General's Accounts to wine sent to Oxford for "Master Henry Beaufort."

[4] e.g. on behalf of his clerk, John Chaterys, M.A., Warden of Clare Hall, Cambridge, for a benefice. (*Papal Petitions*, 529.)

sities, and John of Gaunt, instead of following the notable example of William of Wykeham, preferred to endow and support the more exclusively " religious " foundations, monasteries, friaries, collegiate churches, and chantries.[1]

The influence of that early humanism which was beginning to refine English society, conspicuous in the case of the gentle Philippa of Hainault, was even more strongly marked in the Lancastrian household. The tastes of the Duchess Constance have already been noticed ; the Duchess Blanche also was regarded as a patroness of letters, and Froissart offers her the homage of his verse, as he offered to her husband the more lasting fame of a place among the *preux chevaliers* of the *Chronicles*.[2]

Philippa of Lancaster inaugurates a new era at the Portuguese Court by the careful education of her children. While Prince Henry the Navigator is begining to lead his countrymen towards undiscovered lands, Joan Beaufort, to whom Hoccleve dedicates his verses, is reading the *Tale of Tristan, the Travels of Godfrey of Bouillon,* and the *Chronicles of Jerusalem,* and it is at least suggestive that, as has been remarked,[3] among the first ladies in England who learned to write, were those of the family of John of Gaunt, and that among his friends were men like Sir Thomas Percy, who, with all the cares and ambitions of statecraft and war, found time to appreciate the things of the mind and the gentler graces of life.[4]

Was it the insensible effect of these leanings towards humanism that softened the Duke's nature and saved him

---

[1] There are two interesting appointments in the Register : Henry Barton to be Master of the Grammar School at Higham Ferrers (I. f. 51) ; John Bradley to be Master of the Grammar School in the town of Crofton (I. f. 53).

[2] Froissart, K. de L. ii. 3.

[3] M. A. E. Wood, *Royal Letters*, p. 89.

[4] The Pope recognized Sir Thomas Percy's accomplishments by conferring on him the degree of B.C.L.

Q

from the brutality and cruelty common to the society of the age ? Certainly his record is extraordinarily free from acts of violence and oppression.

Life counted for little in the fourteenth century ; constantly risked in battle, it was lightly thrown away in the tournament. The innumerable pardons for homicide registered on the Patent Rolls show how easily men passed from a word to a blow, and how often their quarrels proved fatal. A man of power like John Holland could defy the law; but though the Duke of Lancaster, if any one, stood above the law, he used his vast power with a rare restraint.

Five times in ten years he was threatened with assassination. Putting aside the conspiracy of the Spaniards who tried to poison him at the close of the invasion of 1387,[1] there remain four distinct plots against the Duke's life hatched in England between 1384 and 1394. Robert de Vere's unsuccessful efforts in 1384 and 1385 have already been related ; the same intriguer must certainly have been responsible for the scheme planned a few years later to seize the Duke on his return from the Spanish expedition,[2] while it is probably that mysterious conspiracy of 1393 in which the Duke of Norfolk avowed his complicity before the Court of Chivalry at Windsor—

> For you, my noble Lord of Lancaster,
> The honourable father to my foe,
> Once did I lay an ambush for your life,
> A trespass that doth vex my grieved soul ;
> But ere I last received the sacrament
> I did confess it, and exactly begg'd
> Your grace's pardon, and I hope I had it.[3]

---

[1] Fernão Lopes, v. 177.

[2] Et outre ceo les ditz Mesfesours et Tretours ordeigneront qe bon espie serroit fait sur la arryvaille Monsr de Lancastre, et q'il serroit arestuz meintenant sur sa arryvaille. *Rot. Parl.* iii. 234a.

[3] *King Richard II.* Act. I. Scene 1. : *Chronicque de la Traïson et Mort*, 16–17. "Si est vray que jauoye mise une embusche pour tuer le duc de Lenclastre qui la est assiz, et est verite

Yet in these cases Lancaster made no attempt to follow
up the feud or to protect his life by destroying his enemies, and Knighton's praise is not undeserved when he
calls the " pious " Duke " Pacis amator et reformator."

Gloucester sent his political rivals to the scaffold ;
Richard himself took life for life, and when the time came
Henry of Bolingbroke punished rebellion with ruthless
severity ; but John of Gaunt shed no blood in his quarrels,
and the assemblies dominated by Lancastrian influence
have no parallel to offer to the deeds of the " Merciless "
Parliament.

Where the common people were concerned the Duke
was never vindictive. Towards the rebels of 1381 and
the insurgents of 1393 he acted with moderation. Northumberland and Arundel were compelled to sue the Duke's
pardon, but if honour exacted reparation from the strong,
pride demanded mercy for the weak, and the Duke was
proud.

Knighton tells an anecdote to illustrate this virtue of
clemency which he claims for his hero. Some servants
of the household once stole a large quantity of silver
vessels ; the Duke's officers caught them and wanted to
have them hanged. But Lancaster refused. Contenting
himself with making the culprits abjure the service of the
King and his family, he let them go, saying that no man
should lose his life on account of his chattels.[1] The Canon
of Leicester is a biassed witness, but his story does not
stand alone. The statute against " Backbiters " was
passed by the Duke's influence and for his own protection, but some of the first prosecutions under the new law
show that it was not administered with undue severity.
A certain clerk called Thomas Knapet, probably a religious

que monsr le ma pardonne et en a estee faicte bonne paix entre
luy et moy de quoy je len mercye." Probably the plot for which
Sir William Bagot was brought to book in 1399 belongs to the same
conspiracy. *Rot. Parl.*, iii 458a.

[1] Kn. ii. 149–150.

fanatic, was proved guilty of speaking " disrespectful and disorderly words of his puissant and most honourable lordship of Lancaster ;" but when he confessed and sued for pardon, the Duke sent one of his esquires to John Philipot the Mayor with a request that the man might be released.[1]

A personal sympathy with the poor and humble is not inconsistent with a reactionary political creed, and that John of Gaunt felt such sympathy there is ample evidence. The attempt to put a stop to " advancement by clergy," made by the Commons after their panic in 1381, found no support from the Duke, who was always ready to manumit a serf that he might take orders,[2] or to release him that he might go on a pilgrimage.

Simple unremembered acts of kindness and charity are vouched for by many a warrant under the Duke's privy seal, nor should posterity neglect the unrecorded testimony of the " poor lazars of Leicester," or the wretched prisoners of Newgate, who drank the wine and warmed themselves in winter at the fires provided for them by John of Gaunt.[3]

Six years before Henry of Bolingbroke was born a greyhaired knight of Queen Philippa was once entertaining her maids of honour at Berkhamstead with stories of ancient days. Froissart, young, eager and inquisitive, was there, and a generation later could recall the words then spoken.[4]

---

[1] *Memorials of London*, 425.

[2] Here is an instance.
Johan *etc* a touz *etc* Sachez que nous de notre grace especiale avons grantez congee a Andrew fitz Symond Grayne notre neif de Stepyng d'estre ordenez si bien as saintz ordres come as autres nient contreesteantz q'il est notre neif come avant est dit issint toutes voies que pur tout le temps q'il ne preigne mye les saintz ordres susditz q'il demure notre nief come reson demande. En tesmoignance *etc*. Donne a notre manoir la Savoye le vi jour de May l'an *etc* tierz (Reg. II. f. 153*d*).

[3] e.g. Reg. I. f. 157*d* and 214*d*.

[4] Froissart, K. de L. xxi. 142–3 ; 235.

The knight was saying how, long ago in the mystic days of Merlin, it had been foretold that " the realm and crown of England shall come neither to Edward Prince of Wales, nor to the Duke of Clarence, nor to the Duke of Lancaster, sons though they be of King Edward, but the realm shall return to the House of Lancaster."

One half the ancient prophecy had been proved ; the other part was soon to have its fulfilment.

Suddenly, in the year in which Lancaster died and the King set out for Ireland, the bay trees withered throughout England, and as suddenly again put forth their leaf.   Was it not a prodigy, portending the reversal of unjust acts, the restoration of fallen fortunes ?

So at least it appeared to the men of that time, believing as they did that—

These signs forerun the death or fall of kings.

But John Plantagenet died before the full measure of his nephew's treachery had been made clear, or the full measure of his son's revenge.   But could those " juggling fiends who palter with us in a double sense " have revealed the future of John of Gaunt, as they revealed it to Macbeth and Banquo on the dreary heath, the wildest dream of ambition, the most eager desire for revenge, must have been satisfied.   Imagine the dying man in Leicester Castle.   The spirits of his children and their children yet unborn, kings of Portugal, kings of Castile, file before him.   As the long procession fades, another scene succeeds. In the Great Hall of Westminster the Lords spiritual and temporal and the Commons of England are gathered, and Henry, no longer Henry of Hereford, but Henry of Lancaster, Henry of England, is saying, " In the name of God, I Henry of Lancaster challenge this realm and this crown," and as the vision fades away the voice of Fate whispers in the ears of the dying man, " Thou shalt get kings though thou be none " !

Appendix I

TESTAMENT OF JOHN, DUKE OF LANCASTER

En noun de Dieu le pier, du filtz, et de seint espirit. Amen.

3 Feb. 1398.

Jeo Johan filtz du Roy d'Engleterre, Duc de Lancastr', en bone memoire le tierz jour de feverer, l'an du grace mil trois centz quatre vingtz dis et sept, ay fait mon testament par maner qu'ensuyt.

(i) To be buried in St. Paul's beside the Duchess Blanche.

En primes jeo devise m'alme a Dieu et a sa tresdouce miere Seinte Marie et a le joy du ciel, et mon corps a estre ensevelez en l'esglise cathedrale de Seint Poule de Londres, pres de l'autier principale de mesme l'esglise, juxte ma treschere jadys compaigne Blanch illeoq's enterre.

(ii) Exequies and burial.

It'm je devise parochiell ou qe jeo moerge tout ceo q' mes executours y voillent donner en noun de mon principall, quelle que par le ley y doit estre donnez pur mortuair ; et ce cas que jeo moerge hors de Loundres jeo voille et devise qe la prim' nuyt que mon dit corps serra apportez a Londres qe soit portez tut droit as frers Carmes en Fletstrete pur ycelle nuyt, y avoir les exequies, et lendemain la haut messe de requiem, apres quelle messe jeo voille soit mon corps removez et portez tut droit a la suisdet esglise de Seinte Poule, pur y avoir ycelle nuyt les exequies, et lendemain la haute messe de requiem et la sepultur' ; et en quelle lieu qe jeo moerg jeo voille et devise que apres mon trespassement mon corps demoerge desur la terre nemy enterez qe quarant jours, et doune en charge a mes executours qe dedeinz yceulx quarant jours nulle encerement de mon corps ne soit fait ne faynez privement n'en appert.

(iii) Alms to be given to the poor for forty days.

Item je voille et devise qe chescun jour des suisditz quarant jours soient pur m'alme donnez ad pov's gentz de pays cynquant marcs d'argent, et la veille de ma sepulture troiz centz marcs d'argent, et la jour de ma sepulture cynk centz marcs d'argent, s'il semble a mes executours qe ceo purra estre fait, considere la quantite de mes biens et autres mes ordinances et devys, les ditz somes ne purront de tout estre donnez as pov's com desuis, adonques mes executours a leur discrecion

420

facent donner as pov's chescune des ditz quarants jours
autielles sommes com faire purront le quantite de mes biens
et mes aultres ordinaunces et devys considere.

(iv) Tapers to be burnt.

Item jeo devise entier pur arde entour mon corps
le jour de ma sepulture primerement dis grossez
ciergez en noun des dis commandementz de n're

ten, in the name of the ten commandments.

seignour Dieu, countre les queux j'ay trop malement trespassez, suppliant a mesme n're seignour
Dieu que ceste ma devocion me puiss' remedier de
tuit cella q'encontre les ditz commandements ay

seven, in memory of the seven works of charity, and of the seven. deadly sins ;

multz sovent et trop malement fait et ferfait, et
qe desuis yceulx dis soient mys sept cierges grosses
en memoire des septz oevres de charite es queux
j'ay este negligent, et pur les septz mortielx
pecches, et desuis yceulx sept jeo voille qe soient
mys cink cierges grosses en l'onur des cink plaies

five in honour of the Five Wounds, and the five senses ;

principalx n're seignour Jesu, et pur mes cynk
scens lesquelx j'ay multz negligentment despendie,
dounte je prie a Dieu de mercy ; et tout amont
yceulx cierges jeo voille qe soient trois cierges en
l'onur de la benoit trinite a la quele jeo me rende

three in honour of the Trinity ;

de touts les malx qe fait ay, ensuppliant de pardon
et de mercy pur la mercy et pite q' de sa benigne
gracc il a fait pur la salvacion de moy et d'autres
peccheours. Et voille bien qe de parentre les
suisditz cierges soient mys entour mon corps
morters de cier tieulx et atentz come a mes ditz executours
plerra de y mettre.

(v) Prayers.

Item je voille qe mes executours facent prier
mes cosyns et amys d'estre a ma sepulture
pur prier pur m'alme, san ce faire de mon devys autre
solempnitie ne feste, si ceo ne soit as pov's gentz a prier Dieux
pur m'alme.

(vi) Payment of debts ;

Item je voille ordeigne et devise qe de l-es-
toutes mes biens et chateulx mes executors
apres ma mort devant lestoutes mes aultres
ordinances et devys facent paier lestoutes mes dettes qe le
jour de mon trespassement serront duz, savant qe si nulle
dettes lors serra demande la quelle pur negligence nounchalure
poverte au temps male talant ou autre defaut soit aderier
noun paie come reason demaunde, et purra par evidence ou par
bon' conscience estre trovee qe soit due, a demandant, qe mes
executours la facent paier si avant s'ils averont de quoi des

421

mes biens et chateulx, except toutz voiez qe je ne voille par nulle voie qu'ils paient ascune dettes pur l'arme en voiage qe mon tresame frere le Duc de Everwyk devant ore fist en Portugole, dount jeo me teigne de tut quites devant Dieu et tout la mounde, mes des toutes autres dettes jeo voille que resonable gree soit fait, et aussi voille et ordenne et devise q'si a asscune temps de ma vie j'ay ehu aucuns terres, ten'tz, rentz, services, ou or ou argent, ou autres biens moebles d'acune autre persone sanz juste et due title, ou a autre a fait tort ou injurie, combien qe de present ne cognoisse nulle en especiale meintenaines, si en temps avenir il puisse estre duement preuvez, mes executors facent plain restitucion et amend, si avant ils averont de quoy de mes biens et chateulx, des quelx facent ils aussi coustage convenables pur ma sepulture et entour mon corps del jour de mon trespassement, jusques au temps qe mon enterment serra acompliz, et auxi paient a mes servitours lours regardes per mon ordenns, et outre ceo q'mes executours pregnent de mes biens en leurs mains un tiel some convenable, de quelle ils purront faire et acompler toutz les chanteries et obitz en ceste mon testament ordennes pur m'alme et pur les almes des mes tres-cheris jadis compaignes Blanche et Constance qe Dieux assoille. Et depuis facent mes ditz executours acomplir mes devys desoubz expresses si averount com de mes biens et chateulx ils averont, de quoy issuit toutz voies q' si apres les coustages affaire entour mon corps apres ma mort et ma sepulture et enterement plainement accompliz et apres qe trestouts mes dettes serront paiez et restitucion faitz des torts et injuries com desous, et les regardes par moy ordennez de tout paies a mes serviteurs et pris et reservez es mains des executours la somme pur les chanteries et obits suisditz, mes biens et chateux lors remainantz es mains de mes executours ne suffisent my pur en acomplir mes devises desoubz expressez, qe de mes dites devys et de chescune de yceulx soit rebatement fait solom la descrecion de mes executours, exceptez toutz voiez les choses desobz limitez a mon tres sovereigne seignour le roy, les queulx jeo voille qe luy soient livrez come chose a luy donne en ma vie.

Item jeo devise a la suisdit aultier du Seynt Poule mon graunt lyt de drap d'ore, le champ piers poudres des roses d'or myses sur pipes d'or, et en chescun pipe

Margin notes:
(expedition of the Duke of York to Portugal 1381, excepted);

restitution;

(legacy to the King to be paid in full).

(vii) Gift to St. Paul's.

deux plums d'ostrich blankes, les curteines de taffeta piers batuz de sembleable ovrage, xiii. capits de tapiterie texes de la suite, et a mesme l'autier mon vestement de satyn blank embroudez d'ore, donc l'ovrage est un raille passant parmy corons d'or le quelle jeo achatay de Courtenay, broudier de Londres, et contient le vestement deux frontiers per l'autier, et un chescun frontiers trois grosses tabernacles d'ore, et grosses images d'or enbroudez en ycelle, un chesible, deux tunicles, iii. aubes, ii. estoles, iii. fanons, iii. copes, et un covertur pur le letton, un corpora, ii. courtins, ii. tonailles pur l'autier l'une aieant petit front ensemble, et mon entierre vestment de camaca noir fait a deserver pur messes de requiem enbroudez d'une crucifix d'or ovesq' les trois corporax et autres pieces a ycelle vestiment appurtenantz. Et voille toutz voiz qe trestouts cestes choses a le suisdit autier prin- cipall de Seint Pouls devisez ovecq' trestouts leurs appur- tenances demoergent a mesme l'autier a toutz jours pur ycelle autier a honuer, et entoure ma sepultur' sanz estre a nule autre oeps convertez, ne d'illoesques esloignez par nule voie. Et voille qe mes executours de mes biens facent purchacer en Londres, ou dehors la ou pluis profitablement ceo faire purront, atant de terre, ou de rent, appropriacion des esglises, ou aultres possessions donc ils me purront faire avoire pur m'alme et l'alme de ma dit nadgairs compaigne Blanch pur toutz jours en la suisdite esglise de Saint Poule

Two obits; one for him- self on the anniversary of his death. deux obite, cest assavoir, pur m'alme un obit solempnement a celebrer chescune an le jour de mon trespassement, et pur l'alme de ma dite nadgaires compaigne Blanch un obit solempne- ment a celebrer chescun an le xii. jour de septembr' a toutz

one for the Duchess Blanche to be celebrated September 12 yearly. jours, et aussi voille jeo, ordenne et devise que de mes biens et chateux mes executoures facent ordeignier et establer en l'avant dite esglise de Seint Poule, un chanterie des deux chapelleins a celebrer divines services en ycells a toutz jours pur m'alme et l'ame de ma dite nadgairs compaigne

Blanch, et que a ce sustenir perpetuelement soient donnez et amortizez certeinz terres et tenementz en Londres des queux la reversion est purchacez a mon oeps, reddant ent par an vint marcs a dame Katerine del Staple a terme de sa vie. Et voille que durant sa vie el en soit paie del issues de manoir de Bernolswyk en counte d'Everwyk des queux issues soit auxi sustenuz la dit chanterie durant la vie de dit Katerine.

APPENDIX

Item, pur estrem devocion, q j'ay a la monstier de Seint Esmon de Bury en counte Suff' jeo devise au dit monstier mon rych vestment de perill c'est assavoir, un chesible ovecq' les parures d'une aube et d'un amitte, un estole, et un fanon de rouge velvet enbroudez d'un frett d'or et en chescune un mascle de la frette un augnell de perill, et en chescun autre mascle un escochon de perill faite des armes de Seint George, et a cella un touaill ovecq' un petit frontier pur l'autier de velvet vert enbroude de perill, l'ovrage testes des xii. apostres ensemble, et l'une des deux pieces de drap pur un autier enbroudez d'or, quelux j'a achatez a Dameux faiz de n're seignour Dieu et de sa tresdouce miere Seinte Marie et des dusz apostres, et trestoutes mes draps d'armes texes d'or pur parcelles q' sont faiz de Dieu et de n're dame, except ceulx qui sount ailliours en mon testament devisez, et mon vestment rouge de drap d'or donc la champ satyn et l'ovrage angils d'or, ovecq' trestoutz parcelles et pieces qe a cele vestment appartiegnent, en paravant a l'abbe et covent de ycelle monstier, qu'ils pur cestes choses me facent avoir en ycelle monstier de Seint Esmond un obit perpetuele a tenir chescune an le jour de mon trespassement.

Item, je devise al monstier de n're dame de Nicol ma tierce chalice d'or fait a Burdeus qu'ad un crucifix grave desuis la pie et en la patens un vernicle grave, ma table d'or en ma chapell, la quell table jeo apelle Domesday achatez a Amien et mes plus grantez chandeleurs d'or faitz pur ma chapell, et mon novell vestment de drap d'or la champe rouge ovez des faucons d'or contenant dieux frontiers et ii. touailles pur l'autier, un chesible, deux tunicles, trois aubes, trois amyttes, ii. estoiles, iii. fanons, iii. copes et un drap pur le lettron, et ii. curteins pur l'autier raiez de soi et l'un piece pur un autier enbroudez d'or lequel je achetaz a Amienx faitz de n're seignour Dieu et de sa tresdouce miere Marie et des xii. apostres.

Item, jeo devise a le nouvell esglise collegialle de n're dame de Leycestre mon rouge vestment de velvet enbroudez de solailes d'or ovesq' trestout l'appareille a ycelle vestment appurtenante et a celle trestouts mes messalx et autres livres de ma chapell qe sont del use et ordinale de la esglise cathedrale de Sarum, et qe sont ne serrout aillours en ma vie devisez.

APPENDIX

(xi) Friars Carmelites. Item, jeo devise a l'autier principale des frers Carmes en Londre mon veille vestment blank de drap d'ore apelle Rakamas, ovecq' tout ceo qe a ycelle vestment appurtient ; a celle xv. marcs d'argent en l'onur des xv. joyes de n're dame.

(xii) Friars Preachers Minor, and Augustins. Item, jeo devise as trois autres ordres des frers en Londres, com as Precheours Minours et Augustins, a chescun ordre x. marcs, dont les v. marcs en l'onur des v. plaiez principalx de n're seignour J'hu, et les autres v. marcs en l'onur des v. joyes de notre dame.

(xiii) Minoresses. Item, jeo devise a convent de Minoresses pres la tour de Londres cent livres d'argent d'estre paie eutre eux.

(xiv) Hermits. Item, jeo devise a chescun pov'e heremite et recluse aiant maison en Londres ou dedeins v. lieues environ, en quel il demoert, trois nobles, en l'onur de la benoit trinite.

(xv) Nuns. Item, jeo devise a chescun des noneignes denis Londres et en les suburbs v. marcs, en l'onur des v. joies de n're dame, et a les noneignes de Clerkenwell, vint livres d'argent.

(xvi) Lazar Houses. Item jeo devise a chescun maison de lepres deins v. leues entour Loundres charges de v. malades, v. nobles, en l'onur de v. plaiz principalx de n're seignour J'hu, et a ceulx qe sont meniz charges troice nobles, en l'onur de la benoit trinite.

(xvii) Charterhouses. Item jeo devise a chescun maison de Charthous en Engleterre vint li'.

(xviii) Prisons. Item, jeo devise as prisons de Newgate et Ludgate en Loundres cent marcs, pur estre departe par entre eulx par mialtz manire come multz leur purra profiter solom la descrecion de mes executours.

(xix) Katharine, Duchess of Lancaster. Item jeo devise a mes trescheer compaigne Katerin deux meillor nouches qe j'ay apres le nouch qe j'ay devise a mon tresredoute seignour et nevu le Roy, et mon pluis grant hanap d'or lequelle le counte de Wyltes donna a Roy mon seignour, et il le donna a moy a mon alee en Guyen darreinement devant la date du cestes, ensemble ove toutz les hanaps d'or qu'ele mesme m'a donne devant ore, lesqueulx serront les meins le jour de mon trespassement, et ensemble ovecq' trestoutz les ferniculs, anelx, diamandes, rubies, et autre

425

choses qe serront trovez en un petit cofre de cypres qe j'ay,
donc jeo porte le clief mon mesmes ; et aussi q'apres ma mort
serront trovez en ma bource, le quel port mesmes desuz
moy ensemble, et mon vestment entier de drap d'or, la lite
et la sale de sa suyt, ovesq' trestoutz les copes, tapites pur
le chambre, cuissins, closet oreillers, drap enbroudes pur la
sepulcre et toutes autres pieces de la suyt, de qel condicion
en entaille qe soient, quels je achatay de ma treschere cousyn
la Duchesse de Northfolk aussi entierement sang riens eut
enbeseiller com jeo les avoy de ele, dont le champ rouge frette
d'un noir traille et en chescun place ou qe le frette se joynte
un rose d'or, en chescun un mascle de la frette un tielle lettre
ꝏ noir, en chescun autre mascle un leopard noir, et a cella
jeo devise mon grant lit de noir velvet enbroude d'un com-
passe de ferures, et gartiers, et un turturell en mylieu de les
compasses avecq' trestout les tapites et tapicerie et cuissins
a ycelle lit ov chambres appurtenantes et a cella jeo le
devise trestouts mes autres lits faitz pur mon corps,
appelles en Engleterre trussyng beddes, ove les tapites
et autres appurtenances, et mon meillour cerf ov le
bonne rubie, et mon meillour coler ovecq' touts les
diamandes ensemble, et mon second covertur d'ermyn, et
deux mes meillors mantils d'ermyn ovecq' les robes de la
suyt ; et a cella jeo devise a ma dit compaigne trestoutes les
biens et chateulx de quelconq' natur ou condicion qe soient,
les queles ele avoit devant les espousailles entre moy et ele
celebres, ovecq' trestoutz les aultres biens et joialx le queulx
jeo luy ay donne depuis les espousailles suisditz, et le quelx
biens et joialx sont en la garde de ma dite compaigne nient
expressez en l'inventoire de mes biens.

(xx) The King. Item jeo devise a ma tresredoute seigneur et
neveu le Roy le meillour nouche qe j'avois le jour
de mon trespassement, et le mein meillour hanap d'or coverez,
le quel moy donna ma treschere compaigne Katerin le jour
de l'an renoef darrein passez, et mon saler d'or ovecq' le
gartir, le coler overez, entour le saler un turturell assis
desuis le covercle, et a cella xii. draps d'or donc la champ
rouge satyn raye d'or, les quelx draps j'avoye ordenuz d'en
faire un lit, lequel n'est uncore comencez, et un covertur
d'ermyn le meillour qe j'ay ovecq' la coverchief de la
suyte ensembler, et la piece d'arras la quelle le Duc de
Burgoyn me donna a darrein qe jeo estoie a Calays devant
la date du cestes:

APPENDIX

(xxi) The Duke of York. Item jeo devise a ma trescher frere Duc d'Everwyk un hanap d'or coverez.

(xxii) The Duke of Hereford. Item jeo devise a mon treschere filtz Henry Duc de Herford, Counte de Derby, deux les meillours peces drap d'arras que jay outre ceulx qu'en especial j'ay en ccst mon testament, dount l'un me donna mon tresredoute seigneur et neveu le Roy, et mon tresame frere le Duc de Gloucestr', qui Dieux assoille, l'autre au temps qe je retourna darreinement d'Espaine devant la date du cestes, et mon grant lit de camaca eschette blank et rouge, enbroude d'un arbre d'or et un turturell assis desuis l'arbre ovecq' xiiii. tapitz de tapiterie, et a cella mon grant lit de draps d'or, le champ piers overez des arbres d'or, et juxte chescun arbre un alant blank liez a mesme l'arbre ovecq' la vestment de la suyt et toutes les tapitez de tapiterie faitz a ycell, et en outre jeo lui devise toutz les armures, espies, et dages, qe serront miens le jour de mon trespassement except ceulx q'aillos sount devisez ou donnez ; et plus outre jeo lui devise iiii. chargeors, deux duzein de escuilles et sis saucers d'argent, et a cela jeo lui devise un fermaile d'or del veile manere, et escriptz les nons de Dieu en chescun part d'ycelle fermaile, la quele ma treshonour dame et mier la reigne qe Dieu assoille me donna, en comandant qe jeo la gardasse ovecq' sa benison, et voille q'il la garde ovecq' la benison de Dieu et la mien.

(xxiii) Philippa, Queen of Portugal. Item jeo devise a ma treschere fille Phylypp' Roigne du Portugale mon second meillour cerf d'or et un hanap d'or coverez.

(xxiv) Katharine Queen of Castile and Leon. Item jeo devise a ma treschere fille Katerine Roigne de Chastill et de Lyon un hanap d'or coverez.

(xxv) Elizabeth, Duchess of Exeter. Item jeo devise a ma treschere fille Elizabeth Duchesse d'Excestre mon blank lit de soi overez des egles bloyes displaies, les curteins de taffeta blank batuz de la suyte, xiiii. tapitz de tapiterie, et mon meillour nouch qe j'ay apres ceulx qe sont devisez.

(xxvi) John, Marquess of Dorset. Item jeo devise a mon trescher filtz John Beaufort Marquis de Dorset deux douzein de escuilles et un douzein saucers, deux pottes demy galons d'argent pur le vin, un hanap d'argent endorrez, ii. bacins et ii eauers d'argent.

Item jeo devise a reverent pier en Dieu et mon tresame

427

APPENDIX

(xxvii) Henry, Bishop of Lincoln. filtz l'evesq' de Nicol un douzein des escuilles et douzein saucers, deux pottes d'argent de galons pur le vin, un hanap d'argent endorrez ovecq' un bacyn et i. eauer d'argent, et mon entier vestment de velvet jane ovesq' les choses appurtante au cell vestment, et a celle mon messale et mon portheus qe furent a mon seignour mon frere Prince de Gales qe Dieux assoille.

(xxviii) Thomas Beaufort. Item jeo devise a mon tres chere fitz Thomas Beaufort leur frere un douzein des escuilles et un douzain saucers, deux pottes d'argent demy galons pur le vin, et sis tasses d'argent.

(xxix) Joan, Countess of Westmorland. Item jeo devise a ma treschere fille leur seure Countesse de Westmorland et dame de Nevyll un lit de soy et un hanap d'or decovrez, ovecq' un eauer.

(xxx) Henry [V]
(xxxi) John [Duke of Bedford]. Item jeo devise a mon tres chere Henry fitz ayzn de mon tres chere filtz le duc de Herford, un hanap d'or. Et a mon tresame filtz John, frere du dit Henry, filtz de mon dit filtz, un hanap d'or.

(xxxii) Residuary legacies ; Item jeo voille et devise qe si apres costages affairs entour mon corps apres ma mort, et entour ma sepultur, et entierement plainement accomplez, et apres qe trestoutes mes dettes serront paiez et pleniere restutcion fait des tortes et injuries par moy et mes ministres a mon oeps faitz, et les coustages de mes executours en faisant execution du cest mon testament, et auxi mez servitors regardes et liveretz regardes a eaulx paiez, et la some gardee es mains des executours pur la fundacion des dites chanteries et obitz com desuis, adonques de les dettes qe lore me serront duz quant ils purront estre levez, soient par mes executurs

Bury St. Edmund's ;

Katharine Swynford ;

Henry, Duke of Hereford ;

John, Marquis of Dorset ;

Thomas Beaufort ;

Sir Thomas Swynford ;

Sir Walter Blount ;

Sir Hugh Shirley ;

Sir Richard Aburbury ;

Sir William Par ;

paiez a la suisdite monstier de Bury mil livres, et a ma suisdit compaigne Katerine deux mils livres, a mon dit filtz le Duc de Hereford mil livres, a mon dit filtz le Marquis mil livres, a mon dit filtz Thomas Beaufort mil marcs, a mon tres chere bachelier Mons'r Thomas Swynneford cent marcs, a Mons'r Waut' Blount, Mons'r Chamblayn cent marcs, a Mons'r Hugh Shireley cent marcs, a Mons'r Ric' Aburbury le fils cynquant marcs, a Mons'r Wyllyam Par cynquant marcs de mon

428

APPENDIX

devys, issint touz voiez que se atant ne puissent lors estre leues des dictes dettes residues, adonques de cest mon devys soit rebatement a chescun person de l'afferant par ordinances et discrecion de mes executours.

Item jeo voille, ordenne, et devise, qe de mes biens et chateulx mes executours facent ordenner et establer en la novel esglise de n're Dame de Leycestre un chanterie de deux chapelleins a celebrer divines services en ycell a toutz jours pour moy, et m'alme et l'alme de ma nadgaies tresame compaigne Dame Constances illeouques enterres, et pur tenir et faire tenir en la diste esglise un obit pur l'alme de ma dite nadgairs compaigne le xxiiii. jour de Mars annuelement as toutz jours.

(xxxiii) A chantry at St. Mary's, Leicester, for the soul of the Duke and of the Duchess Constance ; an obit for Duchess Constance on March 24 yearly.

Et qe a ceo faire et sustenir perpetuelement mes ditz executours par l'avys de gents de loy de mes biens facent sufficantment endower la susdite esglise pur le sustentacion de les chanteries et obits suisditz.

Item com ensi soit qe de l'annuite ou pension annuel de quarant mil frankes en la quell m'este tenuz mon tresame filtz le Roy de Chastiell et de Lion certens summes sont oncore a derier nient paiez, non especial ordenuz d'estre paiez a moy, ne a mes procures a mon oeps, si voille et devise qe de toutz ces tiells sommes par mon dit filtz einsi a moy duez nient paier, ne uncore ordenuz par especiale d'estre paiez a mon ocps, mon tres sovereigne le Roy ait le tierce dernier de ceo qe per son sovereigne aide en serra recouvrez par mes executours, et clerement restez oustre les coustages et expensez.

(xxxiv) Of the arrears of the tribute from Spain one-third to the King on recovery.

Item jeo devise voille et ordeigne imprimerement et principalement de trestouts mes biens et chateulx soient trestoutz mes dettes pleinement acquites, et les extorcions tortz et injuriez par moy et mes ministres a mon oeps faitz restorez et amendez solom la aescrecion de mes executours, et les coustages resonables entour mon corps del jour de mon trespassement jusques au temps que ma sepulture et les coustages de mon entierement serront accomplez, depuis de la residue de mes biens soient mes servitours regardez solom la discrecion de mes executours, et les suisdits mes legats accomplez et parformez par les dit mes executours

(xxxv) The residue (if any) to be expended for the profit of the Duke's soul.

429

si avant com ils averont de quoy de mes biens et chateux, et la residue de mes biens et chateulx si nulle y serra demorez, Jeo voille que par mes executours soit dispose pur m'alme le plus profitablement qu'ils en saveront devisez.

(xxxvi) Arrears of the tribute from Spain ; Item com de la somme des francqs del annuele pension des quarant mille francqs a moy et de clere memoir la suisdite Constance quant il viveit ma compaigne, fille et heir de clere memoir Petre jadys Roy de Castill et de Leon, a terme de vie et de la vie de la dicte Constance lors ma campaigne et de l'autre de nous survivant, grantes constitue et solempnement promys par le puissant Prince Johan jadys Roy de Castill et de Lyon et de Portugale par occasion d'anemys accordez transaccion et amicable composicion sur les drois de roialmes de Castill et de Leon, Tolete, Galicie, Sevile, Cordube, Murcy, Gienn, d'Algarve et Algiozire, et de les seignouriez de Lace, Biscayi et Molyne faitz parentre le dit Johan jadys Roy de Castill et de Leon et du Portugale et moy et Constance lors ma compaigne suisdite, si com pluis au plaine est contenuz en lettres et instrumentz obligatorys sur les traicties, composicions, et transaccions ent faitez, les quelux letres et instruments jeo voille icy avoir pur inserteez, plusours sommes des franqs a moy nottairement soient duz et remaignent nientz paiez, Jeo voille, ordenne et devise qe mes executours desoubz escriptz que les conq'z sommes des francs pur quelconq'z ans termes et temps aderier estieantz, en toutz lieus et en quelconcq' z lieu qe ce soit, demandent, exigent, et levent de quelconq'z persones et person de les queles les ditz sommes des francqs doient estre demandez exiges ou leves, par toutes voies, manere et forme meilliours qe purront yceulx mes executours, et leur serra avys qe serra pluis expedient de faire, solom tout force, fourme, et effect de les letres et instrumentz obligacions des quelx mencion est fait desuis ; et de cest mon testament et darrein volunte, a l'execution d'ycelles bien et loialement faire jeo face, ordeine et constitue les reverents

Executors ; piers en Dieu Richard Evesq' de Saresbure, Johan Evesq' de Wyrcestr' mes tres chere et tresames cousyn et compaignons Thomas Count de Wyrcestre, seneschale del houstell de mon tresredoute Seigneur le Roy, et Wyllyam Count de Wyltes, tresorer d'Engleterre, mon tresame filtz Rauf Count de Westmerland, Mons'r Waltier Blownt, Mons'r Johan Dabruggecourt, Mons'r Wyllyam Par, Mons'r Hugh War'ton, Mons'r Thomas Skelton, et Johan Cokeyn, chief seneschall de mes terres et possessions, Sir Rob't Qwytby mon attornee generall, Piers Melburn, Willyam Keteryng, Robert Haytfield, countrerollour de mon hostiell, Sir Johan Legburn mon receviour generall et Thomas Longley clerk, mes executours, donant a eux et a chescun d'eulx plein pouar et auctorite de trestoutz mes biens et chateulx administrer et de toute ceo faire executier qe as bons executours par quelconqe voie resonable et justifiable il appartient, premierement et en especiale par maniere com jeo lour a devyse desuis, et en autre com lour tres sage discrecion et bone conscience leyr purra sembler qe mieultz soit pur moy affaire et pur la service de Dieu et de sa tresdouce miere Marie, ayantz mes ditz executours de mes biens lour coustages resonables droit come par loure fait ils voillent respondre devant Dieu le haut jour de justice.

(xxxvii)   Item, pur ceo qe auscun foiz un des executours deputez al testatour qi mort est nient sachant, les autres executours, mes de tout ignorantz, pur son singuler profit recevant des grantez sommes dues a son testatour certein pur certie, et ascun foiz la meindre partie apliant et convertant a son propre oeps, ad remys la residue d'icelles sommes fraudelousment et contre bone conscience et graunt prejudice del testatour et de ses executours et en graunt peril d'alme de tiel fraudelens, et de mal ensample des plusours, pur ceo pur eschuir tiel fraude, voille jeo ordenne et despone et aussi charge mes dit executours qe nulle d'eux sans consaile, voulente consent auxi et assent expresse del greindre partie des ditz executours de ct sur grandes et grosses sommes de monnoyes, ne face acquittances generalles ne particuliers a nulz, ne aucun acquite delivre ou absolve : mes que mes ditz executours ne facent le contraire ; je a done et reserve toutes et quelconq' povoir en celle partie. Et pur survoier et faire veir q'ils ensi ferront jusques al complisement de ces mes darrenns voulontes jeo prie et a mon tres redoute seignour tres humblement jeo supplie come a mon Roy et sovereigne seignour terrien en qui devant touts autres jeo me pluis affice, qu'il de sa incomparable bontes et en accomplissement de ses graciousez promesses les qels de sa noble seignorie il m'a fait, en ceo case luy please me estre bon seigneur et du cest mon testament soverein surveoire et comandoir, que soit lesse ne changee ceo que jeo paramont ay devise ; et apres luy son treshonourable estat et honoure tout jour sauvez, jeo face surveoirs de mesme le fait mon trescher et tresentierement bien aime frere Esmon Duc d'Everwyk, mon trescher et tresentierement bien ame neveu Edward Duc d'Aumarle, le tres reverentz piers en Dieu Rog' erchevesque de Cantirbure, Ric' erchevesque d'Everwyk et le reverent pier en Dieu l'evesque de Nicole mon tresame filtz ; en priant a mes suisditz frere naturel et neveu, qui de reason et de nature me deussient estre pluis procheins amys, et as ditz tres reverents piers en Dieu et mon tresame filtz, com a mes peres espirituels qi de reson et d'esprituelte me deussent estre espirituelx amys, q'ils, ovesq' mon tres redoute seignor le Roy susdit, son honur toutzdis sauvez, me voillent estre bons surveoirs de mon dit testament, et s'il eu busoigne pur le meilliour de moy en comfort de mes executours suisdits, comandent et ordenent coadjutors, que pur necgligence, nonchalur, male talent, n'autre defaute, cestes mes dits volentes, ordennances, et darreins devys ne soient par voie de monde lessez, ne en autre manere que par dessous est escript changies, ne tournes, come ils voillent respondre devant luy qu'cest Roy de toutz roys, et ad le seurveue de toutz terriens faits et pensez pur quelx il rendre guerdon a chescun solom son desert. En foy et tesmoignance de trestouts cestes choses pur dessus escripts com a ceste mon testament j'ay fait mettre mon seale de mes armes, de quelle cele pur greindre conissanz et affirmance de mon propre fait j'ay mesme mys en le dorce mon signett quele je porte toutes jours mon mesmes, le jour et an suisditz, et les gentz desoub escriptz en ay requis de les tesmoigner, c'est assavoir mestre Johan Kynyngham doctour en theologie, Sir Johan Neuton parson de l'esglise de Burback, Sire Wautier Piers, person de l'esglise de Wymondham, Wyllyam Harpeden et Robert Symeon escuiers.

Subscripcio. Et ego Johannes de Bynbrok, presbyter, Lincoln' dioc' publicus apostolica et imperiale auctoritate notarius, una cum reverendis et discretis viris fratre Johanne Kyningham in theologia professore, D'no Johanne Newton rectore ecclesie paroch' de Burbach et Waltero Piers rectore ecclesie paroch' de Wymondham, et Willo Harpeden et Roberto Simeon armigeris, Norwyc' Lincoln' et Exon' dioc', Anno Domini, mense, et die supradict' indiccione septima pontificis sanctissimi in X'to patris et domini nostri domini Bonifacii divina providencia pape noni anno decimo, praesens interfui ubi et quando illustrissimus princeps et dominus Johannes filius Regis Angliae Lancastr' Dux supradict' in camera infra castrum suum Leycestr' situat dict' Lincoln'

APPENDIX

dioc', personaliter existens in manibus suit tenuit presentem dcripturam superscriptam, et ipsam in testim' superius sescriptos ad hoc specialiter vocatos et rogatos, et mei presencia palam et publice fatebatur et expresse dixit suum esse testamentum, ac suum protunc ultimam continere voluntatem, quam quidem scripturam sivi testamentum una cum quodam codicello eidem scripture inferius annexo voluit et vult juxta ipsorum tenorem et effectum fieri et compleri, eaque sicut praemittitur fieri vidi et audivi ac de mandato ejusdem principis ac ducis hic me subscribendo ac signum meum hic apponendo consuetum, in hanc publicam formam redegi rogatus et requisitus in fidem et testimonium praemissorum intertinear' illias diccionis *autres* super undecimam lineam, ac rasuras illius dictionis *ordre* in tricesima quarta linea et illarum dictionum (*et les coustages resonables entour mon corps del jour de mon trespassement jusques au temps de ma sepulture*) in sexagesima quarta linea, praesentis testamenti approbo, ego Johannes notarius antedictus.

CODICILLUS.

It'm, la ou jeo Johan filtz du roy d'Engleterre, Duc de Lancastre, ay purchacez et fait purchacer a mon oeps diversez seignouries, manoirs, terrez, tenements, rentes, services, possessions, et advoesons des benefices de seint esglise, ove lours appurtenances, des quelx devant les esposailles d'entre moi et ma tresame compaigne Katerine celebrees, jeo luy a fait doner aucunes parcelles a avoir a terme de sa vie, et d'aucunes parcelles j'ay fait enfeffer mon tresame filtz Johan Beaufort Marquis de Dorset a avoir a lui et a ses heirs de son corps issantz, solom la contenue des feffements sur ceo faitz, et d'aucunes autres parcelles sont de ma ordinance diversez personez enfeffez, au fyne qu'ilz doient as autres feoffement ou feoffements faire a ma volente, ordinance, et devys, quand ils serront achetez, et a ceo de par moy requis, si ay jeo fait faire ceste cedule annexe a yceste mon testa·ment contenante ma darreine et entier volente toucheant les suisditz seignouries, manoirs, terres, tenementz, rentes, services, possessions, reversions et advoesons, ove lour appurtenances, laquelle ma volunte jeo voille que soit a toutz convee et effectuelement accomplee en toutes pointz, des quelx jeo ne ferra autre ordenance en ma vie. Et est tiel ma ordenance et devys : Premierement jeo voille que toutz les seignoiries, manoirs, terres, tenementz, rentes, services,

433

possessions, reversions et advoesons, ove lour appurtenances, par manere que desuis purchases et com desus donnes et grantez a ma dite compaigne a avoir a terme de sa vie, remaignent a ele tuit entierement solonque l'effecte et purpous des douns et graunts a ele faitz, la reversion d'ycelles que de ma ordenance sont taillez per fyn ou autrement, toutz foiz remaignent a celuy ou a ceulx a qui ou as quelx ils sont taillez. Et que la reversion de toutes autres seignouries, manoirs, terres, tenementz, rentz, services, possessions, reversions, et avoesons, ove lours appurtenances, es quelx ma dite compaigne a estate a terme de sa vie, et lesquells ne sont de ma ordeignance taillez, soient donnez a mon trescher filz Thomas Beaufort frere du devant dit Johan, ensemble et avecque la reversion de toutz les seignouries, manoirs, terres, tenementz, rentz, services, possessions, reversions, et avoesons, ove leurs appurtenances, que furent a Edward de Kendale, laquele reversion j'ay fait purchacer de Dame Elizabeth Croiser, et les seignouries, manoirs, terres, tenementz, rentz, services, possessions, reversions, et avoesons, ove leurs appurtenances qe Dame Elizabeth Barry tient a terme de sa vie, a avoir au dit Thomas et a ses heirs de son corps issants; et pur defaut d'issue audit Thomas, la remeindre au dit Johan et a ses heirs de son corps issants; et pur defaut d'issue de dit Johan le remeindre a ma tresame fille Johane leur seur countesse de Westm'land et a ses heirs de son corps issant; et pur defaut d'issue de dit Johane la remeindre a mes drois heirs q'ils serront heirs et heritage de Lancastre.

Item, jeo voille que l'avant dit Johan Beaufort mon filtz ait a luy et a ses heirs de son corps issants toutes les seignouries, manoirs, terres, tenementz, rentz, services, possessions, reversions, et avoesons ove lour appurtenances que de ma ordinance luy sount donnez solom l'effect et purpoys de doun et grant a luy ent faiz.

Item jeo voille que les certeines terres et tenementz en la cyte de Londres a mon oeps nadgairs purchacez d'une Dame Katerine del Staple en rendant a ele vint marcs per an a terme de sa vie soient per le coungie de n're tressovereigne seignour le Roy donnez a un chanterie a estre fundie des deux chapelleins, a celebrer devines services en l'esglise cathedrale de Seint Poule du Londres pur les almes de moy et de ma trescheer nadgairs compaigne Blaunch, que Dieux assoille, quelle chanterie jeo voille que mes executours facent founder en meilliour manere des biens que serront les miens le jour de mon trespassement, si jeo ne face fonder et ordenier en ma vie.

Item jeo voille que mon trescher bachelier Mons Robert Nevill, Wyllyam Gascoigne, mes treschers esquiers Thomas de Radclyf and Wyllyam Kat'yng et mon trescher clerk Thomas de Langley, qui de ma ordenance sunt enfeffez en manoir de Bernolswyk en counte d'Everwyk, facent annuelement paier a mes executours pur outre a l'avant dit Dame Katerine del Staple les suisdites vint marcs par an a terme de sa vie, et outre ce facent les ditz enfeffez paier des issues suisditz a mes ditz executours autres vint marcs per an a estre per eulx outre paiez as deux chapelleins celebrantz divines services en la dit esglise cathedrale de Seint Poule pur m'alme et l'alme de ma dite jadis compaigne Blanch a un aultre jour le leu de n're sepulture tanq' a temps que serra illeoucq' fondue et endowe un chanterie perpetuele de deux chapelleins a celebrer divines services pur les almes de moy et de ma dite nadgairs compaigne Blanch. Et outre ceo paient les ditz enfeffez as dits executours autielle somme per an de laquele somme ils purront faire annuelement estre celebrees deux obitz en la dit esglise de Seint Poule, c'est assavoir un obit pur moy le jour de mon trespassement et un autre obit pur ma dit nadgairs compaigne Blaunch le douzisme jour de Septembre d'an en an, tanque au temps que terres, tenementz, rentz ou autre suffisant possessions soit donne et amortize pur la perpetuelement sustenacion des ditz obitz. Et voille que la residue des ditz issues soit paie a mes ditz executours pour outre paies en partie de paiement de la sustenance de deux chapelleins celebrantz services divines en la novelle esglise collegiale de n're Dame de Leycestre, pur m'alme et l'alme de ma treschiere nadgairs compaigne Dame Constance illeouques entierree, et pur un obit a celebrer illeoques pur l'alme de ma dite nadgairs compaign Constance le vint et quart jour de Mars d'an en an, tanque au temps que en la suisdit novell esglise collegialle serront sufficientement fonduz un chanterie perpetuele de deux chapelleins a celebree divines services pur l'alme de moy et de ma dit nadgairs compaigne Constance illeouques enterree, et aussi un obit pur l'alme de le a celebrer perpetuelement le jour de Mars suisdit.

Adonques soit estate faite du dit manoir a mon tresame filtz aizne Henry Duc de Herford, et a ses heirs de son corps, et pur defaute d'issue de dite Henry la remeindre a mes droitz heirs.

APPENDIX

Item touchant les wapentakes de Hangest, Hangwest et Halykeld en Rychmondschir, les queulx j'ay devaunt ore faite grantier a mon tresame filtz en ley Raufe Counte de Westmerlande et a ma tresame fille Johane sa compaigne, a avoir a terme de leurs vies, jeo voille qu'ils les aient a eulx et a leurs heirs malz de lour corps issantz, et pur defaut d'issue de heir male de lour corps la remeindre a l'avant dite Johan mon filz et a ses heirs de son corps issants, et pur defaut d'issue de dite Johan la remeindre a dit Thomas et a ses heirs de son corps issants, et pur defaut d'issue de dit Thomas la remeindre au dit Johane et a ses heirs de son corps issauts, et pur defaute d'issue de dit Johane la remaindre a mes droiz heirs de Lancastre.

Item jeo voille que toutz aultres seignories, manoirs, terres, tenementz, rentz, services, possessions, reversions, et avoesons ove leurs appurtenances a mon oeps purchases et remaignants uncore es mains des enfeffez pur moy a ceo ordennes, soient apres ma mort si jeo ne face autre ordenance en ma vie, donnez a l'avant dit Thomas mon filtz, a avoir a luy et a ses heirs de son corps issants, et pur defaute d'issue de son corps issants la remeindre a l'avant dit Johan son frere et a ses heirs de son corps issants, et pur defaute d'issue de dit Johan la remaindre a la suisdite Johane leur seur, et a ses heirs de son corps issants, et pur defaute d'issue de la dite Johane la remaindre a mes droits heirs que serront heirs del heretage de Lancastre ; voillantz toutz voies que toutes ycestes mes voluntees, ordinaunces et devys en ceste cedule comprys soient toutz accompliez per ceulx que averont l'estate et povoir, et per l'avys ordenances et conseille de gentz de ley en le pluis sur manere que en ceo purra ordenner.

Appendix II

INVASION OF SCOTLAND, AUGUST, 1385

CEUX sont les ordenances de les trois batailles et de les deux eles du bataille du Roy a son primer viage en Escoce l'an de son regne noefisme.

EN L'AVANTGARDE

Monsr. de Lancastre	m hommes d'armes	iii^m archiers.
Le Conte de Bukyngham	cccc hommes d'armes	viii^e archiers.
Le Conte Mareschall et de Notyngham	cc hommes d'armes	ccc archiers.

EN LA BATAILLE DU ROY

Le Tynell du Roy   viii^c hommes d'armes ii^m archiers.
Monsr de Cantebrigg   cl hommes d'armes cc archiers.
Le Conte d'Arundell   cxl hommes d'armes cc archiers.
Le Conte de Warrewyk cxl hommes d'armes ccc archiers.
Le Conte de Stafford   cxx hommes d'armes cc archiers.
Le Conte d'Oxenford   cxx hommes d'armes cc archiers.
Le Conte de Sar'   l hommes d'armes cxx archiers.
Le Chanceller   lx hommes d'armes iiii^{x[x]} archiers.
Le Tresorer   xl hommes d'armes xl archiers.
Le Gardein du prive seal xxx hommes d'armes xxx archiers.
Le Seneschall del 'ostell du
  Roy   xxx hommes d'armes xxx archiers.
Le Sire du Roos   xx hommes d'armes xxx archiers.
Le Sire de Beaumont   xxx hommes d'armes xl archiers.
Le Sire de Wylughby   l hommes d'armes lx archiers.
Mons. Johan Lovell
Mons. William Botreaux } c hommes d'armes cc archiers.
Le Sire de Seymour
Mons. Johan Deveros   l hommes d'armes iiii^{x[x]} archiers.
Mons. Symon Burley   xx hommes d'armes xxx archiers.
Le Sire de fferers de Groby xx hommes d'armes xx archiers.
Le Sire de Haryngton   xxx hommes d'armes lx archiers.
Mons. Thomas Tryvet   xx hommes d'armes xx archiers.

APPENDIX

Mons. Maheu Gournay   xx hommes d'armes xx   archiers.
Mons. Aubrey de Veer   xx hommes d'armes xx   archiers.
L'evesque d'Everwyk   hommes d'armes   archiers.
Venoit apres l'ordenance faite.

    Et est assavoir q'il covient avoir deux eles pur la dite bataille de la somme susdite come ensuyt.

En la ele dextre

Monsr de Cantebrigg   cl hommes d'armes cc   archiers.
Lovell Botreaux Seymour   c hommes d'armes cc   archiers.
Le Sire de Wylughby   l hommes d'armes lx   archiers.

En la ele sinestre

Le Conte de Warrewyk   cxl hommes d'armes ccc   archiers.
Le Conte de Stafford   cxx hommes d'armes cc   archiers.
Le Chanceller   lx hommes d'armes iiii$^{x[x]}$archiers.

En la Rergarde

Le Conte de Northumbr' cccc hommes d'armes cccc   archiers.
Le Conte de Deveneshire lx hommes d'armes lx   archiers.
Le Sire de Nevill   cc hommes d'armes ccc   archiers.
Mons. Henry Percy   c hommes d'armes c   archiers.
Le Sire de Clifford   xl hommes d'armes lx   archiers.
Le Sire de la Zouche de
    Haryngworth   xxx hommes d'armes xxx   archiers.
Mons. Amory Seint Amant xvi hommes d'armes xxiiii archiers.
Le Sire de Berkele   xxiiii hommes d'armes xxx   archiers.
Mons. Thomas Percy l'eisne lx hommes d'armes lx   archiers.
L'evesque de Duresme   hommes d'armes   archiers.
Venoit apres l'ordenance.

L'ordenance de l'estale pur forreours

Le primer le Conestable et Mareschall sanz plus.
Le Tynell du Roy . . . . . .   i.
Monsr de Lancastre . . . . . . i.
Les deux eles de la bataille du Roy . . . i.
Les autres contes et baneretz du bataille le Roy .   ii.
La tierce bataille . . . . .   ii.

La nombre des gens d'armes iiii^m ccccc. iiii ^{xx}x.⎞ par l'orden-
La nombre des archiers ix   vii^{xx}iiii   ⎠ nance du Roy
Dount en l'avantgarde m. ccccc hommes d'armes et des
    archiers iiii^m c.

APPENDIX

Et en la bataille du Roy ii^m iii^{xx} hommes d'armes et des archiers iii^m ix^c iiii^{xx}

Et en la reregarde ix^c xxx hommes d'armes et des archiers m. lx iiii.

1 This is from *Cotton Nero*, D. vi. f. 91*b* and 92*a*. There are eight other MSS. purporting to give the same thing in the British Museum alone, viz.: (1) *Add MS.* 29901, f. 36–7 (fifteenth century); (2) *Cotton Jul. B.* i. f. 95*b*-96 (early sixteenth century); (3) *Cotton Dom.* xviii. f. 32–3 (sixteenth century); (4) Stowe 140, f. 150*b* (sixteenth century); (5) Stowe 531, f. 296*b* (seventeenth century); (6) Harl. 1309, f. 39–40 (eighteenth century); (7) Harl. 369, f. 92–3 (sixteenth century); (8) *Add MS.* 5758, f. 226 (seventeenth century).

The text of the first five is French; of the last three English.

The two printed by Sir H. Nicolas in *Archaeologia*, vol. xxii. p. 16 (viz.: (6) and (7) above) are obviously of no authority.

Mr. Williams in his edition of *La Chronicque du Traison et Mort de Richard II* (p. 239 note), printed a similar text from Latin MS. 6,409 Bibliotheque de Roi: the figures there given differ slightly from the above and the text contains several obvious corruptions.

Cotton Nero, D. vi. appears to be the most authoritative text.

Appendix III

RETINUE OF JOHN OF GAUNT

The Earl of Derby.
The Earl of Nottingham.
Lord Roos.
Lord Neville.
Lord Dacre.
Lord Welles.
Sir Michael de la Pole.
Sir Richard le Scrope.
Sir John Marmion.
Sir Robert Knolles.

Sir Richard Abbirbury.
Sir Esmon Apleby.
Sir John de Assheton.
Sir Nicholas Atherton.
Sir Richard de Baldreston.
Sir Thomas Banastre.
Sir Robert Barry.
Sir William Beauchamp.
Sir Thomas Beaumond.
Sir Thomas Beek.
Sir Baldwyn Bereford.
Sir Walter Blount.
Sir John Boseville.
Sir Thomas Boseville.
Sir John Botiller.
Sir Ralf Braysbrugg.
Sir William Breteville.
Sir John Bromwych.
Sir Richard Bureley.
Sir John Busshe.
Sir William Cantelowe.
Sir Robert Charles.
Sir Roger Cheynee.
Sir Robert Clifton.
Sir Thomas Colshall.

APPENDIX

Sir Thomas Colvyll.
Sir John Croyser.
Sir William Croyser (*Steward*).
Sir Roger Curson.
Sir John d'Aubrecicourt.
Sir Thomas Dale.
Sir John de Dalton.
Sir Thomas Daventre.
Sir Philip Denys.
Sir John Dodyngsels.
Sir John Dymmok.
Sir John Dypre (*the father. Chief of the Council.*)
Sir John Dypre (*the son*).
Sir Thomas de Erpyngham.
Sir Juan Fernandez.
Sir William Fitzwilliam.
Sir Thomas Fitzsymond.
Sir Thomas Fogg.
Sir Godfrey Foliambe.
Sir William Fraunk.
Sir Esmon de Frithby.
Sir Thomas Fychet.
Sir Otes Graunson.
Sir Henry Grene.
Sir Henry Grey of Codenore.
Sir John Gruivre.
Sir Frank van Hale.
Sir Thomas Harecourte.
Sir Ralf Hastynge.
Sir Robert Hanley.
Sir William Hanley.
Sir Richard de Havering.
Sir Nichol Haywood.
Sir Robert de Herford.
Sir John Herlee.
Sir Richard de Hoghton.
Sir William de Hoghton.
Sir Richard Hoo.
Sir Thomas Hungerford (*the father*).
Sir Thomas Hungerford (*the son*).
Sir Thomas Ildreton.
Sir Richard Kyghley.

APPENDIX

Sir Nichol de Longford.
Sir John de Loudham.
Sir Gerard de Lounde.
Sir William de Lussy.
Sir Andrew Lutterell.
Sir Mauburni de Liniêres.
Sir John Namers.
Sir Thomas de la Mare.
Sir Thomas Marchington.
Sir William Mauleverer.
Sir Thomas de Metham.
Sir Thomas Meaux.
Sir Thomas Morieux.
Sir Baldwyn Monford.
Sir Richard Northlond.
Sir Roger Northwode.
Sir Philip de Okovere.
Sir Ralf Paynell.
Sir Hans Paynewych.
Sir John Payton.
Sir John Pecche.
Sir Walter Penkergarde.
Sir John Playes.
Sir Ralf de Radecliff.
Sir Robert Roos.
Sir David Rocclif.
Sir Richard Rouclif (*the father*).
Sir Richard Rouclif (*the son*).
Sir John de Rocheford.
Sir John de Rondon.
Sir Thomas de Routhe.
Sir John Scott.
Sir John Sentcler.
Sir Matthew Senches.
Sir John Seyntlowe
Sir John Seyville.
Sir John Seyton.
Sir William Skargill.
Sir Nicholas de Sharnsfeld.
Sir Thomas de Southeworth.
Sir Ralf Stanley.
Sir Robert Standyche.
Sir John Straunge.

APPENDIX

Sir Robert Swylyngton (*Chamberlain*).
Sir John Swynton.
Sir Thomas Symond.
Sir John Talbot.
Sir John Thornebury.
Sir Richard Torbok.
Sir Thomas Travers.
Sir Roger de Trumpington.
Sir William de Tunstall.
Sir Walter Ursewyk (*Master of Sports and Hunting*).
Sir Gerard de Usflet.
Sir Thomas Wannesley.
Sir Geoffrey de Workesley.
Sir Richard de Whitefeld.

Hugh de Annesley.
Thomas de Aynfreson.
Richard de Aston.
William Bagote.
Edward Banastre.
Thomas Barley.
Oliver de Barton.
William de Barton.
John Bathe.
Philip Baynard.
Edward Beauchamp.
Thomas Berkeley.
Robert Beyville.
Robert Blakewell.
William Bloumehill.
John Bolton.
Robert Boulot.
Thomas de Braddeley.
William de Bradeshawe.
John Brenchelee.
Roger de Burelay.
William Burgoyn.
Thomas de Burton.
John Care.
Robert de Caunsefeld.
William Chetewynd.
John Collepepir.

APPENDIX

Richard Colman.
Roger Colman.
John Croyser.
Stephen Derneford.
John de Deyncourte.
Thomas de Dryby.
Thomas de Dryffeld.
Raulyn Dyprre.
Thomas de Ecton.
Robert de Ecleston.
Roger de Elston.
William Fifide.
Robert Fitzrauf.
Piers Frank.
Madok Frevill.
Waryn Fresdale.
William Gaskrig.
Piers Geblesen.
Edward Gerberge.
Thomas Goys.
John Gyffard.
William atte Halle.
Hugh Haywode.
Robert de Haytefeld.
William Haybere.
William Hervy.
Thomas de Hesulden (*Controller of the Household*).
Richard de Holand.
William Holme.
John Holt.
John de Halford.
Thomas de Holford.
John de Kendale.
William Keteryng.
John de Kirkeby.
Nicholas Kynbell (*Chief Butler*).
Hugh Lotterell.
William Marschall.
Thomas Maundeville.
Thomas Maistreson.
John Mautravers.
Richard Massy.

APPENDIX

Piers de Melbourne.
Roger Messyngham.
Richard Mikelfeld.
John Moresam.
Symkyn Molyneux.
Robert de Morton.
John Myniott.
Adam de Neusom.
John Newmarche
William Nessefield.
William de Notton.
James Orell.
Walter Oliver.
William Overbury.
Robert de Pylkyngton.
William Par.
Stephen Pulham.
William Paumes.
Richard Perrers.
Roger de Pyrton.
Henry ap Phelipe.
Robert Pershay.
John de la Pole of Hertington.
Roger Perewyche.
William de Querneby.
Lowys Recouchez.
Henry Roose.
John Rous.
Thomas Roos.
Piers Roos.
John Reynald (*Master Cook*).
Robert de Rokkeley.
William Randolf.
John de Roudon.
John de Rixton.
Richard de Rixton.
Alfonso Senche.
John Skargill.
John Skogan.
John de Southenon.
William de Staines.
John Strange.
Hamond Strange.

445

APPENDIX

Robert de Stanfeld.
William de Suddeburry.
John Synnes.
Symkyn Symeon.
Thomas Swynford.
William de Swyllyngton.
John Stynt.
John Tayleboys.
Thomas de Trewennok of Cornwall.
John Topelyf.
Piers Tebaud.
Thomas Tutbury.
Elys de Thursby.
Henry Warde.
John Wanndesford.
Hugh de Waterton.
Richard de Wirley
Robert de Workesley.
John Wrenche.
John White.

1 This list, which does not pretend to be exhaustive, represents the Duke's retinue roughly between 1372 and 1382. The list entitled "Nomina Milit et Scutifer," f. 6 and 7 of the second part of the Register has been supplemented from indentures of service, warrants to pay fees and wages, etc., in the Register II. f. 8-12 and *passim*. The new names given in the confirmation of the Duke's retainers (*Rot. Pat.* 22 Ric. II. part 3) have not been added. Many gaps were made n the ranks by the invasion of Castile in 1387.

Appendix IV

ACCOUNT OF THE RECEIVER GENERAL OF THE DUKE OF LANCASTER

For the Year 2 February, 1394, to 2 February, 1395.

Receipts.	First Half-year, Feb. 2, 1394, to Aug. 12, 1394.			Second Half-year, Aug. 12, 1394, to Feb. 2, 1395.			Total Feb. 2, 1394 to Feb. 2, 1395.		
	£	s.	d.	£	s.	d.	£	s.	d.
I. Issues of land in England and Wales (including £156 11s. 6d. "foreign parcels").	668	7	0	1,957	14	4¼	2,626	1	4¼
II. From Exchequer for custody of Aquitaine and for the Treaty of Calais (£200 paid to the late Duchess and £400 to the Duke's privy purse not included)	2,698	19	8	4,000	0	0	6,698	19	8
III. From Treaty with Spain (per Constable of Bordeaux)	2,697	8	6	3,342	13	9	} 6,550	7	11¾
From Treasure of Spain *en masse* (per Sir T. Tutbury)	510	5	8¾	—					
IV. Loans repaid	225	0	0	490	13	4	715	13	4
V. Arrears of last account (unchanged money)	2	14	0	2	14	0	2	14	0
	£6,802	14	10¾	9,791	1	5½	16,593	16	4¼

PAYMENTS.	First Half-year, Feb. 2, 1394, to Aug. 12, 1394. £ s. d.	Second Half-year, Aug. 12, 1394, to Feb. 2, 1395. £ s. d.	Total. Feb. 2, 1394 to Feb. 2, 1395. £ s. d.
I. Expenses of the Household		5,146 15 0	5,955 0 0 (brace)
,, ,, during the Duke's absence in France	708 5 0		
,, ,, (at Hertford)	100 0 0		
II. Expenses of the Wardrobe	500 0 0	140 0 —	640 0 0
III. Privy Purse	733 6 8	433 6 8	1,166 13 4
IV. Annuities and Wages—			
Annuities of Knights and Esquires	41 5 0	147 18 4*	189 3 4
Chancellor's fee [W. Ashton]	20 0 0		20 0 0
Keeper of the Privy Seal, one term	—	2 10 0	2 10 0
R. de Whitby, Receiver General (first half-year); Attorney General (second half-year)	30 10 0	20 0 0	50 10 0
J. Legbourne, Receiver General (second half-year)	—	13 6 8	13 6 8
Chief Steward in the North, J. Busshe, for fee for one term		20 0 0 (brace)	41 10 0
and for wages of his office		21 10 0 (brace)	
Chief Steward in the North, P. de Tilney	30 15 0		30 15 0
,, ,, South and in Wales, T. Skelton, for one term	40 0 0	40 0 0	80 0 0
Auditor's fee and for sitting in London on accounts of R. de Whitby, J. Elnet, J. Legbourne and others, Feb. 1395	25 0 0	9 18 0	34 18 0
Ministers in the King's Courts at Westminster	11 14 5	23 13 11	35 8 4
Lancaster Herald	—	10 0 0	10 0 0
Clerks of the Chapel	25 3 4	24 3 4	49 6 8
Clerks who chaunt for the soul of the Duchess Blanche in St. Paul's	6 13 4	6 13 4	13 6 8
Falconers	26 6 0	3 6 2	29 12 2
King's sergeants-at-arms travelling on the Duke's voyage from Plymouth this year	—	13 6 8	13 6 8
Writing indentures of service of the Duke's retinue for the voyage to Gascony	—	8 12 10	8 12 10
Notaries going to Brittany on the Duke's business	109 8 4	—	109 8 4
John Malet going abroad on the Duke's business	66 13 4	—	66 13 4
T. Langley, Clerk, going to Wales on the Duke's business	—	5 0 0	5 0 0

	£ s. d.	£ s. d.	£ s. d.
Thomas Chaucer for business transacted	—	13 6 8	13 6 8
The Duke's business: divers times	—	1 10 0	1 10 0
William Ashton: wages out of Court at London with the Duke's council	—	18 13 4	18 13 4
Petrine de Cause at 10d. a day: issues of Bordeaux	—	30 0 0	30 0 0
V. Anniversary of the Lady Blanche	—	10 0 0	10 0 0
VI. Miscellaneous expenses—			
To the late Duchess for her assignment (per J. Elnet)	13 6 8	—	13 6 8
To divers creditors of the late Duchess	409 15 11½	—	409 15 11½
For burial of the late Duchess, black cloth, etc.	544 5 9½	—	584 5 9½
Balance due to the Earl of Salisbury of 5,000 marcs for reversion of manors	2,666 13 4	40 0 0	2,666 13 4
Fine of lands in Sandon in Common Bench	61 13 4	—	61 13 4
Foreign payments by warrant	—	13 6 8	13 6 8
For making new glass window for Friars Preachers at Dunstable	—	20 0 0	20 0 0
For making great gold table for the Duke's chamber	—	10 0 0	10 0 0
For making a stew at Hertford	—	11 16 7	11 16 7
For two horses bought at London	—	14 0 0	14 0 0
VII. Arrears: imprests, loans, etc.—			
Henry Hoghton, by loan	—	66 13 4	66 13 4
Debts due to Hostel in time of W. Ermyn	124 13 4½	1,526 12 11½	1,651 6 4
Debts due to Wardrobe in time of J. Legbourne	—	198 18 5½	198 16 5½
Imprest	200 0 0	—	200 0 0
J. Elnet, Clerk of Wardrobe: imprest	—	170 16 8	170 16 8
Due from Sir W. Beauchamp for which the Duke is suing	14 8 10	—	14 8 10
J. Stenche and other	—	3 18 8	3 18 8
Arrears of last account of the Wardrobe	—	—	3 18 8
Arrears of last account (Receiver General)	248 2 2½	—	248 2 2½
	*6,758 0 3	*8,239 4 2½	*14,997 4 5½
Balance	44 14 7½	1,551 17 3½	1,596 11 10¾
	6,802 14 10½	9,791 1 6	16,593 16 4¼

* And 40 francs.

* Sic in MS.

SPECIE ACCOUNT

FEBRUARY 2, 1394, TO FEBRUARY 2, 1395:

First half-year, February 2 to August 12, 1394

Currency.	Florins (of Florence), Ducats (of Genoa).	Doubles, Scutes.	Bullion.		Currency.	Florins. Ducats.	Doubles. Scutes.	Bullion.
£ s. d.	No.	No.	lb. oz. dwt.		£ s. d.	No.	No.	lb. oz. dwt.
6,802 14 10½	821	11,227	1,383 1 18	To Nicholas Usk Per account .	6758 0 3			
				To Adam Portlewe Trier in bullion .		821	11,227	1,383 1 18
				Balance .	44 4* 7½	821	11,227	1,383 1 18
6,802 14*10½	821	11,227	1383 1 18		6802 4*10½	821	11,227	1,383 1 18

Second half-year, August 12, 1394, to February 2, 1395.

Currency.	French Scutes.	Franks.		Currency.	French Scutes.	Franks.
£ s. d.	No.	No.		£ s. d.	No.	No.
9,791 1 6*	477	335½	Per account. To J. Elvet (in gold) Annuities Valets .	8,239 4 2½	476	0
						180
			Balance .	8,239 4 2½	476	220
				1,551 17 3½	1	115½
9,791 1 6*	477	335½		9,791 1 5¾*	477	335½

450

Appendix V

EPITAPH

HIC IN DOMINO OBDORMIVIT
JOHANNES GANDAVENSIS
VULGO DE GAUNT, A GANDAVO FLANDRIE URBE, LOCO NATALI, ITA DENOMINATUS ;
EDWARDI TERCII REGIS ANGLIE FILIUS ;
A PATRE COMITIS RICHMONDIE TITULO ORNATUS.
TRES SIBI UXORES IN MATRIMONIO DUXIT ;
PRIMAM BLANCHAM, FILIAM ET HAEREDEM HENRICI DUCIS LANCASTRIE,
PER QUAM AMPLISSIMAM ADIIT HEREDITATEM.
NEC SOLUM DUX LANCASTRIE, SED ETIAM LEICESTRIE, LINCOLNIE, ET DERBIE COMES EFFECTUS ;
E CUJUS SUBOLE IMPERATORES, REGES, PRINCIPES, ET PROCERES, PROPAGATI SUNT PLURIMI.
ALTERAM HABUIT UXOREM CONSTANTIAM (QUE HIC CONTUMULATUR) FILIAM ET HEREDEM PETRI REGIS
CASTILLIE
ET LEGIONIS CUJUS JURE OPTIMO TITUTO REGIS CASTILLIE ET LEGIONIS USUS EST.
HAEC UNICAM ILLI PEPERIT FILIAM CATHARINAM, EX QUA AB HENRICO REGES HISPANIE SUNT PROPAGATI.
TERTIAM VERO UXOREM DUXIT CATHARINAM, EX EQUESTRI FAMILIA, ET EXIMIA PULCHRETUDINE FEMINAM ;
EX QUA NUMEROSAM SUSCEPIT PROLEM, UNDE GENUS EX MATRE DUXIT HENRICUS SEPTIMUS REX ANGLIE
PRUDENTISSIMUS
CUJUS FELICISSIMO CONIUGIO CUM ELIZABETHA EDWARDI QUARTI REGIS FILIA E STIRPE EBORACENSI REGIE
ILLE
LANCASTRIENSIUM ET EBORACENSIUM FAMILIE AD EXOPTATISSIMAM ANGLIE PACEM COALUERUNT.
ILLUSTRISSIMUS HIC PRINCEPS JOHANNES, COGNOMENTO PLANTAGENET
REX CASTILLIE ET LEGIONIS, DUX LANCASTRIE, COMES RICHMONDIE, LEICESTRIE LINCOLNIE ET DERBEIE.
LOCUM TENENS AQUITANIE, MAGNUS SENESCHALLUS ANGLIE
OBIT ANNO XXII REGNI REGIS RICARDI SECUNDI
ANNOQUE DOMINI MCCC XCIX.

This epitaph (taken from Weever's *Funeral Monuments*, p. 365) dates from the time of Henry VII ; hence the inaccuracies. It was Blanche and not Constance whose body rested in the same tomb with her husband. The omission of the Dukedom of Aquitaine is stranger still. The funeral monument (engraved in Dugdale's *St. Paul's*, p. 90, and Sandford, *Genealogical History*, p. 254) belongs to the same period. It disappeared in the great fire.

APPENDIX

Appendix VI

COINAGE OF JOHN OF GAUNT

ANTIQUARIAN details often throw a side-light on character. This is so in the present case, for Lancaster's continental ambitions and love of royal state are reflected in his fondness for the regality of coinage. As the recognized authorities on coinage, Spanish and Anglo-French, are meagre in their information about Lancaster's coinage, or silent altogether, the following brief *résumé* of the facts may possibly be of interest to numismatists.

John of Gaunt obtained the right to coin in four ways, viz. :—

I. AS KING OF CASTILE AND LEON

This right extended from 1371, the date of the second marriage, to 1388, the date of the treaty of renunciation.

Baines (*History of the County Palatine of Lancaster*, i. 351) says that " several pieces were struck bearing his superscription " in this character, but quotes no authorities.

Heiss (*Descripcion general de las monedas Hispano-Cristianas desde la invasion de los Arabes*) has no notice of the Duke's coinage, and the doubt as to its existence has been increased by the prevailing confusion of " John, King of Castile and Leon and Duke of Lancaster," and Juan II, his grandson, the successor of Enrique III.

It was not likely that the Duke, punctilious to a degree in the niceties of royal etiquette, would have omitted to put into practice one of the functions most closely identified with royalty, but the following passage from Fernão Lopes (*Chronica de El Rei Dom João I*, vol. v. p. 110–111) removes any doubt on the point :—" Vieram as naus e galés de Portugal que estavam na Corunha ... e em uma vinha todo o thesouro do duque o qual trazia pera fazer moeda, de que fizesse pagamento aos seus, assim como a fez, e depois em Gallizia e n'aquella cidade do Porto, que lavron reales de prata, de sete dinheiros, e de seis, e outra moeda similhante á de dez soldos, quei em Portugal corria, e tinha no cunho armas de Castella com outras mesturadas, e moeda mais pequena faziam outra pera acabar." No specimen of the Duke's coinage, minted at Oporto or in Galicia (probably at Santiago) is to be found in any of the known collections, but the coin described by Venuti in his *Dissertation sur les mon-*

APPENDIX

noyes que les Anglois frapperent en Aquitaine (p. 162), quoted in Ducarel's *Anglo-Gallic Norman* and *Aquitanian Coins* (p. 51), is perhaps a genuine Lancastrian piece.

It is a silver penny, stamped with the King's head and bust, " bearing a crown with large fleurs-de-lys open and adorned with roses, surrounded by the legend, IOANN : REX : CAS-TELLE : ET : LEGIONIS ; in the middle three towers and the letters B.S."

Is B.S. an error for P.S. ? If so, these letters may possibly represent the initials of Lancaster's " Master of the Mint," for the " Register " contains a transcript of a warrant, dated April 15, 3 Richard II (1380), appointing " Mestre Pelegrin de Ser to be Mestre Soverain of all his monies of gold and silver and other metals, and to make money in Spain "(ii. f. 116).

What the " monies " other than those of Spain were will appear below.

II. As Duke of Aquitaine

The right of coinage is expressly mentioned in the terms of the grant of the Duchy of Aquitaine, dated March 2, 1390—

" Et ad honoris et nominis tui validius fulcimentum, hanc tibi auctoritatem et potestatem specialiter impertimur, monetam auream et argenteam et aliam qualemcunque faciendi cudendi et fabricandi, monetamque jam usitatam, seu alias quascunque imposterum per te cudendas, quoties et quomodo tibi videbitur expediens, mutandi (aliqua con-suetudine in contrarium ibidem retroactis temporibus usitata non obstante) ac magistris et operariis earundem indulgentias et privilegia talibus dari solita largiendi," etc.

Henry, Duke of Lancaster, coined as Duke of Aquitaine, and under the Black Prince coinage produced a large propor-tion of the revenue of the principality.

But on Lancaster's creation, as we have seen,[1] the bare possession of the powers described above excited a storm of excitement in Bordeaux. Article XIII of the Treaty of Bor-deaux (March 22, 1395) runs as follows :—

" Item an xiii^e article, en laquel nous supplient que nous ne fassons faire ne faisons nouvelle monoye, ne muer la valeur de l'antique, sinon de consentiment du peuple d'iceulx qui ont part en lez monoyes ; et que soit pourveu suffisantment des changeours ; Nous ne le povons octoyer sans faire assavoir

[1] See above, Ch. XV. p. 378.

453

APPENDIX

a mon seigneur le roy, ne attendons aucune chose octroier ou muer, en cest article contenue, qu'ele soit en prejudice de la royalté dudit duche pour nostre temps, mais toutes choses garder et observer selonc que antiquement est use et observe ; toutesfoiz nous promettons pouvoir des changeours come ils demandent (*Livre des Bouillons*, p. 267).

III. As Lord of Bergerac

The right of coinage is contained in the grant by Prince Edward of the Lordship of Bergerac to his brother, dated Cognac, Oct. 8, 1370,[1] and is repeated in the King's confirmation of the grant [2]—" Concessimus insuper de gratia nostra speciali auctoritate nostra regia et ex certa scientia dicto filio nostro et heredibus masculis de corpore suo ut praemittitur exeuntibus, cussionem monetae in dicto loco, sic quidem ipsi in eodem loco monetam cudere possint seu cudi facere prout sibi visum fuerit faciendam, et quod emolumentum cussionis illius monete suum remaneat, et ad ipsorum utilitatem omnimodo convertatur prout nuper prefato consanguineo nostro concesseramus.

" Ita tamen quod moneta illa ibidem sic cudenda sit ita fortis aut fortior moneta nostra partium prædictarum."

The danger, anticipated in the last clause, of an inferior baronial currency starting from Bergerac to conquer Aquitaine and to drive the royal currency out of circulation was not formidable, for, as has been seen, John of Gaunt held the town with no very certain grip, and if Pelegrin de Ser coined for his master as Lord of Bergerac, his coins have not survived. *A priori* it is probable that the attempt was made, for the privilege of coining in Aquitaine would be all the more valued by the Duke because he could not coin at home. The Counts Palatine of Lancaster had never possessed that regality, and in England the Palatinate of Durham alone was allowed to compete with the royal mints.

IV. By Special Grant

One of the last acts of Edward III was to grant to John of Gaunt for two years the right of coinage in Bayonne Guiche and the Landes, with all its profits.

The date, June 12, 1377, is significant. Obtained during Lancaster's dictatorship, it affords one more proof of his

[1] Register, and Delpit *Collection*, ccxviii.
[2] Dated Havering, Nov. 8, 1376 (Delpit *Collection*, cclxvii.).

APPENDIX

fondness for this particular manner of adding to his revenue and dignity. King Edward grants to the Duke :—

" . . . Quod ipse a data praesentium per duos annos proximo sequentes plenarié completos cudi et fabricari facere possit in civitate Baione, seu in castro de Guissen, vel alio loco ubi voluerit, in Senescalcia Landarum, monetam de auro et argento et alio metallo, de quocumque cunio allaia et tallia prout sibi placuerit (excepto de Anglia et Aquitania) per manus Pelgrini de Ser vel alterius quem per ipsum filium nostrum vel deputatos suos, ordinari seu deputari contigerit in hac parte, volentes quod proficuum inde proveniens eiden filio nostro remaneat et totaliter applicetur"

A similar grant, also for two years, was made by Richard II, March 7, 1380. Neither grant interfered with existing rights, for Prince Edward had resigned the " Principality " on his return to England in 1371, and the " Duchy " of Aquitaine was not revived until Richard II granted it to Lancaster in 1390.

The moneyer is the same in both cases, Pelegrine de Ser. In the first grant the mints named are those of Bayonne and Guiche (near Bordeaux) ; in the second those of Bayonne and Dax, the usual centres of Aquitanian coinage. (See Ruding, *Annals of Coinage of Great Britain* ; and Ainslie, *Supplement to the Illustrations of Anglo-French Coinage.*)

On several occasions Lancaster received power as the King's Lieutenant to coin in his name as King of France, but in the case of these grants (which have been compared to "letters of marque" issued against the French King) the profit would go to the royal exchequer, and the coinage, if ever struck, which is doubtful, would bear the King's image.

It may be worth noticing that the medal supposed by Ducarel to have been struck in commemoration of Lancaster's second marriage really belongs to a much later period. It bears the legend, " Jungimus optatas sub amico foedere dextras " on the obverse, and on the reverse, " Uxor Casta est rosa suavis : sicut sol oriens dei sic mulier bona eius ornamentum."

To Ducarel " rosa " suggested the Lancastrian badge, and " Casta " Castile (p. 77, ibid.), but the medal commemorates the marriage not of John of Gaunt and Constance of Castile, but of Henry VII and Elizabeth of York (*Medallic Illustrations of British History*, i. 19).

APPENDIX

Appendix VII

ARMS AND SEALS OF JOHN OF GAUNT

LANCASTER used several varieties of privy seals. He had also his great seal as King of Castile and Leon, his great seal as Count Palatine of Lancaster, and lastly a private signet ring.

I. PRIVY SEALS

I. Of the Privy seals there are three main varieties belonging to—(i.) the period before his second marriage ; (ii.) the period during which he claimed the throne of Castile ; and (iii.) the period after that claim had been compromised.

(i.) Before the marriage with Constance of Castile (1371) John of Gaunt bore on his privy seal the royal arms of France and England, with a difference (see Fig. 1). There is a very fine specimen of this period attached to Harl. Ch. 43, E 14, in the British Museum. It is No. 12,691 in W. de Gray Birch's *Catalogue of Seals in the Dept. of MSS. of the British Museum* (iii. 386), where it is thus described :—

" A shield of arms, *couché*, quarterly 1 and 4 France ; 2 and 3 England : over all in chief a label of three points ermine ; crest on a helmet and short mantling diapered, on a chapeau a lion statant guardant, crowned, charged on the neck with a label of three points ermine, the tail hanging down ; supporters, two falcons, each standing on a padlock and essaying to open the same : the background replenished with sprigs of foliage :—within a carved Gothic quatrefoil, ornamented along the inner edge with small quatrefoils : surrounded with the legend :—S : p'uat : joh'is : ducis : Lancastr' : comit : richemond' : derb : linc : leyc : senescalle : angl."

(ii.) From 1371 to 1388 the Duke bore the royal arms of Castile and Leon quarterly, impaling the royal arms of France and England quarterly, with a difference. (See Fig. 2.)

There are two specimens of this period in the British Museum—one of A.D. 1386, attached to Ad. Ch. 13,910 (Catalogue, No. 12,694) ; one of A.D. 1380, attached to Harl. Ch. 84, c 17 (Catalogue, No. 23,053). They are described (ibid.) :—

" Armorial bearings not on a shield. Per pale *dexter*, quarterly 1 and 4 Castile ; 2 and 3 Leon ; *sinister*, quarterly 1 and 4 France (ancient) ; 2 and 3 England, with a label of three points ermine. The first and fourth quarters of each

456

FIG. (i.)

FIG. (ii.)

FIG. (iii.)

FIG. (iv.)

PRIVY SEALS AND GREAT SEAL OF JOHN OF GAUNT.

APPENDIX

impalement raised, and the second and third counter-sunk : within a carved border ornamented with cinquefoils along the inner edge, surrounded by the legend :—S : privatū : joh'is : dei : grā : Regis Castelle : et : Legionis : Ducis : Lancastrie."

(iii.) After 1388 the Duke continued to bear the royal arms of Castile and Leon, impaling those of France and England, but he moved the Spanish quarterings from *dexter* to *sinister*. (See Fig. 3).

There is a fair specimen of this later period in the British Museum attached to Ad. Ch. 8,125, A.D. 1392 (Catalogue, No. 12,695), and to Ad. Ch. 11,310 of the same year (Catalogue, No. 12,696).

II. The Great Seal of Castile and Leon

The plate here reproduced (Fig. 4) is from a cast in the possession of the Society of Antiquaries. There is a reverse, with the usual equestrian figure bearing the royal arms of Castile and Leon quarterly (engraved in Rymer's *Foedera*, vol. vi.), but I have not been successful in finding the original.

Unlike the other monarchs of Europe, the Kings of Castile and Leon did not use the ordinary wax seals ; instruments issuing from their chanceries, like those of the Papacy and Empire, bore a metal " bulla."

John of Gaunt did not follow precedent in this, but impressed wax with a silver seal in the manner common to the other royal chanceries. (See Reg. Warrant dated Dec. 11, 1375, to Ralf de Erghum, Bishop of Salisbury, his Chancellor, to deliver to his Chamberlain and his Receiver-General . . . the two seals in his possession, viz., the Privy Seal and the Silver Seal, with the arms of Spain.) The leaden " bulla " preserved in the Museum of the Public Record Office, which used to be described as the seal of John of Gaunt, is now recognized as that of his grandson, Juan II of Castile and Leon (A.D. 1406–1454).

III. The Great Seal of the County Palatine.

John of Gaunt, after February, 1377, had of course his " magnum sigillum pro regimine regalitatis comitatus pala-tini " (*Record Report*, xxxii. App. I. xl. and App. IV. 17), but I have not found an impression as old as 1377–1399.

457

APPENDIX

The arms of the Duchy of Lancaster were—" Gules, three lions passant guardant in pale or ; a label of three (sometimes of five) points azure, charged with fleurs-de-lys of the second." (*Notes and Queries*, sixth series, x. 208.)

IV. THE DUKE'S SIGNET RING.

I have not found an impression of this. The antiquary may possibly find the following extract from the Register (I. f. 149) of interest :—

" Trescher et tresbien ame pour divers choses et busoignes moult chargeantz quelles nous avons affaire volons et vous mandons que a nostre bien ame Johan Gutier Dean de Segovy qi nons avons chargez des ditz choses et busoignes vous deliverez notre seal plat de nos entiers armes de Castille et de Leon pur ycelles exploiter et expedir prenant de luy serement de bien et loialment garder le dit seal sanz preiudice damages ou desheretison a nous faire le temps quil sera en sa garde. Et cestes etc. Donne sous le signet de notre auel a notre manoir de la Savoye le xii jour d'avril l'an *etc* xlvi.'

APPENDIX

Appendix VIII

NOTES ON LANCASTER'S FAMILY

(i)˙ ELIZABETH OF LANCASTER

MALVERNE is the only authority for the scandal about Elizabeth of Lancaster, but he is usually so full and accurate that there can be little hesitation in accepting the story, especially as it squares with everything known of John Holland's character and the manners of the English court at the time. Here it is :—

Altera vero (Elizabeth) fuit desponsata comiti Penbroke puero immaturae aetatis ; sed illa viripotens tunc (i.e. 1386) effecta, in regalem curiam est delata ad conspicandum gestus aulicos et mores eorum. Quam ut aspexit dominus Johannes Holand frater domini regis nunc ex parte materna vehementer captus est ejus amore propter quod die nocteque eam sollicitavit tamen (*sic*) per temporum intervalla tandem tam fatue illam allexit sic quod tempore transitus domini ducis patris sui ad mare per eum extitit impregnata. Unde illam incontinenti postea ducc acceptante duxit in uxorem ante prolis exortum transivitque in Hispaniam cum illo (Higden, ix. 96–97). Is this last fact the basis of the myth of the Religieux de Saint Denys, i. 443, who says that a daughter was born to the Duke on his arrival at Coruña ?

Elizabeth was a younger sister of Philippa. How much younger is uncertain, and the fact that she was " viripotens " in 1386 does not give much help. The sisters were sufficiently near in age to have the same mistress, Katharine Swynford.

The betrothal to John Hastings (b. 1372, s. 1375, d. 1389), third Earl of Pembroke, took place in 1380 (warrant to the Clerk of the Great Wardrobe to make several payments amounting to £257 6s. 5½d., several of which are on account of the marriage (i.e. betrothal) of the Duke's daughter Elizabeth, dated June 24, 4 Rich. II [Reg. II. f. 38 ; 42], and warrants to pay the Countess of Pembroke £100 for the expenses of her household and wardrobe, *ibid. passim*).

After the betrothal was annulled (Kn. ii. 208) Pembroke married a daughter of the Earl of March. On the death of his favourite, Michael de la Pole, Richard II granted Elizabeth,

APPENDIX

then Countess of Huntingdon, his Inn in Lombard Street (*Rot. Pat.* April 30, 1391). Their usual residence was Pulteney House.[1]

(ii) DAME BLANCHE MORIEUX

Of this mysterious daughter little is known. Her parentage rests on the authority of a single passage of Froissart, who speaking of the Duke's army in 1386 says : " Et maréchal (étoit) messire Thomas Moriaux lequel avoit aussi par mariage une de ses filles à femme ; mais elle étoit bastarde, et fut mere à la Dame Morielle demoiselle Marie de Saint-Hylaire de Haynau [K. de L. xi., 326]. The English chroniclers, curiously enough, have nothing to say about the Duke's daughter Blanche. From the Register it appears (i) that on her wedding day Lancaster gave her twelve silver spoons, twelve silver saucers, two basins with ewers, a basket with a silver top, etc. (March 6, 1381) ; (ii) that he settled upon Blanche and her husband for their lives £100 a year out of the issues of the manors of Snettisham and Fakenham in Norfolk (June 1, 1382). There is one unimportant reference to Dame Blanche Morieux in the Patent Rolls, a pardon for homicide "at the supplication of Blanche, wife of Thomas de Murrieux, the King's knight." [2]

Her mother, Marie de Saint Hilaire, is equally obscure. The facts are (i) that as late as 1399 Marie is in receipt of a pension from the Duke " for the good and agreeable service she has rendered for a long time to our honoured Lady and mother Philippe, late Queen of England " (confirmation of grant dated April 7, 22 Rich. II, *Rot. Pat.* Part. III. m. 3) ; (ii) that in 1360 she received a pension of £20 per annum from Edward III to be paid at the Exchequer, which was exchanged in 1390 for an annuity of £20 charged on the issues of the Counties of Cambridge and Huntingdon.[3] Marie was therefore a maid of honour of Queen Philippa, and a native of Hainault. Kervyn de Lettenhove (Froissart 1 a, 443-4) gives as her probable ancestry—

Jean *dit* Vilain de Saint Hilaire = Mahaut de Wasnes.
|
John of Gaunt = Marie de Saint Hilaire.
|
Blanche = Sir Thomas Morieux.

[1] D. N. B. Articles, Holland, John ; Hastings, John.
[2] *Rot. Pat.* Rich. II, vol. ii. 295, dated Aug. 1, 1383.
[3] *Issue Roll of Brantingham*, p. 359, and *Rot. Pat.* Feb.19, 1390.

APPENDIX

In determining the date of this *liaison* the significant facts are (1) that Marie received the considerable pension of £20 per annum as early as 1360, and (2) that Blanche her daughter was already married in 1381.

There is no evidence that any *amour* disturbed the married life of John of Gaunt and Blanche of Lancaster. The Duke married Blanche in 1359. Probability therefore points to the conclusion that Blanche, afterwards wife of Thomas Morieux, was the fruit of a very early *liaison* (? 1358 or 9), before the first marriage, and before the Duke's actions were being scrutinized by the chroniclers. An *amour* with one of the Queen's maids of honour would have delighted the Monk of Saint Albans, and would certainly not have passed unnoticed in later years.

The problem has been complicated by the existence of a second Blanche, daughter of Katharine Swynford, vouched for by the Register (e.g. grant to Katharine Swynford for her, and for her daughter Blanche, of the wardship of the lands and heir to Sir Robert Deyncourt, Jan. 1374, Reg. I. f 41).

But the attempt to identify the Duke's daughter and the daughter of his later mistress breaks down hopelessly. (It was made by Sir N. Nicolas, *Scrope v. Grosvenor Controversy* ii. 185). For (i) there is Froissart's explicit statement quoted above ; (ii) Blanche is never mentioned among the Beauforts ; (iii) there is the insuperable difficulty of age. Katharine Swynford, born in 1350, and married to Sir Hugh Swynford in 1367, whose elder child, Sir Thomas Swynford, was born in 1368, could not possibly have been the mother of Blanche, who was married to Sir Thomas Morieux in 1381.

The matter is settled by a passage in the last published volume of *Papal Letters*. In 1396 the Duke and Katharine pray the Pope to sanction their marriage. Among the impediments recited are, first, the fact that they have been living in adultery during the lifetime of the Duchess Constance ; second, the fact that they are already united by the bond of compaternity (a canonical bar to marriage), the Duke having been godfather to *Blanche, a daughter of Katharine by another husband*, i.e. Sir Hugh Swynford.[1]

As for Sir Thomas Morieux, there is no mystery. He was a well-known public character in the reigns of Edward III and Richard II. A son of Sir Thomas Morieux, of Thorpe

---

[1] *Papal Letters*, Kal. Sept. 7, Boniface IX, 1396, iv. 545.

S

APPENDIX

Morieux, Suffolk, he was a sheriff of Norfolk and Suffolk in 1367 and 1368, and from time to time held a score of commissions of the Peace and of Oyer and Terminer. In 1376 he was one of Lord Latimer's sureties ; in 1381 he was made Constable of the Tower, and two years later Master of the Horse to Richard II. In 1384 he was one of the knights who tortured the Carmelite Friar. In all the campaigns in France, Gascony, Spain and Scotland he had his share. The campaign in Castile was his last. He died worn out by fighting in Galicia before May 5, 1387. (See Nicolas, *Scrope and Grosvenor Case*, ii. 183).

(iii) KATHARINE SWYNFORD

It is difficult to fix an accurate date for the beginning of the *liaison* of John of Gaunt with Katharine Swynford.

The Monk of Evesham, speaking of Katharine, says : " Quam ut concubinam multo tempore *vivente uxore Constancia* carnaliter cognovit (p. 128)," which, if true, limits it to 1371–1394, while Froissart's account narrows the period still further, viz. : "Quant . . . celle seconde duchesse Constance fut morte, le duc de Lancastre, *la dame vivante*, avoit tenu celle Katherine de Ruet, qui aussi avoit esté mariée à ung chevallier d'Angleterre. *Le chevallier vivant et mort,* tousjours le duc Jehan de Lancastre avoit amé et tenu celle dame Katherine . . ." [K. de L. xv. 239].

Only the years 1371 and 1372 fit in with this statement, a. conclusion which harmonises with the other available evidence For instance, the petition to the Pope above quoted mentions the adultery in the life of Duchess Constance, not in that of the Duchess Blanche. The *Chronicon Angliae* (p. 196) speaks of the notoriety of the affair almost as something new in 1378, while, according to Knighton (ii. 147), it was a well-established fact in 1381. No contemporary evidence supports the statement of Percy MS. 78 (quoted below), which places the birth of the Beauforts in the life of the Duchess Blanche. There is no doubt, however, that most historians have postdated the birth of the Beauforts, or at least of the eldest of them, for in 1390 *Monseigneur Jehon de Biaufort, bastart de Lancastre*, was old enough to bear himself with credit at the jousts of Saint Inglevert [Froissart, K. de L. xiv. 416], though on the other hand Henry Beaufort could be described as *admodum puer*, when in 1398 he obtained the Bishopric of

462

APPENDIX

Lincoln, and Thomas Beaufort, being described in the patent of legitimation as *domicellus* in 1397, was evidently too young for knighthood in that year.

The evidence of the Register, though inconclusive because incomplete, points to the same conclusion, viz., that the *liaison* began in 1371 or 1372.

At that date the Duke's gifts and grants to Katharine are no greater than might have been made to any other member of his household; immediately after they begin to become significant. Here are the principal instances :—
(i) May 1, 1372, gift of £10 ; (ii) May 15, 1372, grant of an annuity of 50 marcs, on surrender of a former annuity of 20 marcs ; (iii) June 20, 1372, grant of the wardship of the lands of her late husband, excepting the marriage fees and advowsons ; (iv) June 23, 1373, gift of three bucks ; (v) June 28, 1373, gift of oaks ; (vi) Jan. 1, 1375, grant of the wardship of the lands and heir of Sir Robert Deyncourt, and the marriage of the heir for her daughter Blanche ; (vii) Jan. 1377,, grant of the manors of Gringley and Wheatley, and gift of a tun of wine ; (viii) July 23, 1377, grant of tenements, late of Geoffrey de Sutton, in St. Botolph's ; (ix) July 24, 1377, gift of fifty oaks for the repair of her houses at Ketelthorp ; (x) July 25, 1379, grant of the wardship of the lands and heir of Bertram de Savenby ; (xi) Jan. 20, 1381, grant of the wardship of the lands, and the marriage of the heir of Elys de Thorsby ; (xii) Sept. 7, 1381, grant of an annuity of 200 marcs.

The presents, already noticed, made to Katharine by the Mayor of Leicester belong to the years 1375 and 1379.

(iv.) NOTE ON LANCASTER'S DEATH.

Recordasse pudet, materna lingua scribere abhorret quae sequuntur, sed quo perfectius opusculum istud de Ganda-vensi nostro existat, citare cogimur obscœnam quamdam fabulam quam primus edidit Thomas Gascoigne, qui natus anno domini MCCCCIII., defunctus MCCCCLVIII. librum insulsum conscripsit, cui falsilatem sic dissimulans nomen, " Loci e Libro Veritatum " finxit. Audi deliramenta :—

Novi enim ego Magister Thomas Gascoigne, licet indignus sacre Theologiae doctor qui haec scripsi et collegi, diversos viros qui mortui fuerunt ex putrefactione membrorum suorum et corporis sui, quae corruptio et putrefactio causata fuit, ut ipsi dixerunt,

463

APPENDIX

per exercitium copulae carnalis cum mulieribus. Magnus enim dux in Anglia scil. J. de Gawnt mortuus est ex tali putrefactione membrorum genitalium et corporis sui, causata per frequentationem mulierum. Magnus enim fornicator fuit, ut in toto regno Angliae divulgabatur, et ante mortem suam jacens sic infirmus in lecto eandem putrefactionem regi Angliae Ricardo II° ostendit, cum idem rex ipsum ducem in sua in— firmitate visitavit, et dixit michi qui ista novit unus fidelis thelogiae bachillarius.[1]

Nota bene callide lector clericum audisse clericum rettulisse fabulam istam. Enimvero qui odio habuit Lollardos et illustrem illum Lancastrensium domum huiusmodi mendaciis fundatoris, qui vir robustus et valens miles strenuus vixit ad summam senectutem, famam denigrare concupiscit.

Ætatis suæ malignitatem, posterum obscœnitatem immerito luit Dux noster.

(v) PERCY MS. 78 (ALNWICK CASTLE).

The following extract from Percy MS. 78, preserved at Alnwick Castle, contains some genealogical facts not otherwise known, and is therefore (for the first time, I believe) here reproduced. The nickname "Fairborn" given to the Beauforts is interesting. Is this mentioned in any other record?

The MS. is in a late fifteenth-century hand (or early sixteenth-century), and breaks off suddenly.

Iste Johannes Gaunt Dux Lancastrie et quartus filius Edwardi III primo duxit in uxorem Blanchiam filiam Henrici Ducis Lancastrie et heredem de qua genuit Johannem qui moritur Henricum regum IIIItum Elezabetham Comitissam Huntyndonie Phelippam Reginam Portingalie Edwardum et Johannem qui moriuntur.

Mortua domina Blancia idem Johannes superduxit Constanciam filiam Regis Hispaniarum de qua genuit Katerinam post hereditariam reginam Hispaniarum et obtinuit a regibus Anglorum et Hispaniarum quod captivi Anglorum a piratis Hispaniarum et captivi Hispaniarum a piratis Anglorum puppis (*sic*) et bonis retentis captivi abirent illesi. Quod servatum est in hodiernum diem.

Iste etiam Johannes Gaunt post mortem Constancie secunde uxoris sue adhuc superduxit dominam Katerinam de Swynfurth de qua genuit in diebus domine Blanchie prime uxoris

---

[1] *Loci e Libro Veritatum Thomae Gascoigne*, pp. 136-7. Oxford, 1881.

APPENDIX

sue Johannem Bowfurth comitem Somersissie Johannam Bowfurth comitissam Westmorelandie Henricum Bowfurth presbiterum cardinalem et episcopum Wyntonyensem ; qui potenti manu et sumptu proprio invitis Franciis coronari fecit Parisiùs Henricum VIum in Regem Francorum anno regni et aetatis sui X° et eum ibi secure retenuit, et in Angliam iterum similiter cum magna prosperitate et pompa militari reduxit : Thomam Bowforth ducem Exoniensem vel Exeter. Et legitimari fecit omnes istos quatuor a domino Papae unde vocebantur Bowfurthes aut Faerborne.

Henricus (*sic*) rex Hispaniarum habuit tres filias quibus intalliavit coronam Regni Hispaniarum propter defectum maris, quarum primogenita in virginitate defuncta secunda nupta erat Johanne (*sic*) de Gaunte ut supra duci Lancastrie, qui ex ea genuit Katerinam que nupta (*sic*) hereditavit coronam Hispaniarum : tertia vero filia nupta erat isti Edmundo Langley duci Ebor fratri ejusdem Johannis ducis Lancastrie qui ex ea genuit Edmundum Ducem Ebor qui occiditur in bello apud Agyncourt, et Ricardum fratrem ejus comitem Cantabregie quem decapitari fecit Henricus Vus apud Southamptonam.

Iste Ricardus comes Cantabrigie ex herede Marchie et Ulton genuit Ricardum ducem Ebor qui Ricardus dux anno Domini m.cccc.liv, infirmitate regie Henrico sixto (*sic*) in consilio quorundam dom norum apud [West]monasterium ordinatus erat Protector Anglie et duxit in uxorem Mariam filiam Radulphi Nevelle primi comitis.

Iste Johannes Bowfurth comes Somersecie genuit Johamem aliter Henricum comitem Somersecie qui cito moritur, Thomam qui moritur, Edmundum ducem Somersecie Joh[anname reg[inam] Scotorum et Margaretam comitissam Devoni] Ista Johanna Bowfurth prima maritata fuit domini de Ferrers et genuit ex ea duas filias unam maritatam Baroni de . . . (*desinit* MS.).

Index I—Persons

A.

Abbirbury or Aburbury, Sir Richard : 428, 440
Adam of Usk : 162
Aderby, Sir Richard : 186
Albert of Wittelsbach : 346
Albret, Sieur de : 38 and *note* ; 45, 51, 68, 69
—— House of : 366
Albuquerque, Dom Fernando Affonso de, Grand Master of St. James of Portugal : 274, 275
Alcántara, Grand Master of : 42
Alençon, Count of : 387
ALFONSO X. of Castile : 314, 325 *note*
ALFONSO XI. of Castile : 35, 36
Alfonso, " de la Cerda " : 315 and *note*
Alfonso : *See* Denia, Count of
Alvarez, Brother : 358
Amand, St. : 1
Andeiro, João Fernando de : *See* Ourem, Count of
Andrade, Fernand Perez de : 312
Angoulême, Guiscard de : *See* Huntingdon, Earl of
Anjou, Louis, Duke of : 59, 71, 78, 111, 118, 200 and *note*, 383
—— Charles of : 90
Anne of Bohemia, Queen of England : 259, 294, 357, 362
Annesley, Sir John : 410, 411
Anthony, the Falconer : 220
Antwerp, Lionel of : *See* Clarence, Duke of
Appleton. William de, physician to the Duke of Lancaster : 248 and *note*

Appleby, Sir Esmon : 137, 440
—— Thomas de : *See* Carlisle, Bishop of
Apulia and Sicily, King of : *See* Lancaster, Edmond, Earl of
Aquitaine, Duke of : *See* Lancaster, John, Duke of
Armagh, Richard Fitz Ralf, Archbishop of : 165, 169
Armagnac, Count of : 269 *note*
Artevelde, James van : 2, 3, 12, 30
Arthur, King : 27, 186
Arundel, Richard Fitz Alan, Thirteenth Earl of : 148, 185 *note*, 192, 233, 280, 281, 282, 295, 338, 339, 351, 352, 353, 354, 355, 356, 398, 400, 401, 417, 437
Ashton, William, Chancellor to the Duke of Lancaster : 302 *note*, 448, 449
Aston, Sir Robert, Chamberlain to Edward III. : 147, 157
Atterbury, Sir Richard : 302 *note*, 303 *note*
Aubrécicourt, Eustace de : 38
—— Jean de : 229, 430, 441
Audley, James, Lord : 409
Aumâle, Edward, Duke of : *See* York, Edward, Duke of
Auxerre, Count of : 59
Avis, House of : *See* João I. of Portugal
—— Order of : 274, 317
Ayala, Péro Lopez de : 52, 287, 309

B.

Badby, John, Confessor to the Duke of Lancaster : 172 *note*
Bagot, Sir William : 395, 417
Bajazet, Sultan : 161

467

INDEX

INDEX

469

INDEX

INDEX

INDEX

France : *See* Philip VI., John I., Charles V., Charles VI., Louis XI.

Francis, St. : 164

Froissart, Jean : 6, 10, 16, 52, 54, 75, 82, 84, 92, 102, 106, 108, 132, 139, 186, 198, 246, 296, 321 *note*, 326, 328, 329, 350, 365, 380, 383, 384, 385, 393, 395, 398, 409, 412, 415, 418, 459, 460, 461

Frondsberg, George of : 151

Furtado, Affonso, Admiral of Portugal : 309

Fychet, Sir Thomas : 137, 326, 441

G.

Galeazzo (Visconti) II., Lord of Milan : 24

Gandia, Duke of : *See* Denia, Count of

Gascoigne, Thomas : 463

—— William : 435

Gaston, Phoebus : *See* Foix, Count of

Gaveston, Piers : 22, 24, 292

Gilbert, John : *See* Hereford, Bishop of

Glasgow, Bishop of : 245, 288

Gloucester, Thomas of Woodstock, Earl of Buckingham, Duke of : 25, 152, 189, 191, 231, 268 *note*, 281, 286, 291, 292, 295, 296, 338, 340, 342 and *note*, 346, 351, 352, 382, 385, 386, 394, 395, 397, 398, 399 and *note*, 400, 403, 417, 427, 437

Gower, John : 165, 397

Graily, Jean de, Captal de Buch, Constable of Aquitaine : 51, 53, 88, 185, 385

—— Jean de, bastard son of : 385

—— Archambaud de : 376, 377, 385

Grayne, Andrew Fitz Symond : 18 *note*

Gregory XI : 91, 160, 185 *note*

Grene, Sir Henry : 285

—— Henry : 395

Grey de Ruthyn, Lord : 141

Greystock, Baron of : 243, 253 *note*, 277

Grosvenor, Robert : 13, 310

Guadelupe, Prior of : *See* Serrano, Don Juan

Gueldres, Duke of : 72

Guesclin, Bertrand du, Constable of France : 46, 51, 53, 54, 59, 63, 64, 71, 79, 81, 87, 98, 111, 114, 140, 200 and *note*, 233, 331

Gurney, Sir Matthew : 438

Guttierez, Juan, Dean of Segovia : *See* Dax, Bishop of

Guzman, Fernan Perez de : 335 and *note*

—— Leonor de, Mistress of Alfonso XI., 36, 300

H.

Hainault, Count of : 385

Hapsburg, House of : 12

Hardyng, John : 360, 361, 362

Harpeden, Sir John : Seneschal of Saintonge : 199 *note*

—— William, 432

Harrington, Lord : 437

Hastings, Sir Hugh : 326

—— John : *See* Pembroke, Earl of

Hauley, Robert : 234 *note*, 235-7, 240 *note*

Haxey, Thomas : 398

Haytfield, Robert, 431

Henrique (Prince Henry, the Navigator) : 308, 336, 415

Henry II. of England : 35, 206

Henry III. : 22, 89, 90

Henry IV. : Earl of Derby, Duke of Hereford, Duke of Lancaster : 131, 181, 191, 204, 209, 214, 226, 248, 310, 338, 340, 345, 346, 351, 357, 359, 360, 381, and *note*, 383, 386, 392 *note*, 395, 401–7, 417–9, 427, 428, 435, 464

Henry V. : 387, 414, 428, 464

Henry VI. : 464

Henry VII. : 389, 451, 455

Henry VIII. : 388

INDEX

INDEX

474

INDEX

INDEX

Montague, William de : *See* Salisbury, Earl of
—— Sir John : 284
Montfort, Simon de, Count of Toulouse, 365
—— Simon de : *See* Leicester, Earl of
—— John de : *See* Brittany, Duke of
Morieux, Sir Thomas : 285, 310, 321, 326, 459–461
—— Blanche, 310, 459–461
Mortimer, Roger, 5 : 10, 23
Mowbray, Thomas, Earl of Nottingham : *See* Norfolk, Duke of

N.

Namur, Robert de : 72
Narbonne, Amaury de, Admiral of France : 103
Navarre : *See* Charles I. (The Bad), King of ; Henry III. Count of Champagne, King of.
Neillac, Guillaume de : 313 *note*
Nero : 135
Nevill of Hornby, Sir Thomas : 389
—— Margaret, daughter of : 389
Neville of Raby, John, Lord : 128, 228, 231 *note*, 243, 253 *note*, 254, 266–7, 295, 438, 440
Neville of Raby, Ralf, Lord : *See* Westmorland, Earl of
—— Cicely : 389
—— Sir Robert : 435
Newman, Isolda (Nurse to John of Gaunt), 4
Newton, John : 432
Norfolk, Thomas Mowbray, Earl of Nottingham, Duke of : 191, 281, 289 and *note*, 291, 294, 338, 391, 399, 401, 404, 416
—— Margaret Brotherton, Duchess of : 189, 426, 437
—— John de : 245 *note*, 246
Northumberland, Henry Percy, Earl of : 51, 53, 72, 125, 140, 141, 148, 150–5, 189, 191, 206, 218, 236 *note*, 243, 244, 246, 249, 252, 253 *note*, 254, 255 and *note*, 256 and *note*, 257, 258 *note*, 279, 295, 297, 361, 417, 438

Northumberland, Margaret, Countess of : 255 *note*
Norwich, Henry le Spencer, Bishop of : 125, 270, 271, 305
Nottingham, Thomas Mowbray, Earl of : *See* Norfolk, Duke of

O.

Okovere, Sir Philip : 137, 442
Orleans, Duke of : 347
Orozco, Iñigo Lopez de : 54
Osorio, Alvar Perez de : 325
Ostrevant, William, Count of : 346
Ourem, João Fernando d'Andeiro, Count of, Grand Master of St. James', and Chancellor of Portugal : 262 and *note*, 264, 274
Overbury, William de : 284 *note*, 445
Owen of Wales : 140, 198
Oxford, Robert de Vere, Earl of : Marquess of Dublin, Duke of Ireland : 24, 189, 191, 281-7, 289 and *note*, 290-92, 294, 295, 296 and *note*, 297 *note*, 298, 337, 338, 339, 340, 353, 395, 416

P.

Pacheco, João Fernandes : 321 *note*, 325
Padilla, Maria de (wife of Pedro I. of Castile and Leon) : 37, 314
Par, William : 428, 430
Passac, Gaucher de : 313 *note*
Patrington, Stephen : 181, 182 *note*
PEDRO IV. of Aragon : 38, 46, 59-61, 63, 239
PEDRO I. of Castile and Leon : 35-37, 38 and *note*, 39-41, 42 and *note*, 43, 45, 47, 54-56, 58, 61, 63-65, 68, 70, 90, 92, 100, 269, 301, 312, 314-16, 318, 329, 334, 355, 357, 358, 363, 430, 451, 464
PEDRO I. of Portugal : 39, 232, 274

476

INDEX

INDEX

Stafford, Ralf, Earl of: 125, 141, 178 *note*, 294, 437, 438
—— Ralf, Son of: 294
—— Richard, Lord: 125, 192
Staple, Katharine del: 423, 434, 435
Stenche, John: 449
Stury, Sir Richard: 385
Suffolk, William de Ufford, Earl of: 105, 125, 256 and *note*, 296
—— Michael de la Pole, Earl of, Chancellor of England: 228, 272, 281, 282 and *note*, 290, 295, 296, 297 *note*, 339, 340, 440, 459
Sulny, Sir Avery: 137
Surrey, Thomas Holland, Earl of Kent, Duke of: 401
Sutton, Geoffrey de: 462
—— William de: 174
Swaffham, John: *See* Bangor, Bishop of
Swylyngton, Sir Robert: 102, 209
Swynford, Sir Hugh: 390, 391, 460, 461
—— Katharine: *See* Lancaster, Duchess of
—— Sir Thomas: 390, 428, 461
—— Blanche: 390, 460-2
Swynton, Sir John: 154, 156, 443
Symeon, Robert: 432
Symond, Sir Thomas: 326, 443

T.

Tacitus: 135
Telles de Meneses, Leonor: 264, 308
Tello, Don: 48, 49, 52, 53
Thelwall, Thomas de, Chancellor of the County Palatine of Lancaster: 209
Thomas of Woodstock: *See* Gloucester, Duke of
Thorsby, Elys de: 462
Tilney, Sir Philip de (Chief Steward of the Duke of Lancaster): 448
Tovar, Fernando Sanchez de, Admiral of Castile: 230, 261 *note*, 264 *note*
Trastamare, House of: 13, 97, 101, 235, 239, 263, 274, 316, 331.

See also Enrique II., Juan I., Enrique III., Juan II., of Castile and Leon
—— Count of: *See* Enrique II. of Castile and Leon
Tresilian, Robert, Chief Justice: 340
Tryvet, Sir Thomas: 437
Tudor, Edmund: *See* Richmond, Earl of

U.

Ufford, William de: *See* Suffolk, Earl of
Ulster, Elizabeth de Burgh, Countess of: 4, 10
—— Lionel of Antwerp, Earl of: *See* Clarence, Duke of
Urban V.: 26, 31, 37, 38, 59, 91, 160, 177, 270
—— VI.: 270, 304, 333
Ursewyk, Sir Walter: 219, 229, 443
Usk, Sir Nicholas: 450

V.

Vaca, Cabeza de, Admiral of Castile: 97
Valois, House of: 13, 29, 31, 97, 370, 395. *See* also Philip V., John I., Charles V., Charles VI.
—— Chronicler of the first four: 115, 185
Vere, Aubrey de: 155, 185 *note*, 438
—— Robert de: *See* Oxford, Earl of
Vienne, Jean de, Admiral of France: 71, 103, 108, 230, 232, 293 and *note*, 296
Villareal, Alvar Martinez de: 314
Villemur (*or* Vinemur), Jean de: 81, 412
Villena, Marquess of: *See* Denia, Count of
Visconti, Galeazzo II., Lord of Milan: *See* GALEAZZO
Vivonne, Sir Regnaut: 199 *note*

W.

Waldemar III. of Denmark: 27

479

INDEX

Wales, Edward, Prince of, Duke of Cornwall, Earl of Chester, Lord of Biscay and Urdiales : 5–7, 9, 10, 12, 19, 23, 25, 40–7, 50, 51, 54–63, 68–70, 78–86, 90–2, 95, 97, 98, 100, 108, 110, 126, 130, 131, 139, 142, 143, 155, 170, 185 *note*, 196, 199, 200, 235, 294, 325 *note*, 363, 366, 367, 371, 380–2, 384, 409, 410, 419, 428, 453–5

—— Joan, Princess of : 25, 59, 131, 142, 149, 154, 155, 186, 237, 238, 291, 294

Walsingham, Thomas : 136

Walworth, William : 194, 241

Warwick, Thomas de Beauchamp, Thirteenth Earl of : 72, 105, 125, 141, 148, 190, 256, 281, 338, 398, 400, 401, 437, 438

Waterton, Sir Hugh : 430

Welles, Lord : 229, 440

WENCESLAUS, Emperor : 397

Wennesley, Sir Thomas : 137

Westminster, Abbot of : 342, 398

Westmorland, Ralf, Sixth Lord Neville, of Raby, First Earl of : 389, 401, 430, 436, 464

—— Joan (Beaufort), Countess of : 389, 391, 401, 415, 428, 434, 436, 464

Whitby, Robert de, Receiver-General, Attorney-General of the Duke of Lancaster : 174 *note*, 431, 448

Willoughby, Lord : 437, 438

Wiltshire, William le Scrope, Earl of (Treasurer of England) : 371, 401, 425, 430

Winchester, William of Wykeham, Bishop of : 19, 104, 132, 136, 141, 148, 155, 157, 162, 175, 181, 184, 185 *note*, 187, 190, 415

—— Henry Beaufort, Bishop of : *See* Lincoln, Bishop of

Windsor, William de : 411

Woodstock, Thomas of : *See* Gloucester, Duke of

Worcester, Thomas Percy, Earl of : 199 *note*, 244, 255 *note*, 310, 317, 318, 346, 384, 401, 402, 415 and *note*, 430, 438

—— Bishop of : 91, 190, 430

Wycliffe, John : 26, 32, 133, 134, 149–52, 156, 162, 165, 166, 168, 169, 172–4, 176, 177 *note*, 178–83, 220, 242, 270, 271, 304, 305, 355, 392, 406, 409, 413, 414

Wyn, John : 198

Y.

Yerdburgh, John de, Clerk of the Wardrobe, Receiver-General of the Duke of Lancaster : 174 and *note*

York, Edmund of Langley, Earl of Cambridge, Duke of : 15, 25, 27 and *note*, 28–30, 71, 83, 93, 190, 192, 262, 263 and *note*, 264, 265, 267 and *note*, 268 *note*, 272, 296, 304, 309, 346, 398, 402, 410, 411, 422, 427, 432, 437, 438, 464

—— Edmund, Duke of : 464

—— Edward, Earl of Rutland, Duke of Aumâle, Duke of : 263 *note*, 264, 267 and *note*, 272, 399, 401, 432

—— Richard, Duke of : 389, 464

—— Isabella of Castile, Duchess of : 93, 178, 357 and *note*

York, House of : 451

—— Alexander Neville, Archbishop of : 340

—— Richard, Archbishop of : 432, 438

Z.

Zealand, William of Bavaria, Duke of : 13, 19

—— Maude, or Matilda, of Lancaster, Duchess of, 13, 19, 20, 143, 210

Zouche, of Haringworth, Lord la : 284–86, 438

Index II—Places

A.

Abbeville : 72, 73, 74
Abchester : 250, 251 *note*
Acre : 22
Agen : 382
Agincourt : 396, 464
Aire : 106
Alava, Province of, 47 and *note*, 57
Albuquerque : 39
Alcañices : 324
Alconeta : 318 *note*
Alcuéscar : 318 *note*
Aldgate, Convent of St. Clair of, 22
Alemtejo, Province of : 264
Alexandria : 28
Alfaro : 38
Algarve : 302 *note*, 331 and *note*, 430
Algeciras : 23, 35, 302 *note*, 331, 430
Aljubarrota : 235, 298, 301, 313, 317, 325, 412
Allier, River : 111, 113
Almazán : 331
Almeida : 327
Alnwick : 206, 244, 255 *note*
Amiens : 108, 109, 347, 348, 382, 424
Amonderness : 208 *note*
Amusco : 57
Añastro : 47, 50
Angoulême : 68, 78, 99, 366 *note*, 382
Anjou : 196
Annandale : 254, 277
Antolin, St., Church of, at Palencia : 333
Antwerp : 1, 2, 3

Aquitaine : 40, 58, 59, 61, 62, 67, 68, 69, 79, 84, 87, 91, 92, 97, 98, 99, 101, 104, 116, 117, 122, 123, 196, 200, 322, 327, 328 *note*, 342, 343, 353, 354, 363–388, 391, 447, 448, 451, 453, 454, 455, 461
Aragon : 34, 37, 60, 61, 231, 236, 239, 240 *note*, 269 *note*
Ardres : 105, 106, 396
Arga, River : 45
Ariñez : 49
Arras : 106
Arruiz, Pass of : 47
Artois : 16, 28, 105, 111, 196
Ashdown, Chace : 219
Assisi : 164
Astorga : 325
Asturias, Province of the : 34, 63
Atienza : 331
Attalia : 28
Aube (Department) : 197
Authie, River : 106
Auvergne : 111, 112, 113
Auxerre : 111, 112
Avallon : 111, 112
Avignon : 8, 26, 27, 31 *note*, 59, 109, 121, 142, 160, 165, 175, 313
Ayton : 251 *note*

B.

Babé : 323 *note*
Badajóz : 265, 273
Bamborough : 9 *note*, 245 *note*, 251 and *note*, 252, 256
Bañares : 47
Barcelona : 38

481

INDEX

Barlings Abbey : 179
Bassingbourn : 175 *note*
Bayeux : 328 *note*
Bayona : 322 and *note*
Bayonne : 40, 41, 44, 55, 56, 62, 90, 96, 232, 241, 327, 328, 329, 332, 363, 364, 368, 374, 385, 454, 455
Beaufort : 196, 197 and *note*, 198 and *note*, 199
Beauquesne : 106 *note*
Beauvais : 71
Becherel : 103, 127
Bedford : 246
Belloc : 114
Benavente : 324, 325, 326, 327
Bergerac : 28, 78, 84, 114, 196, 199, 200 and *note*, 201 and *note*, 382, 454
Berkhamstead : 98, 255, 256, 257, 258 *note*, 418
Bernolswick, Manor of : 423, 435
Berwick : 9, 206, 243, 250 *note*, 251 *note*, 252 and *note*, 254, 278, 279
Betanzos : 322
Bethlehem : 147
Beverley : 310
Beyford : 201, 202 *note*
Biddlesdon Abbey : 168 *note*
Bicêtre : 263 *note*
Bigorre : 59
Biscay : 42, 53, 57, 59, 61 and *note*, 331, 430
Bishopthorpe : 294
Blackburnshire : 208 *note*, 219
Blanchetaque : 73
Blaye : 44
Bohemia : 397
Bolbec : 74
Bolingbroke Castle : 218
Bordeaux : 6, 44, 52, 62, 71, 81, 86 and *note*, 87, 92, 96, 100, 102, 112, 114, 115, 116, 199, 229, 232, 241, 325 and *note*, 329, 333 *note*, 340, 363, 364 and *note*, 365, 366 and *note*, 368, 371, 372 and *note*, 373, 374, 375, 376 and *note*, 378 and *note*, 379, 380 and *note*, 381, 382, 383 and *note*, 384, 385, 388, 412, 424, 449, 453, 455
Borja : 46, 62
Boroughbridge : 169 *note*, 251 *note*

Boulogne : 72, 276, 287, 349
Brabant : 2, 12, 104
Brackley : 251 *note*
Bradford, Church of : 175 and *note*
Braganza : 262 *note*, 323 and *note*, 411
Bray-sur-Somme : 106, 107, 109
Brentford : 402
Brest : 103, 232, 241, 311 and *note*, 397
Brétigni : 18, 27, 67, 70, 110, 348
Brie : 78
Bristol : 79 *note*, 128, 403
Brittany : 13, 44, 117, 127, 142, 387, 448
Brive la Gaillarde : 114
Briviesca : 38, 55, 332 *note*
Bruges : 27, 29, 30, 118 and *note*, 119 and *note*, 122, 133, 270, 301, 345
Burbage, Church of : 432
Burgos : 38, 39, 46, 47, 50, 55 and *note*, 57, 331 *note*
Burgundy, Duchy of : 17, 28, 108, 111
—— County of : 28
Bury St. Edmunds, Abbey of : 406, 424, 428

C.

Cáceres : 318 *note*
Carmarthen : 206, 217
Calahorra : 38
Calais : 5, 16, 27, 29, 30, 40, 67, 71 and *note*, 72, 74, 104, 105 and *note*, 110, 114, 115, 196 *note*, 198, 232, 241, 276, 287, 325, 346 and *note*, 347 and *note*, 348, 349, 396, 397, 399, 400, 426, 447
Calatayud : 58
Cambrésis : 16
Cambridge : 172 *note*
—— County of : 203, 460
—— University of :
—— Clare Hall : 41 *note*
—— Corpus Christi College : 414 and *note*
Camelot : 27
Camillo : 315 *note*

482

INDEX

483

INDEX

E.

Eagle, Honor of : 204, 216, 219
East Anglia : 270
Ebro, River : 38, 39, 47, 50, 53
Edinburgh : 9, 10, 251 *note*, 252
note, 254 and *note*, 278, 298, 301
Eltham : 385
Elvas : 265
Ely, Diocese of : 175 *note*
Empire, The : 29, 54
England : 366, 367, 370, 371,
374, 376, 378, 380, 381, 383,
386, 387, 388, 395, 396, 397,
402, 404, 405, 419, 447, 451,
455, 456, 457, 464
Esplechin : 4
Essendon : 201, 202 *note*
Essex : 247, 251, 264, 341
Essigni : 106
Estouteville : 74
Estremos : 262 *note*, 264
Étampes : 17
Étienville : 74
Evesham : 217
Exeter : 93
—— Diocese of : 432

F.

Fakenham, Manor of : 459
Ferrol : 322
Firth of Forth : 278
Flanders : 6, 11, 28, 29, 30, 32,
33, 54, 121, 142, 270, 271, 272,
287, 288, 364, 451
Fleet Street : 189, 408 and *note*,
420
Foix : 142, 321 *note*, 329
France : 5, 13, 17, 29, 38, 40, 54,
160, 190, 196, 230, 231, 266,
272, 287 and *note*, 293, 295,
302, 303, 311, 325, 328, 330,
333, 363, 366, 367, 368, 370,
379, 382, 385, 386, 396, 448,
455, 456, 457, 461
Fregenal : 318 *note*
Frendles, Wapentake : 169 *note*
Fuentarrabia : 333
Fuente del Maestre : 318 *note*
Fulham : 256
Furness : 168

G.

Galicia : 39, 302 *note*, 311, 312,
314, 321, 322 and *note*, 323,
331, 430, 452, 461
Galloway : 243, 254, 276
Garonne, River : 111, 363, 368,
374
Gascony : *See* Aquitaine
Germany : 5, 7, 104, 346. (*See*
Empire, The)
Ghent : 1, 2, 3, 30, 119, 270, 271,
299 *note*, 451
Gibraltar : 96
Gironde, River : 44
Glamorgan : 206, 217, 219
Gloucester : 137, 241
Gomerville : 74
Gracechurch Street : 299, 317
Granada : 34
Gravelines : 271
Gravesend : 230, 261
Grimaldo : 318 *note*
Gringley, Manor of : 462
Grosmont : 217, 250 *note*
Guadalajara : 331
Guadiana, River : 264, 265
Guárdia, La : 50
Guiche : 454, 455
Guildford : 93
Guillon-sur-Serain : 17
Guines : 30, 71 *note*, 105, 396
Guipuzcoa : 47, 57, 287
Guyenne : *See* Aquitaine
Gyé : 106 *note*, 111

H.

Haddington : 254, 278
Hainault : 11, 104, 384, 393, 459,
460
Halton : 218
Halykeld, Wapentake of : 435
Hampshire : 99
Hangest, Wapentake of : 435
Hangwest, Wapentake of : 435
Harfleur : 71 74, 232
Hastings : 230
Hatfield : 10, 11
Havering-atte-Bower : 184 *note*,
454 *note*
Havre, Le : 74
Hawdenstank : 406 *note*
Hereford : 125, 162, 206, 216, 217

484

INDEX

485

INDEX

INDEX

INDEX

INDEX

INDEX

490